Counseling and Professional Identity titles tied to CACREP standards
Titles in Counseling and Professional Identity series

CACREP Standards	Introduction to Professional Counseling	Counseling Assessment and Evaluation	Group Work	Essentials Of Becoming A Skilled Counselor	Theories of Counseling and Techniques	Counseling Individuals Through the Life Span	Becoming a Multiculturally Competent counselor	Research Methods For counseling	Career Development and Counseling	Essentials of Becoming a Skilled Consult.	Ethical, Legal and Professional Issues for Counselors in the 21st Century
1. PROFESSIONAL ORIENTATION AND ETHICAL PRACTICE	1a 1b 1d 1e 1f 1g 1h 1i 1j	1j	1b 1j	1b 1d 1e 1j	1j	1j	1j	1j	1b 1j	1b 1j	1b 1d 1e 1f 1h 1i 1j
2. SOCIAL AND CULTURAL DIVERSITY	2c 2f 2g	2g	2d 2e 2g	2b 2c 2g	2c 2e 2g	2a 2b 2c 2d 2e 2g	2c 2e 2f 2g	2g	2g	2d 2g	2c 2e 2f 2g
3. HUMAN GROWTH AND DEVELOPMENT			3f		3b	3a 3b 3c 3d 3e 3f 3g	3d 3e		3e		3g
4. CAREER DEVELOPMENT		4f							4a 4b 4c 4d 4e 4f 4g	4c	
5. HELPING RELATIONSHIPS	5a 5b 5c 5f 5g 5h		5b 5c 5d 5e	5a 5b 5c 5d	5b 5c 5d 5e 5g	5b	5b 5e		5b 5c	5b 5c 5f 5g 5h	5b 5d 5h
6. GROUP WORK			6a 6b 6c 6d 6e								6d 6e
7. ASSESSMENT		7a 7b 7c 7d 7e 7f 7g	7b	7b		7f		7c 7d 7e			
8. RESEARCH AND PROGRAM EVALUATION								8a 8b 8c 8d 8e			8d

COUNSELING AND PROFESSIONAL IDENTITY

Series Editors: Richard D. Parsons, PhD and Naijian Zhang, PhD

Becoming a Skilled Counselor—Richard D. Parsons and Naijian Zhang

Research Methods for Counseling—Robert Wright

Group Work Leadership: An Introduction for Helping Professionals—Robert Conyne

Introduction to Professional Counseling—Varunee Faii Sangganjanavanich and Cynthia A. Reynolds

Becoming a Multiculturally Competent Counselor—Changming Duan and Chris Brown

Counseling Individuals Through the Lifespan—Daniel Wai Chung Wong, Kim Hall, Cheryl Justice, and Lucy Wong Hernandez

Career Development and Counseling: Theory and Practice in a Multicultural World—Mei Tang and Jane Goodman

Counseling Assessment and Evaluation: Fundamentals of Applied Practice—Joshua C. Watson and Brandé Flamez

Ethical Decision Making for the 21st Century Counselor—Donna S. Sheperis, Michael Kocet, and Stacy Henning

Counselor As Consultant—David Scott, Chadwick Royal, and Daniel Kissinger

Counseling Theory: Guiding Reflective Practice—Richard D. Parsons and Naijian Zhang

COUNSELING and
PROFESSIONAL IDENTITY

Group Work Leadership
An Introduction for Helpers

Robert K. Conyne
Professor Emeritus, University of Cincinnati

Los Angeles | London | New Delhi
Singapore | Washington DC

Los Angeles | London | New Delhi
Singapore | Washington DC

FOR INFORMATION:

SAGE Publications, Inc.
2455 Teller Road
Thousand Oaks, California 91320
E-mail: order@sagepub.com

SAGE Publications Ltd.
1 Oliver's Yard
55 City Road
London, EC1Y 1SP
United Kingdom

SAGE Publications India Pvt. Ltd.
B 1/I 1 Mohan Cooperative Industrial Area
Mathura Road, New Delhi 110 044
India

SAGE Publications Asia-Pacific Pte. Ltd.
3 Church Street
#10-04 Samsung Hub
Singapore 049483

Acquisitions Editor: Kassie Graves
Editorial Assistant: Elizabeth Luizzi
Production Editor: Stephanie Palermini
Copy Editor: Lana Todorovic-Arndt
Typesetter: Hurix Systems Pvt. Ltd.
Proofreader: Wendy Jo Dymond
Indexer: Wendy Allex
Cover Designer: Candice Harman
Marketing Manager: Erica DeLuca
Permissions Editor: Adele Hutchinson

Printed in the United States of America.

Library of Congress Cataloging-in-Publication Data

Conyne, Robert K.

Group work leadership : an introduction for helpers / Robert K. Conyne, University of Cincinnati.

pages cm. — (Counseling and professional identity in the 21st century)
Includes bibliographical references and index.

ISBN 978-1-4522-1790-1 (pbk. : alk. paper)

1. Group counseling. 2. Group problem solving. 3. Group counseling—Case studies. 4. Group problem solving—Case studies. I. Title.

BF636.7.G76C664 2014

361.4—dc23

2013004012

This book is printed on acid-free paper

13 14 15 16 17 10 9 8 7 6 5 4 3 2 1

BRIEF CONTENTS

Chapter List of Case Illustrations, Figures, and Learning Exercises   xiii

Editors' Preface: Introduction to the Series   xix

Preface   xxiii

Acknowledgments   xxix

Section I: *Group Work Is a Comprehensive and Unique Approach*

Chapter 1:   **Introduction to Group Work**   3

Chapter 2:   **Foundations of Group Work: Multiculturalism, Social Justice, and Ethics**   29

Chapter 3:   **Group Dynamics and Group Process**   63

Chapter 4:   **Group Development: The Beginning, Working, and Ending Stages**   91

Section II: *Critical Elements of Group Work*

Chapter 5:   **Group Work Leadership**   115

Chapter 6:   **Group Work Theories**   139

Chapter 7:   **Group Leader Styles and Functions**   177

Chapter 8:   **Group Work Methods, Strategies, and Techniques**   203

Section III: *Meaning, Action, and Professional Identity in Group Work*

Chapter 9:   Reflecting in and on Group Work Practice   239

Chapter 10:   Selecting Effective Interventions   261

Epilogue: From the Author's Chair   297

References   305

Index   327

About the Author   341

DETAILED CONTENTS

Chapter List of Case Illustrations, Figures, and Learning Exercises   xiii

Editors' Preface: Introduction to the Series   xix

Preface   xxiii

      Introduction   xxiii

      Organization   xxiv

          Sections and Chapters   xxiv

          Format   xxv

      Highlighting Some Unique Aspects of Group Work   xxv

          Group Work Is Interdependent, Interactive, and
             Collective   xxv

          Group Work Comes in Different Types   xxvi

          Group Work Has a Range of Purposes   xxvi

      Be Forewarned!   xxvii

      Let Me Know Your Reactions   xxvii

Acknowledgments   xxix

Section I: Group Work is a Comprehensive and Unique Approach

Chapter 1: Introduction to Group Work   3

      Introduction: Welcome, Book Framework, and Structure   3

          Chapter Objectives   5

      Groups Are Everywhere   5

      What Is Group Work?   7

          Five Perspectives Underlying Group Work   7

          Group Work Is an Umbrella Term   10

          Various Conceptualizations of Group Methods   10

          Group Work Is Effective   10

      ASGW's Conception of Group Work   11

          Core Group Work Competencies   11

          Four Advanced Types of Group Work   14

ASGW Group Work Definition 17
   Group Work Definition, Part I: Group Work Is
    a Broad Professional Practice 17
   Group Work Definition, Part II: Giving Help or
    Accomplishing Tasks in a Group Setting 18
   Group Work Definition, Part III: Involving the
    Application of Group Theory and Process 18
   Group Work Definition, Part IV: By a Capable
    Professional Practitioner 21
   Group Work Definition, Part V: To Assist an
    Interdependent Collection of People 24
   Group Work Definition, Part VI: To Reach Mutual
    Goals 25
   Group Work Definition, Part VII: Goals May Be
    Personal, Interpersonal, or Task Related 25
Group Work Keystones 27
Recommended Resources 27

Chapter 2: Foundations of Group Work: Multiculturalism,
Social Justice, and Ethics 29

Introduction 29
   Chapter Objectives 31
A Brief Look at Relevant History in Group Work's
   Development 31
   A Broad Sweep Examination 31
ASGW's Foundation Documents: Training Standards, Best
   Practice, Ethics, and Multicultural and Social Justice
   Competencies Principles for Group Workers 33
   ASGW Document #1: Professional Training
    Standards 35
   ASGW Document #2: Best Practice Guidelines 39
   ASGW Document #3: Multicultural and Social
    Justice Competence Principles for Group
    Workers 49
   Multicultural Competency and Social Justice 49
   The Multicultural and Social Justice Competence
    Principles for Group Workers 52
Accreditation Standards and Group Work 56
   The Council for the Accreditation of Counseling
    and Related Educational Programs (CACREP) 57

ASGW's Recommended Clock Hour Training   60

Group Work Keystones   60

Recommended Resources   61

Chapter 3: Group Dynamics and Group Process   63

Introduction   63

Chapter Objectives   64

What Are Group Dynamics?   64

Defining Group Dynamics   66

What Is Group Process?   70

Managing Exploding Data in Groups   71

Group Work Keystones   89

Recommended Resources   90

Chapter 4: Group Development: The Beginning, Working, and Ending Stages   91

Introduction   91

Chapter Objectives   92

Why Is Group Development Important?   92

Perspectives on Group Development   93

Cyclical Models   93

Contemporary Models   93

Progressive Stage Models   94

Exploring Four Group Development Models   98

Tuckman's Model   99

AGPA's Model   99

Jones' Model   101

Brabender and Fallon's model   103

Group Work Keystones   110

Recommended Resources   111

Section II: Critical Elements of Group Work

Chapter 5: Group Work Leadership   115

Introduction   115

Chapter Objectives   115

Leadership   116

What Leadership Is Not   116

What Leadership Is   116

Group Work Leadership Elements   118

Group Counseling Leadership Definition, as a Model   118

Group Work Leadership Definition   130

Group Coleadership   132

General Statements About Group Work Leadership   134

Group Work Keystones   135

Recommended Resources   136

Chapter 6: Group Work Theories   139

Introduction   139

Having a Theory Is a Very Good Thing   139

Chapter Objectives   141

Existing Theories Fall Short of What Is Needed   142

A Need for Theories Particularly Congruent With Groups   142

No Overarching Theory of Group Work Exists   145

Group Work Theory Sources: The Current Status   145

Group Counseling and Group Psychotherapy Theories   145

Task Group and Psychoeducation Group Theory and Models   153

Identifying Six Transtheoretical Orientations in Group Work: Contextual, Interpersonal, Interactive, Interpersonal Neurobiology, Process, and Purposive   158

Contextual Orientation   159

Interpersonal Orientation   161

Interactive Orientation   163

Interpersonal Neurobiology Orientation   163

Process Orientation   165

Purposive Orientation   166

Toward an Overarching Theory of Group Work   170

Your Personal Theory in Action   170

Group Work Keystones   174

Recommended Resources   175

Chapter 7: Group Leader Styles and Functions   177

Introduction   177

Chapter Objectives   177

Looking at Personal Experience With Group Leadership   178

What Do Group Leaders Do?   179

Group Leader Functions and Styles   180

Group Leader Competencies   193

Group Work Keystones   202

Recommended Resources   202

Chapter 8: Group Work Methods, Strategies, and Techniques   203

   Introduction   203
      Chapter Objectives   204
      Group Leader Methods: *Blueprints Guiding Action*   204
      Ten Examples of Methods   204
   Group Leader Strategies and Techniques: *Action Tools
      of the Trade*   226
   Five Selected Strategies and Techniques in Group
      Leadership   226
      Focusing   227
      *Shifting Interaction by Loosening and by
        Tightening*   228
      Pre-Planned, Structured Exercises   230
      Intuitive Experiments   232
      Psychoeducation Lecturettes   233
   Group Work Keystones   235
   Recommended Resources   235

Section III: Meaning, Action, and Professional Identity in Group Work

Chapter 9: Reflecting in and on Group Work Practice   239

   Introduction   239
      Chapter Objectives   240
   Reflecting in Group Work Practice: Focusing on One
      Group at a Time   240
      Lessons Learned   240
      *Reflective Practice, or Processing, Between
        and Within Group Sessions*   244
   Reflecting on Group Work Practice: Taking Perspective   251
      *The Deep Processing Model (Conyne, 1999):
        Toward Personal and Professional Development*   251
      Self-Care   254
      Professional Practice and Accountability   258
   Group Work Keystones   259
   Recommended Resources   259

Chapter 10: Selecting Effective Interventions in Group Leadership   261

   Introduction   261
      Chapter Objectives   262
   The Role of Practice and Processing in Accomplished
      Group Leadership   262

Practice: Providing Opportunities to Learn From
    Successes and Failures   263
Processing: Converting Experience and Practice
    Into Meaning   266
Leader Choices in Group: Those Made, Those Not Made   269
Intervention Selection Cases From Four Group
    Work Types   270
    Task Group Illustration: Student Representative
        at the Weekly Faculty Meeting   270
    Psychoeducation Group Illustration: Lifestyle and
        Healthy Functioning Group   275
    Counseling Group Illustration: Stress Management
        During Deployment Group   281
    Psychotherapy Group Illustration: Struggling With
        Lifestyle and Family   287
Group Work Keystones   294
Recommended Resources   294

Epilogue: From the Author's Chair   297

References   305

Index   327

About the Author   341

CHAPTER LIST OF CASE ILLUSTRATIONS, FIGURES, AND LEARNING EXERCISES

Preface   xxiii
      Figure P-1: Did Not Work Well in Groups   xxiii

Section I: Group Work Is a Comprehensive and Unique Approach

Chapter 1: Introduction to Group Work   1
      Case Illustration 1–1: A Day in the Life   6
      Learning Exercise 1–1: Take a Life Sample   7
      Learning Exercise 1–2: Assessing Some of Your Core Competencies   12
      Case Illustration 1–2: Four Types of Group Work   15
      Figure 1–1: The Group Work Rainbow   16
      Case Illustration 1–3: People Are Connected   20
      Learning Exercise 1–3: What About *Your* Social Support Network?   20
      Case Illustration 1–4: Four Tried and True Learning Strategies   22
      Learning Exercise 1–4: Assessing How You Are Learning About Group Work   23

Chapter 2: Foundations of Group Work: Multiculturalism, Social Justice, and Ethics   29
      Figure 2–1: Some Major Group Professional Associations and Journals   32
      Case Illustration 2–1: Please Lead This Group!   33
      Figure 2–2: Highlights of Important Group Work Components   36

Case Illustration 2-2: Knowledge and Skills in
Group Work   37

Learning Exercise 2-1: Observing and Identifying Group
Process   38

Figure 2-3: Best Practice Guideline Domains   41

Learning Exercise 2-2: A Knotty Challenge   41

Case Illustration 2-3: When Adjustment Is Needed   44

Learning Exercise 2-3: Your Turn: When Adjustment Is
Needed   45

Figure 2-4: Examples of Best Practice Guidelines: Planning,
Performing, Processing   47

Learning Exercise 2-4: Practice With a Group Plan   48

Case Illustration 2-4: Observing Group Process
Multiculturally   54

Learning Exercise 2-5: Examining Your Multicultural
Identities   55

Figure 2-5: CACREP Group Work Core Curricular
Experiences   58

Figure 2-6: ASGW Professional Training Standards
Related to Direct Experience   61

Chapter 3: Group Dynamics and Group Process   63

Learning Exercise 3-1: Identifying Relative Strengths and
Limitations   66

Case Illustration 3-1: Specific Group Dynamics   68

Learning Exercise 3-2: Tying Strengths and Limitations to
Specific Group Dynamics   69

Case Illustration 3-2: What to Look for in Groups:
Excerpts   72

Learning Exercise 3-3: Jeremy's Out of Whack Content
and Process   76

Learning Exercise 3-4: Give Jeremy Some Helpful
Feedback   77

Figure 3-1: Ideal Balance in Content and Process   80

Figure 3-2: Modified Grid for Processing Experiences
and Events in Group Work   82

Learning Exercise 3-5: Analyzing Group Content
and Process   82

Figure 3-3: Roles of Group Members   87

Learning Exercise 3-6: What Roles Fit Whom?   89

Chapter 4: Group Development: The Beginning, Working,
    and Ending Stages   91

    Learning Exercise 4-1: How Might Leadership Promote
        Positive Group Development?   96
    Figure 4-1: Tuckman's Group Development Model   99
    Figure 4-2: Jones' Task-Personal Relations Group
        Development Model   101
    Learning Exercise 4-2: Playing With Task and Personal
        Relations   103
    Case Illustration 4-1: Group Development Begins Early   104
    Learning Exercise 4-3: Getting a Handle on Group Work's
        Ultimate Purpose   109

Section II: Critical Elements of Group Work

Chapter 5: Group Work Leadership   115

    Case Illustration 5-1: Bombarded!   119
    Learning Exercise 5-1: Alternative Leader Responses to
        Feeling Bombarded   121
    Figure 5-1: Yalom's Therapeutic Factors   124
    Learning Exercise 5-2: From There-and-Then to Here-and-
        Now   126
    Learning Exercise 5-3: Looping Back   128
    Case Illustration 5-2: Misapplication   131
    Learning Exercise 5-4: How to Correct It   132
    Figure 5-2: Some Coleadership Advantages and Concerns   133
    Learning Exercise 5-5: Sylvia Is Going to Colead a Group   134

Chapter 6: Group Work Theories   139

    Case Illustration 6-1: Your "Every Day" Theory   140
    Figure 6-1: Desirable Group Qualities Theory
        Might Reflect   144
    Learning Exercise 6-1: Illustrate Group Qualities   144
    Learning Exercise 6-2: Antwan's Heart Races: Feelings   148
    Case Illustration 6-2: Dilemma   149
    Learning Exercise 6-3: Your Dilemmas   149
    Case Illustration 6-3: "Here's What I'd Like You To Do"   151
    Learning Exercise 6-4: Relaxing ...   153
    Case Illustration 6-4: Context   156
    Figure 6-2: Experiential Learning Cycle: One Example   158

Figure 6-3: Six Transtheoretical Orientations for
    Group Work   159
Learning Exercise 6-5: Outline an Oral Presentation:
    Part 1   171
Learning Exercise 6-6: Outline an Oral Presentation:
    Part 2   171
Learning Exercise 6-7: Outline and Share Your
    Developing Personal Theory of Group Work   173

Chapter 7: Group Leader Styles and Functions   177

Case Illustration 7-1: Bob's First Group Leading
    Experience   178
Learning Exercise 7-1: Your First Group Leading
    Experience   180
Learning Exercise 7-2: What Did the Group Leaders Do?   181
Figure 7-1: Group Leader Functions and Some Sample
    Behaviors   185
Learning Exercise 7-3: A Group Leadership Functions
    Activity   185
Learning Exercise 7-4: Avi's Test: Match Functions
    With Types   194
Learning Exercise 7-5: Assessing the "Provider" Type and
    Yourself   194
Figure 7-2: Core Competencies, Functions, Types,
    Methods, Strategies, and Techniques   195
Learning Exercise 7-6: Tom's Group Visits yalOMMM, the
    Group Guru With Feedback   196
Learning Exercise 7-7: Using Group Work Core
    Competencies   199

Chapter 8: Group Work Methods, Strategies, and Techniques   203

Figure 8-1: List of 10 Examples of Generic Methods   205
Learning Exercise 8-1: What's the Big Deal About
    Personhood, Anyway?   205
Figure 8-2: A Context of Interconnection in Group   209
Learning Exercise 8-2: Weighing Group Leader
    Intervention Choices   210
Learning Exercise 8-3: Walk With a Book on Your Heads   213
Learning Exercise 8-4: Use of Language: "Yes, but;"
    "Yes, and"   214
Learning Exercise 8-5: Match Up Stages With Activities   215

Figure 8-3: Switchboard Method Supporting Group
Leadership: A Relic? 217

Figure 8-4: Network Method Supporting Group
Leadership: A "Web of Life" 217

Learning Exercise 8-6: Activating the "Web of Life"
in Group 218

Figure 8-5: Suggestions for Conducting Pre-group
Preparation 220

Learning Exercise 8-7: Some Ways to Establish a Positive
Group Culture 221

Learning Exercise 8-8: Good Luck, Mr. Phelps 224

Case Illustration 8-1: Establish, Hold, and Shift the Focus:
Sample Group Leader Strategies and Techniques 227

Case Illustration 8-2: *Drawing Out* Strategy, With
Techniques 229

Case Illustration 8-3: *Cutting Off* Strategy, With
Techniques 229

Learning Exercise 8-9: Role Playing *Cutting Off* as a
Strategy? 230

Figure 8-6: A List of Some Types of Structured Exercises 231

Case Illustration 8-4: Using the "Life Line" Exercise 232

Learning Exercise 8-10: Content and Process in
Psychoeducation Lecturettes 234

Section III: Meaning, Action, and Professional Identity in Group Work

Chapter 9: Reflecting *in* and on Group Work Practice 239

Case Illustration 9-1: Some Difficult and Enjoyable
Situations in Group Leading 241

Learning Exercise 9-1: A Possible Life Lesson From the Difficult
Group Leading Situation 242

Learning Exercise 9-2: Are you a Seneca or a Wallace? 243

Case Illustration 9-2: Arcing Back, Looking Forward 246

Case Illustration 9-3: Pausing the Action 247

Case Illustration 9-4: At the End of a Session 248

Learning Exercise 9-3: Schedule Coleader Between-Session
Processing 250

Figure 9-1: Steps in the Deep Processing Model 252

Learning Exercise 9-4: Excerpts From *Assessing Self Care
Assessment Worksheet* 255

Chapter 10: Selecting Effective Interventions 261

Figure 10-1: The Purposeful Group Techniques Model (PGTM) 267
Learning Exercise 10-1: Personal "Sliding Doors" 268
Learning Exercise 10-2: Your Thoughts for Chairperson
Fulbright 273
Learning Exercise 10-3: Your Thoughts for Frederica and
William: What Might They Do? 277
Learning Exercise 10-4: How to Address Monopolizing? 283
Learning Exercise 10-5: Your Thoughts for How Rhonda Might
Intervene 290
Learning Exercise 10-6: Other Therapeutic Issues in the Group 291
Learning Exercise 10-7: Your Concluding Comments 295

Epilogue: From the Author's Chair 297

Learning Exercise E-1: Where Are You? Where Do You
Want to Go? 303

EDITORS' PREFACE: INTRODUCTION TO THE SERIES

COUNSELING AND PROFESSIONAL IDENTITY IN THE 21ST CENTURY

Group Work Leadership: An Introduction for Helpers is a text written by a true expert in the field, Robert K. Conyne, PhD. This text will not only introduce to the *what* and *why* of group work but will also inspire you to see the unique value of group work for those in the helping profession. Bob Conyne's knowledge and experience helps to make the theory, the research, the concepts of group work come alive. In addition to facilitating your developing knowledge and skills, the text will stimulate further development of your professional identity (see Table EP-1).

As is obvious, one text, one learning experience, will not be sufficient for mastery of group work, nor for the successful formation of your professional identity and practice. The formation of both your professional identity and practice will be a lifelong process—a process that we hope to facilitate through the presentation of this text and the creation of our series: *Counseling and Professional Identity in the 21st Century.*

Counseling and Professional Identity in the 21st Century is a new, pedagogically sound series of texts targeting counselors in training. This series is *not* simply a compilation of isolated books matching that which is already in the market. Rather, each book, with its targeted knowledge and skills, will be presented as but a part of a larger whole. The focus and content of each text serve as a single lens through which counselors can view their clients, engage in practice, and articulate their own professional identity.

Table EP-1   Knowledge and Skills by Chapter

Group work studies that provide both theoretical and experiential understandings of group purpose, development, dynamics, theories, methods, skills, and other group approaches in a multicultural society, including all of the following:

Focus: Knowledge and Skills	*Addressed in Chapter(s)*
Principles of group dynamics, including group process components, developmental stage theories, group members' roles and behaviors, and therapeutic factors of group work	Chapter 1 and throughout whole text
Group leadership or facilitation styles and approaches, including characteristics of various types of group leaders and leadership styles	Chapters 3, 7
Theories of group counseling, including commonalities, distinguishing characteristics, and pertinent research and literature	Chapters 5, 7, 8, 10
Group counseling methods, including group counselor orientations and behaviors, appropriate selection criteria and methods, and methods of evaluation of effectiveness	Chapters 6, 5, 9, 10
Direct experiences in which students participate as group members in a small-group activity, approved by the program, for a minimum of 10 clock hours over the course of one academic term, and where internship requires at least 240 clock hours of direct experience, including group work	Chapters 10, 2
Professional identity is a theme running through all entries in this series. It is emphasized within this text.	Chapters 9, 10, and the Epilogue

Counseling and Professional Identity in the 21st Century is unique not just in the fact that it "packaged" a series of traditional text but also in that it provides an *integrated* curriculum targeting the formation of the readers' professional identity and efficient, ethical practice. Each book within the series is structured to facilitate the ongoing professional formation of the reader. The materials found within each text are organized in such a manner as to move the reader to higher levels of cognitive, affective, and psychomotor functioning, resulting in his or her assimilation of the materials presented into both his or her professional identity and his or her approach to professional practice. While each text targets a specific set of core competencies (cognates and skills), competencies identified by the Council for Accreditation of Counseling and Related Educational Programs (CACREP) as essential to the practice of counseling, each book in the series will emphasize the following:

a. the assimilation of concepts and constructs provided across the text found within the series, thus fostering the reader's ongoing development as a competent professional;

b. the blending of contemporary theory with current research and empirical support;

c. a focus on the development of procedural knowledge with each text employing case illustrations and guided practice exercises to facilitate the reader's ability to translate the theory and research discussed into professional decision making and application;

d. the emphasis on the need for and means of demonstrating accountability; and

e. the fostering of the reader's professional identity and with it the assimilation of the ethics and standards of practice guiding the counseling profession.

We are proud to have served as coeditors of this series, confident that texts just like *Group Work Leadership: An Introduction for Helpers* will serve as a significant resource to you and your development as a professional counselor.

Richard Parsons, PhD

Naijian Zhang, PhD

PREFACE

Welcome to this text on group work and its leadership. I hope you will find reading it beneficial to you both personally and professionally.

Let's begin by taking a look at the following figure.

Figure Preface-1   Did Not Work Well in Groups

Source: www.CartoonStock.com

Don't be *that* guy/gal, the one whose tombstone epitaph decries the inability to work well in groups!

It is really important for counselors and other helping professionals to be able to work well in groups. Why? Well, you don't want to wind up at the end put outside the "in" group, do you? On a serious note, today's and certainly tomorrow's professional helpers use groups frequently as a way to help people and to solve problems. You see, groups by their very nature contain unique forces for healing and for production that cannot be found in other helping modes. These forces, or dynamics, are centered around therapeutic conditions (e.g., cohesion, the sense of "we-ness" that can develop in a group and among members) through which members can progress. The group leader needs to work well in groups both as a personal participant and as a facilitator of important dynamics, helping to establish and maintain these conditions so positive outcomes can be realized.

Group work is a comprehensive and unique service delivery method for counselors and other helping professionals. It is at once a core competency area within counseling program accreditation (Council for the Accreditation of Counseling and Related Educational Programs, or CACREP), and it stands apart from other forms of counseling and professional helping because of its particular origins, premises, and applications. It is an approach that is valued within all helping professions and is a part of their training curricula as well. In this text, you will become acquainted with why group work and the leadership of groups are so central to helping.

● ORGANIZATION

Sections and Chapters

The text covers major content in the area of group work, and it is intended for the central group work course in the curriculum. It is organized by three sections: (a) "Group Work Is a Comprehensive and Unique Approach," (b) "Critical Elements of Group Work," and (c) "Meaning, Action, and Professional Identity in Group Work."

Section I describes the breadth of group work (Chapter 1), its foundations, including best practice and ethical considerations (Chapter 2), dynamics and processes in group work (Chapter 3), and how groups tend to develop over time (Chapter 4).

Section II explores group work leadership (Chapter 5); theories in group work that are both traditional and innovative (Chapter 6); the building blocks of group leadership that include functions, style, and competencies

(Chapter 7); and group leadership methods, strategies, and techniques, that is, its "action tools of the trade" (Chapter 8).

Section III examines the role of reflection in and on group practice (Chapter 9) and selecting effective interventions in group leadership, where interaction examples are provided, analyzed, and discussed for each of the four group work types (task, psychoeducation, counseling, and psychotherapy) from the perspective of choices made (Chapter 10).

The Epilogue is an innovative conclusion that is part of each book in this series; in it, I comment on the text, discuss how I've become excited about transtheoretical orientations to group leadership and to the emerging implications of interpersonal neurobiology (IPNB), and highlight the importance of meaning attribution and professional identity.

Format

The general format for the chapters of this book is consistent with that used in the series. Following the chapter title and a quotation especially chosen for the chapter's contents, chapter sections will include (a) introduction, (b) chapter objectives, (c) substance of the chapter, (d) group work keystones (summary highlights), and (e) recommended resources. A complete reference list is presented at the end of the text. The material is presented with the goal of providing information in such a way as to engage you in reading, providing ample opportunities for you to try out and apply your learning. To that end, the text includes more than 100 case illustrations, learning exercises, and figures; see the Chapter List of Case Illustrations, Figures, and Learning Exercises for a compilation.

The content of all books in the larger series on counselor professional identity, of which this book is a part, seeks to connect with CACREP accreditation standards. For those of you especially interested in the relationship between the accreditation standards and the chapters in this book, please refer to the Preface of the Editors by Richard Parsons and Naijian Zhang.

HIGHLIGHTING SOME UNIQUE ASPECTS ● OF GROUP WORK

Group Work Is Interdependent, Interactive, and Collective

Group work stands alone as a comprehensive and unique service delivery method, which I mentioned previously. Certainly, it is compatible with individual counseling and therapy and fits squarely within the overall values and premises of the counseling profession.

However, it is becoming more widely appreciated among scholars that group work is not based primarily on the individual helping model, or with individual counseling theories. Rather, it is more closely aligned with an interdependent and collective model. Connections among group members receive dominant importance in group work. *Attention is given by group leaders to work with members to create and maintain therapeutic conditions—it is through this facilitative milieu that members learn, grow, change, and create.* You will read about all this in the chapters to come.

But, for now, just picture in your mind's eye individual members interacting with each other within a circle of helping—that's group work. This interaction also may occur online, in a non-face-to-face manner. This emerging area, which I touch lightly on in Chapters 3 and 7, will become a focal point for research and development in the future. But, for the most part, we tend to think of group work as a direct, face-to-face contact activity. However it may occur, though, group work holds much in common with multicultural approaches to helping and with ecological and systems thinking, where interactions of people with environments are salient.

Group Work Comes in Different Types

Group work also is distinguished by its variety of types. The Association for Specialists in Group Work (ASGW), for instance, has identified four main types: task or work groups, psychoeducation/skill-based groups, counseling/interpersonal problem-solving groups, and psychotherapy/personality reconstruction groups.

Indeed, other important group-focused professional associations, such as the Society of Group Psychology and Group Psychotherapy, the Association for the Advancement of Social Work with Groups, and the American Group Psychotherapy Association, all view groups as a multifaceted method. All affirm that group work is robust.

Group Work Has a Range of Purposes

Implicit in this "robustness" are the range of purposes that characterize group work. It can be used for remedial reasons, to help members to correct and repair damage and difficulties. It can be employed for developmental reasons, helping members to learn and enhance knowledge and skills. And group work can be applied for preventive purposes, to inoculate members against future challenges and threats.

BE FOREWARNED ●

I write in the text about how I got "bit" by the group work bug. The "infection" that resulted did not make me ill. Rather, it was like some kind of life-giving force running though my arteries. It's said that the great former manager of the Dodgers Tommy Lasorda bleeds "Dodger Blue." I suppose I bleed "Group Work," which is composed of a rainbow of colors to reflect its variety and range. I'm not the only one; rest assured, many others also find group work an essential and compelling method of help giving, and they care deeply about it.

Of course, it's my desire that you may get bit by this very same bug, at least a tiny bite. Then you, too, may feel the joy and wonder of what groups can do to improve the lives of clients and others with whom you work. And it may be said of you: She (or he) "worked well with groups."

LET ME KNOW YOUR REACTIONS ●

Finally, I invite you to contact me at any time (robert.conyne@uc.edu), to give feedback, to ask questions, or just to communicate about group work. It would be my pleasure to be in touch with you!

ACKNOWLEDGMENTS

There always is dancing around in my imagination, so many wonderful associations that have contributed to my own development as a group leader. The little church in the valley in Sciota, New York, where services were conducted as the six or maybe eight of us sat in a circle around an old pot-belly stove during a cold winter Sunday; Mooers Central School and all that I learned in that wonderful but "undermanned setting," tucked against the Quebec and Vermont border in upstate New York; Syracuse University course work in the behavioral and social sciences; my professors at Purdue University; the National Training Laboratories (NTL) at Bethel, Maine (the "holy grail"), and at the Midwest Group for Human Relations; Illinois State University and the University of Cincinnati—which allowed me to learn, teach, research, and write in this area; wonderful students and faculty colleagues of more than 40 years; ASGW and Division 49 of APA, that serve as my "group work homes"; all my group work friends and colleagues, too numerous to mention (and, besides, what if I started and then forgot some?); the continual support of my wife and colleague (Lynn Rapin) and my family; our dog, Lucy, who sits patiently every day at my feet as I write; Kassie Graves of SAGE for encouraging and supporting my writing in the group and prevention areas; and Rick Parsons and Naijian Zhang for the opportunity to participate in this unique book series.

While writing this book was my solo effort, I also benefited from comments made by a group of reviewers, selected by the publisher. Their comments were always enlightening and often very helpful. I want to cite and thank them publicly for their assistance: David Tobin, Diana Hulse, Kerri Augusto, Hamilton Baylon, Karen Cathey, Betty Watts, Bill Casile, Judith Bachay, and Nancy Meyer-Adams.

Thank you, everyone!

I dedicate this book to

The memory of my parents, Robert Karlton Conyne, Sr., and Elizabeth Maida Brownell Conyne: For all their love and sacrifice.

And to my sisters, Mary and Julie, and my brother, John: A really good group, over the decades and across the miles. Take it to the limit!

Lynn, my wife, and our children, Suzanne and Zack. The joys of my life!

Those who will read this book, perhaps especially to you, hoping it will contribute to your growth as group leaders—May you all get bitten by the "group work bug"!

And last—but certainly not least—a grateful thank you to Professors Allan Dye and Richard Diedrich, who taught and nurtured me in group work as a doctoral student at Purdue. I am forever grateful.

SECTION I

GROUP WORK IS A COMPREHENSIVE AND UNIQUE APPROACH

The four chapters contained in the first section of this book, *Understanding Group Work*, are focused on increasing knowledge and understanding.

The first chapter considers the *breadth* of group work, using the metaphor of an "umbrella." Groups are discussed as being ubiquitous—everywhere—in our society, occurring in all manner of shapes and forms. A definition of group work is given and elaborated throughout the chapter: "a broad professional practice that refers to the giving of help or the accomplishment of tasks in a group setting. It involves the application of group theory and process by a capable professional practitioner to assist an interdependent collection of people to reach their mutual goals, which may be personal, interpersonal, or task related in nature."

Chapter 2 places group work in a historical context. It then proceeds to focus on three *foundational documents* that have been instrumental in supporting group work's evolution: training standards, best-practice guidelines, ethics, and multicultural principles. The role of accreditation in counseling and, particularly, in group work, is enumerated and specific recommendations are provided on how to further shore up training in this important area.

Chapter 3 addresses *group dynamics and group process*. Group dynamics and group process are essential forces in group work. Major categories of group dynamics include group evolution and organization, control and direction, working and performance, maintenance and conflict, and context. Important group processes include balancing content and process, the processing of group events and experiences, and group member roles.

Chapter 4 emphasizes how important good group work is dependent on leaders understanding *how groups can develop* over time and even within any one session or meeting. Knowledge of group development is invaluable. It strongly contributes to designing a group, observing what is occurring, and in selecting appropriate and effective interventions. Some examples of group development models are described, with connections suggested between any one group development stage and actions that leaders might take.

Chapters in subsequent book sections extend these emphases while increasingly adding specific concentration to competencies, experience, and application.

CHAPTER 1

INTRODUCTION TO GROUP WORK

My wife, a retired social work administrator, is offering training work-shops to Boards of Directors of non-profit agencies . . . she sure puts group dynamics to work . . . My son-in-law directs the Emergency Room at a large local hospital. He sure puts group dynamics to work. Harold Kelman has been applying group dynamics to the tinder-box of the Middle East . . .

—Morris Goodman (1995, p. 2)

And so it goes.

—Linda Ellerbee (1986)

INTRODUCTION: WELCOME, ● BOOK FRAMEWORK, AND STRUCTURE

It is a pleasure to welcome you to this book on group work and its leader-ship. I hope you will find its contents to be inviting and informative.

I'm excited to present this information to you because group work is such an important method for counselors and other helpers to include in their helping repertoire. As Goodman, a past president of the Society of Group Psy-chology and Group Psychotherapy, implies in his earlier quote above, group dynamics—a key part of group work—are used in a variety of ways, in a range of settings, and for a number of reasons. Those of us in the helping professions—counselors, psychologists, social workers, human service providers, human relations consultants and coaches, and more—most often think of group work in terms of group counseling and group psychotherapy, no doubt. Fair enough, they are essential forms. But, as you will come to see, group work also is employed in organization change, discussion groups, teaching skills, community development, management, and in many other ways. It is used to heal, to promote, to facilitate, and to change; it is applied in schools, clinics, the workplace, and communities. *And so it goes.* Indeed, group work truly is a robust method that applies group dynamics in a variety of ways, and it takes a broad umbrella to span it. We will talk more on this topic later in the chapter.

This book is developed to advance the evolving group work competencies of students and trainees and to provide instructional opportunities for faculty to incorporate within and outside of class. Text materials will inform you about the theory and practice of group work, which is a comprehensive and unique service. More than 100 case illustrations, figures, and learning exercises are provided and are geared to promote group work leadership skills within counseling and all helping professions.

Although we will give closest attention to the products and services of the American Counseling Association (ACA) and its "group" division, the Association for Specialists in Group Work (ASGW), each helping profession has its own professional association, supportive academic disciplines, and professional literature (Figure 2-1 in Chapter 2 contains basic contact information). For instance, the Association for the Advancement of Social Work with Groups (AASWG) has produced its own training document, *Standards for Social Work Practice with Groups* (2010), and the American Group Psychotherapy Association has developed its *Practice Guidelines for Group Psychotherapy* (2007). The Society for Group Psychology and Group Psychotherapy, as many of these associations, has its own unique journal— *Group Dynamics: Theory, Research, and Practice.* Clearly, group work as a practice results from the contributions of many professions and influencing academic disciplines, such as psychology, counseling, education, social work, management, sociology, and social psychology.

Chapters in this book draw from many of these sources. They are intended to help enhance group work training and practice in such a way as to foster your ongoing development as a competent helping professional, regardless of your professional affiliation.

In general, all chapters in this text are developed to

a. blend contemporary theory with current research and empirical support;

b. help you translate theory and research discussed into professional decision making and application through inclusion of case illustrations, figures, and learning exercises;

c. foster your professional identity and with it the assimilation of the ethics and standards of practice guiding the helping professions;

d. attend to diversity and multicultural influences; and

e. illustrate the comprehensiveness and uniqueness of group work as a service delivery method for counselors and other professional helpers.

CHAPTER OBJECTIVES

As a result of reading this chapter you will be able to

- Show how group work is a broad helping methodology
- Show that groups are commonplace in our lives
- Discuss five perspectives supporting group work
- Explain how all groups are interpersonal phenomena
- Indicate that research on group work (especially group counseling and psychotherapy) generally attests to its effectiveness
- Describe various conceptualizations of working with groups
- Understand the framework used by the ASGW as a general model that can be applied to other situations
- Present that group work can be thought of as an umbrella term, spanning core group work competencies and four types/specializations of group work
- Define group work and its major components
- Define the four types of group work, as defined by the ASGW: task, psycho-education, counseling, and psychotherapy

Let's move ahead now by considering the umbrella of services that characterizes group work.

GROUPS ARE EVERYWHERE ●

To understand group work, one must first understand groups themselves, their basic nature and the processes that characterize them (Forsyth, 2011). Humans generally enjoy being around others and choose to engage together for any number of outlets.

Note the following: "People, no matter what they are doing—working, relaxing, studying, exercising, worshiping, playing, socializing, watching entertainment, or sleeping—are usually in a group rather than alone" (Forsyth, 2011, p. 19).

Groups, then, are ubiquitous in our society and around the world, both in daily living and, increasingly, as an intentional method to induce growth and development and/or the alleviation and resolution of life problems.

Case Illustration 1–1 and Learning Exercise 1–1 are intended to sensitize you to the presence of groups in your life.

Case Illustration 1–1: A Day in the Life

*The **object** of this case illustration is to demonstrate how being connected with others occurs on a daily basis for many people. This daily interaction with others suggests that working with people in groups is a natural approach.*

Antwan is a sophomore at State U. In his Introduction to Sociology course, the professor has assigned each student the task of observing their daily activities over the course of one week. Here is a sample of some of Antwan's activities for the preceding week:

- Friday night, socialized and went drinking with four friends
- Saturday afternoon, went to basketball game with my roommate
- Saturday night, went to dinner with my girlfriend and another couple
- Sunday, slept in until noon; hung out with friends later
- Monday–Thursday, went to class every day
- Tuesday night, studied with my study group
- Wednesday night, worked on group project for Careers class

Returning to the first question, how Antwan spent his time, among other things, it seems apparent from Antwan's report that many of his activities involved him with other people. This situation is not unusual but, rather, is consistent with what we know of how most people live their daily lives—they are involved with others, whether by choice (e.g., going to a basketball game with a roommate) or by circumstance (e.g., participating in assigned group projects). Such ongoing daily interaction with others represents a support for working with people in groups.

Learning Exercise 1–1: Take a Life Sample

*The **object** of this learning exercise is to help readers examine how they spend their own daily lives and what this might possibly imply for group work.*

Now, take a sample of your world during a typical week. What did you do during that weekend? During the weekdays, Monday–Friday?

1. List five activities with which you were involved, as Antwan did in the previous case illustration:

   _____

   _____

   _____

   _____

   _____

2. Record the number of activities in which you were involved with others: _____

3. Hypothesize how your general involvement with others might relate to your working style in groups.

WHAT IS GROUP WORK? ●

Five Perspectives Underlying Group Work

Five major perspectives undergird group work:

a. *Individual* perspective, having its basic origins and primary focus on the individual person

b. *Group* perspective, focused on the group unit itself as the main point of reference, the group

c. *Interpersonal* perspective, where member interaction and the relationships among participants is key

d. *Contextual* perspective, which takes the interactions of people with each other *and* with the group environment as central

e. *Multicultural-diversity* perspective, which posits that all group work is multicultural

Note that these five perspectives are not mutually exclusive. In the real world, there is overlap among them.

The individual person perspective. The individual perspective occupies a hallowed position in Western culture (e.g., humanistic philosophers, such as John Locke), American history (notably, the Declaration of Independence), and in the counseling profession as well. According to Kitchener (1984), there is the principle of autonomy as a core moral value guiding ethical practice. Certainly, a "group" would not exist without individuals, and the growth, development, and welfare of individuals is essential in all of forms of counseling practice, including group work.

The group perspective. However, it needs to be stressed that a *group* is more than a number of separate individuals occupying the same space at the same time. As you have seen from reading the preface, when people gather in a group and begin to interact, a number of dynamics and processes are generated. In fact, a group is an excellent example of an organism being more than the sum of its individual parts because of the multiplicative impacts that result from member-to-member interactions. In a group, $1 + 1 + 1$ does not equal 3, but some other integer greater than 3. Another way to think of this multiplicative factor is in relation to the number of paired interactions possible in a group, which greatly exceeds the obvious. For instance, in a group of eight members, if you'd think that four possible member pairings exist (as many might, at least at first glance), you would be wrong; in this case, the number of possible paired interactions is 28. (For those of you interested in the math, the calculation of number of pairings is $n(n - 1)/2$ or, in this instance, $8(7)/2 = 56/2 = 28$ pairs. Of course, additional combinations occur in groups beyond pairing, such as when a subgroup of three of more people interacts. Although a group is comprised of individual members, once they begin communicating, more complicated and powerful dynamics are generated.

The interpersonal perspective. Participating in a group is above all an interpersonal experience. By definition, a group is not a group without individual members being in relation to each other. So, an interpersonal perspective is tied to ongoing interactions and the relationships that develop over time among group participants. The quality of these relationships—their positive or negative valence, their degree of intimacy or distance, their level of safety or danger, their activity or passivity—strongly influences whether the group will coalesce and its members will enjoy a meaningful and productive experience.

The contextual perspective. This perspective is based on the assumptions that people do not exist in a vacuum but they are embedded within environments and that people and environments are mutually influencing. Thus, to understand persons, it is necessary to understand them within their milieu, their context. George Stern (1970), a pioneering ecological researcher, referred to this condition as the congruence of "people in context." Fritjof Capra (1996), an innovator in understanding living systems, captured the interaction between people and environments as the "web of life."

The group offers a prime example of people in context. In a group, individual participants, their relationships, and their connection within the total group all are in context and subject to a dynamic and reciprocal influencing process. For instance, how a person feels about being a group member is a function not only of his or her personal characteristics, but also is influenced by such variables as the kinds of relationships that exist with other members, and the climate of the group. Lewin (1936) represented this situation as $B = f(PxE)$, or Behavior is a function of Persons interacting with levels of their Environment.

The multicultural-diversity perspective. This perspective is based on the assumption that all groups are microcosms of the community and the world. That is, each member brings to the group a unique set of demographic characteristics (e.g., age, gender, socioeconomic condition, educational level, relationship status, religious/spiritual beliefs), cultural background (e.g., ethnicity, race, worldview), lifestyle (e.g., sexual orientation, family life), awareness of identities (of self, others, self in relation to others), status similarities and differences (e.g., rank, power, and influence), experience (e.g., work, travel, involvements with others), and derived meaning (beliefs, values, assumptions) that mirror the world from which they come (Anderson, 2007). This world is both multicultural and diverse (DeLucia-Waack & Donigian, 2004; Salazar, 2009). In turn, multiculturalism and diversity are inherent in all of group work (DeLucia-Waack, 2006b).

When members interact with one another in the group, then, a major part of what is happening is an exercise in diversity, which can yield both positive and negative consequences. That is, it can yield an environment teeming with abundance through which members can learn remarkable things about themselves and others. Or, it can produce an environment fraught with defensiveness and fear, where members learn or reiterate distrust others who are unlike themselves.

It is an ethical responsibility of group work leaders to acquire the awareness, knowledge, and competencies allowing for effective functioning in the diverse and multicultural context of the group.

Group Work Is an Umbrella Term

Like an umbrella that spans and covers space, group work is an expansive term covering a comprehensive set of group mediated methods, which I mentioned at the start of this chapter. These methods, sometimes referred to as types or specializations (Note: I use these terms interchangeably), are intentionally used to help people cope and be more effective in their personal lives, in their involvements with others, and in the tasks they perform with others in organized settings. Working with people in groups provides an important way for counselors to reduce dysfunction, develop competencies, promote prevention of future life problems, and collaborate with others in solving problems and achieving task goals. Group methods provide a viable alternative—a unique way—to other counseling approaches, such as individual counseling and consultation, and often complement them in practice (Bemak & Conyne, 2004).

Various Conceptualizations of Group Methods

Group methods have been conceptualized in different ways (Conyne, 2011, 2012). For instance, the Society for Group Psychology and Group Psychotherapy (Division 49 of the American Psychological Association) organizes the range of group methods under "group psychology and group psychotherapy." The American Group Psychotherapy Association (AGPA) uses *group psychotherapy* as the overarching term covering, as Yalom and Leszcz (2005) put it in the preface to their classic text, *group therapies*, rather than *group therapy* (p. xii). The Association for the Advancement of Social Work with Groups (AASWG) uses the term common in social work, *group work*, as the organizing construct. The Association for Specialists in Group Work (ASGW of the American Counseling Association) also employs the broad term, group work, to contain a range of group methods.

Group Work Is Effective

Are group work approaches effective? The overwhelming research indicates they are. Group counseling, psychotherapy, and psychoeducation are the forms of group work receiving the most research attention (e.g., Barlow, Fuhriman, & Burlingame, 2004; Conyne, 2011, 2012; Leszcz & Kobos, 2008). Empirical research is accumulating to indicate that they are at the minimum as effective as individual therapy in producing client change. As well, research in the area of task groups, especially those that are based on teams that use interactive processes, has been shown to be effective in many circumstances (e.g., Cohen & Bailey, 1997; Hackman, 2002; Kozlowski & Ilgen, 2006; Mathieu, Maynard, Rapp, & Gilson, 2008). Moreover, all group work affords many additional benefits, including those of efficiencies and cost benefits (e.g., Bauman, 2009; Spitz, 1996), belonging, social support, and other advantages that can result from positive interactions with others (Forsyth, 2010). After reviewing hundreds of studies, Barlow, Burlingame, and Fuhriman (2000) concluded that "the group format consistently produced positive effects with a number of disorders using a variety of treatment models" (p. 122).

The mounting evidence supporting the effectiveness of group approaches, however, does not mean that all questions have been answered. Although variables such as cohesion (i.e., the sense that group participants matter to one another) clearly contribute to overall effectiveness, the mechanisms for change are not so clear in any type of group work. "There remains a critical need for empirically supported group processes and conditions, for development of more measures to accurately detect them, and for the actionable group leadership that is tied to these group processes and conditions" (Conyne, 2011, p. 612). For those of you who may find research of high interest, take note. The field of group work needs not only good practitioners but also good researchers. A lot has been accomplished and there is so much more to do.

ASGW'S CONCEPTION OF GROUP WORK ●

Core Group Work Competencies

In the ASGW framework, a set of *core competencies* (attitudes, knowledge, and skills) is held out as the supportive platform of all group work. Examples of these core competencies, drawn from the *ASGW Professional Standards for the Training of Group Workers* (ASGW, 2000) include encouraging participation of group members, knowing therapeutic factors, and demonstrating collaborative consultation with targeted populations to enhance the ecological validity of planned group interventions—among many others.

Group work core competencies undergird what all counselors who lead groups should be able to do at the minimum (ASGW, 2000). They are conceptualized as Knowledge and Skills and are arranged into seven categories:

a. Nature and scope of practice

b. Assessment of group members and social systems in which they live and work

c. Planning group interventions

d. Implementation of group interventions

e. Leadership and coleadership

f. Evaluation

g. Ethical practice, best practice, diversity-competent practice

Learning Exercise 1–2 gives you the opportunity to examine a few of your core competencies.

Learning Exercise 1–2: Assessing Some of Your Core Competencies

The **object** of this learning exercise is to help you identify strengths and areas for improvement in group work core competencies.

The following checklist contains a sample of core competency items, one from knowledge and another from skills within each of the seven categories. Use the "OK" and "Needs Improvement" columns to indicate present status:

	OK	NEEDS IMPROVEMENT
1. Nature and scope of practice		
Knowledge: Nature of group work and its various specializations	_____	_____
Skill: Preparing a professional disclosure statement for practice	_____	_____
2. Assessment of group members and social systems		
Knowledge: Principles of assessment of group functioning in group work	_____	_____
Skill: Observing personal characteristics of individual members in a group	_____	_____

(Continued)

3. Planning group interventions

   Knowledge: Principles of planning for _____ _____
   group *work*

   Skill: Planning for group work activity _____ _____
   (e.g., purpose, methods)

4. Implementation of group interventions

   Knowledge: Therapeutic factors in _____ _____
   group work and when group approaches
   are indicated and counterindicated

   Skill: Giving and receiving feedback in _____ _____
   a group setting

5. Leadership and coleadership

   Knowledge: Group leadership styles and _____ _____
   approaches

   Skill: Engaging in collaborative group _____ _____
   processing

6. Evaluation

   Knowledge: Methods for evaluating _____ _____
   group process in group work

   Skill: Contributing to evaluation _____ _____
   activities during group participation

7. Ethical practice, best practice, diversity-
   competent practice

   Knowledge: Best practices in group work _____ _____

   Skill: Evidencing ethical practice in,
   planning observing, and participating in
   group activities

   Skill: Demonstrating awareness of _____ _____
   other cultures

SUM UP: Review your responses and write a summary paragraph about the present status of your core competencies.

Four Advanced Types of Group Work

Resting on and extending these core group work competencies are four advanced types, methods, or specializations of group work (ASGW, 2000; Conyne, Wilson, & Ward, 1997). All of these forms of group work also make full use of group processes, dynamics, and therapeutic conditions. These advanced types of group work are the following:

(a) *Task/work groups,* which facilitate accomplishing specific project-oriented goals (Arrow, McGrath, & Berdahl, 2000; Conyne, 1989; Conyne, Rapin, & Rand, 1997; Fatout & Rose, 1995; Forsyth, 2009; Hackman, 2002; Hulse-Killacky, Killacky, & Donigian, 2001; Kormanski, 1999, 2001; Reddy, 1994; Schwarz, 2002; Wheelan, 2004). Schwarz's (2002) description of a work group fits well: "a set of people with specific interdependent roles who are collectively responsible for producing some output (service, product, or decision) that can be assessed, and who manage their relationships with those outside the group" (2002, p. 20). Note the emphasis on interdependent functioning, output production, the types of output, and connections with the external environment (Larson & LaFasto, 1989; Sundstrom, DeMeuse, & Futrell, 1990). The primary focus in task groups is on the work, but attention also must be paid to human interactions that support or detract from work accomplishment. An example can be found in a classroom discussion group, where the main purpose is to learn content through the process of group members interacting with one another (see Hill, 1969). In the work setting, task groups often are referred to as work groups or teams that can be used for a range of purposes: planning, decision making, setting policy, and a number of other activities aimed at reaching organizational goals (Wheelan, 2004). Problem-solving processes are prime elements of a task or work group (Conyne, Rapin, et al., 1997).

(b) *Psychoeducation groups,* which teach life competencies through education and skill training (Brown, 1998, 2005; DeLucia-Waack, 2006a; Furr, 2000; Rivera et al., 2004). Psychoeducation groups use planned, structured activities with the group leader functioning as a facilitator, teacher, and trainer. Didactic presentation, skill demonstration and practice, and use of group process are interwoven throughout group sessions. The overall focus of a psychoeducation group is on development and prevention.

(c) *Group counseling,* which resolves typical stressful problems of daily living (Conyne, 2011, 2012; Corey, 2012; Delucia-Waack, Gerrity, Kalodner, & Riva, 2004; Gladding, 2011b; Kline, 2003; Posthuma, 2002; Trotzer, 2006). While these issues present challenges, they generally tend not to impede daily functioning. In addition to helping members work through desig-nated life problems, such as loneliness or mild anxiety, group counseling also can promote interpersonal growth and development. While group counseling is useful primarily for people who may be experiencing transitory maladjustment, it "occupies a broad middle section of the helping goals continuum where prevention, development, and remediation all play important roles, depending on member needs and situational supports and constraints" (Conyne, 2012, p. 615).

(d) *Group psychotherapy,* which remediates psychological and emotional dysfunction (Agazarian, 2004; AGPA, 2007, 2012, n.d.; Bernard & McKenzie, 1994; Delucia-Waack et al., 2004; Leszcz & Kobos, 2008; Weinberg, 2012; Yalom & Leszcz, 2005). It addresses maladaptive conditions of group members, those that serve to interfere with their daily functioning. It may involve attending to both historical, past behavior as well as to present circumstances in efforts to help correct distortions and repetitive patterns of dysfunctional behavior and to promote healthier personal and interpersonal attitudes, feelings, and behavior.

Case Illustration 1–2 announces the four types of group work through a university counseling center flyer.

Case Illustration 1–2: Four Types of Group Work

The **object** of this case illustration is to further acquaint you with definitions of group work types.

Groups at the Counseling Center Flyer

Groups are a great way for people to learn, to improve, and even to change in needed directions.

We invite participation in the groups we are offering this semester. All of them provide opportunities for connecting with others to reach goals. Below are brief descriptions. To indicate your interest in participating, or just to ask questions about any of the groups, call XXX-YYYY or just stop by. The groups are

Task Groups: Solving Real World Tasks and Problems. These groups are intended for organizations on campus, whether they are for students or for faculty and staff. The groups are arranged to fit circumstances and can assist with clarifying organizational goals, helping the organization to reduce conflict and improve cooperative functioning, or facilitating planning and evaluation.

Psychoeducation Groups: Building Life Skills. These groups help members enhance their knowledge and skills in everyday and necessary

(Continued)

(Continued)

skills for living, such as maintaining relationships and coping with academic stressors. They use some structured exercises and practice, along with open discussion, to help members deal even more successfully with college life.

Group Counseling: Resolving Problems of Living. Everyone is challenged by life's demands. On a residential college campus such as ours, some of these life challenges may include loneliness, roommate conflicts, managing newfound "freedom," finding ways to cope satisfactorily with academic pressures, developing and maintaining relationships, and many more. Group counseling builds interpersonal connections and support among members to learn effective methods for better handling life's never-ending challenges.

Group Psychotherapy: Correcting Deeper Personal Problems. Sometimes the challenges of college life can become excessive, outstripping a student's available resources to handle them well or with ease. This situation can lead to feeling out of control, and possibly to feelings of depression and low self-worth. When this happens, it often is harder to study and to be with other people. Group psychotherapy is available to help qualifying students develop the deeper level of support they need to develop corrective strategies that can get them back on a positive track.

Figure 1–1 depicts the relationship between the core group work standards and the four group work types (Conyne-Rapin, 1996).

 Figure 1.1 The Group Work Rainbow

Source: From Conyne-Rapin, Z., 2006. Used with permission.

In this book, which is part of a series of books concerned with both the helping professions and, more particularly, with counseling as a profession, we will pay close attention to materials published by ASGW. Founded in 1973, the Association for Specialists in Group Work is a division of the American Counseling Association. According to its website, ASGW is comprised of counseling professionals who are interested in and specialize in group work. They value creation of community and service to their members, their clients, and their profession. They likewise value leadership as a process to facilitate the growth and development of individuals and groups (www.asgw.org).

ASGW GROUP WORK DEFINITION ●

As defined by ASGW, group work is a broad term encompassing a range of group methods, known singularly as task groups, psychoeducation groups, group counseling, and group psychotherapy. By extension, group work also embraces related group applications, such as support groups, prevention groups, and self-directed groups, among others.

By definition,

> Group work is a broad professional practice that refers to the giving of help or the accomplishment of tasks in a group setting. It involves the application of group theory and process by a capable professional practitioner to assist an interdependent collection of people to reach their mutual goals, which may be personal, interpersonal, or task-related in nature. (ASGW, 2000, p. 3; Conyne, Wilson, & Ward, 1997, p. 14)

Let's break this definition into its seven parts (Conyne, Wilson, et al., 1997).

Group Work Definition, Part I: Group Work Is a Broad Professional Practice

Group work is a professional practice just as is individual counseling, consultation, or family counseling (Conyne & Bemak, 2004a, 2004b). Associated with it are sets of knowledge and skills, training standards, best-practice guidelines, diversity principles, theory, and research.

Group work emerges from no single academic discipline, profession, or association. Rather, it is a broad professional practice that has been influenced by divergent sources including, but not limited to (a) *academic disciplines* of sociology, psychology, and political science; (b) *professions* of counseling, clinical psychology, counseling psychology, social work, community psychology, organization development, social psychology, public health, and teacher education; and (c) *professional organizations* such as the National Training Laboratories, Esalen, American Association of Group Psychotherapy and Psychodrama, American Group Psychotherapy Association, Association for Specialists in Group Work, the Society for Group Psychology and Group Psychotherapy; and (d) the *research and publications* of numerous scholars across many fields over the last 110 years (Barlow, Fuhriman, & Burlingame, 2004; Conyne, 2011; Leddick, 2011).

Group Work Definition, Part II: Giving Help or Accomplishing Tasks in a Group Setting

Group work is a method with two central concentrations, to (a) provide help to group members who seek resolution, change, or growth in relation to personal and interpersonal domains, and (b) assist group members to achieve tasks and goals and to produce desired products and outcomes.

Personal and interpersonal concentration. Group work leaders collaborate with members to establish a positive therapeutic climate in the group. Such a climate, which is both safe and challenging, allows the leader opportunities for encouraging members to join together cohesively to help each other to improve or to change aspects of their lives (Corey, 2012; Gladding, 2011b; Marmarosh & Van Horn, 2011; Trotzer, 2006).

Task concentration. In task groups, such as committees and staff meetings, leaders place priority on helping group members join together to accomplish tasks and produce concrete products. Examples include strategic plans, position papers, organization development activities, training and staff development, prevention program plans, team teaching, focus groups, and program evaluations (Conyne, 1989; Conyne, Rapin, et al., 1997; Hulse-Killacky, 1996; Hulse-Killacky, Killacky, & Donigian, 2001; Johnson & Johnson, 2008).

Group Work Definition, Part III: Involving the Application of Group Theory and Process

Group work grew out of individual counseling and continues to be strongly influenced by it. For example, most textbooks in group counseling or group psychotherapy (e.g., Corey, 2009; Gladding, 2011b; Yalom

& Leszcz, 2005) prominently feature content addressing theories of counseling. Generally, these are theories of individual counseling, the helping mode that has typified the profession and the practice of counseling. Yet it is the case that group work emerges not from the individual frame of reference but from an interpersonal and group perspective, as I noted earlier.

Individual counseling quickly assumed the dominant helping method in the United States because it best matches the individualistic and independent Western European ethos that has historically characterized American culture. Arguably, it also is less complex and complicated to understand and deliver than other counseling interventions that involve larger numbers of people and may be embedded within bigger systems, such as group work, family counseling, and consultation. So, individual counseling was a natural first choice for counseling.

However, our culture is broadening to include people from other races, ethnicities, and places of birth. For instance, U.S. census bureau statistics reveal that one-third of the population identified as part of a racial or ethnic minority group (e.g., Latino([a])/Hispanic, African American, Asian), including 45% of children under age 5 (Population Reference Group, 2012). In such minority populations, a group, family, and more collectivist orientation tends to be characteristic. As our society grows ever more multicultural and diverse, accompanied by a collectivist, group-centered conception of life (Herr, 2004), group and other interpersonal modes of counseling will continue to gain attention and use.

Likewise, the reliance upon individual counseling is now expanding to embrace group and family approaches more fully, in part due to the need to mirror the variety of populations seeking counseling assistance (Bemak & Conyne, 2004; Conyne, 2003; Conyne & Bemak, 2004a, 2004b) and to increase the cultural appropriateness of counseling. In turn, a more authentic counseling that matches the worldview and values of clients and group members is ethically right and is a best practice.

While group work is its own professional practice, what needs to be more fully developed is a theoretical base that is unique from theories of individual counseling. As has been suggested (e.g., Conyne, 2003) this theoretical foundation "will emerge from an interdependent and collectivistic orientation, giving close attention to contextual circumstances" (p. 294). Bemak and Conyne (2004) have expanded upon this point to recommend an interdependent, ecological theoretical framework to support group work. This framework emphasizes the connections among group members and between the group and its external environment (Conyne & Cook, 2004). Therefore, it is very different from an individualistic orientation, which is much more sensitive to individual counseling. Instead, it would support how people in a group interact and connect with one another, which is the essence of group work. Note that Chapter 6 is devoted to the topic of theories in group work.

See Case Illustration 1–3 and Learning Exercise 1–3 to explore the place of interpersonal connections in your life.

Case Illustration 1–3: People Are Connected

*The **object** of this case illustration is to underline the importance of social support.*

Sylvia worried about her sister, Carmelita. Where was she? She was supposed to have come home by 6:00 p.m. Already an hour late. She called her mother, her brother; no answers there. She thought about Sylvia's many friends, some of them whom she knew. She called Julio, but no answer. She tried Frieda and was answered by a message system. What should she do?

In the end, after another half hour, it turned out that Carmelita was simply delayed by "good times." She came home, albeit late.

Looking back at it, Sylvia thought, what a wonderful network of supportive people Carmelita has in her life. Maybe, she thought, I should not worry so much.

Learning Exercise 1–3: What About Your Social Support Network?

*The **object** of this learning exercise is to provide you with a way to take a look at your own social support network and to estimate its meaning for group work.*

Sometimes a social network is more important than at other times. Sylvia's situation was one of those times. But at nearly any time connections with friends and family can be important, not only for pleasure but also for the support and sustenance they can provide. This condition also is very important in a group. How connected are you with other members? How supported do you feel? How much assistance are you able to provide to others?

(Continued)

Consider your social connections. How are you with other people? Think about the following three questions, rate your responses, and be prepared to discuss with others (Circle the appropriate response, where "1" = Not at all, and "5" = Totally.)

1. I am connected with other people in my life. 1 2 3 4 5

2. If I needed help, I could turn to others. 1 2 3 4 5

3. I see myself as being available to help others. 1 2 3 4 5

Reflect on your responses to these three questions. What is the meaning? What implications might there be for group work?

Group Work Definition, Part IV: By a Capable Professional Practitioner

Effective group work leadership doesn't just happen, although some people may be more naturally adept at it than others. In the main, though, group leaders are trained, not born (Barlow, 2004; Bennis & Nanus, 1997; Kottler, 1981).

How to prepare effective group work leaders has been the subject of considerable study, trials, guidance, and research over the decades. Examples include the professional training standards of ASGW (1983, 1991, 2000), special issues of the *Journal for Specialists in Group Work* (1981, 1996, 2004) devoted to group leader preparation and training, and a treasure trove of other scholarly products, such as summaries of effective group leadership (Riva, Wachtel, & Lasky, 2004; Stockton, Morran, & Krieger, 2004) and group leadership teaching and training (Brown, 2011).

Presented in the following are what a capable group work practitioner generally needs to be able to do and how these assets can be developed:

a. Possess a positive attitude and be personally and interpersonally at ease and effective, achievable through a combination of natural characteristics and nurturing training

b. Demonstrate attitudes, knowledge, skills, techniques, and best practices required for leading groups, achievable through a comprehensive training program

   c. Apply learning effectively and appropriately, achievable through guided practice in both simulated and real situations

   d. Continuously improve their group leadership abilities and skills, achievable through ongoing processing and supervision

Four tested strategies for teaching students about group work leadership are presented in Case Illustration 1–4, and following you can identify which strategies so far seem to be a part of your group work learning.

Case Illustration 1–4: Four Tried and True Learning Strategies

*The **object** of this case illustration is for you to understand four proven ways to learn about group work and associated leader skills.*

Barlow (2004) outlined four "tried and true learning strategies" (p. 115) for teaching group leaders the skills they need to be effective. These four strategies enjoy considerable empirical support and include the following:

a. Experiential learning strategy. Students need to learn what it is like to be in a group. This experience gives them a reality base to draw from and helps them to empathize with the experience of the group members who will be in their own groups. Many programs include it.

b. Observation learning strategy. Watching experts in live or taped demonstrations of group leadership can reveal a lot about group work leadership in a relatively low threat manner. Intentionally teaching group process observation skills, such as who seems to open doors for others to enter conversations and who seems to close them, in combination with viewing a group can sharpen knowledge and skills.

c. Academic learning strategy. The amount of content material that needs to be mastered by those in training to be group practitioners is "daunting" (Barlow, 2004, p. 120), ranging across theory, practice, and research in groups and in various applications of groups with differing populations. While the domains of education and training in content and skills have been identified yet still await empirical support according to Brown (2011), the "current state of only one course to teach all of the dimensions of groups and group leadership does not meet the entry level needs for knowledge and skill as group leaders (Brown, 2011, p. 366). Academic programs that prepare students to become practitioners, such as those in social work, counseling, or psychology,

(Continued)

are guided by training standards. In the counseling profession, for instance, the Council for the Accreditation of Counseling and Related Educational Programs accreditation standards for group work, coupled with the professional training standards and best practice guidelines of ASGW, lay out a basic blueprint of what is needed, as Chapter 2 of this book will show. Evidence-based research is needed about how to best deliver this training.

    d. Supervision learning strategy. Group leaders in training must receive adequate supervision in order to develop their competency. Supervision is the learning strategy that can best yield an integration of theory, research, and practice into one's own evolving personal and professional application. As pointed out by Riva (2011), the supervisor needs to be competent in two essential areas: (a) supervision methods and (b) the complexities of group applications. The supervision of group work leadership is a critically important part of how novice leaders advance toward expert stage.

Learning Exercise 1–4: Assessing How You Are Learning About Group Work

*The **object** of this learning exercise is to provide you with a means for assessing how you are learning about group work.*

    I wonder how you and fellow students are being taught group work leadership? Or, if you are a graduate of a professional helping program in counseling, psychology, or social work, how were you taught about it?

1. Turn your attention to that question of how you are (or were) being educated and trained in group work leadership.

2. Use the scale attached to each strategy below to judge the presence or lack of it in your own training and then provide any relevant comments.
   a. *Experiential* learning strategy (e.g., participation in a group): Extent to which your group work leadership learning springs from this strategy ("1" = Not at all through "5" = Very much):

   1   2   3   4   5

   Comments:

(Continued)

(Continued)

    b. *Observation* learning strategy (e.g., observing a group in action): Extent to which your group work leadership learning springs from this strategy ("1" = Not at all through "5" = Very much):

      1   2   3   4   5

      Comments:

    c. *Academic* learning strategy (e.g., from an academic course dedicated to group work): Extent to which your group work leadership learning springs from this strategy ("1" = Not at all through "5" = Very much):

      1   2   3   4   5

      Comments:

    d. *Supervision* learning strategy (i.e., your group work leadership being supervised): Extent to which your group work leadership learning springs from this strategy ("1" = Not at all through "5" = Very much):

      1   2   3   4   5

      Comments:

Group Work Definition, Part V: To Assist an Interdependent Collection of People

One of the most important aspects involved with becoming a capable group work leader is developing conditions in the group that allow members to interact directly with each other (Stockton et al., 2004). In some ways, this requires that group leaders learn how to "let go" of ideas that leaders take charge or dominate proceedings, in favor of adopting an approach to nurture the creation of therapeutic factors (e.g., instilling hope, promoting cohesion), which, in turn, sets the stage for member-to-member connections. Likewise, group leaders in training may need to unlearn some other conceptions, such as group leadership is the performance of individual therapy within the group (Barlow, 2004). While sometimes engaging in one-to-one intervention with a group member is called for by the group leader, this "telephone switchboard" model of group leadership—where everything goes through the leader—is not recommended for general practice. Rather, a "network" model is where the group leader seeks to foster interconnections of members with each other, freeing them to interact directly.

Group Work Definition, Part VI: To Reach Mutual Goals

Goals are motivating. Setting goals in a group can help direct and maintain action in a cohesive way and then provide a yardstick for measuring if the effort expended led to desired results.

In group work, there usually are general goals for the group itself and more specific ones for each of the members. In both cases, these goals can be process- and outcome-oriented. By *process-oriented*, I mean goals that are centered on the ongoing activities of the group; by *outcome-oriented*, I mean goals that focus on what will be accomplished by the group's end point.

An example of a *process-oriented group* goal might be "to allow members opportunities to interact with each other during each session." An example of an *outcome-oriented group* goal might be "to assist members in reaching their stated goals by the end of the group." As I mentioned, individual members are encouraged to establish their own goals within the larger goals of the group. An example of a *process-oriented individual member* goal might be "to listen carefully to what other members say during sessions," while an example of *an outcome-oriented individual member* goal might be "to increase my ability to be supportive to my wife by the group's end."

An important aspect of goal setting in group work is that the goals be collaboratively designed and mutually reinforcing. In terms of individual member goals, the group leader's role is to encourage their creation by each member and then to ensure with the members that these goals are generally consistent with the overarching group purpose and its goals. This is what I mean by *collaborative and mutually reinforcing*—that is, the group work leader and members cooperate to set goals that are meaningful to members and that are reachable within the context of the group itself. The quality of this process of goal setting, which occurs early in the group's development, can contribute substantially to the emerging group climate and to the eventual success of the group experience for everyone.

Group Work Definition, Part VII: Goals May Be Personal, Interpersonal, or Task Related

Group work is a robust method that majors in multiplicity. It spans four types of groups. It is influenced by numerous academic disciplines and professions. And its goals may be personal and interpersonal—especially interpersonal—or task related.

Personal goals. Personal change and growth, emerging from targeting personal goals, are the sine qua non of counseling. Examples of personal goals include becoming more appropriately self-disclosive, losing 10 pounds of weight, developing improved communication skills, and resolving feelings of sadness.

As I've pointed out earlier, this attention to individual personal goals in the United States emerges from our earliest heritage in Western Europe. The individual level of intervention so dominates the counseling profession that the term *counseling* still is nearly synonymous with individual counseling. In fact, try this yourself. When you consider what counseling is, what first comes to mind? Chances are, it's one-on-one counseling. But as Morrill, Oetting, and Hurst (1974) showed the profession decades ago, counseling is not limited to an individual intervention level. It also includes group, organizational, and community levels.

Interpersonal goals. Group work is naturally conversant with interpersonal (and ecological) models. Examples of interpersonal goals in a group include learning how to relate better with others, developing skills to effectively support others and becoming more adept at providing and receiving constructive feedback. Because group work is an interdependent process, one of a group work leader's chief responsibilities is to help foster an interpersonal, interconnected network among group members. This is what spawns member interaction that, in turn, is what leads to change and growth in members.

Task and maintenance/personal relations functions in groups. Task and maintenance/personal relations functions are a part of any group, to be sure. The classic work, *Interaction Process Analysis* (Bales, 1950), and an updated version, *Systematic Multiple Level Observation of Groups (SYMLOG)* (e.g., Bales, 1999), catalogued how group members function in groups according to task and to socioemotive (maintenance) functions. Think of your experience in any group—a counseling group, some committee you've served on, even a family gathering. As you reflect, you may quite easily be able to identify that some people in the group may have pushed for some things to be done (task function example), while others may have been more inclined to listen to others and provide encouragement (maintenance/personal relations function examples).

Task functions, such as giving suggestions, serve to propel a group forward, while maintenance/personal relations functions, such as providing support, aid in honoring personal relations by helping members feel encouraged and respected.

Task group goals. Beyond task and maintenance/personal relations functions occurring within any group, the goals of some groups center primarily around improving personal relations (e.g., therapy groups) while goals of other groups are primarily to problem solve or to produce tangible output (task groups). Examples of task groups include neighborhood councils developing watch groups, study groups to help students master subject material, task forces, and commissions aiming to produce policies. Even in these task groups, where members sometimes may be consumed by achieving concrete goals, maintenance/personal relations issues are involved: members may feel elated or rejected, there may be restless vying for control, sluggish wallowing in confusion, or the exhilaration that can accompany a smoothly running and effective group. Group work principles apply just as well to task groups as they do to personal and interpersonal ones (Conyne, 1989). Group workers can be very helpful in task group facilitating, just as they can with the other more familiar applications, such as group counseling.

GROUP WORK KEYSTONES

- Groups are a central part of most people's lives.
- Group work is a comprehensive and unique approach to helping.
- Research generally supports the effectiveness and value of group work and of group counseling and therapy particularly.
- All groups are interpersonally based, and group work leaders rely on both core and advanced competencies.
- Group work as a term can be thought of as an umbrella, spanning core group work competencies and four types/specializations of group work.
- Task groups, psychoeducation groups, group counseling, and group psychotherapy are the four broad specializations of group work endorsed by ASGW, and these can serve as a general model.

RECOMMENDED RESOURCES

American Group Psychotherapy Association. (2007). *Practice guidelines for group psychotherapy*. New York, NY: American Group Psychotherapy Association. Retrieved from http://agpa.org/guidelines/AGPA%20Practice%20Guidelines%20 2007-PDF.pdf

American Group Psychotherapy Association. (2012). Publications: Group psychotherapy book list. Retrieved from http://www.agpa.org/pubs/Booklist.htm

American Group Psychotherapy Association. (n.d.). Group works! Evidence on the effectiveness of group therapy. Retrieved from http://agpa.org/efficacy-brochure.htm

Brown, N. (2005). Psychoeducational groups. In S. Wheelan (Ed.), *The handbook of group research and practice* (pp. 511–529). Thousand Oaks, CA: Sage.

Conyne, R. (Ed.). (2011). Group counseling. *The Oxford handbook of group counseling.* New York, NY: Oxford University Press.

Conyne, R. (2012). Group counseling. In E. Altmaier & J. C. Hansen (Eds.), *The Oxford handbook of counseling psychology* (pp. 611–646). New York, NY: Oxford University Press.

Corey, G. (2012). *Theory and practice of group counseling* (8th ed.). Pacific Grove, CA: Brooks Cole.

DeLucia-Waack, J., Gerrity D., Kalodner C., & Riva M. (Eds.), *Handbook of group counseling and psychotherapy.* Thousand Oaks, CA: Sage.

Gladding, S. (2011). *Groups: A counseling specialty* (6th ed.). Upper Saddle River, NJ: Prentice Hall.

Hulse-Killacky, D., Killacky, J., & Donigian, J. (2001). *Making task groups work in your world.* Upper Saddle River, NJ: Merrill Prentice Hall.

Leszcz, M., & Kobos, J. (2008). Evidence-based group psychotherapy: Using AGPA's practice guidelines to enhance clinical effectiveness. *Journal of Clinical Psychology: In session, 64,* 1238–1260.

Mathieu, J., Maynard, M. T., Rapp, T., & Gilson, L. (2008). Team effectiveness 1997–2007: A review of recent advancements and a glimpse into the future. *Journal of Management, 34,* 410–476.

Trotzer, J. (2006). *The counselor and the group: Integrating theory, training, and practice* (4th ed.). New York, NY: Routledge.

Wheelan, S. (2004). Groups in the workplace. In J. DeLucia-Waack, D. Gerrity, C. Kalodner, & M. Riva (Eds.), *Handbook of group counseling and psychotherapy* (pp. 401–413). Thousand Oaks, CA: Sage.

Yalom, I., & Leszcz, M. (2005). *The theory and practice of group psychotherapy* (5th ed.). New York, NY: Basic Books.

CHAPTER 2

FOUNDATIONS OF GROUP WORK

Multiculturalism, Social Justice, and Ethics

All counselors should possess a set of core competencies in general group work.

—Association for Specialists in Group Work (2000, p. 2)

INTRODUCTION ●

Let's expand the preceding quotation to read "All *helping professionals* should possess a set of core competencies in general group work." As we shall see throughout this text, group work is a central practice for all helpers.

Standards, principles, and guidelines serve important functions. They give institutions and people within their sway something larger than themselves to shoot for while serving to keep them on target toward achieving desired goals and purposes.

Apart from institutions, they can serve as reference points for individuals. Think about it. Your parents held expectations for you, no doubt, and in some cases, these expectations may have reached the level of standards, or principles, or guidelines. The Ten Commandments, the Boy Scout and Girl

Scout oaths, the Pledge of Allegiance, the policies and procedures set out in the handbook of your counseling program, a mother's requirement for her children to be home by 9:00 "sharp!" All these are examples. You can probably think of some others from your own life.

A professional association also develops standards, guidelines, and principles to represent jointly held values, missions, goals, and procedures that then serve to motivate and guide actions of the association itself as well as the behavior and conduct of its members. The presence and quality of these measures provide an indelible mark of an association's maturity.

The purpose of this chapter is to orient you to the standards, guidelines, and principles contained in important documents related to group work and to how these emerged historically. These materials are important for guiding training, practice, supervision, and research.

Particular focus is given to how the foundation documents of the Association for Specialists in Group Work (ASGW), and the *2009 Standards* of the Council for the Accreditation of Counseling and Related Educational Programs (CACREP) have supported the development of group work. Important for readers from sister helping professions, such as psychology, human services, and social work, is this point: While the documents to be considered are directly connected with the counseling profession, they also are generalizable and applicable to other helping professions, too. I encourage you to access documents that are specifically associated with your discipline and profession, if it differs from the counseling profession.

These major documents are to be considered, which address academic standards, best practices and ethics, minimal training standards, and diversity competence. They serve as touchstones to help shape practice, research, and training. As stated by Wilson, Rapin, and Haley-Banez (2004) with regard to the ASGW documents,

> The ASGW foundational documents are responses to a unique challenge: to describe and provide grounding for the field of group work taken as a whole . . . ASGW has increased the recognizability of our profession and raised the standard to which group workers may aspire. (p. 21)

Rapin's (2004, 2011) two extended summaries of these foundation documents within the counseling profession and across related helping professions (psychology, social work) are especially important to consider because they compare and contrast against such key factors as ethics, law, best practices, and training.

CHAPTER OBJECTIVES

As a result of reading this chapter you will be able to

- Appreciate major milestones in the evolution of group work
- Understand the contribution of ethics, program accreditation and ASGW foundation documents in group work to counseling specifically and generally to the helping professions
- Learn the main elements of both CACREP and ASGW definitions of *group work* and *core competencies*, with their specific and general applications
- Learn the author's perspective on what needs to be done to advance group work through accreditation standards

A BRIEF LOOK AT RELEVANT ● HISTORY IN GROUP WORK'S DEVELOPMENT

A Broad Sweep Examination

Briefly reviewing major epochs in the historical development of group work provides a context for understanding when foundation documents emerged. You will note that about 100 years of evolution preceded their development; see especially Period 4, below.

Essentially, this historical development can be divided into four broad periods (Conyne, 2012): (a) Period 1, the "years of development" (1900-1939), with the professional beginnings of working with people and at group work being targeted at changing adverse social conditions; (b) Period 2, the "years of early explosion" (1940-1969), marked by exceptional expansion, including the spread of groups throughout society; (c) Period 3, the "years of setting in" (1970-1989), where group research and training began to take root and several professional organizations were established; and (d) Period 4, the "years of standardization and further expansion to the age of ubiquity," (1990-Present), where foundation documents and increasingly sophisticated research were produced, and where the use of a wide range of groups, including online groups, aimed at an ever-increasing diverse population, appeared. If you would like to read more about the historical development of group work, additional sources also are recommended (e.g., see Barlow, Burlingame, & Fuhriman, 2000; Barlow, Fuhriman, & Burlingame, 2004, 2005; Blatner, 2007; Leddick, 2011).

Beginning with the latter years of Period 3 and continuing, professional associations in the area of "group" (the Association for Specialists in Group Work, ASGW, of the American Counseling Association, ACA; the Society for Group Psychology and Group Psychotherapy, Division 49, of the American Psychological Association; the American Group Psychotherapy Association, AGPA; American Society of Group Psychotherapy and Psychodrama, ASGPP; and the Association for the Advancement of Social Work with Groups, AASWG, among others) organized, with each adding needed support from their own discipline and profession to advance practice, training, research, and advocacy in the area of groups.

All of these professional associations contribute valuable resources (such as training standards). For instance, the *Standards for Social Work Practice with Groups* published by AASWG (2010) sets out desired practices organized by beginning, middle, and ending stages of a group, as well as detailing ethical standards. AGPA's *Practice Guidelines for Group Psychotherapy* (2007) addresses such important topics as creating successful therapy groups, therapeutic factors and mechanisms, and therapist interventions.

The focus of this book, in this book series aimed at advancing practice and professional identity within the counseling profession, will be limited to the work of one group work professional association, the ASGW (and to the accreditation body most associated with the counseling profession, CACREP). See Figure 2-1 for a list of these associations.

Figure 2–1:   Some Major Group Professional Associations and Journals

- Society for Group Psychology and Group Psychotherapy, Division 49 of the American Psychological Association
  www.apa.org/about/division/div49.aspx
  Journal: *Group Dynamics: Theory, Research and Practice*
- Association for Specialists in Group Work (ASGW)
  www.asgw.org
  Journal: *Journal for Specialists in Group Work*
- American Group Psychotherapy Association (AGPA)
  www.apga.org
  Journal: *International Journal of Group Psychotherapy*
- Association for the Advancement of Social Work with Groups (AASWG)
  www.aaswg.org
  Affiliated Journals: *Social Work with Groups—A Journal of Community and Clinical Practice; and Groupwork*
- American Society of Group Psychotherapy and Psychodrama (ASGPP)
  http://www.asgpp.org/
  Journal: *The Journal of Group Psychotherapy, Psychodrama and Sociometry*

One of the most significant contributions of ASGW to the development and support of group work is to be found in the three guiding foundation documents for group work that it has commissioned. Let's take a look at these documents next.

ASGW'S FOUNDATION DOCUMENTS: TRAINING STANDARDS, ● BEST PRACTICE, ETHICS, AND MULTICULTURAL AND SOCIAL JUSTICE COMPETENCIES PRINCIPLES FOR GROUP WORKERS

Before beginning our discussion of foundational documents in group work, I am imagining you may be wondering something like "Why is this stuff so important, anyway?" Let me try to respond to this very understandable question.

First, the delivery of groups is a critically important part of what counselors are expected to do. The first case illustrates this situation and the learning exercise that follows asks you to look ahead at the value of training standards and best practices for group work practice.

Case Illustration 2–1: Please Lead This Group!

*The **object** of this case illustration is to show a not too uncommon way that school counselors, social workers, psychologists and mental health staff in community agencies may be asked by administrators to "do a group." The urgency of this kind of request can be, at the least, uncomfortable.*

You are a school counselor. For the third time in a 2-month period a complaint has been received about a student being bullied. A series of action steps is being considered, including developing a comprehensive policy about bullying prevention. The principal also has approached the school counseling staff, asking for a bullying prevention group to be created and offered during the next semester. She obviously is feeling some political heat to get something underway as quickly as possible, and something that will work.

As you talk with other staff about this, it becomes clear that no one else has had experience with leading prevention groups of any kind, let alone in the area of prevention. You have the benefit in your training program of taking a course in group work. But it's been a while since you have led a group.

Where to start? You recall the ASGW materials related to training standards and best practice guidelines. Maybe that will be a good place to start researching; you decide.

Case Illustration 2–1 highlights the value of group as a service delivery modality. But the employment of group, as with any counseling service, cannot be done without a foundation of what constitutes best practices in the field. Thus, these specific documents contribute to synthesizing important elements of the field of group work, something which had been needed as the group work field emerged. Being informed by scholarly and empirical work in the field of group work, taken together these sources integrate an understanding of group work with best practices for its training and delivery with diverse populations in various settings. In a very real sense, they provide a foundation for group work practice in the counseling profession.

As has been pointed out by Wilson, Rapin, and Haley-Banez (2004), other values of these documents are that they have (a) enhanced the professional recognition and scope of practice of group workers; (b) expressed the common values inherent in the profession of group work based on ecology and diversity; and (c) provided a common frame of reference in support of training goals linked to conceiving, organizing, delivering, processing, and evaluating group interventions. As a triumvirate, then, the foundation documents have consolidated guidance for effective group work practice, making it readily accessible for application.

Now let's consider these three influential sources.

The three sets of ASGW foundation documents began with its *Professional Training Standards,* first edition, in 1983 which was followed by two revisions (1991 and 2000). The other two sets are its *Best Practice Guidelines* (1998, 2007) and the *Multicultural and Social Justice Competence Principles for Group Workers* (2012). While the content of each of these documents is essential in serving to guide ethical and effective group work practice, as stated in the preamble of the ASGW *Best Practice Guidelines,* note that the ethical code of ACA (2005), ASGW's parent organization takes precedence in all cases:

> The Association for Specialists in Group Work (ASGW) is a division of the American Counseling Association whose members are interested in and specialize in group work . . . The Association for Specialists in Group Work recognizes the commitment of its members to the Code of Ethics (as revised in 2005) of its parent organization, the American Counseling Association, and nothing in this document shall be construed to supplant that code. (ASGW, 2007)

Combined, these documents are intended to provide guiding frameworks to assist with

a. learning about, gaining competency in, and teaching group work (*Training Standards,* aimed at students, trainees, and faculty),

b. guiding effective group work practice and ethical behavior (*Best Practice Guidelines,* aimed at faculty, trainers, and agency staff), and

c. demonstrating how group workers can become more aware of diversity issues and how they can incorporate diversity principles more fully in their group work practice (*Multicultural and Social Justice Principles,* aimed at everyone). Each of these documents is addressed next.

ASGW Document #1: Professional Training Standards

ASGW was founded in 1973. Ten years later, the Association produced its initial set of professional training standards, the *ASGW Training Standards for Group Counseling* (1983), introduced 2 years earlier by an article by Kottler (1981). These group counseling training standards included competency areas in knowledge and clock hour baselines for supervised clinical experience in group counseling. Two revisions of these training standards have emerged since then (ASGW, 1991, 2000).

In the first revision (1991), training standards were broadened to address group "work" instead of group "counseling" only, and they differentiated training into four separate yet overlapping group work "types" or "specialties," which we discussed in Chapter 1: (a) task groups, (b) psychoeducation groups, (c) counseling groups, and (d) psychotherapy groups. In addition, a set of "core competencies" was enumerated as the basic minimum of mastery for all master's degree graduates in counseling programs and those upon which all group work types rested. Finally, clinical contact hours for core competencies and for each of the four group work types were recommended (Note: This information is presented at the end of this chapter). In the second revision of the *Training Standards* (2000), refinements were conducted to increase clarification of terminology and to connect training with the recently emerged ASGW documents on best practices (1998) and on diversity competence for group workers (1998), now revised as *Multicultural and Social Justice Competence Principles for Group Workers* (2012).

Highlighting Key Group Work Definitions. In Chapter 1, you were introduced to the definition of group work and its various aspects. You may recall that group work is intended "to assist an interdependent collection of people to reach their mutual goals." This is a very important concept because it implies a whole class of group work leader interventions that pivot around the goal of fostering positive interrelationships of group members as a primary route to member change and growth and to the accomplishment of task goals. A summary of these highlights is contained in Figure 2-2.

Figure 2–2   Highlights of Important *Group Work* Components

Core competencies: Basic platform knowledge and skills, obtainable in one academic course

Group work types/specializations: Four applications needing advanced and specific training

Task/work groups: Facilitate accomplishing specific project-oriented goals

Psychoeducation groups: Teach life competencies through education and skill training

Group counseling: Resolves typical problems of daily living

Group psychotherapy: Remediates psychological and emotional dysfunction

If you are interested in unraveling the incremental steps that occurred between the publication of the *Training Standards* edition in 1991 to its revision in 2000, see the 25th anniversary issue of the *Journal for Specialists in Group Work* (Vol. 23, Number 2, 1998), which contained several articles reviewing and reacting to the 1991 version of the standards. You might find the following publications of particular interest, some of which appeared in the *JSGW* issue just mentioned (Bauman & Waldo, 1998; Conyne, 1996; Conyne & Wilson, 1998; DeLucia-Waack, 1998), and otherwise (Conyne, 1996; Conyne et al., 1992; Conyne, Wilson, Kline, Morran, & Ward, 1993; Dye, 1996; Hulse-Killacky, 1996; Ward, 2006; Wilson & Newmeyer, 2008), as well as the book by Conyne, Wilson, and Ward (1997).

The core group work competencies contained in the *Training Standards* are essential building blocks for effective group work practice. They also are largely consistent with the core curricular experiences in group work that are part of the accreditation standards of CACREP, which you will discover later in this chapter.

It is important that you begin to get a sense of the knowledge and skills comprising the core group work competencies. Case Illustration 2–2 and Learning Exercise 2–1 are intended for that purpose.

Case Illustration 2–2: Knowledge and Skills in Group Work

*The **object** of this case illustration is to increase your understanding of exemplary knowledge and skills domains thought to be important in group work.*

1. Let's take a quick look at some areas included within the *Training Standards*. What is a competent group worker supposed to be able to do?

2. Ask this question, "Can I perform these illustrative activities successfully?" Because only three examples drawn from Knowledge and three from Skills are presented in the following, I encourage you to review the entire *Training Standards* document for necessary detail.

Three Knowledge objectives examples, which ask you to identify and describe

1. Theories of group work, including commonalities and distinguishing characteristics among the various types/specialization within group work

2. The impact of group member diversity (e.g., gender, culture, learning style, group climate preference) on group member behavior, group process, and dynamics in group work

3. Best practices in group work

Three Skills objectives examples, which ask you to demonstrate skill in

1. Applying theoretical concepts and scientific findings to the design of a group and the interpretation of personal experiences in a group

2. Observing and identifying group process

3. Attending to, acknowledging, clarifying, summarizing, confronting, and responding empathically to group member behavior

Learning Exercise 2–1: Observing and Identifying Group Process

*The **object** of this learning exercise is to identify group processes that occur and then, if you were a leader of the group being observed, how you might have used your observations effectively.*

1. Consider example Skill #2, listed earlier: "Observing and identifying group process." Examples of group process observation include noting patterns of interaction (e.g., who talks to whom and when?), sources of influence in the group, how decision making occurs, feeling expression, and others (Bieschke, Matthews, Wade, & Pricken, 1998; Conyne, 1997a, 1998b; Hanson, 1972).

2. Watch a movie, such as *12 Angry Men, The Breakfast Club, The Big Chill,* or *The Dream Team* (DeLucia-Waack, 2001; Koch & Dollarhide, 2000), with a partner who also is interested in group work. Parenthetically, you might find Armstrong and Berg's (2005) discussion of how *12 Angry Men* demonstrates group process to be valuable. These movies are easily accessible. An alternative is to observe a meeting of a school or community group, again with the goal of identifying group processes.

3. Look for the processes I referred to earlier:

   Patterns of interaction: Who talks to whom?

   Influence: Who seems to hold high influence and how does that occur? Who seems to have low influence?

   Decision making: How do decisions get made in the group (e.g., by compromise, by fiat, by acquiescence).

   Feelings: What kinds of feelings seem to be expressed? What others are not?

4. Following your independent observations:

   a. Hold a discussion with your partner to compare and contrast your findings.
   b. Ask yourself, If you were leading the group, how might you have used your observations?

ASGW Document #2: Best Practice Guidelines

The ACA Code of Ethics. The *ACA Code of Ethics* (2005), as previously mentioned, is the primary source of ethical guidance for all members of the American Counseling Association, including group work specialists. For those holding state licensure, that ethical code also shares precedence. Seventeen of 52 U.S. jurisdictions, including Puerto Rico and Washington, D.C., as well as the 50 states, use the ACA ethics code (ACA, 2010a).

As the Preamble to the *ACA Ethical Code* indicates,

> When counselors are faced with ethical dilemmas that are difficult to resolve, they are expected to engage in a carefully considered ethical decision-making process. Reasonable differences of opinion can and do exist among counselors with respect to the ways in which values, ethical principles, and ethical standards would be applied when they conflict. While there is no specific ethical decision-making model that is most effective, counselors are expected to be familiar with a credible model of decision making that can bear public scrutiny and its application. Through a chosen ethical decision-making process and evaluation of the context of the situation, counselors are empowered to make decisions that help expand the capacity of people to grow and develop.

It is important to realize that, with regard to group work, the *Code* addresses important considerations, but only a narrow set of them. Issues that are addressed (Rapin, 2011) deal with

> Screening of prospective group members (Item A8a): Counselors screen prospective group counseling/therapy participants. To the extent possible, counselors select members whose needs and goals are compatible with goals of the group, who will not impede the group process, and whose well-being will not be jeopardized by the group experience.

> Client protection (Item A8b): In a group setting, counselors take reasonable precautions to protect clients from physical, emotional, or psychological trauma.

> Confidentiality (Introduction, Section B): Counselors recognize that trust is a cornerstone of the counseling relationship. Counselors aspire to earn the trust of clients by creating an ongoing partnership, establishing and upholding appropriate boundaries, and maintaining confidentiality. Counselors communicate the parameters of confidentiality in a culturally competent manner.

Groups and families (Item B4a): In group work, counselors clearly explain the importance and parameters of confidentiality for the specific group being entered.

Peer relationships (Item F6e): Counselor educators make every effort to ensure that the rights of peers are not compromised when students or supervisees lead counseling groups or provide clinical supervision. Counselor educators take steps to ensure that students and supervisees understand they have the same ethical obligations as counselor educators, trainers, and supervisors. (ACA, 2005.)

Other complex specific issues and challenges that can occur in group work are unaddressed, and this is where the *Best Practice Guidelines* of ASGW become particularly useful.

The *Best Practice Guidelines* Supplement the *Ethical Code*. As stated in the Preamble to the *Guidelines*:

These *Best Practice Guidelines* are intended to clarify the application of the *ACA Code of Ethics* to the field of group work by defining group workers' responsibility and scope of practice involving those activities, strategies and interventions that are consistent and current with effective and appropriate professional ethical and community standards.

It is essential, therefore, to understand that the purpose of the *Best Practice Guidelines* is to provide a reference point for how to behave ethically as a group worker; that is, *Best Practice Guidelines are intended to help group workers deal with the often knotty challenges occurring in group work situations and to help them make sound ethical choices.*

Areas Covered by the *Best Practice Guidelines*. Group workers do not function in a vacuum, apart from the rest of the world. Rather, they are part of the larger profession, the community, and larger society, and they are subject to its various forces, laws, and influences. The *ASGW Best Practice Guidelines* (2007, Section A.1) acknowledge this condition through their clear statement about professional context and regulatory requirements:

Group Workers actively know, understand and apply the *ACA Code of Ethics* (2005), the *ASGW Professional Standards for the Training of Group Workers*, these ASGW *Best Practice Guidelines*, the ASGW diversity competencies, and the *AMCD Multicultural Counseling Competencies and Standards*, relevant state laws, accreditation requirements, relevant National Board for Certified Counselors Codes and Standards, their organization's standards, and insurance requirements impacting the practice of group work.

Any group, too, exists within a context. It never stands alone but always is subject to external (and, of course, internal) influence. Is the room too hot or too cold? Are the chairs moveable or locked into position? Is the group supported by its sponsoring agency? How are its members being affected by the economic downturn or by threats of war? These are just a few examples of how a group and its members function ecologically within a dynamic set of influencing factors (Conyne & Bemak, 2004b; Conyne & Mazza, 2007). The guidelines call for group leaders to be cognizant of these kinds of contextual influences on a group, of its ecology, as well as a range of other important factors.

The guidelines are grounded in the view that ethical processes are integral to group work and that group workers are ethical agents. As I mentioned, but want to reinforce and now specify, the *Best Practice Guidelines* complement the *ACA Code of Ethics* by defining the specific responsibilities of group workers in the planning, performing, and processing of all forms of groups they lead. These three key group work leadership domains sometimes are referred to colloquially as the "three *P*'s" of group leadership (Rapin & Conyne, 2006) and are contained in Figure 2–3.

Figure 2–3   Best Practice Guideline Domains

> a. *Planning* and preparing for the group
>
> b. *Performing* or leading the group
>
> c. *Processing* and evaluating the group

Learning Exercise 2–2: A Knotty Challenge

*The **object** of this learning exercise is to draw from the ACA Code of Ethics and the **ASGW Best Practice Guidelines** to address an ethical issue and then to compare responses with another person.*

Confidentiality in a group is a vitally important concept and process. The group needs to be a safe place where members can interact freely and genuinely. However, confidentiality cannot be ensured or certainly not guaranteed by the group leader, as it can be within individual counseling.

1. Refer to the *ACA Code of Ethics* and to the *ASGW Best Practice Guidelines* for assistance, remembering that these documents provide reference points for how to behave ethically as a group worker.

(Continued)

(Continued)

2. In counseling, therapy, and psychoeducation groups you may lead, present how you would generally describe to group members how confidentiality would be handled:

_____

_____

_____.

3. Discuss your approach with another student. Compare notes and learn from one another.

Let's now take a closer look at each of these best practice domains in some detail.

Best practice in planning. Suppose you are heading on a 3-week vacation to Europe, or Asia, or some place across the globe that is largely unfamiliar to you. Once there, you intend to rent a car to drive to a number of destinations that are quite distant from one another. What do you do? Well, if you are like most people, you might do some (or a lot of) planning, perhaps even being sure to bring with you, or get there, a global positioning satellite device to assist with getting around with greater ease and confidence. Or, consider a different scenario. You are a licensed pilot of a small aircraft and are about to fly it 900 miles to a family reunion. You are required to develop, file, and follow a flight plan for this journey. In a third example, scuba diving, there is a mantra among divers: "Plan your dive and dive your plan."

Best practice planning in group work leadership is analogous in many ways to these examples.

Early in its development, though, leading groups was considered similar to an expressive art form, where spontaneity and being open to one's experience in the group were prized. Pre-planning was low on the priority list perhaps, in part, because in the earliest days knowledge about just what was needed or involved with effective group leading was yet to be discovered. Group work theories and research awaited development and production.

The practice of group work leadership has come a long way since its beginnings. Research and theory have accumulated so that evidence-based knowledge and skills that enhance effective practice have been identified. The ensuing chapters of this book will introduce you to much of this material. And, certainly, the best practice guidelines have benefitted from this information and, in turn, have contributed to the wisdom needed to guide effective group work leadership.

In Planning, group work leaders get ready and prepare the conditions necessary for the group to be formed, delivered, and evaluated. *Guidelines* address nine planning areas:

1. *Professional context and regulatory requirements:* For example, know the *ACA Code of Ethics.*

2. *Scope of practice and conceptual framework:* For example, identify rationale for techniques used.

3. *Assessment:* Appraising self and ecological assessment of community

4. *Program development and evaluation:* For example, developing a concrete plan to guide action

5. *Resources:* For example, funding, marketing, appropriate space

6. *Professional disclosure statement:* For example, specify qualifications and experience.

7. *Group and member preparation:* For example, screening, informed consent, as appropriate

8. *Professional development:* For example, remain current with competencies.

9. *Trends and technological changes:* For example, shifting demographics, new technologies

Best practice in performing. Performing, or leading the group, is what is usually thought of first and foremost in group work leadership. Rightly so, because member change, growth, learning, and productivity occur through the group plan being implemented effectively and appropriately in real time. This statement is not intended to be an endorsement for a strict application of a group plan to action, such as what may occur in a manualized treatment group program. Rather, best practice in performing demands that the leader apply a plan with sensitivity, being continuously open to ongoing events and processes occurring by the moment in the group and being able to make adjustments, as needed, to fine tune the plan for a better fit with changing circumstances.

Case Illustration 2–3 and Learning Exercise 2–3 address the importance of adaptation and flexibility in group ledership.

Case Illustration 2–3: When Adjustment Is Needed

*The **object** of this case illustration is to show how group leaders need to be sensitive to when a previously developed group session plan may need to be adapted on the spot, due to changing circumstances.*

Here is one example of when adjustment is needed. Two students in a group practicum were leading an after-school psychoeducation group of middle school students that was held in a community center. Approaching the third of nine sessions, their plan was to begin a series of steps to teach a basic problem-solving method that the members would then apply against some current issues they were confronting in their lives. When the coleaders arrived for the group that late afternoon, they learned from the first student who came to the group session that a teacher in their school had died 2 hours earlier in an automobile accident. This might have explained why two of the seven students did not show for group, when attendance the first two sessions was high. It also was obvious from the five students who did come that they were understandably very emotional about the teacher's death. It was time for the group leaders to modify their plan to fit the present circumstances, and they did, completely ditching the problem-solving plan to allow an opportunity for group members to share their thoughts and feelings. You know, there is a saying from gestalt psychology: "Don't push the river." It fits this situation.

So the domain of performing means that group leaders sensitively apply their plan while being aware of and open to current dynamics occurring within and without the group, holding out the possibility of making appropriate adaptations.

Learning Exercise 2–3: Your Turn: When Adjustment Is Needed

*The **object** of this learning exercise is to provide you with an opportunity for suggesting an alternative group leader approach for the situation contained in Case Illustration 2–3 and to compare your suggestion with another student.*

1. Now it's your turn. Put yourself in the situation just described. You read what the student coleaders did then.

2. Provide a rationale for their action. _____
   _____.

3. Develop another approach that you think might have been sound and describe it.

   _____

   _____.

4. Provide a rationale for your suggested action. _____
   _____.

5. Discuss your work with another student, focusing on these three questions:

   (a) What do you find in common?

   (b) What do you find different?

   (c) What is the likelihood that your possible other approaches might have worked effectively?

Guidelines address nine Performing areas:

1. *Self-knowledge:* For example, being aware of and monitoring personal strengths and weaknesses

2. *Group competencies:* Basic knowledge and skills and in-group types they practice

3. *Group plan adaptation:* For example, monitor group's progress toward group goals and plan.

4. *Therapeutic conditions and dynamics:* For example, group development, process observation

5. *Meaning:* Assist members in generating meaning from the group experience.

6. *Collaboration:* For example, respect members as coequal partners in the group experience.

7. *Evaluation:* Include evaluation, formal and informal, between sessions and at group's end.

8. *Diversity:* For example, show broad sensitivity to client differences and cultural issues.

9. *Ethical surveillance:* Use appropriate ethical decision-making model.

Best practice in processing. The domain of processing rests on evidence that direct experience in a group is necessary but not sufficient for member learning (Lieberman, Yalom, & Miles, 1973). Rather, it is important that group members be led to examine their experience and that of others in the group, to reflect on its meaning, and to identify potential applications both within and—of higher value—outside the group in their "real" lives (Bridbord, 2002; Conyne, 1999; Kees & Jacobs, 1990; Ward & Lichy, 2004). Processing, then, is about reflecting on experience, what Yalom termed the "reflective arc" in group psychotherapy. Group work leaders need to create with their members group conditions allowing for direct interpersonal experiences *and* opportunities for them to review especially salient experiences for their meaning and future application. Much more about this important best practice is presented in Chapters 9 and 10.

The *Guidelines* include four Processing areas:

1. *Processing schedule:* Process group events within sessions, before and after sessions, at end.

2. *Reflective practice:* For example, synthesize theory and practice to incorporate learning outcomes.

3. *Evaluation and follow-up:* Evaluate process and outcome, and conduct follow-up contacts.

4. *Consultation and training with other organizations:* For example, seek consultation as needed.

Talking about best practice guidelines is important, but it is instructive to see some actual examples of how these guidelines are stated. Figure 2–4 contains selected examples of best guideline items drawn from the sections of planning, performing, and processing. It is followed immediately by a learning exercise aimed at providing you with an opportunity to get a little practice in planning a group.

Figure 2–4   Examples of Best Practice Guidelines: Planning, Performing, Processing

---

The sample items, below, are extracted from the *ASGW Best Practice Guidelines.*

Planning

A.3b.   *Ecological assessment:* Group workers assess community needs, agency or organization resources, sponsoring organization mission, staff competency, attitudes regarding group work, professional training levels of potential group leaders regarding group work, client attitudes regarding group work, and multicultural and diversity considerations. Group workers use this information as the basis for decisions related to their group practice, or to the implementation of groups for which they have supervisory, evaluation, or oversight responsibilities.

A.4.   *Program development and evaluation:* Group workers (a) identify the type(s) of group(s) to be offered and how they relate to community needs and (b) concisely state in writing the purpose and goals of the group. Group workers also identify the role of the group members in influencing or determining the group goals; (c) set fees consistent with the organization's fee schedule, taking into consideration the financial status and locality of prospective group members; (d) choose techniques and a leadership style appropriate to the type(s) of group(s) being offered; (e) have an evaluation plan consistent with regulatory, organization, and insurance requirements, where appropriate; (f) take into consideration current professional guidelines when using technology, including but not limited to Internet communication.

Performing

B.4.   *Therapeutic conditions and dynamics:* Group workers understand and are able to implement appropriate models of group development, process observation and therapeutic conditions. Group workers manage the flow of communication, addressing safety and pacing of disclosures as to protect group members from physical, emotional, or psychological trauma.

B.5.   *Meaning:* Group workers assist members in generating meaning from the group experience.

Processing

C.1.   *Processing schedule:* Group workers process the workings of the group with themselves, group member, supervisors or other colleagues, as appropriate. This may include assessing progress on group and member goals, leader behaviors and techniques, group dynamics and interventions, developing understanding and acceptance of meaning. Processing may occur both within sessions and before and after each session, at time of termination, and later follow up, as appropriate.

C.2.   *Reflective practice:* Group workers attend to opportunities to synthesize theory and practice and to incorporate learning outcomes into ongoing groups. Group workers attend to session dynamics of members and their interactions and also attend to the relationship between session dynamics and leader values, cognition and affect.

Source: Association for Specialists in Group Work (1998, 2007).

Learning Exercise 2–4: Practice With a Group Plan

The **object** of this learning exercise is to gain practice in developing a group plan, based on the material contained in Figure 2–4.

1. Think of one kind of group you might like to provide.

2. Sketch a response to each of Steps 1 through 4 that follow. There is no need for perfection or comprehensiveness here; just jot down some ideas for each step.

3. In Step 5, hold a discussion with a partner.

Step 1: Identify the type of group (e.g., task) to be offered and how it relates to community needs. _____

_____

Step 2: Concisely state in writing the purpose and goals of the group.

a. Purpose: _____

_____

b. Goals: _____

_____

Step 3: Indicate techniques and a leadership style appropriate to the group.

a. Techniques: _____

_____

b. Leadership style: _____

_____

Step 4: Indicate one way to evaluate outcomes of the group.

_____

Step 5: Compare your work with a partner. Focus on what came easy for you in this exercise and what might have been a bit more difficult or confusing. Get and give tips and suggestions.

ASGW Document #3: Multicultural and Social Justice Competence Principles for Group Workers

Working with people in groups is an exercise in multiculturalism. Members bring diverse cultural issues, often are diverse demographically, and the unfolding group events and experiences are guaranteed to contain diverse dynamics (Lee, 2013). As stated by Bemak and Chung (2004), "Given the dramatically changing diversity in the U.S. population, it is critical that group workers are culturally competent" (p. 33). Of course, it also is the right thing to do, to become culturally competent so as to be of maximal assistance to the diverse populations that can benefit from group work participation. Moreover, and importantly, becoming culturally competent is much more than an obligation. It also can be rewarding, health producing, and inspiring for group members and leaders alike (Brinson & Lee, 1997; Conyne & Diedrich, 2013).

As Conyne, Tang, and Watson (2001) observed, one of the ways to promote diversity in group work is for the leaders to work with members to create a social ecology in the group allowing for differences to be acknowledged and respected and also where commonalities can be recognized and accepted (p. 359). DeLucia-Waack and Donigian (2004) and DeLucia-Waack (2011) expand and elaborate these and other points.

Because group work is inherently multicultural, it is necessary for group workers to become aware of how issues of diversity, multiculturalism, and social justice affect all aspects of group work including group process and dynamics, group facilitation, training, research, and group leaders and members themselves. A central goal is that group workers possess the confidence, competence and integrity to lead groups that are diverse along a wide range of dimensions, and to advocate for injustices as is possible and needed.

Prior to examining the *ASGW Multicultural and Social Justice Competence Principles for Group Workers* directly, let's consider some more relevant background material (see Conyne & Diedrich, 2013). You also will find continued coverage of this topic in Chapters 6 and 8.

Multicultural Competency and Social Justice

Groups can become a "safe place," providing an opportunity for members to discuss topics they avoid approaching in the rest of their life. These interactions can range from interpersonal feedback that is considered taboo or highly charged in other social settings, such as deep questions about one's sexual identity, to intergroup dialogue discussions helping to build awareness and understanding of others representing disparate life circumstances. Some of the most challenging topics to explore in group (and elsewhere) include issues of discrimination, oppression, and privilege. Group leaders often can feel underequipped to guide these discussions and interactions in ways that are beneficial and not harmful to the group members (Conyne & Diedrich, 2013).

In any case, group workers are ethically and morally obligated that they deal with issues of oppression and marginalization, which also requires that they address issues of privilege (ASGW, 2012; Burnes & Ross, 2010). Striving toward social justice and empowerment takes courage, skill, and dedication. We need only to recall the bold steps and sacrifices taken by such social justice advocates as Martin Luther King, Cesar Chavez, Nelson Mandella, and Rosa Parks, for example. Indeed, in a famous expression of courage, Ms. Parks said about her refusal to move to the back of that Montgomery, Alabama, bus in 1955: "The only tired I was, was tired of giving in" (cited in Arredondo & Perez, 2003, p. 287).

Intrapersonal Awareness. As they progress along the continuum of multicultural awareness, social justice, and action, group workers engage in a "process of self-reflection, learning, and action" (ASGW, 2012, p. 3). This is an active process, not an end result, in which "group workers move towards multicultural and social justice advocacy competence" (ASGW, 2012, p. 3) and strive to create an inclusive and empowered group environment (Ratts, Anthony, & Santos, 2010) that promotes social justice (Burnes & Ross, 2010).

An initial step toward social justice requires that the group worker focus on himself or herself first. Self-development in this area is vitally important. Group workers should strive to develop an awareness of their own identity that is based on their own experiences and histories with privilege and oppression (ASGW, 2012). This awareness can evolve through structured activities and discussions in class or supervision, such as through genealogical interviews, spiritual history exercises, and reflections in group supervision. However, it is crucial for development to continue throughout one's career and not just in the process of formal schooling. Reflecting on Western, middle-class values and how they play out in the norms and expectations of group leaders, such as a goal of self-development, not giving advice, and opening up to strangers about personal issues, is part of this awareness process. White group workers who are culturally competent are able to identify how they have benefited from privilege and institutional racism, both in their present lives and through their family history. *Building this self-awareness is essential, as the extent to which social justice is incorporated depends on a counselor's expertise, comfort, and familiarity in dealing with issues of privilege and oppression* (Ratts et al., 2010).

Interpersonal Factors. Culturally skilled group workers strive to become knowledgeable about the families, values, and communities where their group members live. Through this knowledge, combined with their own self-awareness, they are better able to identify and address differences in communication styles between group members and/or leaders (ASGW, 2012). One example of this is by recognizing the differences between high-context and low-context communication styles (ASGW, 2012). Conyne and Diedrich (2013) elaborate on these styles. With high-context communication, the speaker typically uses fewer words and lets the cultural context help explain. In contrast, with low-context communication the speaker is more explicit. If group leaders or members come from a background where a high-context communication style is the norm, they could assume that another individual (who has a low-context communication style) is rambling or adding in irrelevant details or facts. They may then assume the member has communication and interpersonal problems that need to be addressed through the group. However, this perspective privileges the high-context method of communicating and does not value the diversity that is present in the group.

Social Justice Factors. Culturally competent group workers not only attend to individual and interpersonal differences in their groups, but also to how larger systems, such as sociopolitical and economic forces, influence group members (Ratts et al., 2010). Enacting social justice in group work means that group leaders take action based on four factors: (a) *Equity,* focused on a culture-centered approach; (b) *Access,* centered on understanding identity construction based on a differences and deficiency model; (c) *Participation,* highlighting mutuality and authenticity; and (d) *Wellness,* spotlighting a culturally defined state of being in which mind, body, and spirit are integrated in a way that enables a person to live a fulfilled life (ASGW, 2012).

In a nutshell, a social justice approach requires group work leaders to "Expand the concept of 'client' to include systems and communities when examining change" (ASGW, 2012, Section III-13). This broadened level of awareness includes exploring issues such as immigration and poverty, for instance, and understanding how lack of health care access can affect the well-being of group members. When working with members who are bilingual, group workers strive to actively value bilingualism (ASGW, 2012) and not view a client's language as a barrier to counseling. Social justice also goes beyond awareness and valuing to include taking action, as appropriate, to improve the profession and the welfare of group members.

● THE MULTICULTURAL AND SOCIAL JUSTICE COMPETENCE PRINCIPLES FOR GROUP WORKERS

Now, let's take up the *Principles* directly. They emerge from the context described above and are organized into three areas:

a. Awareness of self and of group members

b. Strategies and skills in the best practice areas of planning, performing, and processing

c. Social justice advocacy

Due to space considerations, a selective discussion of the multicultural and social justice principles follows. Three example principles for each area will provide you with a sense of the document's contents. Please refer to the *Principles* document for needed detail.

a. Example of **Awareness of Self and Group Members:** As group workers move toward multicultural and social justice advocacy competence, they will

> 1. Demonstrate movement to being increasingly aware of and sensitive to their own multicultural identity and how their race, ethnicity, socioeconomic class, age, gender identity and expression, sexual orientation, religion, and spirituality, are impacted by their own experiences and histories.

b. Example of **Strategies and Skills**: As group workers move toward multicultural and social justice advocacy competence, they will incorporate the ASGW Best Practice Principles of Planning, Performing, and Processing.

Group workers demonstrating multicultural and social justice competence in group *planning* will

> 1. Develop multiple ways to demonstrate respect for group members' multicultural worldviews, which affect psychosocial functioning and expressions of distress . . .
>
> b) Example of *Group Worker Performing and Processing:* Group workers demonstrating multicultural and social justice competence in group performing and processing will

> 1. Establish group norms to accept, value, and respect cultural differences. The group leader needs to be intentional about such norming very early in the group to allow for open discussion of dynamics related to cultural issues.

c. **Example of Social Justice Advocacy:** As group workers move toward social justice advocacy competence they will

1. Discuss why social justice and advocacy issues are important within a group setting and how these issues influence the practice of group work.

Here are three illustrations of contributions that have emerged from the original version of the *Principles* (1998), and more are expected to flow from the current edition. As one example, different types of diversity groups have been conceptualized (Merchant, 2009): (a) culture-specific groups, focusing on the needs of a particular cultural group; (b) intercultural learning groups, addressing relations between cultural groups; and (c) other content-focused groups that are not specifically geared toward diversity issues but which do so because they are important. A second illustration is found in the supervision of group work (SGW) model (Okech & Rubel, 2007) that is used to develop diversity competence in group work among supervisees. Another example of how the *Principles* have generated innovation is the compilation of multicultural group work activities edited by Salazar (2009). This resource contains entries addressing such topics as how to select, use, and process group exercises, with the majority of attention given to practical group exercises focused on a range of multicultural factors including race, culture, ethnicity, gender, age, ability, socioeconomic status, sexual orientation, and spirituality. As a final illustration, a number of useful training videos addressing multicultural and diversity issues in group work have been produced, helping to translate sometimes complicated concepts and principles into action strategies. See, for example, training videos by Banez, Ivey, and Ivey (2002) on group microskills applied to diversity; Bauman and Steen (2009) on multicultural considerations when working with adolescents in groups; and Pack-Brown, Whittingham-Clark, and Parker (2002) on an Afrocentric approach to group work. All of these videos are listed in the Recommended Resources section of Chapter 5 on Leadership.

How do group leaders include a multicultural focus in their work? One way is to become sharply aware of how group processes may be expressing themselves in terms of the multicultural factors we have discussed. The following questions can aid in this process and are adapted from Conyne (1998b):

● Are members resentful they have to understand others?
● Do some members act as if their ideas are similar?
● Do members from minority identities/cultures make suggestions for the best way to proceed?
● Which topics does the group spend time on? Are these related to cultural background?
● Are certain topics, such as racism, avoided in the group?
● How do the group norms related to current societal issues, such as empowerment, oppression, etc.?
● Are subgroups based on cultural identity?
● What are the levels of verbal participation? Who talks to whom?

- What are the levels of influence between members?
- Do members hesitate to discuss their unique cultural concerns?

See Case Illustration 2–4 and Learning Exercise 2–5, which bring attention to these matters.

Case Illustration 2–4: Observing Group Process Multiculturally

*The **object** of this case illustration is to help sensitize you to the importance of viewing group process from a diverse and multicultural perspective.*

You considered group process observation earlier in Learning Exercise 2–1, and I now want you to have an opportunity to build on it. Observing group processes (e.g., Hanson, 1972), such as levels of participation and how decisions get made—among many others—is a critically important function for all group work leaders, and it can be very useful to help group members to become more aware of them, as well. These processes take on more particularized meaning when considering diversity issues in a group. I developed a "multicultural sensitizer" (Conyne, 1998b) to assist with how essential group processes might be viewed from a multicultural perspective. Consider the following example:

Group Member Participation

One indication of involvement in a group can be found in the activity levels of members as determined through their verbal participation. Group work leaders can gain valuable information by observing differences in the amount and kind of verbal participation engaged in by group members—including such items as who are high and low participators and shifts in verbal participation over time.

From a multicultural perspective, a group leader might also wonder if such factors as ethnicity, race, gender, and any other multicultural aspects (see discussion earlier) might affect verbal participation. Therefore, in any group the leader might give close attention to considerations such as the following:

1. In general, what cultural similarities and differences may exist in the group that may influence amount of participation? In what way?
2. How might silence relate to cultural differences?
3. How are any members from different cultures participating, based on your knowledge of that culture? For example, high and low participators?
4. Who talked to whom? Do member of different cultural backgrounds interact with each other? (Conyne, 1998b, p. 25)

Learning Exercise 2–5: Examining Your Multicultural Identities

*The **object** of this learning exercise is for you to examine yourself from aspects of a multicultural perspective and to underscore the value of multicultural self-awareness for group work leaders.*

Introduction: This learning exercise is adapted from the EdChange project (Gorski, 1995–2012). It allows group members to identify, compare, and then to discuss some of the multiple dimensions of their identities. I have modified it to fit more closely the particular forms of multicultural identity that are consistent with the *ASGW Diversity-Competent Principles* (1998) and with the *ASGW Multicultural and Social Justice Competency Principles for Group Workers* (2012).

Instructions:

1. Place your name in the center circle below.

2. Write an important aspect of your multicultural identity in each of the satellite circles—an identifier or descriptor that you think is important in defining you. This can include any multicultural aspect, drawn from race, ethnicity, age, gender, sexual orientation, socioeconomic status, ability, religion, or spirituality. For instance, one constellation might be the following: Asian American, female, straight, senior citizen.

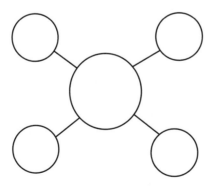

3. Pair up with a partner (or, if you are part of a group, with fellow group members) and share your identities, using one of the suggestions listed next.

(Continued)

(Continued)

30 minutes:

   a. Share a time when you were especially proud to identify with one of the descriptors you used earlier.
   b. Share a time when it was especially painful to be identified with one of your identifiers or descriptors.
   c. Name a stereotype associated with one of the groups with which you identify that is not consistent with who you are. Fill in the following sentence:

     I am (a/an) _____, but I am *not* (a/an) _____ .

     (So if one of your identifiers was young adult, and you thought a stereotype was that all young adults tend to be wild and crazy, your sentence might be:
     I am a young adult, but I am not wild and crazy in my thoughts and actions.)

Adapted with permission from EdChange project, Gorski (1995–2012).

● ACCREDITATION STANDARDS AND GROUP WORK

"Accreditation is a term to define a quality-assurance review process whereby individuals, schools, or other organizations are deemed to meet a set of standards" (Bobby, 2009, p. 2). Specialized accreditation addresses programs within a unique area of preparation, such as psychology, social work, law, or counseling for their adherence to quality standards. To stand for program accreditation review is an elective choice made by an academic program for it to be assessed and evaluated for quality.

Because a program is not accredited, however, does not by itself indicate that quality is absent. While it could mean that the program is unable to qualify for accreditation, it also could be the case that the program in question chooses not to pursue accreditation or that its program design intentionally is different from that espoused by the accreditation body.

Within the counseling professions, which (arguably) broadly span counselor education and counseling psychology, there are three accreditation bodies. CACREP is the primary body for accrediting master's-level counseling and doctoral-level counselor education and supervision programs. The

American Psychological Association's Commission on Accreditation is aimed at doctoral degree academic programs in the psychological specialty of counseling psychology (and other specialties). The Council on Social Work Education set its *Educational Policy and Accreditation Standards* (2008) to address bachelors, master's, and doctoral programs in social work. The Master's in Psychology and Counseling Accreditation Council (MPCAC) accredits master's degree academic programs in psychology and also, more recently, in counseling. I limit the discussion to CACREP as it has been and remains the "default" accreditation body for academic training programs in counseling.

The Council for the Accreditation of Counseling and Related Educational Programs (CACREP)

CACREP provides specialized program-level accreditation for master's- and doctoral-degree academic preparation programs in counseling. It is an independent accreditation agency recognized by the Council for Higher Education Accreditation. It is the primary accreditation agency of academic programs in counseling. In addition to accrediting doctoral degree programs in counselor education and supervision, CACREP accredits masters programs in counseling with these specialties: addiction; career; clinical mental health; marriage, couple, and family; school; student affairs and college counseling.

CACREP holds that its *Standards* are written to ensure that students develop a professional counselor identity and master the knowledge and skills to practice effectively. If an academic program is accredited, that status indicates to the public at large that a program has accepted and is fulfilling its commitment to educational quality (CACREP, 2009).

The 2009 CACREP master's-degree standards examine multiple areas of a counseling program, including its learning environment, resources, professional identify, eight common core curricular experiences, professional practice (practicum and internship), and the specialty areas that were pointed out above. Common core curricular experiences and demonstrated knowledge in each of the eight common core curricular areas are required of all students in an academic program. In addition, a set of doctoral-degree standards build on and extend those at the master's level.

Group work education and training are relevant for two sections of the master's-degree standards: (a) the common core curricular experiences area and (b) the practicum and internship of professional practice. Let's first examine common core area #6 of the CACREP standards: Group Work.

Group work core curricular experiences. Figure 2–5 contains the CACREP standards language for group work core curricular experiences at the master's level.

Some supportive observations. I would like to make a few supportive observations about the group work study areas that are described in Figure 2–5. Studies that address group purpose, group development, group dynamics, group theories, group methods, group skills, and other group approaches in a multicultural society are in tune with what it takes to produce effective group work leaders. This book is guided by those key elements as we move forward.

Consistent with CACREP standards, the ways that theoretical and experiential understandings can be met are not prescribed but, rather, counseling programs are required to provide what are called "curricular experiences." These most often are courses, but they might also include other types of training activities that can be documented. Allowing flexibility in how standards can be met is advantageous to program integrity.

The content included within group work studies has resulted, in part, from a continuing dialogue over the years with the ASGW representative on the CACREP Board who seeks to advocate appropriately for inclusion in the CACREP standards the perspective of group work that is contained in the *ASGW Standards for the Training of Group Workers* document you have become familiar with in this chapter. There is considerable agreement

Figure 2–5   CACREP Group Work Core Curricular Experiences

6. GROUP WORK—Studies that provide both theoretical and experiential understandings of group purpose, development, dynamics, theories, methods, skills, and other group approaches in a multicultural society, including all of the following:

a. *Principles of group dynamics,* including group process components, developmental stage theories, group members' roles and behaviors, and therapeutic factors of group work;

b. *Group leadership or facilitation styles and approaches,* including characteristics of various types of group leaders and leadership styles;

c. *Theories of group counseling,* including commonalities, distinguishing characteristics, and pertinent research and literature;

d. *Group counseling methods,* including group counselor orientations and behaviors, appropriate selection criteria and methods, and methods of evaluation of effectiveness; and

e. *Direct experiences* in which students participate as group members in a small group activity, approved by the program, for a minimum of 10 clock hours over the course of one academic term.

between, for example, the CACREP core curricular experiences for group work and the core competencies of ASGW's training standards.

Some critical observations. However, some issues remain to be solved, in my opinion. For instance, while the CACREP core area is termed *group work,* much of the language contained in points (a) through (e) refers not to group "work" but to group "counseling," which certainly is an important group work method, but just one of the four types of group work defined by ASGW.

The emphasis of the CACREP standards is on curricular experiences that lead to student theoretical and experiential "understandings." Coupled with the introduction to the common core curricular experiences section, which reads "Common core curricular experiences and demonstrated *knowledge* [italics added] in each of the eight common core curricular areas are required," one could conclude that knowledge and understanding are primarily the province of the Standards, with the attention to *skills* of lesser importance. The uncertain place of skills in the group work curricular experiences combined with clear emphasis on understanding could easily lead counseling programs to focus their curricular experiences on didactic- and knowledge-centered training. Not there's anything wrong with that per se. But when group work training is the focal point, an integration of knowledge, awareness, skills, experience, and supervised practice are all critically important (e.g., ASGW Professional Training Standards, 2000).

Professional practice: Practicum and internship. The CACREP standards indicate that the application of theory and the development of skills under supervision occur through professional practice—that is, through the practicum and internship. According to the *Standards*, those experiences provide the opportunities for students to "*counsel clients* [italics added]" (p. 15).

Previous versions of the *Standards* for practicum included a minimum number of clock hours to be devoted to group work practice, but these are no longer included. The *ASGW Professional Training Standards* call for a minimum of 10 clock hours, with 20 hours desirable (out of the 40 clock hours required by CACREP) for core group work experience in the practicum. In the internship, at least 240 clock hours of 600 total clock hours are to be devoted to direct service, and these 240 hours are to include experience leading groups (p. 16). While the inclusion of group leadership is commendable, no number of hours for leading groups is set, which weakens the standard. The *ASGW Training Standards* call for at least 60 of the 240 clock hours be devoted to supervised group leadership or coleadership experience.

Given that the intent of the professional practice standards addresses providing opportunities for students to counsel clients, a statement obviously encouraging of individual counseling, professional practice standards would seem to lend only limited support for students gaining supervised experience in the application of group work knowledge and development of group work skills. Note that extended attention to practicum and internship in group work are given in Chapter 8.

Doctoral degree standards in terms of group work. The doctoral-level standards related to group work are largely silent, except to indicate that theories pertaining to the principles and practices of group work are one of the content areas where learning experiences beyond the entry level are required.

Accreditation, in sum. CACREP accreditation standards contain considerable agreement with the *ASGW Training Standards*. In my opinion, though, the CACREP core curricular experiences could serve to guide training more effectively if they contained a fuller balance of theory *and* supervised practice, while emphasizing knowledge *and* skills. CACREP could build on its present foundation for group work by clarifying definitions of group work and group counseling, strengthening attention to skill development and supervised practice in group work, reintroducing clock hours for group work experience in practicum, specifying a minimum number of direct service clock hours in group work for the internship, and by legitimizing group work as an advanced training area at the doctoral level.

● ASGW'S RECOMMENDED CLOCK HOUR TRAINING

ASGW recommends more extensive course work and direct training in group work than is required by CACREP, including the specification of clock hours. Please refer to the association's Professional Training Standards for detail (ASGW, 2000). As a sampler, refer to Figure 2-6, which presents clock hour training recommended for each of the four group work types: task, psychoeducation, counseling, and psychotherapy. These hours are in addition to training in the core competencies involving observation of and participation in a group experience as a group member and/or as a group leader (10 clock hours minimum, which is comparable to the CACREP standard in this area, and 20 clock hours recommended).

Moving toward this direction would improve group work training.

● GROUP WORK KEYSTONES

- Group work's development has occurred over the last 100 years and longer.
- Group work professional associations (e.g., Association for Specialists in Group Work, American Group Psychotherapy Association, Association for the Advancement of Social Work with Groups, Society for Group

Figure 2–6   ASGW Professional Training Standards Related to Direct Experience

1. *Task/Work Group Facilitation:* A minimum of 30 clock hours (45 clock hours recommended) supervised practice facilitating or conducting an intervention with a task or work group appropriate to the age and clientele of the group leader's specialty area (e.g., school counseling, student development counseling, community counseling, mental health counseling)

2. *Group Psychoeducation:* A minimum of 30 clock hours (45 clock hours recommended) supervised practice conducting a psychoeducation group appropriate to the age and clientele of the group leader's specialty area (e.g., school counseling, student development counseling, community counseling, mental health counseling)

3. *Group Counseling:* A minimum of 45 clock hours (60 clock hours recommended) supervised practice conducting a counseling group appropriate to the age and clientele of the group leader's specialty area (e.g., school counseling, student development counseling, community counseling, mental health counseling)

4. *Group Psychotherapy:* A minimum of 45 clock hours (60 clock hours recommended) supervised practice conducting a psychotherapy group appropriate to the age a clientele of the group leader's specialty area (e.g., mental health counseling)

Psychology and Group Psychotherapy) have played a significant role in this development.

- ASGW has created exemplary foundation documents to help guide group work's emerging practice, training, and research, as well as its commitment to diversity.
- The core curricular experiences of CACREP and the core competencies of ASGW are compatible and represent a basic blueprint for group worker training.
- In my opinion, CACREP could build on its present foundation for group work.
- The CACREP and ASGW documents are specific to counseling programs but generalizable to other helping professions.

RECOMMENDED RESOURCES

American Group Psychotherapy Associations. (2007). *Practice guidelines for group psychotherapy*. New York, NY: Author. Retrieved from http://agpa.org/guide lines/AGPA%20Practice%20Guidelines%202007-PDF.pdf

Association for the Advancement of Social Work with Groups. (2006). *Standards for social work practice with groups.* Alexandria, VA: Author. Retrieved from http://www.aaswg.org/files/AASWG_Standards_for_Social_Work_Practice_with_Groups.pdf

American Counseling Association. (2005). *ACA code of ethics.* Alexandria, VA: Author.

American Counseling Association. (2010). *ACA's taskforce on counselor wellness and impairment.* Retrieved from http://www.counseling.org/wellness_taskforce/PDF/ACA_taskforce_assessment.pdf

Association for Specialists in Group Work. (2000). *Professional standards for the training of group workers.* Alexandria, VA: Author. Retrieved from www.asgw.org/training_standards.htm

Association for Specialists in Group Work. (2007). *Association for Specialists in Group Work best practice guidelines.* Alexandria, VA: Author. Retrieved from http://asgw.org/pdf/Best_Practices.pdf

Association for Specialists in Group Work. (2012). *Multicultural and social justice competence principles for group workers.* Alexandria, VA: Author. Retrieved from http://asgw.org/pdf/ASGW_MC_SJ_Priniciples_Final_ASGW.pdf

Blatner, A. (2007). A historical chronology of group psychotherapy and psychodrama. Retrieved from www.blatner.com/adam/pdntbk/hxgrprx.htm

Conyne, R., & Wilson, F. R. (1998). Toward a standards-based classification of group work offerings. *Journal for Specialists in Group Work, 23,* 177–184.

Council for the Accreditation of Counseling and Related Educational Programs. (2009). *2009 standards.* Alexandria, VA: Author.

Rapin, L. (2011). Ethics, best practices, and law in group counseling. In R. Conyne (Ed.), *The Oxford handbook of group counseling* (pp. 61–82). New York, NY: Oxford University Press.

Rapin, L., & Conyne, R. (2006). Best practices in group work. In J. Trotzer (Ed.), *The counselor and the group: Integrating theory, training, and practice* (4th ed., pp. 291–318). New York, NY: Routledge.

Wilson, F.R., & Newmeyer, M. (2008) A standards-based inventory for assessing perceived importance of and confidence in using ASGW's core group work skills. *Journal for Specialists in Group Work, 33,* 270–289. doi: 10.1080/01933920802196146

Wilson, F. R., Rapin, L., & Haley-Banez, L. (2004). How teaching group work can be guided by foundational documents: Best practice guidelines, diversity principles, training standards. *Journal for Specialists in Group Work, 29,* 19–29. doi: 10:1080/01933920490275321

GROUP DYNAMICS AND GROUP PROCESS

Architects in the past have tended to concentrate their attention on the building as a static object. I believe dynamics are more important: the dynamics of people, their interaction with spaces and environmental condition . . .

—John Portman, 1977

INTRODUCTION ●

Picture, for a moment, a group as a building (a far stretch maybe, but try it). Observe its properties that, like a building's, can be described concretely. Examples include the group's size (large or small), configuration (circle or rows), composition (similar or diverse members), formation (natural or configured), history (brief or longer term), structure (formal or informal), location (public or private), and type (therapeutic or task). While these kinds of elements capture important aspects of a group, just as they can of a building, John Portman's quotation highlights an essential truth about each object— they are static qualities that fail to capture the object's essential essence— that is, its *dynamics*. These dynamics refer to the forces and processes that ebb and flow, the ongoing interchange and interaction of properties to yield energy, movement, friction, and constant change.

Just as you pictured a group as a building, referencing the quotation again, now picture a group leader as an architect. In this metaphor, group leaders collaborate with others to envision the overall concept for the group and then design the group blueprint, or plan. This plan, which you read about in Chapter 2, serves to guide the group's evolution over time, subject to redesign based on the dynamics that occur. Group leaders remain vigilant architects of the group's blueprint, redrafting and applying it to reflect the ongoing dynamics of the group in order to better serve member needs.

CHAPTER OBJECTIVES

As a result of reading this chapter you will be able to

- Define group dynamics and its major properties
- Define group process and how to observe it
- Discuss two important processes:
  - Group development
  - Group member roles

● WHAT ARE GROUP DYNAMICS?

I coedited a book about professional identity and development called *Journeys to Professional Excellence: Lessons from Leading Counselor Educators and Practitioners* (Conyne & Bemak, 2005). We were very moved by the candid ways that these leaders described their professional life journeys.

We tripped on to the subject of this book accidentally, through a series of informal discussions at a national meeting of the Association for Counselor Education and Supervision (ACES). One of these events was an informal and unplanned table discussion that sprang up over lunch (parenthetically, it is not unusual to find, but perhaps somewhat heretical to put in print, that some of the more impactful and meaningful interactions I've experienced over the decades at professional conferences have occurred spontaneously, over a lunch, say, with colleagues).

Back to the story. We simply mentioned to the six others who happened to be eating their lunch at our table that we had just had a vigorous conversation with some other conference attendees (all of whom were well-known counselor educators) about how they went about doing their professional work, and how they had managed to arrive at the present point in their professional lives. As we said in the book,

Others around the table began to connect with this issue, and soon there was a lively and in-depth interaction occurring. One person talked about how growing up in poverty had led to a certain set of values that had informed her work style; another, about how a childhood of international travel had shaped him in specific ways. The energy level was high, and the connections being made were palpable. (Conyne & Bemak, 2005, p. 1)

In other words, the group dynamics running through this lunch-time discussion were noticeably engaging. People were involved and connected.

It is these kinds of group dynamics—the continual interaction of people with processes and actions in a group—that attract, motivate, and sustain people to work with groups; or, perhaps the reverse can occur, too, that these very same group dynamics may lead some others to feel anxious about and unattracted to groups. In any case, it can be said without any exaggeration that groups are alive and dynamic.

What I have found over the decades in my own experience and in talking with the small cadre of people who—there is no other way to say it—*love* to work with groups, is that group dynamics provide the raw material that draws them in, and keeps them there. While I commented in Chapter 3 that there is one and *only* one reason for leading groups, which is to help members to grow, change, and be productive, I also mentioned that there is indeed another reason why people who are committed to group leadership became and remain so: the *power of group dynamics.*

I reference earlier a research article that explored personal experience and meaning in group work leadership (Conyne, 1998a). In that study, I asked a panel of experienced and committed group leaders a series of questions. Among them was a set that probed their motivation for becoming a group work leader and another asked them to identify what factors defined a group that is really "cooking," or working well.

Note the following two comments. The first comment addresses motivation for becoming a group leader, while the second one describes signs of a productive group:

When the group is "working" and the "field" is activated, I get a charge from the experience. Some practitioners call it a "high." It's a different kind of feeling than derived from individual counseling. My extraverted personality thrives on the multiple focus and activity level of the group. So there is a powerful payoff of doing group work besides a therapeutic one. (Conyne, 1998a, p. 249)

The next comment relates to a group working at a high level:

There is a great air of expectancy. The air itself seems rarified, electric. Spaces among people are filled, there is a palpable "hum," as if a network is fully connected and communicating. Time passes very quickly, everything is light. Members are carrying the load, no need to stimulate, lots of need to process. (Conyne, 1998a, p. 250)

Defining Group Dynamics

Group dynamics have been defined in different ways. Lewin (1951) referred to *group dynamics* as the powerful processes that take place in a group, including the group's continuous movement and progression, and the interacting forces that affect it and its functioning (Brown, 2009). He was especially interested in how these processes and forces influenced the interaction among group members, eventually leading to outcomes (Gladding, 2011b). For Forsyth (2009), group dynamics are "the influential actions, processes, and changes that occur within groups and between groups over time" (p. 2). In a third definition, group dynamics are "the interactions that influence the attitudes and behavior of people when they are grouped with others, through either choice or accidental circumstances" (group dynamics, n.d.). In addition to group dynamics referring to a set of activities involving a group, the term's second meaning is "the scientific study of group processes" (Forsyth, 2009, p. 2).

Drawing from these sources, the following definition of group dynamics may suffice:

Group dynamics include the actions, processes, forces, and changes occurring over time that affect and influence the group, its members, and leader.

Follow Learning Exercise 3-1 as it explores strengths and limitations.

Learning Exercise 3–1: Identifying Relative Strengths and Limitations

The *object* of this learning exercise is to increase your ability to identify strengths and limitations in task groups.

(Continued)

Here are descriptions of two task groups. Both are small groups whose purpose is to plan a community fund-raising event taking place in 3 months. The planning groups have been functioning for about 1 month. Each has a group facilitator and 10 members.

Planning group 1: Members are quiet. The group facilitator sets goals and "runs" each meeting with precision. Tasks get assigned quickly with the facilitator clearly indicating responsibilities and timelines. Meetings begin and finish on time, sometimes early, with the facilitator being clearly in charge. When finished, members promptly exit the building.

Planning group 2: Members are active. The group facilitator works with members to set goals. Meetings include considerable member discussion. Tasks emerge from discussion, with their assignment negotiated, occasionally at some length, and then agreed upon. Meetings sometime appear to be "run by committee," with facilitation being shared. At the close of meetings, members and facilitator typically linger some, chatting and laughing.

Step 1: Identify the *relative strengths* and *limitations* within each planning group:

Planning group 1:

Relative strengths: _____

_____.

Relative limitations: _____

_____.

Planning group 2:

Relative strengths: _____

_____.

Relative limitations: _____

_____.

Step 2: Describe the factors you think account for these differences:

_____

_____

_____.

Finally, keep these factors in mind as we move toward discussing specific group dynamics in this chapter.

Specific group dynamics. What are these actions, processes, forces, and changes that are an integral, and often powerful, part of groups, whether these groups are concerned with helping people change or with problem solving around tasks? Case Illustration 3–1 identifies and briefly describes 17 of them, arranged into five categories (adapted from Forsyth, 2009):

1. *Development and organization:* A group's evolution and structure

2. *Control and direction:* A group's management and guidance

3. *Working:* A group's way of proceeding to accomplish group and member goals

4. *Maintenance and conflict:* A group's capacity to sustain itself

5. *Context:* A group's external and internal influences

Case Illustration 3–1: Specific Group Dynamics

*The **object** of this case illustration is to identify and briefly describe important and specific group dynamics so you can be better prepared to identify and work with them.*

   A. *Development and organization*

   Inclusion: How are members incorporated into a group by others?
   Group development: How does a group form and evolve over time?
   Cohesion: How connected do members of a group feel to the group and to each other?
   Structure: How is a group organized? What roles and responsibilities are defined?

   B. *Control and direction*

   Influence: What factors affect performance in a group? How do norms emerge?
   Power: Where is authority lodged in a group? How is control exercised?
   Membership: What roles and behaviors are engaged in by members as they participate?
   Leadership: How does direction and facilitation occur in a group? What style predominates?

   C. *Working in groups*

   Goals: How do individual and group goals get set and influence behavior?

(Continued)

Interaction: How do members participate? Actively or passively? Connected or independent?

Performance: How are goals and tasks worked on in a group? How are resources used?

Decision making: How do members make choices in a group? How are decisions reached?

D. *Maintenance and conflict*

How does a group manage its functioning? How are relations accommodated?

Communication: How do members talk with each other, the leader?

Conflict: What causes discord in a group? How is it expressed?

Support: How do members demonstrate concern, care?

E. *Context*

External influences: How is a group affected by outside factors (e.g., physical, economic)?

Expectations: How is a group impacted by external expectations and those of participants?

Group types: How is group functioning influenced by its purpose and type?

Learning Exercise 3–2 provides some practice with connecting strengths and limits to particular group dynamics.

Learning Exercise 3–2: Tying Strengths and Limitations to Specific Group Dynamics

*The **object** of this learning exercise is to increase your ability to identify group dynamics occurring in group descriptions.*

1. Return to the relative strengths and limitations you identified in the two planning groups contained in the first case illustration.

2. Now, after having read the descriptions of specific group dynamics, see if you can link any of these group dynamics to particular

(Continued)

(Continued)

strengths and limitations you noted in each planning group. For instance, are there certain group dynamics that seem associated with the behavior of the two facilitators?

Planning group 1:

Strengths and group dynamics: _____

_____.

Limitations and group dynamics: _____

_____.

Planning group 2: _____

_____.

Strengths and group dynamics: _____

_____.

Limitations and group dynamics: _____

_____

● WHAT IS GROUP PROCESS?

Group dynamics, just discussed, and *group process* share much in common. In fact, some authors treat them the same (e.g., Posthuma, 2002; Hanson, 1972; Jacobs, Masson, Harvill, & Schimmel, 2012). Others view the two terms as sharing much in common, with some distinctions, typically that group process is a subset of group dynamics. Following are some definitions of group process.

Gladding (2011b) views group process as the interactions and relationships among group members. It is an important part of group dynamics, spanning the evolution of a group from its formation to conclusion (Corey, Corey, & Corey, 2010). Jacobs et al. (2012) define group process (as well as group dynamics) as the "interaction and energy exchange between members and leaders, how the leader reacts to members, and how the members talk to each other and the leader" (p. 39). Brown expands on these views, explaining further that group process involves here-and-now experiencing and reflecting how a group is functioning, the relationship quality among group members and with the group leader(s), and the expressed and hidden issues and concerns of group members (Brown, 2009).

Drawing from these sources, then, the following definition of group process may suffice. Note how it builds on the previous definition of group dynamics:

> **Group process** *results from the experiencing by group participants of influential group dynamics as they occur separately and in combination over a group's development.*

Some examples of group process include levels of member participation, influence, communication patterns, content and feelings expressed, resistance, norms, defenses, trust, and conflict management by the group (Brown, 2009; Corey et al., 2010; Hanson, 1972).

Managing Exploding Data in Groups

Group interaction can be challenging sometimes to keep track of, and sometimes group leaders can feel overwhelmed. Such a state is not at all uncommon for novices as they are learning group leadership and, in fact, is to be expected. So, it's necessary to develop methods for managing high volumes of input from a group. Aids for observing and categorizing group processes can be very helpful to this end. One of the most useful guides was developed decades ago by Hanson, *What to Look for in Groups* (1972), which is presented in its entirety in Case Illustration 3-2, focuses on these two areas, and it provides a structured and concrete approach to conduct observations. In Hanson's words,

> In most interactions, very little attention is paid to process, even when it is the major cause of ineffective group action. Sensitivity to group process will better enable you to diagnose group problems early and deal with them more effectively. Since these processes are present in all groups, awareness of them will enhance a person's worth to a group and enable him [*sic*] to be a more effective group participant. (p. 1)

I have excerpted material from Hanson's group process observation guide in Case Illustration 3-2.

Case Illustration 3–2: What to Look for in Groups: Excerpts

The **object** of this case illustration is to make available a set of group process observation descriptions that can be very useful for leaders and members of groups.

AUTHOR'S NOTE: I have considered Hanson's discussion of group process/dynamics (he doesn't differentiate the two) as one of the classic and practical treatments available. Included in following are excerpts from Hanson's guide. Please refer to the original source for a complete document.

In all human interactions there are two major ingredients—content and process. The first deals with the subject matter or the task upon which the group is working. In most interactions, the focus of attention of all persons is on the content. The second ingredient, process, is concerned with what is happening between and to group members while the group is working . . . Since these processes are present in all groups, awareness of them will enhance a person's worth to a group and enable him to be a more effective group participant.

Below are some observation guidelines to help you process analyze group behavior.

Participation

One indication of involvement is verbal participation. Look for differences in the amount of participation among members.

- Who are the high participators?
- Who are the low participators?
- Do you see any shift in participation, e.g., highs become quiet; lows suddenly become talkative? Do you see any possible reason for this in the group's interaction?

Influence

Influence and participation are not the same. Some people may speak very little, yet they capture the attention of the whole group. Others may talk a lot but are generally not listened to by other members.

- Which members are high in influence? That is, when they talk, others seem to listen.
- Which members are low in influence? Others do not listen to or follow them. Is there any shifting in influence?

(Continued)

Styles of Influence

Influence can take many forms. It can be positive or negative; it can enlist the support or cooperation of others or alienate them. *How* a person attempts to influence another may be the crucial factor in determining how open or closed the other will be toward being influenced.

- *Autocratic:* Does anyone attempt to impose his or her will or values on other group member, or try to push them to support his decisions?
- *Peacemaker:* Who eagerly supports other group members' decisions?
- *Laissez-faire:* Are any group members getting attention by their apparent lack of involvement in the group?
- *Democratic:* Does anyone try to include everyone in a group decision or discussion?

Decision-Making Procedures

Many kinds of decisions are made in groups without considering the effects of these decisions on other members. Some people try to impose their own decisions on the group, while others want all members to participate or share in the decisions that are made.

- Does anyone make a decision and carry it out without checking with other group members (e.g., decides on the topic to be discussed and immediately begins to talk about it).
- Does the group drift from topic to topic? Who topic-jumps? Do you see any reason for this in the group's interactions?

Task Functions

These functions illustrate behaviors that are concerned with getting the job done, or accomplishing the task that the group has before them.

- Does anyone ask for or make suggestions as to the best way to proceed or to tackle a problem?
- Does anyone attempt to summarize what has been covered or what has been going on in the group?

Maintenance Functions

These functions are important to the morale of the group. They maintain good and harmonious working relationships among the

(Continued)

(Continued)

members and create a group atmosphere that enables each member to contribute maximally.

- Who helps others get into the discussion?
- Who cuts off others or interrupts them?

Group Atmosphere
Something about the way a group works creates an atmosphere that is revealed in a general impression.

- Who seems to prefer a friendly congenial atmosphere? Is there any attempt to suppress conflict or unpleasant feelings?
- Do people seem involved and interested? Is the atmosphere one of work, play satisfaction, taking flight, sluggishness, etc.?

Membership
A major concern for group members is the degree of acceptance or inclusion in the group. Different patterns of interaction may develop in the group that give clues to the degree and kind of membership.

- Is there any subgrouping? Sometimes two or three members may consistently agree and support each other or consistently disagree and oppose one another.
- Do some people seem to be "outside" the group? Do some members seem to be "in"? How are those "outside" treated?

Feelings
During any group discussion, feelings are frequently generated by the interactions between members. These feelings, however, are seldom talked about.

- What feelings do you observe in group members: anger, irritation, frustration, warmth, affection, excitement, boredom, defensiveness, competitiveness, etc.?
- Do you see any attempts by group members to block the expression of feelings, particularly negative feelings? How is this done? Does anyone do this consistently?

Norms
Standards or ground rules may develop in a group that controls the behavior of its members. Norms usually express the beliefs or desires of the majority of the group members as to what behaviors *should* or

(Continued)

should not take place in the group . . . Some norms facilitate group progress and some hinder it.

- Are certain areas avoided in the group (e.g., sex, religion, talk about present feelings in group, discussing the leader's behavior, etc.)?
- Are group members overly nice or polite to each other? Are only positive feelings expressed? Do members agree with each other too readily? What happens when members disagree?

Adapted from Hanson, *Annual Handbook of Group Facilitators* (1972, pp. 21–24).

Group content and process. Considerable attention has been given to group content, which is a part of group process, and how content and process interrelate. Content refers to *what* group members and leaders actually talk about during sessions—and process refers to *how* they talk about that content, the style they use.

Hill Interaction Matrix. The *Hill Interaction Matrix* (HIM) (1965), created by William Fawcett Hill, provides an example of how group content and process can be organized and better understood. The *HIM* is a system for categorizing member verbal interaction in therapeutic groups, and it is a helpful tool for research and training in groups. The *HIM* is formed by the dimensions of *content* (what is discussed) and work style (*process,* or how content is discussed).

In Hill's view, the kinds of content that can be discussed in a group include four categories that range from low risk/gain successively to high risk/gain. These content categories are (a) *topics,* that are external to the group, such as the weather or last night's ball game, which is lowest risk, and (b) the *group* itself, such as wondering where everyone is today or comments about how the group is doing; (c) *personal,* comments about oneself or about another, and (d) *relationship,* comments about interactions occurring between two or among more people in the group, which is highest risk and, potentially, highest gain.

Each kind of content can interact with the how (the process) people discuss content. Hill again divided these ways into four categories, graded from low risk/gain successively to high risk/gain. These process (or work style) categories are (a) *conventional,* a kind of social "chitchat," like what might occur at a reception, involving little to no risk; (b) *assertive,* taking stands and arguing or defending a point, behavior, or position; (c) *speculative,* or hypothesizing about one's own or another's behavior; and (d) *confrontive,* directly engaging with others in the group about their behavior, which is highest risk and, potentially, highest gain.

Generally, the highest risk and potential gain results from combinations of personal or relationship content with speculative or confrontive process. However, the therapeutic potential accruing from any form of verbal interaction is a function of context, especially the group's level of development, a topic to be addressed in more detail later in the chapter. Briefly, early in a group's development, it may be appropriate for conversations to be relatively low risk because participants are just beginning to become acquainted with each other and with the group itself. As the group matures, perhaps accompanied by increased trust and a positive working climate, then interactions can begin to deepen, embracing higher levels of risk.

Appropriate balance of content and process. As a group develops over time, leaders always need to be concerned with helping group members achieve an appropriate balance between content and process, that is, between the information that is being communicated and how it is being delivered. Appropriate balance is a function of the group's level of development (Kraus & Hulse-Killacky, 1996; Hulse-Killacky, Killacky, & Donigian, 2001), and of other factors, such as skill of delivery.

See Learning Exercise 3–3 for an example of how a misbalance of content and process can occur in a group.

Learning Exercise 3–3: Jeremy's Out of Whack Content and Process

*The **object** of this learning exercise is to give you a concrete case situation for applying process observation.*

1. Read the brief case situation.

Jeremy comes to the group "sick and tired," as he admitted during the first session, "of boring people all the time." When asked to say a little bit more about what he meant, he explained in a 10-minute nonstop monotone all the minutiae of how he bores others. The group leader was quite sure that Jeremy had no awareness of how he was "coming across." After just 2 minutes, the group leader began to see other members fidgeting; Suzie even rolled her eyes at about the 4-minute

(Continued)

mark. Jeremy used no affect in his presentation, no variation in tone. He looked no one in the eyes, and he just kind of droned on in the driest of ways. The group leader let Jeremy ramble on until he was finished. No one else intervened along the way, either, but early in a group that is not to be expected usually. At that point, once he was finished, the leader thanked Jeremy for his explanation and then asked him if he would like some feedback. Jeremy paused, took a deep breath, but then said yes.

2. Respond to the two questions following:

   a. Identify what about Jeremy's presentation could be said to be "out of whack."

   _____

   _____.

   b. List what group process observations you referred to in making the above statement:

   _____

See if you could be helpful to Jeremy in Learning Exercise 3–4.

Learning Exercise 3–4: Give Jeremy Some Helpful Feedback

*The **object** of this learning exercise is to learn about ways to give effective feedback and to practice doing it, giving and receiving feedback.*

1. Place yourself in the role of group leader in the above case illustration involving Jeremy.

2. Jeremy has agreed to receive feedback. Keep the general guidelines that follow in mind for giving corrective feedback. Feedback seems to be best received and most helpful when

   a. Its purpose is to help and be corrective
   b. The recipient requests the feedback
   c. It is offered tentatively, not as if you hold the answer key

(Continued)

(Continued)

    d. Something positive (if it can be found) is presented first
    e. It is given immediately, rather than after a long time has gone by
    f. It is descriptive, rather than judgmental or evaluative
    g. It is specific and concrete, rather than general and diffuse
    h. It is concise rather than complex
    i. It is feasible, not impossible
    j. It connects with feedback from others

3. What might you say to Jeremy that could be helpful, remembering this is happening during the group's first session?

Following are two examples:
Person 1: "Thanks for being open to feedback, Jeremy. I know how sometimes that can be kind of anxiety producing, and I admire your risk taking, especially so early in the group."
Person 2: "I second that. You know, I'll admit to wishing that you might have stopped a bit earlier in your talking, and I noticed you didn't look at any of us when you were speaking."

4. Now, follow up the feedback examples by

    a. pairing up with another.
    b. discussing the guidelines about effective feedback. What do these mean to each of you?
    c. evaluating the two examples of feedback that are given: What do you think of each?
    d. taking turns presenting two of your own feedback statements to Jeremy, following the guidelines.
    e. give each other feedback on your statements.

Person 1:

Feedback statement #1:

_____

_____.

Feedback statement #2:

_____

_____.

(Continued)

Person 2 provides feedback to Person 1.
Person 2:

Feedback statement #1:

_____

_____ .

Feedback statement #2:

_____

_____ .

Person 1 provides feedback to Person 2.
Person 1:

Feedback statement #1:

_____

_____ .

Feedback statement #2:

_____

_____ .

Hulse-Killacky et al. (2001), in their analysis of appropriate balancing of content and process in a group, indicate that the ideal relationship can be seen in a bell-shaped curve. See the next figure, which depicts the shape of content and process together in one line across 18 sessions of a group. At Session 4, early in the group, content and process are warming up. At Session 10, around this group's midpoint, content and process are in high action. At Session 16, approaching the group's end, content and process are ebbing toward closure. When significant divergence from the ideal curve occurs in content and process lines, the possibility of inappropriate balance needs to be considered.

See Figure 3-1 to view an "ideal" relationship between content and process.

Processing events and experiences in group work. As we are seeing, successful practice of group work requires that the group leader understand and be skilled in observing, assessing, harnessing, and leveraging appropriately the

Figure 3–1   Ideal Balance in Content and Process

*The **object** of this figure is to depict the idealized balance between content and process, a function of productivity in relation to the number of sessions, in a group.*

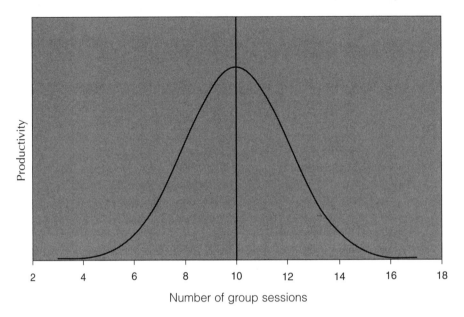

Source: Reprinted with permission from Tushar Mehta (http://tushar-mehta.com/).

group dynamics that occur within group sessions. In this chapter, you are being introduced to some methods geared to helping leaders organize and make sense of the sometimes bewildering and confusing interaction in groups.

A route toward making sense of group activity is found in processing. You already are acquainted with processing, which is one of the three ASGW best practice guidelines in group work (refer to Chapter 2 for review; Chapters 9 and 10 will elaborate). As you recall, processing can occur during group sessions, and leaders also are encouraged to process group actions between sessions. The purpose is to help members, and leaders, to examine group experiences and from those experiences identify their meaning and what can be put to use in their lives inside and outside the group.

The *Modified Grid for Processing Experiences and Events in Group Work,* adapted from Conyne (1997a) is an example of one approach to aid processing. It "can be used within the ongoing context of a group to enable members and leaders to process more efficiently group experiences, thereby improving understanding, meaning attribution, and application" (p. 167). The *Modified Grid* is composed of two dimensions: (a) content (*what*) of the conversation, and (b) process (*how*) of the conversation.

Content refers to what group members discuss. There are five levels of content identified in the *Modified Grid*:

> "It": Topics that are external to the group, for instance, "Sure is nice out today."

> "*I*": Self disclosure, for instance, "I feel very comfortable right now in this group."

> "*You*": Feedback to another, for instance, "Jorge, I really like how you are so helpful to others in here, how you listen and then reach out."

> "*We*": Interrelationships among members, for instance, pointing out similarities and differences among four different members: "Jean and Bill, I've seen you working together to support each other, while Tom and Phyllis, it seems you have been more at odds; I'm not sure, what do you think about this?"

> "*Us*": The group as a whole, for instance, "Our group seems restless today, or listless, to me, anyway. How do the rest of you feel?"

Process refers to how group members discuss the content. The *Modified Grid*, borrowing from the *HIM*, discussed earlier, has four levels of process:

Conventional: Social chitchat style, for instance, "Last night my wife and I saw a great new movie."

Assertive: Taking a firm position while not being interested in learning or changing, for instance, "Are you kidding me? I wouldn't trust another person completely with anything!"

Speculative: Theorizing or hypothesizing about why something is occurring in an effort to understand (but not necessarily opening up for change), for instance, "I wonder if we could analyze what's our best next step to take?"

Confrontive: Taking the most risk by talking directly and openly to others about an issue occurring with oneself, others in the group, or the group itself, for instance, "George and Martha (looking directly at these members), I am wishing you both could drop your attacking style and begin to listen to each other, instead."

The *Modified Grid* is at its most useful when interactions between levels of content and process are considered. Twenty possibilities emerge from these levels of interaction.

See the *Modified Grid* in Figure 3-2, and then try applying it in Learning Exercise 3-5.

Figure 3–2   Modified Grid for Processing Experiences and Events in Group Work

*The **object** of this figure is to show relationships between Process styles of interacting and levels of Content in a group.*

PROCESS

CONTENT

	Conventional	Assertive	Speculative	Confrontive
It	1	2	3	4
I	5	6	7	8
You	9	10	11	12
We	13	14	15	16
Us	17	18	19	20

*The *Modified Grid* has been adapted from its original form by incorporating in the Process dimension the work style categories from the *HIM*. Each of the 20 cells contained in the *Modified Grid* represents a unique interaction between a level of content with another level of process.

Source: Adapted from Conyne (1997).

Learning Exercise 3–5: Analyzing Group Content and Process

*The **object** of this learning exercise is to provide experience in applying the Modified Grid by generating selected examples of interaction.*

1. Now try your own hand with using the *Modified Grid*. Usually, of course, you would be trying to categorize an existing communication into its content and process levels. Here, though, reverse it by trying to generate examples of conversation.

(Continued)

2. Review examples of interaction statements for Cells 3 and 8.

   Cell 3 and 8 Examples
   Cell 3 example ("It" by Speculative): "Why is it that people are curious about their histories? Where does this come from? I wonder, don't you?"
   Cell 8 example ("I" by Confrontive): "I look at myself—when I do, I mean honestly, that is—and I see not a lot to be proud of, a bunch of failures . . . but I don't think I'm a failure. Does that make any sense?"

3. Now try filling in Cells 1, 7, 11, 16, and 18:

   a. Cell 1: ("It" by Conventional): _____

   _____.

   b. Cell 7: ("I" by Speculative): _____

   _____.

   c. Cell 11: ("You" by Speculative): _____

   _____.

   d. Cell 16: ("We" by Confrontive): _____

   _____.

   e. Cell 18: ("Us" by Assertive): _____

   _____.

Group development. You no doubt have noticed that running through much of the discussion in this chapter is the concept of *group development*, one of the key means by which groups can be understood. In fact, group development is of such practical importance for group work leaders that Chapter 4 is devoted to it exclusively. As Brabender (2011) indicates, "Models of how change occurs within a group vary. Yet, they all contain the notion that how groups change over time is systematic rather than random and that from group to group some common features can be discerned" (p. 182).

When one stands apart and looks at a number of groups, patterns of development can be identified. This, in fact, is how group development models—and there are over 100 of them and still counting (Conyne, 1989)—have emerged, through the systematic study and analysis of lots of groups over time. William Fawcett Hill was so taken by group development theory that he collected them over the decades, diligently filing them away. After passing 100 of them in his collection, he declared, "the collecting bug was exterminated, as the object of the quest had lost its rarity" (Hill & Gruner, 1973, as cited in Forsyth, 2009, p. 129).

Brabender (2011), in her comprehensive review of group development in group counseling, provides a summation of empirical evidence attesting to both the reality and the significance of group development, and of its importance as representing a predictable pattern of performance. At the same time, it is important to remember that in any one group, the presence of a general pattern may be fuzzy to discern or even not realized. This important point is yet another reason to underscore the importance of leaders becoming adept at group process observation.

However, being guided by group development is a key element of good theory, practice, and training. Wheelan (2005) discussed the _developmental perspective_ as one of the major theoretical conceptions of groups, alongside the psychoanalytic, functional, social identity, and communication, systems, and nonlinear dynamics perspectives. Group development is recognized and included prominently in the best practice guidelines of the American Group Psychotherapy Association (AGPA, 2007), the Association for Specialists in Group Work (ASGW, 2007), and the Association for the Advancement of Social Work with Group (AASWG, 2006). As I mentioned in Chapter 2, the AASWG standards are organized by group development phases: pre-group planning, recruitment, and group formation; beginning, middle, and ending phases. AGPA's practice guidelines devote considerable attention to group development. The planning, performing, and processing steps of the ASGW best practice guidelines are structured implicitly from a group development perspective. Texts on group counseling (e.g., Corey, 2012; Corey et al., 2010; Gladding, 2011b) and group psychotherapy (e.g., Yalom & Leszcz, 2005) typically explicate group development, organizing discussions of group intervention according to one model of group development or another. The next chapter will be devoted to group development considerations and connect leadership approaches with group development stages.

Group member roles. Over time group members tend to take on roles, which can be understood as a cluster of behaviors and functions. Sometimes these roles stabilize but, in other cases, they may shift. As well, these roles can exert positive and negative effects in the group.

In general, group member roles coalesce around two major dimensions of group life that you have read about previously: (a) _task_ and (b) _maintenance._

Task roles, information seeker, serve to propel a group forward. Maintenance roles, such as encourager, address personal relations among participants. A third set was termed by Benne and Sheats (1948), who wrote the classic source on functional roles of group members, as *individual* roles. These roles are focused on the individual at the expense of the group (e.g., attention seeker) and typically exert a dysfunctional effect.

Task and maintenance roles are vital to group functioning, and their appropriate generally contributes positively to group functioning. However, a member who gets locked into rigidly performing any one of these roles can cross over to being unhelpful. For instance, Nigel at first was helpful to the group by reminding members of time limits. Yet as the group progressed, he seemed to become nearly obsessed with time, showing agitation when others—in his view—were slow, late, or talked excessively. He became an enforcer. In doing so, Nigel had become rigid and disproportionate in what had been at first a positive role (technician); it was now fixed at the individual level at the expense of the group and had become dysfunctional.

Let's consider three examples of each of these types of roles, beginning with task roles:

Information seeker: A group member performing this role typically seeks to clarify suggestions of others based on facts.

"Tariq, how much do you think it might cost to rent the town hall?"

Summarizer: In this role, a group member attempts to pull together various inputs that has been made and checks these out with the rest of the group.

"Well, we covered lots of stuff in the last half hour or so, and I think the theme of it all can boil down to how pleased most of us are feeling with how our group is doing."

Technician: This member role involves executing routine tasks, such as keeping time.

"I think we stayed right on course and respected the time we'd set for the exercise."

A complementary set of roles is termed *maintenance* because these roles focus on personal relationships among participants. Three examples of maintenance roles are the following:

Encourager: This member role supports and praises the behavior of other members.

"I'm so glad you were able to talk to your mother, finally, Sophie!"

Process Observer: In this role a group member notes events and experiences in the group and brings this information back to the group.

"Let's see, I saw Harold supporting Gretchen over the last few minutes with the rest of us kind of sitting back and watching; is that on track?"

Gatekeeper: This group member role seeks to open opportunities for other members to become involved.

"I've been seeing Toni wanting, I think, to get into the conversation (looking invitingly at Toni). Want to jump in?"

A third set of member roles are those that is nearly always negative. Termed "dysfunctional," here are three examples:

Monopolizer: In this role, a group member talks excessively, usually about topics that are tangential to the group, putting himself or herself in the spotlight, diverting the group form its mission.

After three minutes of monologue, " . . . and I really think it's best if people just forget about succeeding at all or even trying to figure it all out, no matter what the cost is. My grandfather believed that, too, and he never liked politicians, which is something I believe . . ." (continuing to drone on).

Avoider: A group member in this dysfunctional role continually veers away from the center of discussions by "zoning out," talking about side issues, or fooling around.

Group members are highly engaged in processing an experience that just occurred. Sheila says, "Who wants to fly this pop stand and go get some wings?"

Rescuer: In this negative role, a group member perseverates in rushing to the aid of any group member who seems to be experiencing anxiety or even challenge, which really is a way to protect the rescuer from experiencing personal discomfort.

"Billie, are you all right, here, I think we should all lay off her because we are just piling on, and Billie needs our help. Billie, what can I do to help?"

A larger listing of member roles, arranged into task, maintenance, and dysfunctional ones is contained in Figure 3-3.

Figure 3–3   Roles of Group Members

*The **object** of this figure is to make available task and maintenance roles in groups, with brief descriptions, for your use as a group leader or member.*

Group members can perform a variety of roles. Some relate to helping the group perform its duties; these are termed *task roles*. Other roles are focused on personal relationships among participants; these are termed *maintenance roles*. Not all roles are positive. Some of them can actually harm a group's functioning. These can be called individual, dysfunctional roles, where behavior is directed more often toward personal rather than toward group needs.

Below is a list and brief description of different roles performed in groups.

Task Roles

Initiator	proposes goals, new ideas, and solutions; suggests procedures; points out benefits
Information giver	offers facts and relevant information or experience
Opinion giver	states belief about alternatives; focuses on values rather than facts
Information seeker	seeks ideas, thoughts, facts and suggestions the problem
Opinion seeker	asks for views and perspectives of group members
Coordinator	clarifies and links various suggestions, ideas, and opinions
Summarizer	reviews and restates back to the group; draw member's activities together; offers conclusions
Clarifier	interprets; gives examples; defines terms; clears up confusion or ambiguity
Evaluator	holds the group's activity to some criterion, for example, practicality, logic, etc.
Orient	tries to show the group the position it is now taking and may raise questions about its direction
Technician	performs routine tasks for the group such as secretary/treasurer or timekeeper
Energizer	stimulates the group to act

Maintenance Roles

Encourager	praises good points, exhibits accepts, promotes group solidarity
Harmonizer	attempts to mediate differences among members or their points of view
Gatekeeper	attempts to encourage communication, bringing persons into the discussion who have not given their ideas

(Continued)

Figure 3–3   (Continued)

Standard setter	expresses goals for the group to attempt to achieve and applies them to evaluating the group process
Compromiser	can negotiate or yield his or her idea or point of view, or admit an error
Process observer	notes group events and experiences and introduces observations into group
Follower	tends toward being a passive and accepting person; goes along with the ideas of others

Individual, Dysfunctional Roles

Aggressor	may express disapproval of others, tends to be on the offensive, attacks the group
Blocker	is negativistic and resistant, disagreeing and opposing beyond reasonable objections; getting discussion off on a tangent; focuses on personal concerns rather than on group problem; argues
Dominator	tries to assert authority to control group at expense of other members
Avoider	withdraws from discussion; daydreams; wanders off, talks to others; fools around
Joker	does not involve self in group process but sits back in horseplay, whispering, etc.
Self-confessor	this person brings in personal feelings, ideas, etc., not pertinent nor oriented to the group
Help-seeker	expresses insecurity through gaining sympathy, or in other ways, deprecates self
Special interest pleader	expresses own biases or prejudices by pleading for the minority groups within the group
Rescuer	"Red Crossing," a style of coming to the aid of any group member who seems to be struggling some, even in times of growth
Monopolizer	pattern of excessive talking, commanding the stage; calls attention to self, boasts; loud or unusual behavior; excessive talker

General Leader-Type Roles

Task leader	person whose behavior contributes strongly to accomplishing work of the group
Maintenance leader	person whose behavior contributes strongly to building and maintaining group relationships
Self-focused leader	person whose behavior was directed toward meeting his or her own needs; hindered or ignored group needs

See now if you can apply some of these roles in your own life by working with Learning Exercise 3-6.

Learning Exercise 3–6: What Roles Fit Whom?

*The **object** of this learning exercise is for you to apply member roles to a group example you envision and thereby increase your ability to assess and work with roles in groups.*

If you are a member of a group currently, reflect on its members. Which roles might fit which members, including yourself? If you are not currently a member of a group, think about people you have known. Any fits?

Use the format below to assist your work.

Person	*Role*
_____	_____
_____	_____
_____	_____
_____	_____
_____	_____

Group dynamics and group process are essential aspects of group work. As was implied about groups by the architect, John Portman, at the chapter's beginning: group is not a static object, but a dynamic, living entity. Group work leaders are obligated to become aware of the many dynamics and processes that can and do occur and then develop methods and strategies for maximizing positive effects. We examine some of these methods in the following chapter.

GROUP WORK KEYSTONES ●

- Group dynamics and group process are essential forces in group work.
- Group work leaders need to harness those forces effectively.
- Considerable attention has been given to group content, which is a part of group process, and how content and process interrelate. Content refers to

what group members and leaders actually talk about during sessions—and to *how* they talk about that content, the style they use.

● Group development is an important part of group process that addresses the evolution of a group over time.

● Group member roles tend to coalesce around two major dimensions of group life: (a) task and (b) maintenance.

RECOMMENDED RESOURCES

Benne, K., & Sheats, P. (1948). Functional roles of group members. *Journal of Social Issues*, *4*, 2.

Brown, N. (2009). Group work dynamics: Content and process. In American Counseling Association (Ed.), *The ACA encyclopedia of counseling* (pp. 229-230). Alexandria, VA: American Counseling Association.

Conyne, R. (1997). A developing framework for processing experiences and events in group work. *Journal for Specialists in Group Work*, *22*, 167-174.

Corey, M., Corey, G., & Corey, C. (2010). *Groups: Process and practice* (8th ed.). Pacific Grove, CA: Brooks/Cole.

Forsyth, D. (2009). *Group dynamics* (5th ed.). Belmont, CA: Wadsworth.

Hanson, P. (1972). What to look for in groups: An observation guide. In J. Pfeiffer & J. Jones (Eds.), *The 1972 annual handbook of group facilitators* (pp. 21-24). San Diego, CA: Pfeiffer.

Wheelan, S. (Ed.). (2005). *The handbook of group research and practice*. Thousand Oaks, CA: Sage.

4

GROUP DEVELOPMENT

The Beginning, Working, and Ending Stages

Group development: Patterns of growth and change that emerge across the group's life span ...

—Forsyth (2009, p. 19)

INTRODUCTION ●

You're driving at night in hilly terrain. It's 32 degrees, foggy, with some windy turns. The speed limit is posted as 65 miles per hour, which you can do more than handily in your 6-speed roadster. Your spouse has a different idea, advising you (in no uncertain terms) to slow down and take the turns more carefully. Wisely, you comply.

It's important to keep in mind that preposted signs don't always match shifting conditions. Driving at the speed limit in harsh conditions would be inappropriate at the least and, most likely, highly dangerous. Signs always need to be considered in context.

Group development "signs" need to be considered similarly. Expecting a group that is about midway through the number of planned sessions, say, 11 of 20, to be entering a working and productive stage of functioning may be consistent with the general predictions of a group development model, yet, for any particular group, such as one that has been dealing with high member turnover, its level of development may be much more nascent, not anywhere near what the group development sign may have predicted. As mentioned in Chapter 3, group process observation of any group you are leading is necessary, as is exercising prudence in making intervention decisions.

Understanding the evolution of groups, whether they be counseling, therapy, psychoeducational, or task in scope, is essential to effective group work. In addition, group development is dependent on leadership style and other important group dynamics, such as membership roles and levels of group activity.

CHAPTER OBJECTIVES

As a result of reading this chapter you will be able to

- Understand the importance of group development in group work
- Become more familiar with selected models of group development
- Become aware of how group development stages can guide leader interventions

● WHY IS GROUP DEVELOPMENT IMPORTANT?

The extent to which a group develops over time is associated with productivity and outcomes (Conyne, 2011). Brabender (2011), whose work I discussed briefly in Chapter 3, summarized a number of studies showing that members of groups that operate at progressively more mature levels tend to do better, for instance on personal outcomes (MacKenzie, Dies, Coche, Rutan, & Stone, 1987) or on grade point averages (Wheelan & Lisk, 2000).

As well, models of group development can assist group leaders in planning, delivering, and evaluating groups. These models also can provide direction for group training programs. Group development models, which are arranged linearly from beginning to ending of a group, provide sign posts along the way, much as the highway road sign that was mentioned above, suggesting direction through what might ordinarily be experienced as a maze and lending some predictive power to the group's future. But, as with the roadster driver, the group leader must exercise judgment along the way.

PERSPECTIVES ON GROUP DEVELOPMENT ●

That groups develop is not deniable, yet there is no guarantee they will do so positively. Some groups literally go nowhere; they get to a certain point and then get stuck, like a car mired hopelessly in the muck. No spinning of the wheels, revving of the engine, or rocking back and forth of the vehicle can seem to produce forward movement. Other groups may go somewhere but not in the desired direction, as if the GPS got fouled up. No measure of "recalculating," so familiar a patiently corrective injunction, if you've ever used a GPS device, can serve to redirect the group from its downward spiral.

Two dominant perspectives on group development exist, the progressive stage model and the cyclical model. Additional contemporary perspectives are being developed, as well. We focus on the progressive stage model, which provides a particularly helpful roadmap for group leaders. First, let's consider each of the perspectives.

Cyclical Models

In *cyclical* models, a group may move forward and backward over time (or within one session) with growth not necessarily being anticipated (Bales, 1950; Bion, 1961). That is, there is no progression implied in cyclical models. Beck (1997) and Mackenzie (1997) separately indicated that progressive and cyclical models can be accommodated, suggesting that groups hold the potential to both evolve sequentially over time and to cycle back and forth within stages. Beck suggested that groups cycle within stages from differentiation to integration, while Mackenzie highlighted how they can cycle between a focus on task and on personal relations within any one sequence or stage (Brabender, 2011).

Contemporary Models

A number of contemporary models also are emerging, such as the *Punctuated Equilibrium Model* (e.g., Gersick, 1988), where revolutionary and discontinuous change may suddenly appear in bursts (Brabender, 2011). For instance, a task force on the prevention of bullying was stymied for a protracted period, seemingly unable to gather any traction as it sought to produce a schoolwide plan. However, passage of a new school levy with its provision to generate additional revenues served to suddenly spur the group forward, with its members now more confident in being able to fund any plans produced.

Progressive Stage Models

As I indicated, the literature contains a vast number of group development models. These include a huge number of *progressive* step models (depicted by stages or phases), where sequential and patterned progress builds successively upon previous accomplishments (e.g., Brabender & Fallon, 2009; Conyne, Crowell, & Newmeyer, 2008; Corey, Corey, & Corey 2010; MacKenzie & Livesley, 1983; Tuckman, 1965; Tuckman & Jensen, 1977; Ward, 2009). These progressive models are said to have derived from the model first described by Bennis and Shepard (1956), "establishing what has been the dominant perspective on group change over time" (as cited in Brabender, 2011, p. 185).

In the progressive stage model of Bennis and Shepard, groups are theorized to develop in four phases that build successively on each other, that is, Phase 4 evolves systematically because of what occurred in Phases 1, 2, and 3. These four phases (each of which includes important subphases) are (a) *dependence* phase, dealing with relationship and authority figures; (b) *interdependence and personal relations* phase, where members evolve from a preoccupation with authority figures, such as the group leader, to a focus on each other, their needs and interactions; (c) *consensual validation* phase, where formerly competing or conflicting positions now can be accepted; and (d) *integration of similarities and differences* phase, permitting closure and moving ahead.

General consensus and some empirical evidence supports the idea that groups develop through a common orderly sequence of stages in a way similar to the development of individuals described by developmental psychology theory (Wheelan, 2004). A five-stage model, consistent with major literature reviews by Tuckman (1965), Tuckman and Jensen (1977), and Wheelan (1994) garners much support. Although some authors identify various numbers of group development stages, ranging from 3 to 19 described by Carl Rogers (1967), with the Bennis and Shepard model consisting of four stages, most models containing more or fewer stages than five differ primarily in how they differentiate and organize similar behaviors occurring across these stages. For instance, my colleagues and I (Conyne et al., 2008) have found a three-stage model to be very useful: (a) beginning stage: *getting established and transitioning,* (b) middle stage: *connecting and producing,* and (c) ending stage: *consolidating and forecasting*.

Linking group development and psychological issues. To understand group developmental stages, it is useful to link psychological and interpersonal issues or themes that seem associated. Let's consider these linkages (Ward & Ward, 2013), without naming the stages other than to assign each a number.

Stage 1. The most salient themes representing the first stage of group development revolve around emphasizing similarities, making a personal commitment to other members and the group, and becoming included. Although a myriad of related issues are important early in the group, such as trust, security, hesitant participation, and diffuse anxiety, finding similarities to allow for the potential members to make a personal commitment to others and to be included within the parameters of the emerging social system seems to be necessary if the group is to become a cohesive, collaborative group achieving maximum productivity.

Stage 2. As fears of being left out are resolved, another set of issues arises to confront the group. These issues include how power, control, conflict, and differences will be expressed and handled. Especially in groups with psychosocial purposes, members must learn to deal with their own and others' differences and challenges, which sometimes can be volatile and potentially divisive.

After bonding and initial acceptance into the group have been established, tolerance for differences becomes more normative. Members are able to find ways to differentiate and still maintain the group integrity and respect for members. This step forward allows the members to relate more closely.

Stage 3. Critical processes of cohesiveness and collaboration are deepened and confirmed. These processes are characteristic of cooperative, productive working groups.

Stage 4. Cohesion and interdependence foster the conditions underlying this working stage. Productivity emerges through the convergence of supportive task and personal relations functions. High levels of productivity can be achieved, as members are drawn to work together and with leaders to realize goals amidst a satisfying interpersonal environment.

Stage 5. Groups that are open ended are constructed to continually allow for a flow of new members and the exiting of current members, when appropriate. Open-ended groups are common within in-patient settings. In such groups, there is no predetermined and common end point.

For those groups that do plan to end at the same time, known as closed groups, a fifth stage was identified in the second literature review of proposed group development stage models (Tuckman & Jensen, 1977). Many person change groups, such as counseling groups, are closed as are many task groups. Task groups, for example, typically set ending points because products are expected or required according to a preexisting time line; this might include responding to a Request for Proposal (RFP)—a process whereby a funding institution requests bids for a project, almost always, one laments, with a very tight timeline—that is due by a specific date and time. In other cases, a task group may be continuing, such as an agency staff meeting that convenes every Tuesday at 1:30.

In this final group development stage, attention is given to summarizing, reviewing, and consolidating learning. In addition, separation and unresolved issues are addressed. A key purpose in this stage is to maximize transfer of learning and accomplishments from the group situation to outside of the group. *In fact, the external application of accomplishment (e.g., learning in a psychoeducation group and a new policy in a task group) is the ultimate purpose of all group work because group is a vehicle for enabling growth and change to occur "in the real world."*

Leadership in relation to group development stages. Group development stages reflect member interactions undertaken to explore, test, norm, and resolve issues of team development. Group leaders can behave in certain ways to both fit within and to facilitate different group development stages; in turn, each developmental stage calls for certain group work leadership actions. See Learning Exercise 4-1.

Learning Exercise 4–1: How Might Leadership Promote Positive Group Development?

*The **object** of this learning exercise is to help you to begin thinking about group leadership in relation to group development stages.*
Group work leadership will become a center of attention in the chapters to come. But let's begin to think about it now.
As you have been reading in this chapter about group development the idea is surfacing that there is a positive correlation between issues characterizing the stages of group development and what kind of leadership might be appropriate or needed.

Here, I want you to brainstorm. What do you imagine a leader should do in each stage to promote positive group development? Follow these four steps:

1. Briefly describe each stage of development: What's going on?

    Stage 1: _____

    _____.

(Continued)

Stage 2: _____

_____.

Stage 3: _____

_____.

Stage 4: _____

_____.

Stage 5: _____

_____.

2. What do you think a group work leader should be doing in each stage? What actions?

Use action verbs: *direct, listen, guide, stop, protect, connect,* etc.

Write three actions for each stage:

Stage 1 actions: _____ _____ _____

Stage 2 actions: _____ _____ _____

Stage 3 actions: _____ _____ _____

Stage 4 actions: _____ _____ _____

Stage 5 actions: _____ _____ _____

3. What general group work leader style (circle one) do you think is suggested?

a. Autocratic: Firm, decisive, taking control
b. Democratic: Participative, collaborative, facilitative
c. Laissez-faire: Permitting, distant, avoiding direction

4. Explain: _____

_____.

In general, a democratic leader may be most appropriate for group work leadership. Of course, what is needed in any group circumstance is often a delicate question, and it requires consideration of various factors in addition to the stage of group development, such as the context, type of group, member resources, and leader ability. Yet, all things considered, a democratic style generally is desired because it is grounded in shared decision making, collaboration with members, and the fostering of member engagement with one another and with the group—among many other factors. Effective democratic leaders provide appropriate amounts of group structure to support the members in their risk-taking normative ventures early in the group until the more relevant and risky issues emerging at each stage are addressed and become normative. As the stages are resolved the leader should be able to spend much less time addressing structural issues directly, because group members learn to work together to become a positively functioning system.

Group composition, psychological maturity, and motivation of group members. Ward and Ward (2013) indicate that an important element influencing the progressive nature of group work can be attributed to the psychological maturity of group members and their motivation to become involved in the central group purpose or task. When group development unfolds positively, members discover together how to actively share responsibility for process and outcome. But for this to occur, members need to possess the necessary knowledge, skills, attitudes, and maturity necessary to assume the demands of group participation in the group. If they do not, either because of deficit (e.g., lacking intellectual or physical capacity), age (e.g., young child or elderly), or context (e.g., a short-term task group, or an emergency situation), a more direct style of leadership might be needed where the leader actively guides and controls the action. Such a style appropriately would tend to include the use of structure, provision of information and guidance, concrete tasks, and shorter periods.

As examples, young children can share responsibility for appropriate tasks and function as a team in some situations, whereas adults with low intelligence or with severe psychiatric dysfunction are likely to have difficulty working effectively and cooperatively on many tasks. In general, it is desirable that leaders keep group composition in mind when they have the opportunity to form groups. Selecting those who are homogeneous in psychological maturity or ego strength will assist the group to coalesce and move ahead positively, helping to ensure a successful experience for group members.

● EXPLORING FOUR GROUP DEVELOPMENT MODELS

There have been over 100 different models of group development made available. In this section, you will become acquainted with four models: (a) Tuckman's; (b) American Group Psychotherapy Association's; (c) Jones's; and (d) Brabender and Fallon's. Note the similarities and differences as you read about them.

Tuckman's Model

A group development model by Tuckman (1965) and expanded by Tuckman and Jensen (1977) is one of the most frequently cited. It is a five-stage model consisting of (a) forming, (b) storming, (c) norming, (d) performing, and (e) adjourning. See Figure 4-1.

The steps of Tuckman's influential model—forming, storming, norming, performing, and adjourning—are incorporated in the American Group Psychotherapy Association (AGPA) model that follows.

Figure 4.1   Tuckman's Group Development Model

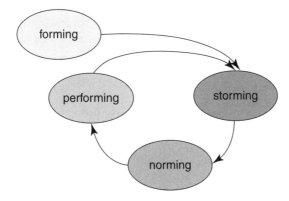

Source: Tuckman & Jensen (1977).

Note: Later, a fifth stage was added to capture termination. Consistent with the rhyming pattern used in this model, this stage is called adjourning. See "Stages of Small Group Development Revisited," by B. Tuckman and M. Jensen, 1977, *Group Organizational Studies, 2,* 419–427.

AGPA's Model

This is the model summarized by AGPA in its *Practice Guidelines for Group Psychotherapy: A Cross-Theoretical Guide to Developing and Leading Psychotherapy Groups* (AGPA, 2007, pp. 30–35), that I mentioned in the preceding chapter. This model is a progressive five-stage one, extending from birth to death, as it were, in the group. It hews closely to the stages suggested by Tuckman, as you will see. The AGPA guidelines point out that there is a strong consensus for a five-stage model of group development emerging.

Stage 1: *Forming* stage including issues of dependency and inclusion.

Members are unsure of what is to happen, and they are motivated by becoming accepted.

Group leaders aim to educate the members (e.g., about group purpose, rules, and roles of participants), inviting trust and highlighting commonalities.

Stage 2: *Storming* stage, focused on issues of power or status and the resolution of the associated conflicts.

Members may question leader authority, and some may test for control.

Group leaders seek to promote a safe and successful resolution of conflict, encourage group cohesion, and facilitate interpersonal learning.

Stage 3: *Norming* stage, signifying the establishment of trust and a functional group structure (norms).

Members develop a sense of greater cohesion and understandings of how to work together.

Leaders promote cohesion and a positive group working environment with interventions reflecting a balance of support and confrontation.

Stage 4: *Performing* stage is characterized by a mature, productive group process and the expression of individual differences.

Members engage with one another and come to accept their uniqueness

Leaders allow the group to function at an optimally productive level and to highlight the individuality of the members.

Stage 5: *Final or termination* stage, which Tuckman and Jensen (1977) called *adjourning*. The group experience is reviewed in this phase, and closure is reached.

Members identify their learning, say good-bye to one another, and anticipate the future.

Leaders facilitate a focus on separation issues, a review of the group experience, and help members prepare for the ending of the group. Leaders strive to encourage the expression of feelings associated with saying good-bye and to help members attend to unfinished business in the group.

Jones' Model

The group development model of Jones (1973) depicts both the progressive stages of a group's evolution and also *the relationship* that is posited to exist between *task* and *personal relations* at each stage in a group. *Because the model sets out these two dimensions and their interactions clearly, I have found it to be a very useful generic schema that is easily adaptable to both task and person change (psychoeducation, counseling, therapy) groups.* This framework suggests a method group leaders can use for planning groups, guiding interventions, and predicting general future directions. It consists of four progressive stages of development, with attention given to both task and to personal relations dimensions. A group leader's style needs to permit him or her to appropriately balance the task and personal relations dimensions associated with each stage.

Take a look at Figure 4-2, which presents the model, and then work with Learning Exercise 4-2 that follows.

As you have learned, in all group interaction—whether occurring in a task focused or in a personally focused group—involves *both* task and personal relations dimensions. However, it also is the case that emphasizes that within these two group foci typically vary.

The major concern of a *task* or *work* group, such as a committee that you could be leading or consulting with, is on accomplishing tasks and goals set out to the group; attention to personal relations usually plays a supportive role. The major concern of a *personally focused* group—such as a therapy group you could be leading or coleading—is on individual and relationship growth, development and change, which largely result from member interaction with each other, and the kind of personal relations they create and maintain; attention to task functions usually takes a supportive role. Note in

Figure 4.2   Jones' Task-Personal Relations Group Development Model

Stage	Task Dimensions	Personal Relations Dimensions
1	Orientation	Dependency
2	Organizing	Conflict
3	Data flow	Cohesion
4	Problem solving	Interdependence

Source: Jones (1973).

all cases that "supportive" does not mean unimportant; it is more like a sub-theme alongside a theme.

So, to break this out, let's assume you have been contracted to provide group process observation of a governing body's meeting—think of one of the divisions of a professional association, for example. Your observations will be fed back to the meeting chair at the end of the first day as he or she readies for the next day's meeting, and at the end. Because this is a task group, you likely will give the keenest attention to task dimensions, such as those listed above in the figure. You will note the degree to which the chair assists members in becoming oriented (Stage 1) to the task (e.g., to review, rank order, and select the top three of 15 funding proposals) at the start, how members become organized (Stage 2) to work on the task, how fully and effectively data and information flow among the members (Stage 3), and their capacity to implement problem-solving strategies successfully as they seek to reach their goals (Stage 4). At the same time, you will be noting how personal relations dimensions support task accomplishment: Do members resolve dependency (Stage 1) issues commonly present in the beginning, work through disagreements and conflict (Stage 2), are they able to become connected and cohesive (Stage 3), and then work together in joining their resources to accomplish their goals (Stage 4). With a task group, success is measured by goal accomplishment, in this case, did the proposals get selected effectively, but it almost always is the case that goal accomplishment is enhanced through satisfactory personal relations.

The situation is flipped over in groups that are organized to help their members directly improve. If you are leading a counseling group, for instance, you will give primary importance to the personal relations dimensions and how the group progresses through them (or not). In the beginning (Stage 1), members typically are unsure, dependent on the leader, and looking for structure. As the group progresses, they then may turn their attention to challenging leadership and the procedures and processes being used to guide the group (Stage 2). As conflict works itself out, the group members are able to align themselves more fully with each other and the group itself, developing a sense of belonging and connection (Stage 3), which then allows them to work collaboratively in giving and getting help (Stage 4). It is through resolving issues stimulated in these personal relations stages that members learn and grow. Again, though, the task dimensions support this movement. Dependency is dealt with through becoming oriented (Stage 1), conflict gets resolved through becoming organized in joint effort (Stage 2), cohesion depends on sharing information and feelings (Stage 3), and interdependence is aided by effective interpersonal problem solving (Stage 4).

Learning Exercise 4–2: Playing With Task and Personal Relations

The **object** of this learning exercise is to sharpen your understanding of how task and personal relations fit within one group development stage.

The preceding model suggests, for instance, that early in a group's development (typically at around Stage 1), the group leader may need to pay attention to the task of orienting members to the experience to come while, at the same time, being concerned with helping members deal positively with their personal and interpersonal dependency needs. For example, the leader might provide members with a set of general group goals and then ask for their feedback before moving toward assisting them to identify one of two personal goals. By doing this, she anticipates clarifying goals will help with becoming oriented while alleviating some anxiety and uncertainty.

Now, it's time for you to take a turn playing with task and personal relations. Select any other stage in the model and suggest how the group leader might positively address both the task and the related personal relations dimensions:

Stage selected: _____

How to address task dimension: _____

_____

How to address personal relations dimension: _____

_____

_____

Discuss your product with a fellow student.

Brabender and Fallon's model

Brabender (2011) points out that group development "is one of the core concepts by which groups are understood" (p. 182), reinforcing a theme you have probably been noticing. The practical value of understanding about group development is that it affects what leaders know and can do in their groups. Again, referring to Brabender,

> When group development is the centerpiece of the therapist's conceptualization of, and intervention in, the group, it informs all of the therapist's activities such as the creation of a group design, the selection of members, and the ongoing manner in which the therapist intervenes with the group. (p. 196)

Take a look at Case Illustration 4-1.

Case Illustration 4–1: Group Development Begins Early

*The **object** of this case illustration is to exemplify one aspect of group development, starting before a group ever gets into the first meeting.*

About half the day was gone now, Sgt. Lopez realized, as she glanced angrily—once again—at her watch. "What a waste of time," she muttered to herself. "Why in the world do we have to attend these deployment reunions is way beyond me!"

The reunion leader, Capt. Tomlinson, was wondering too. "Why isn't this going better?" he ruminated to himself.

Just then he saw the military consultant, Lisa Black, walk by. Tomlinson caught Lisa's attention and asked her if they could spend a moment.

Reaching out, the captain asked Lisa if she had any idea why the event was slogging along, at best. After some discussion, it now seems pretty clear to him of at least one problem: The event had been organized too close to the deadline, and its purpose was never made clear to attendees.

"Well," Tomlinson decided, "Guess we'll have to press on through this one and then in the future be sure to do much better due diligence in getting the retreats organized earlier and with more clarity. Maybe before people get out of here today, I'll check in with some of them informally to get their ideas of what they might need down the road . . ."

Group development starts before a group ever gets in the room, by following necessary planning steps that allow people to get oriented to the task and find ways to become involved.

In this final model description, I provide a group interaction sample for each stage. Observe how the group leader behaves.

Stage 1: Formation and engagement. Brabender draws from Agazarian's (1997) systems view of group by pointing out that the first stage in group development can be characterized as a struggle between opposing forces. Doubts and attractions compete for the potential value of participating in the group. Resistances against revealing oneself battle with the realization that this will be necessary. Wanting to be an independent person butts up against the strong forces of being dependent on the leader for guidance, structure, and orientation.

What does the leader do in this stage to assist? An overriding contribution is to begin creating a safe and welcoming environment. Leaders listen to members, provide information about general group goals and procedures, and encourage and support members becoming involved. They seek to help members realize they are not alone and, in fact, may have much in common with the others. They help members introduce themselves to each other and to the group. They try to ensure that everyone in the group has an opportunity to talk, leaving no one out, attempting to avoid monopolization. As Conyne et al. (2008) put it, "the group leader functions as a new social system 'host or hostess,' who helps members get oriented to the group's surroundings and to what is available" (p. 74).

Consider the following interaction from a counseling group (we will follow this group over the next three stages and come back to end at the termination stage):

Hank:	"I'm not sure about being here. I mean, I think sometimes I do and sometimes I don't want to be here right now."
Scilla:	"I was in a group like this once before, and it took me quite a while to get comfortable. I can sure remember that . . ."
Betsy:	"Oh, come on, let's get off it and get goin'!"
Leader, Felicity:	"You know, this is often how it is at the start. It's okay. We'll get there. Anyone else want to comment?"

In this example, the leader in just a few words conveys that "all is well." This reassurance can be comforting to members and helps to begin a climate of safety. The leader also encourages others to enter the discussion.

Stage 2: Conflict and rebellion. The group members are getting involved within an environment that seems welcoming. Yet, they are in no way as yet self-initiating. They have been largely looking to the group leader for direction. A sign of Stage 2 emerging is that members begin to question, to "stick their heads out," to make some of their own ideas and needs known. A key aspect of this increasing self-expression is that leadership gets questioned subtly and sometimes strongly and directly. This can be a very trying time for group leaders, but it helps greatly to know—and this is one of the palpable values of a group development model—that expressions of conflict and rebellion at this point are entirely normative and to be expected. Importantly, a leader should not take such challenges personally. It really is a systemic response, and healthy, too, where members begin to assert themselves as they seek to contribute to creating a system of which they are a part.

Take a look at the following:

Tommy: "Yeah, and I'm right now feeling kind of angry at how [he looks at the leader, Felicity] you've been controlling us, making us do what *you* want!"

Betsy: "Like it's all *her* show, or somethin' . . ."

Miguel: "Hey, man, no way . . . she's been cool, helping us move."

Leader, Felicity: "I'm really interested in what each of you thinks about this. Let's see what we have and then take a look at next steps, okay?"

You can see in this interchange that Felicity does not defend herself and her position. Rather, she takes the opposite tack, sailing with the wind, so to speak. She sanctions the expression of viewpoints about leadership, encouraging members to share, while suggesting an end result of coming to some sort of collaborative resolution. This approach demonstrates a "trust in the process," in which the leader conveys a sense of openness and optimism that they will be able to work this conflict out positively.

Stage 3: Intimacy and unity. This stage is marked by a sense of satisfaction resulting from the recasting of control from leader centered to leader *and* member centered. This stage is a transitional one, in which the group is lurching from getting established to becoming productive.

A kind of "high" infuses the group at this point where members feel more connected, positive, and sometimes playful. Boundaries can become porous during this stage due to the exuberance members feel. Brabender points out two examples, where sexual attraction may get activated outside the group and refreshments may be brought to the group by some members. Such boundary infringements need to be guarded against through examining them.

The kind of feedback occurring during this transitional phase tends to be uniformly positive. Group leaders can help members to make their feedback more effective through teaching them simple guidelines, such as describing and not evaluating, being immediate and not delayed, and being concrete rather than vague.

Here is an excerpt from this stage:

James:	"I really think you're great, Scilla. Really, I must say, I like everything about you."
Scilla:	"Hmm, it's nice to be liked. Better than the reverse, by a long shot! Thanks for saying that, James."
Leader, Felicity:	"Let's see if we might work some on trying to sharpen up the kind of feedback we can give to each other so it is as useful and meaningful as possible. Are you game?"

Members nod.

Felicity:	"Okay, good. Let's go back to James's first comment to Scilla . . . what was that, James?"
James:	"Oh, I said something like I think she's great."
Felicity:	"Oh, yes, thanks. Okay, let's see if you might try being more concrete and specific. Can you identify what it is about Scilla that you find to be 'great'?"

Here, you see the group leader encouraging feedback while beginning to help members learn how to provide it in a more effective way.

Stage 4: Integration and work. During this period, members begin to realize, in a sense, that "life is more than a bowl of cherries." That is, they recognize that they are not all alike, that all is not always absolutely wonderful, and that differences among them exist. Further, their deepening connection allows them to want to explore some of these variations. Brabender (2011) concludes, "how they affect others is precisely what they came into the group for" (p. 199). Thus, members become involved with integrating positives and negatives in a constructive way, which can then promote productive work.

Productive work is the essence of group work. In a task group, this term refers to an open flow of communication among members that is on task and supported by good group skills—listening, clarifying, offering suggestions, giving effective feedback, and pooling resources. This combination of task and personal relations functions allows a task group to problem-solve and reach its goals. These goals can range from mastering learning, as in a seminar, or creating a product, such as a report or program plan. Productive

work in a group aimed at personal improvement—such as a psychoeducation, counseling, or psychotherapy group—means that members get to the
point where they can take interpersonal risks to self-disclose and to give and
get feedback, all leading to accomplishing goals that can be generalized and
applied outside the group.

Let's examine the following transaction, this time switching to a *task*
group aimed at producing a community safety plan:

Leader, Carlos: "So, let's see if we can together develop a list of possible
strategies that the community could apply to become
safer."

Christina: "Sounds good, I'm ready for it. How should we get
started on this?"

Carlos: "Good question, Christina. How about each of us listing
three possible strategies on a note card, and then we
can round-robin it to give us a kind of master list that
we can gradually winnow down? What do you think?"

Felipe: "Yeah, like we did before; that worked well."

You can see how the group was ready to move ahead. The leader, when
asked, provided a possible way to develop the needed information, which
involved a structured activity. He checks it out and gets support, and it
appears this task group is about to move ahead.

Stage 5: Termination. As I've pointed out, this final stage is part of any
group that has a predetermined ending point. There are several goals for the
final group stage.

In a task or work group the main one is to consolidate the work and to
apply it outside the group. In the previous stage example, the task group has
been charged with producing a safety plan for the community, for instance. What
members learned about themselves along the way in a task group typically is
secondary—except in a learning group, such as a seminar or a book discussion
group, examples of task groups where what members learn is paramount.

In other types of groups aimed at personal and interpersonal change,
consolidation of learning and application outside the group also is critically
important. How, for instance, newly found communication skills might be
used appropriately in one's work setting or family. In addition, in such groups
it also is important to help members to say good-bye to each other, to reach
some form of genuine interpersonal closure. Likewise, helping members to
resolve any lingering issues—so-called unfinished business—is also at issue

during termination, such as when a member feels incomplete and has more to say about his or her anxiety when around others, or when a member continues to feel a strong need to close off an interaction with another that feels lingering and unsettled.

In general, one of the key elements of termination is providing a guided opportunity for members to reflect and process their experience. Doing so will assist them in making sense of what has occurred and facilitate application elsewhere.

After all, it is *application elsewhere* that really is the central reason for doing group work. See Learning Exercise 4–3.

Learning Exercise 4–3: Getting a Handle on Group Work's Ultimate Purpose

*The **object** of this learning exercise is to underscore the ultimate purpose of group work.*

1. *Context:* Imagine you're at lunch with friends that haven't seen each other for a couple years. You're all talking about what you've been doing during that time. Your turn comes up, and you mention you've been excited about learning group work in your graduate program.

   One of your friends, Jake, known for being a provocateur, jokes, "Hey, I've always thought this group work thing is for 'weak knees' and 'the forlorn.' Tell us, what's it all about, anyway?"

   Not wanting to fall into a trap of joshing around with this question or blowing it off, you decide to answer it straight. You remember your professor using the shorthand phrase "application elsewhere" when emphasizing group work's fundamental purpose, and that always has stuck with you.

2. *Explain this phrase*—or another of your choosing—as you respond to Jake and your other friends:

   _____

   _____

   _____.

Consider the following interaction, back to the counseling group of Stages 1–3:

Leader, Felicity: "Now that we're closing in on finishing our group, it's important that we take some time to reflect on what happened and what it meant, and to see what you might use in the future. I'll just leave it open here, for anyone to jump it. What have you gotten out of this?"

James: "I think I'm learning how to connect with other people in a more direct way. I recall way back to when you helped me do that with Scilla. I've been trying being more, what is it, concrete [his voice rises in question] with some of my friends. Well, sometimes they kind of don't know what I'm doing, but I think it works usually."

Tommy: "I'm still chewing on stuff for me. I know I need to not jump so fast on people, to calm down some, to listen . . . I'm workin' on that."

Felicity: "Good to hear what you both are working with! We can come back, if you'd like, but let's give others a chance to jump in . . . also, consider if any of you have any "unfinished business" with anyone else in here you'd like to clear up before getting away tonight. Still open to us is our follow-up session in 4 weeks, just a reminder . . . anyway, back to anyone else now."

Here, you see the group leader guiding members to reflect on some important topics for a group's termination—what has been learned, what can be applied, any unfinished business. Also, note that this group has scheduled a 1-month follow up meeting, which can provide a timely opportunity to check in and to identify how postgroup life has been going.

● GROUP WORK KEYSTONES

- Group development models can assist group leaders in planning, delivering, and evaluating groups. They also can provide direction for group training programs. Examples of group development models were provided.
- Some experts suggest that a group development model can be a central organizing feature to guide practice.

● Group is a vehicle for change. The ultimate value of group work is to help members become more fulfilled outside the group (personally oriented groups) and to enable accomplishments developed in the group to be transferred to the external environment (task groups).

RECOMMENDED RESOURCES

American Group Psychotherapy Assocation. (2007). *Practice guidelines for group psychotherapy*. New York, NY: Author. Retrieved from http://agpa.org/guide lines/AGPA%20Practice%20Guidelines%202007-PDF.pdf

Brabender, V. (2011). Group development. In R. Conyne (Ed.), *The Oxford handbook of group counseling* (pp. 182–204). New York, NY: Oxford University Press.

Wheelan, S. (2004). Groups in the workplace. In J. DeLucia-Waack, D. Gerrity, C. Kalodner, & M. Riva (Eds.), *Group handbook of group counseling and psychotherapy* (pp. 401–413). Thousand Oaks, CA: Sage.

Wheelan, S. (2005). The developmental perspective. In S. Wheelan (Ed.), *The handbook of group research and practice* (pp. 119–132). Thousand Oaks, CA: Sage.

DVD

Corey, G., Corey, M. S., & Haynes, R. (2000). *Evolution of a group*. Belmont, CA: Brooks/Cole.

SECTION II

CRITICAL ELEMENTS OF GROUP WORK

Section II addresses the critical elements of group work leadership. These elements constitute the engine that makes groups run.

Chapter 5 examines *leadership.* Leadership in general is defined, followed by tearing apart and then putting together definitions for group counseling leadership and for group work leadership. Coleadership as a model also is considered.

Chapter 6 is focused on *theories* in group work leadership. The point is made that group theory needs to be connected less with individual counseling theory and more with systemic and interdependent ones. Traditional theories are discussed, and attention is given to six transtheoretical orientations that are especially compatible with group work. The need for a comprehensive theory of group work is emphasized as is the importance of practitioners adapting a personal theory that is credible, reflects their personality and values, and fits the type of group and the client population at hand.

Chapter 7 focuses on what I term the "building blocks of group leadership," its *functions, styles and competencies.* These elements are the foundations for delivering group leadership and for how group leaders can promote learning, growth, and change.

Chapter 8 highlights examples of generic *methods* in group work leadership. I think of them as "blueprints for action" because they serve to guide how to intervene. These methods include the following: (a) draw from one's personhood; (b) consider context; (c) be intentional; (d) be creative and spontaneous; (e) be guided by a group development framework; (f) facilitate connection and interaction; (g) build cohesion; (h) create and use therapeutic factors; (i) endorse diversity, multiculturalism, and social justice; and (j) draw from and appropriately adapt evidence-based practice when possible.

This chapter also addresses some of the major *strategies and techniques* of group work leadership, which I term the "action tools of the trade." Five strategies and techniques are described: (a) focusing; (b) shifting interaction; (c) preplanned, structured exercises; (d) intuitive experiments; and (e) psychoeducation lecturettes.

CHAPTER 5

GROUP WORK LEADERSHIP

But of a good leader ... when his [sic] work is done, his aim fulfilled,
they will say, "We did this ourselves."

—Lao Tse

INTRODUCTION ●

Group work experiences that lead to productive outcomes for participants typically do not just happen naturally. Rather, they are the result of many interrelated and complex factors. As might be expected, group work leadership is an important factor in what occurs in a group, and it is the focus of this chapter. It is the leader (or coleaders) who collaborates with group members to develop a cooperative environment through which change, learning, and growth can occur. When all works well, as the above quotation from Lao Tse suggests, the members can feel justifiably empowered.

CHAPTER OBJECTIVES

As a result of reading this chapter you will be able to

- Define leadership
- Define and discuss group counseling leadership as a model
- Define and discuss group work leadership
- Consider coleadership from different vantage points
- Provide a set of especially helpful training DVDs and other special resources on aspects of group work leadership

● LEADERSHIP

What Leadership Is *Not*

Many perspectives exist about leadership, some of which we consider in this chapter. But first, let's think about what leadership is *not*.

Contrary to popular belief, leadership is not tied to a "great person" view. Leadership really is not an inborn set of abilities allowing a person to possess some uncanny, even mystical, abilities that serve to propel members and a group forward (Forsyth, 2009).

I typically asked brand-spanking-new first-year students early in my Group Theory and Process course to indicate their understanding of leadership. I always was surprised to find that a common thought expressed is that leaders possess some special charisma, they take charge in a group crisply and certainly, discerning somehow (divinely?) what is needed and then providing it, with members gratefully following their "lead."

This wrongheaded view of leadership is based on the leader possessing super inborn abilities and on one-way power and control over others. It could not be further from the truth for leadership in general and certainly in the instance of group work leadership. So, one of the first steps in teaching students about group leadership is to dissuade many of them from such a popularized view of leadership with a more subtle and accurate understanding.

What Leadership Is

Leadership is a complex function and one that is the subject of extensive research in a number of disciplines. Social psychology, sociology, and management are major sources of research on the topic.

While a "great man" notion of leadership may not hold, it is the case that certain personal characteristics do correlate positively with leadership. One of the most important qualities may be *flexibility*. Research findings (e.g., Zaccaro, Foti, & Kenny, 1991) demonstrated that skilled leaders were able to shift their expertise to fit the demands of the group; if tasks needed to be accomplished, these leaders could assist, but if interaction called for attention to relationships, these leaders could adapt to provide people-oriented skills. Representative qualities associated with the emergence of leadership include authenticity, character strengths (such as honesty, hope), self-efficacy for leadership (belief that "I can do it"), emotional intelligence, and a moderate amount of assertiveness (Forsyth, 2009).

You may recall one of the classic studies on leadership that was conducted by Lewin, Lippitt, and White (1939). They placed young boys in small groups and examined how satisfied and productive they were when working for a leader who behaved autocratically, democratically, or in a laissez-faire style. The autocratic leader made all decisions for group members, the democratic leader encouraged members to arrive at their own decisions, and the laissez-faire leader refrained from providing assistance and guidance. Results showed that boys in the autocratic groups were most productive, followed by those in the democratic and laissez-faire groups, respectively. However, when the leaders left the room for periods, another story surfaced. Boys in the autocratic group ceased to work, while those in the democratic group continued to work. Moreover, higher aggression typified the autocratic groups, with a tendency for scapegoating (targeting a person for criticism) appearing. These results suggest the value of a democratic style of leadership in promoting member satisfaction, responsibility, and productivity.

There are a number of leadership theories and views of leadership. These center around different concepts, including group dynamics, influence, reciprocity, compliance, personality, persuasion, power, interaction, situations, exchange, and more (Bass, 1995; Forsyth, 2009; Scholl, 2003). As Gladding (2011b) observed about leadership, it is "a concept in search of a definition" (p. 54).

However, the following definition of leadership as an interpersonal process works well for our purposes: "Leadership is a complex of interpersonal processes whereby cooperating individuals are permitted to influence and motivate others to promote the attainment of group and individual goals" (Forsyth, 2009, p. 376).

In addition to its interpersonal orientation, note what I would call the *empowering* tone that runs through this definition. It is the polar opposite of a top-down expression of power. Rather, leadership induces; it permits members to connect and work together, thereby unleashing positive forces existing in the group so that the goals of the members and of the group itself can be reached. In a sense, leadership eases rather than forces; it connects rather than tells; it yields mutually desired goal accomplishment rather than goals the designated leader might set independently. Such an understanding of leadership seems highly consistent with counseling, in general, which is a facilitative, collaborative, and compassionate process of help giving—and with group work more particularly.

● GROUP WORK LEADERSHIP ELEMENTS

Group work leadership is a variant of leadership, in general. When discussing this area, I will refer to either *group work leadership* or its shorter form, *group leadership*, and to *group work leader*, or to *group leader*; I mean these terms to be interchangeable.

Group leadership suffers from a lack of common definition. Common treatments (e.g., Chen & Rybak, 2004; Corey, Corey, & Corey, 2010; Gladding, 2011b; Trotzer, 2006; Yalom & Leszcz, 2005) examine important aspects of it, usually without defining the whole: leadership styles, functions, roles, skills, theory, personality, and others. These parts are important for group work leadership, as you will note in succeeding chapters of this book, but I think it is important for you to be introduced to an overview definition of group leadership.

Let us begin with a definition of group counseling leadership.

Group Counseling Leadership Definition, as a Model

I first draw from the domain of group counseling for a definition of group counseling leadership and then spend some time exploring its major elements, before moving to a generic description of group work leadership. The definition of group counseling leadership also can be generalized, with some caution, to the leadership of psychoeducation groups and group psychotherapy, a point to keep in mind as you read this next section.

Group counseling leadership can be conceptualized as

> the ability to draw from best practice and good professional judgment to create a group and, in collaboration with members, build and maintain a positive group climate that serves to nurture here-and-now interaction and its processing by leader and members, aimed at producing lasting growth and change. (Conyne, 2012, p. 629)

Let's amplify the key ingredients of this definition of group counseling leadership.

Best practice and good professional judgment. Group counseling leadership is not a rote, static, or routine endeavor. It is not best delivered from a set of manualized instructions, but it relies upon activation of ongoing processes occurring within the group.

While reading about various forms of group leadership can be helpful and instructive, it also can be enlightening to see how these can occur. This is where live demonstrations, such as what might be able to happen in an academic course or in a training workshop, are important. Also of value is being able to view training videos. In the latter case, the field is fortunate to have several such training videos available.

In the area of group counseling leadership, you might find these training videos to be helpful: *Group Counseling for Children: A Multicultural Approach* (Bauman & Steen, 2009); *Group Counseling with Adolescents* (Bauman, 2012); *Group Counseling in the Here and Now* (Carroll, 1985); *Evolution of a Group* (Corey, Corey, & Haynes, 2000), *Developmental Aspects of Group Counseling* (Stockton, 1995). In group therapy leadership, you might find the following training video of value: *Group Therapy: A Live Demonstration with Yalom and Leszcz* (n.d.).

From its beginnings in planning and preparing for a group, through performing leadership functions in group sessions, and through postgroup processing and evaluation, group work leadership is guided by applications of best practice principles (discussed in Chapter 2) and the sound professional judgment of the group leader. Group interaction is highly dynamic, the product of a bewildering number of separate factors. Therefore, group counseling leaders always are confronted with variable conditions that demand real time choices. At these points, being informed by best practice guidelines and one's own well-honed professional judgment is not only comforting, but also, it is highly beneficial.

Consider the next two applications, Case Illustration 5–1 and Learning Exercise 5–1.

Case Illustration 5–1: Bombarded!

*The **object** of this case illustration is to demonstrate the complexity of group interaction and how group leaders need to adopt ways to help them make sense of it.*

Jonah and Sally are coleading a 10-session psychoeducation group on communication skills with teenagers at the local YMCA. This is part of their internship in the university's mental health counseling program. The first two sessions had gone fairly much in line with their plan with the eight group members, split equally between males and females, slowly beginning to become involved. In the middle of the third session, the tenor and tempo of the group suddenly changed.

(Continued)

(Continued)

Here is a sample:

The group had just finished a communication exercise on listening skills, functioning in pairs. Coming back to the group as a whole, Sally asks if anyone would be willing to share something about his or her experience working together as pairs. All seems to be going according to expectations.

But, then, Sally's request is met by what seems to be a long, thundering silence. This is the first time something like this has happened in the group. Sally and Jonah decide to wait this out, to allow members some space.

Suddenly, Alex bursts out, "I hate this [expletive] group!" He continues defiantly. "What's with always asking us to *share?* Over and over, share, share, share. What if I don't wanna share?"

Now there are no gaps. Some nod their heads. Adrian jumps in. "Yeah, I've got better things to do, and then this huge silence . . . what's that all about?" Looking at the coleaders, he implores, "Why can't you do something about that!"

Bettina takes a different tack. "Hey, what's going on in here? I've been likin' the group until now; where is all this coming from?" she asks, looking at Adrian and Alex directly.

At this point, Jonah and Sally are catching each other's gaze, trying to glean from one another what they should do. Intervene? Yes, but how? With one of the members, with the whole group? To provide some perspective taking, or to challenge, or maybe to support?

The leaders feel bombarded. They need not only to find a way to recognize their state and that of the group but also to de-escalate their affective state so they can positively assist group members. There is no particular theory or technique that will work for sure. What they need is to be able to find some calm in the overwrought sea. Then they need to exercise their own professional judgment, guided by knowledge of best practice, theory, techniques, and experience and delivered through their own skillful style.

Learning Exercise 5–1: Alternative Leader Responses to Feeling Bombarded

*The **object** of this learning exercise is to develop ideas for how group leaders can calm themselves during fast-moving group interaction and can access good professional judgment.*

So, put yourself in the preceding "Bombarded!" scenario. What might you do as you try to calm yourself (e.g., deep breathing) and then to exercise your own professional judgment (e.g., consider helping members to generate meaning from the group experience: *ASGW Best Practice Guideline* B.5).

Because there typically is no one right answer to challenging practice questions in group work leadership (such as there is to the arithmetic question, "What is 9 x 7?") but, rather, plausible alternatives that might best fit the circumstances, develop three such approaches and write them below, with a rationale for each one.

Plausible Alternatives for Self-Calming

1. Rationale:

2. Rationale:

3. Rationale:

Plausible Alternatives for Exercising Professional Judgment

1. Rationale:

2. Rationale:

3. Rationale:

To create a group. Group counseling leadership, as we noted in Chapter 2, involves not only delivering a group but also creating it (e.g., American Association for Social Work with Groups [AASWG], 2006; Association for Specialist Group Work [ASGW], 2007; Bertcher & Maple, 1977; Fujishin, 2001) and evaluating it. Group work leaders can set the table properly for effective group interaction to occur by attending to planning and preparation principles, such as those found in Section A, Planning, of the *ASGW Best Practice Guidelines* (1998, 2007).

For instance, note Guideline A.7, Group and Member Preparation:

(a) Group workers screen prospective group members if appropriate to the type of group being offered. When selection of group members is appropriate, group workers identify group members whose needs and goals are compatible with the goals of the group.

Collaboration with members. You already noted in the first definition of leadership a theme related to cooperation and empowerment. Leaders do not do things to members or tell them what to do, except perhaps in crisis situations where a quick and decisive action must be taken to avert a disaster; think of a fire in a crowded theater as an example, where someone best take charge.

In most group work circumstances, effective leadership also is appropriate leadership. That is, the kind of leadership provided broadly matches the culture of the group, which is assessed through ongoing collaboration with members. Another way of stating this is that group counseling leaders take care not to impose goals and strategies brought in from the outside or delivered in a one-way, top-down direction by the leaders to the members. A third way to highlight collaboration is that group work leaders engage with members horizontally rather than vertically. They bring with them their own personal and professional expertise to be joined with the life experience and localized expertise of members. A result is that leadership is both collaborative and appropriate.

It takes a special kind of professional attitude to work laterally with group members. Respect, kindness, and empathy all are part of this professional attitude, plus the belief that working together with people will produce higher quality and longer lasting effects than behaving autocratically, as was noted earlier in the study by Lewin et al. (1939). In extreme cases, we've all encountered professional arrogance, haughtiness, and smugness where expertise is dispensed seemingly from "on high," with no apparent concern for the recipient. Collaborative help-giving, by contrast, levels the playing field. Group counseling leaders who display this kind of professional attitude mediate their expertise through positive relationships with members.

Build and maintain a positive group climate. *Group climate* is a concept in the therapeutic group literature of long-standing, generally thought of as "the atmosphere, culture, or the general personality of a group" (Conyne, 2012, p. 625). Yalom (1995) indicated that a group leader needs to develop a positive group climate that maximally supports effective group interaction, a point that is supported by research (e.g., Ogrodniczuk & Piper, 2003).

Yet, group climate is a term that often is confused with other relevant concepts, such as therapeutic alliance, culture, therapeutic factors, and cohesion. McClendon and Burlingame (2011) report on a large multinational series of studies (AGPA/TransCoop cooperative), a set of which investigated various group relationship variables, including those mentioned earlier. A number of conclusions were drawn, including that group climate can be understood as a perception of the member–group atmosphere containing three broad factors: (a) positive bonding relationship (connections of members with group), (b) positive working relationship (atmosphere of the group supporting work), and (c) negative relationship with negative affect (e.g., tension, avoidance, conflict).

A group can be experienced as having a positive, negative, or neutral climate. In a positive group climate, members feel cohesive, connected to one another and the group. They are encouraged to engage with one another as they attempt to learn, change, or generate solutions to problems. And they feel generally safe from damaging experiences and outcomes.

Related *therapeutic factors* contribute substantially to a positive climate (or may be a product of it, an issue that is the subject of ongoing research). These therapeutic factors are the core mechanisms in the interpersonally centered approach to group psychotherapy (Yalom, 1995; Yalom & Leszcz, 2005).

Cohesion is one of these central therapeutic factors. Cohesion refers to the feeling of "we-ness" in a group, the sense of connection among members and with the group itself. Yalom (1985) describes cohesion as the equivalent of the relationship in individual counseling, and a primary and necessary condition for effective therapy to occur. Marmarosh and Van Horn (2011) described in detail the role of cohesion in counseling and therapy groups, how to foster it, and the need for continuing research.

Cohesion is important in task-oriented groups, too. The effective functioning of committees and teams depends on the active presence of cohesion. Take, for instance, a sports team. Faherty (2012) discussed how what he termed "camaraderie" has been instrumental in the successful performance of the Cincinnati Reds baseball team during the 2012 season. A couple of quotations are illustrative: One fan observed, "The way they get along, the way they root for each other . . . you can see it from up here." Another said, "There is a lot of communication on this team. You can hear them yelling, 'I got it, I got it.' You hear them telling each other when to cut it off. They talk" (A-13).

How do these therapeutic factors, so critically important in counseling and therapy groups, apply to other types of groups, such as psychoeducation and task groups? After all, these other groups are generally less focused on

Figure 5–1   Yalom's Therapeutic Factors

Altruism	Group member offers help to other members
Catharsis	Group member expresses affect strongly
Imparting information	Providing instructive information about mental health, life problems, coping skills, and other matters
Corrective recapitulation of the primary family group	Group member reexperiences negative events from family life in a more positive way
Development of socializing techniques	Group member gains skills through interaction.
Existential factors	Group member confronts deep issues of life and death.
Group cohesiveness and group.	Group member feels connected to others
Imitative behavior	Group member learns through modeling from others.
Instillation of hope	Group member gains inspiration from group
Interpersonal learning	Group member learns and gains interpersonally
Universality	Group member learns he or she is not alone
Existential factors	Group member confronts life realities and the human condition; search for life meaning

Source: Yalom, 1995.

affect, open interaction, and processing. Instead, they typically use higher amounts of structure, imparting of information, and attention to skill development (psychoeducation groups) or to production and goal accomplishment (task groups).

Some theorists have conjectured that the change mechanism in task groups, for instance, travels through group processes and structures (e.g., see

Schwarz, 2002, discussed in the following), suggesting a similarity. Some research has shown that instillation of hope, imparting of information, and existential factors may be of greater salience in guidance-psychoeducation groups than the other factors (e.g., Waldo, Kerne, & Van Horn, 2007). Kivlighan has conducted and reported numerous empirical studies of therapeutic factors in groups (e.g., Kivlighan & Holmes, 2004; Kivlighan, Miles, & Paquin, 2011), recently to conclude that future research needs to examine more closely the role of the *group* itself in promoting and using therapeutic factors. This suggestion means that, like other aspects of group work, therapeutic factors are not a function of the leader but of leadership that is rooted in collaboration with members and with cocreating a group environment or team that is positive, supporting, and challenging. I comment on this point at greater length at this chapter's conclusion.

More research, then, is needed to more fully understand how the therapeutic factors operate in psychoeducation and task groups. It seems likely that all factors are important but that a unique constellation of them may apply.

Nurture here-and-now interaction. To think about "here-and-now" interaction, it is helpful to think of its counterpart, "there-and-then" interaction. An important strategy for group counseling leaders is to maintain the former and to help members convert the latter into the former. To be less obtuse, though, what I mean is that verbal interaction that is in the past tense and outside the group (i.e., "there-and-then") generally is of lesser therapeutic value than verbal interaction that is in the present tense and inside the group (i.e., "here-and-now"). If a group member persists in discussing his childhood experiences with her father, now some 40 years ago, and her presentation remains centered there, it is of considerably less value for change than if she were to focus on what those experiences mean for her currently in her life right now, and also right here in this group.

Leaders of counseling, psychotherapy, and psychoeducation groups generally seek to encourage group members to interact with one another in the here-and-now (Corey et al., 2010). It vitalizes interaction and provides real time material with much change potential. As well, leaders of task groups need to keep attention focused on here-and-now events. Goal accomplishment is in many ways a product of group member resources being harnessed during each and every group meeting.

Of course, at times in any group, there-and-then interaction may be called appropriate and necessary. For instance, a task group, such as ongoing meetings of a Red Cross Disaster Mental Health committee, needs to attend to its context—why has it been formed, what are expectations for it, what disaster events have been occurring in the community, how have its members been performing when responding to requests, and more, and the meeting chair needs to both allow for that kind of discussion and be able to marry it with attention to ongoing processes occurring within the meeting itself. Another example when attention to there-and-then material is important can be found as a group is nearing its conclusion, when attention needs to be given to what has been learned or produced, so that transfer and application outside the group can occur. In a psychoeducation group, for instance, learning constructive confrontation skills in the group need to be transferred appropriately to specific situations in the "real world" outside the group for them to be of any use.

See Learning Exercise 5-2, which aims to show how converting there-and-then to here-and-now language can happen.

Learning Exercise 5–2: From There-and-Then to Here-and-Now

*The **object** of this learning exercise is to note how verbal statements in a group that are historical and outside the group ("there-and-then") might be converted to present and inside the group ("here-and-now").*

Before moving ahead, please note this disclaimer: Some interaction that is historical and/or outside the group is useful and can be important. The problem is when it becomes an entrenched pattern.

There-and-then example, which is part of a 25-minute presentation:

Lawrence goes on, " . . . And my dad just always belittled me, making me feel so small. He would scowl, smirk, sometimes yell and scream at me. He never gave me the time of day either. Why, one time—I think I was 6 or 7 then—he took me to get an ice cream cone; boy, *that* was something, he almost never got me anything! And when I said I wanted chocolate covering on it, he blew up in front of everyone there, and dragged me home by the wrist. And then . . ." (this goes on for another 10 minutes to its conclusion).

The group work leader attempts to move Lawrence to here-and-now:

"Wow, as you describe it, Lawrence, your father really diminished you, so much so that now, some—what—40 or so years later, you still are affected, right?"

Lawrence nods.

"I wonder, Lawrence, if you could put in words how you feel *right now* about your experience with your father?"

(Lawrence struggles, but does this.)

(Continued)

"Thank you, Lawrence; I think that was not easy to do for you. I imagine those feelings may even affect you here in this group, with us. Is that possible? I wonder if you could talk a little about that, about how those feelings lead you to be right here in our group?"

_____

Do you see how the group work leader is trying to nudge Lawrence to try converting past and out-of-group language into current and in-group terms? If Lawrence is able to converse more frequently in the here-and-now, then his potential for learning and change increase. Yet, of course, it is riskier to do so than to stay in the there-and-then, which is the trade-off and the challenge.

_____

Now, let's see if you can try one, as follows.

A sample of there-and-then language:

Fiona, a group member, says, "You know, I've told all of you before about how my first boyfriend turned out to be such a creep. I know, I know, that was about 10 years ago now. But I can't keep thinking about what he did to me. Throwing me over without so much as the common courtesy to come see me and explain. For that fat redhead, too, I was so much better looking and I'll bet you anything on it—I no doubt still am! Boy, is he missing something. I just really hate him for it, and if I ever see him again—which I won't, he lives like in Utah or somewhere—I'd give him a piece of my mind, you can bet on it . . ." (Fiona continues in this vein for another 5 minutes.)

The group work leader attempts to move Lawrence to here-and-now:

Now, this is where you come in. How might you try to redirect Fiona from her historical and out-of-group statements into a present and in-the-group focus? Try this out by writing below a couple of tries at doing this:

1.

2.

Discuss your attempts with another student or reader of this book.

  a. What did you each find?
  b. Identify and discuss similarities and differences.
  c. What did you learn that you might be able to apply in your own group work leadership?

Processing. Although important for generating therapeutic potential, here-and-now interaction is insufficient by itself. It needs to be illuminated (Yalom, 1985), much as one might shine a flashlight to locate an important but otherwise hidden object. As Yalom described it, illumination occurs when group members are asked *to "double back" in a self-reflective loop* to examine and learn from here-and-now experience that has just occurred. Doing so exemplifies the "power cell" of the group: learning from the here-and-now process and experiences that are occurring. Group leaders might ask members about an experience: "What happened here?" "What learning might you get from this?" "How might you apply it to your life outside the group?"

Processing can occur anytime it is appropriate during group sessions. As I pointed out in the last chapter when discussing the *ASGW Best Practice Guidelines*, processing also can and should be engaged in by group leaders between sessions and prior to sessions. Chapters 9 and 10 elaborate.

Learning Exercise 5–3 provides an experience with processing.

Learning Exercise 5–3: Looping Back

*The **object** of this learning exercise is to provide experience applying the self-reflective loop to a sample of group interaction and to identify your learning.*

How might you ask group members to "loop back" following the here-and-now interchange that just happened:

Jessica:	"I'm feeling very vulnerable right now, in here, and that worries me."
Francie:	"I can sense that and I respect you for sharing with us; I, for one, want to be helpful."
Group leader:	"How 'bout the rest of you?" as he scans the others.
Others:	[all nod]
Jessica:	"Hmm . . . I appreciate that, it helps . . ."

Now, remembering what you just read about the "self-reflective loop," try doing this:

1. Indicate how you might ask members to take a pause in the action (assuming this might be an appropriate pausing point) in order to reflect on the here-and-now interaction that just occurred? Jot down some possible invitations.

(Continued)

2. Discuss your invitations with a classmate or another reader of this book.

3. What did you learn? (Note: This last question is an example, itself, of the self-reflective loop.)

Lasting growth and change. While group counseling leaders must attend continuously to *process* issues, or the events and experiences that take place during group sessions, *outcomes* are the bottom line of all group work. We offer and lead groups for one and *only* one reason: they are a way to foster positive outcomes—desired change, growth, learning, or productivity in the members who compose these groups.

That purpose is simple and direct. We do not lead groups to help us feel competent and useful, or for members to experience something powerful in their lives. These are important parts of group work, but in a sense—speaking to those of you comfortable with statistical terms for a moment to help underscore a point—they can be considered examples of its positive *side effects*. But they are not its *main effect*. No, the only justifiable reason we lead groups is to help members to progress in desired or necessary ways. A related goal also is that any change that occurs will be sustainable. It will last over time.

It is accurate, though, that an important reason that people become attracted to leading groups—and then may become committed to this work—is because of the engagingly positive group dynamics that typically are part of groups that function well. These group dynamics exert their own special pull. In my experience and research (e.g., Conyne, 1998a), when those who really, *really* find working with groups meaningful (in fact, it could easily be said that they "love" the process), it often is due to the allure and power of group dynamics, and to the built-in satisfaction they afford. See Chapter 3 for more discussion of the topic of group dynamics.

Yet, having now spoken about the motivational aspects of group dynamics for group leaders, the main theme here is that we provide groups to benefit group members, and this needs to be our laser focus. The good news is that groups work. There is considerable evidence attesting to the general effectiveness of group therapeutic approaches. As Barlow (2011) summarizes it in a comprehensive review of evidence bases for group practice, "Group treatments represent an efficacious and efficient mental health intervention that rivals and at times exceeds individual therapy outcomes" (p. 207). At the same time, researchers are at work measuring what empirically supported group processes account for effectiveness, how this occurs, and what group approaches work best with which client populations (Barlow, 2011; Burlingame, Fuhriman, & Johnson, 2004). As Ward (2004) noted, "We are very confident that group work is effective, but less clear as to which variables in which combinations lead to this effectiveness in various types of groups" (p. 156). As these issues get sorted out through continuing research, results need to be tied closely to actionable group leadership and to training programs that support it (Conyne, 2012).

Group Work Leadership Definition

Now, let's broaden our view from group counseling leadership (and, by extension, psychoeducation groups and group psychotherapy) to group work leadership. This generic description is intended to also embrace task groups.

Group work leadership is

the ability to apply best practice and good professional judgment to collaborate with group members in order to build and maintain a positive working and problem-solving climate through which lasting member growth, change, and/or task productivity is attained.

This generic definition rests generally upon the points discussed earlier on group counseling leadership. However, there are some unique features.

Psychoeducation groups. As you have read, psychoeducation groups aim to help participants enhance or gain needed coping skills to better manage existing life demands and/or to assist in anticipating and dealing more effectively with future ones. Although all therapeutic factors are relevant, psychoeducation groups typically employ more structure, teaching, demonstrating, practice, and direct feedback than other forms of groups. They are, in a very real sense learning groups, environments where group interaction is used to support the acquisition and application of life skills, such as those in communication, conflict, problem solving, decision making, study skills, cultural competence, and relationship development and maintenance.

Psychoeducation training videos are available. Among them are *Leading Groups with Adolescents* (DeLucia-Waack & Segrist, 2006), *Talking Troubles: A Teen Problem Solving Program* (Tellerman, 1998), and *Psychoeducation Group Demonstration: A Career Development Group for International Students* (Conyne & Wilson, 1999).

Task groups. When task groups are added to a conception of group counseling leadership, some broadening needs to occur. Task groups may not necessarily be created, although they can be. Usually, they already exist, and the group leader (who also could function as a consultant or trainer) is challenged to help these groups to move forward in accomplishing their assigned responsibilities. For instance, one might be contracted to assist an existing work group, such as a mental health staff, to improve its functioning, or to consult with a city management group as it labors to develop a strategic plan. Likewise, the emphasis within counseling (and the other helping groups) on here-and-now interaction and on processing may not be as central to task groups, although those processes certainly can apply at times.

In task groups, the accent is placed more on helping people work together using effective problem-solving strategies aimed at accomplishing concrete goals, with the focus of energies placed on task accomplishment as opposed to personal and interpersonal dynamics. Productivity rules in task/work groups with personal and interpersonal relations serving to support that mission. The training video *Task Group Demonstration: Learning through Discussion* (Conyne & Wilson, 1999) illustrates these points.

See what you can do with Case Illustration 5–2 and Learning Exercise 5–4.

Case Illustration 5–2: Misapplication

*The **object** of this case illustration is to show how group approaches can be wrongly applied, where the purpose and the method used are at odds.*

Time for staff meeting in this counseling agency. "Ugh," thought Armand, one of the staff counselors. What a waste of time. Everything always seemed to be out of kilter, he fretted, and he didn't know why. As this meeting wound on, though, he tried to pay attention, to figure out what was not working. Suddenly, it hit him. The agency director, who leads the meeting, misses the point, decided Armand. She keeps asking us to express our feelings, focuses on process issues, maintains long silences . . . all this feels like a therapy group, Armand concluded. But we're supposed to be solving problems, coming up with new plans, revising policy, and all those work-related issues. Damn it, he cursed to himself, she's actually running a therapy group instead of leading a task group, no wonder it's all messed up!

Learning Exercise 5–4: How to Correct It

The **object** of this learning exercise is to give you practice in identifying ways that might better match group purpose with method.

Taking Armand's analysis as accurate, what could the agency director who leads the staff meetings do differently to better fit the purpose of the meeting? How might she appropriately include attention to member feelings and other processes?

Here is one example to get you started: The director might begin to set an agenda to follow for each meeting, including goals and tasks.

List three other ways she might try to improve subsequent meetings.

1. _____

   _____

2. _____

   _____

3. _____

   _____

Group Coleadership

When a group has two leaders rather than one, it is said to be *coled*. Coleadership of groups, then, involves "two or more individuals sharing the organizational, directive, and motivational duties of the leadership role" (Forsyth, 2011, p. 489).

Gladding (2011b) points out that coleadership of groups is common, especially in larger groups of 12 or more. For instance, in a review by Dies (1994), 50% of the groups that were studied employed a coleading model (Riva, Wachtel, & Lasky, 2004). Coleading also is very popular in counselor training, and it "typically involves either the pairing of a counselor-in-training and an experienced counselor or the pairing of two trainees with careful supervision by an experienced counselor" (Luke & Hackney, 2007, p. 280). Bridbord and DeLucia-Waack (2011), based on findings from their study of group coleader satisfaction, suggest that counselors be able to "choose their co-leaders and address issues of compatibility, confrontation, and relationship" (p. 219).

Although this model is used frequently (both in training and in practice), little research evidence—but considerable anecdotal support—has been produced about their desirability and effectiveness (Luke & Hackney, 2007; Riva et al., 2004), along with other informal reports of how coleadership can pose problems. Research into this area is needed.

Group coleadership's advantages and concerns. Corey et al. (2010) and Gladding (2011b) has summarized the advantages and limitations that have been gathered largely through shared experience over the decades of coleadership usage. Refer to Figure 5-2 that organizes advantages and concerns related to group coleadership and then to the Learning Exercise 5-5 that invites you to think about coleadership.

Figure 5–2   Some Coleadership Advantages and Concerns

Some Advantages

Modeling: Especially in an "apprentice" model, the novice learns directly from the expert. As well, members are able to experience not one, but two leader styles.

Division of responsibilities: Leaders can assume separate but complementary roles. For instance, one might focus on task and the other on maintenance.

Feedback: Leaders can provide each other with direct feedback when processing outside the group, and members can benefit from two feedback sources.

Covering: If one leader cannot make a session (e.g., due to sickness), the other most likely will be able to, ensuring consistency of meeting.

Some Concerns

Competition: Leaders can get caught up with who is "better" and also try to gain the upper hand with members.

Tacit collusion: Although unintended, leaders can align with a member to undermine the other leader (e.g., unconsciously ignoring the other leader's suggestions).

Lack of task coordination: Failure of leaders to work well together can derail a group.

Leader incompatibility: Leaders being interpersonally at odds can diminish the group.

Learning Exercise 5–5: Sylvia is Going to Colead a Group

The **object** of this learning exercise is to increase knowledge related to selecting a group coleader.

Context: Sylvia is being asked to colead a 7-week, 2-hour per session, psychoeducation group as part of her internship experience. It is the leaders' responsibility to plan, perform, and process the group, all under close weekly supervision.

She realizes one of her first tasks is to select a coleader because one has not been assigned. She wants to avoid experiencing the possible concerns associated with coleadership while enjoying its advantages.

Address these points:

1. Identify three factors Sylvia might keep in mind in selecting a coleader.

    a. _____

    b. _____

    c. _____

2. Drawing from the contents of Figure 5–2, develop a coleadership plan that she might use and describe it. _____

    _____

    _____

    _____

3. Compare your responses to Items 1 and 2 with those of a fellow student or reader.

● GENERAL STATEMENTS ABOUT GROUP WORK LEADERSHIP

There is considerable support for the perspective of group work leadership that you just have read. This support applies across the range of group work, from task groups through group psychotherapy.

Starting with group psychotherapy, Yalom and Leszcz (2005), drawing from research and clinical experience in psychotherapy groups, emphasize that interpersonal interactions in the here-and-now, coupled with its intentional illumination, are critically important for effective group therapy. It is the group therapist's responsibility to collaborate with group members to promote cohesion (Marmarosh & Van Horn, 2011), a positive group climate (McClendon & Burlingame, 2011), and the development and use of therapeutic conditions (Kivlighan & Holmes, 2004; Yalom & Leszcz, 2005). While remembering the issue of definitional confusion addressed by McClendon and Burlingame (2011), these factors suggest the processes through which members are able to grow and change. It is not the personal traits or characteristics of the leader that account for positive group experiences; rather, it is the leader's capacity to work with members to foster and maintain the necessary conditions through which change can occur.

From the perspective of teams and task groups, Hackman (2002) also points out that it is not a leader's personality or management style that determines how well a team performs, but how effectively a leader designs and supports a team so that members can manage themselves. Schwarz (2002), writing about task group facilitation, supports this viewpoint, too, observing that task group facilitators intervene through a group's processes and structures, with less importance attributed to the group leader's personal characteristics. Group processes that leaders need to attend to include problem solving, decision making, communication, conflict management, and boundary management. Salient aspects of group structure include elements of clear mission and shared vision, effective group culture, clear goals, motivating task, clearly defined roles (including leadership), appropriate membership, group norms, and sufficient time (Schwarz, 2002, pp. 22, 27). Cohen and Bailey (1997), in a far-ranging summary of group effectiveness research in varieties of task groups, demonstrate how group processes occurring both within the group (e.g., communication) and outside it (e.g., conflict) affect what a group can accomplish.

In sum, I conclude this chapter where it began, by returning briefly to the thoughts of Lao Tse. If group work leaders can facilitate goal accomplishment effectively and in such a way that group members genuinely feel that they are the ones responsible for it, then the work probably was well done.

GROUP WORK KEYSTONES ●

- *Leadership* is an important concept for group workers. Many different conceptions of it exist. The understanding emphasized in the chapter underscores interpersonal processes of empowerment, collaboration, and interdependence in goal accomplishment.

- General definitions of *group work leadership* are largely missing from the professional literature.
- A description of *group counseling leadership* was presented as a model for examination, and it was suggested that this definition also extends generally to leading psychoeducation and psychotherapy groups.
- A definition for *group work leadership* was provided, adapting and broadening the definition of group counseling. When *task groups* are considered, then the leadership attention shifts to problem-solving and goal accomplishment issues, with personal relations in an important, but supportive, role.
- *Coleadership* of groups was discussed and analyzed for its relative advantages (e.g., modeling) and concerns (e.g., coordination).

RECOMMENDED RESOURCES

Burlingame, G., Fuhriman, A., & Johnson, J. (2004). Process and outcome in group psychotherapy: A perspective. In J. DeLucia-Waack, D. Gerrity, C. Kalodner, & M. Riva (Eds.), *Handbook of group counseling and psychotherapy* (pp. 49–61). Thousand Oaks, CA: Sage.

Hackman, R. (2002). *Leading teams: Setting the stage for great performances.* Boston, MA: Harvard Business Review Press.

Kivlighan, D. M., Jr., & Holmes, S. (2004). The importance of therapeutic factors: A typology of therapeutic factors studies. In J. DeLucia-Waack, D. Gerrity, C. Kalodner, & M. Riva (Eds.), *Handbook of group counseling and psychotherapy* (pp. 23–48). Thousand Oaks, CA: Sage.

Kivlighan, D. M., Miles, J., & Paquin, J. (2011). Therapeutic factors in group counseling: Asking new questions. In R. Conyne (Ed.), *The Oxford handbook of group counseling* (pp. 121–136). New York, NY: Oxford University Press.

Lewin, K., Lippitt, R., & White, R. K. (1939). Patterns of aggressive behavior in experimentally created social climates. *Journal of Social Psychology, 10,* 271–279.

Luke, M., & Hackney, H. (2007). Group coleadership: A critical review. *Counselor Education and Supervision, 46,* 280–293.

Marmarosh, C., & Van Horn, S. (2011). Cohesion in counseling and psychotherapy groups. In R. Conyne (Ed.), *The Oxford handbook of group counseling* (pp. 137–163). New York, NY: Oxford University Press.

McClendon, D. T., & Burlingame, G. (2011). Group climate: Construct in search of clarity. In R. Conyne (Ed.), *The Oxford handbook of group counseling* (pp. 164–181). New York, NY: Oxford University Press.

Riva, M., Wachtel, M., & Lasky, G. (2004). Effective leadership in group counseling and psychotherapy. In J. Delucia-Waack, D. Gerrity, C. Kalodner, & M. Riva (Eds.),

Group counseling and psychotherapy (pp. 637–640). Thousand Oaks, CA: Sage.

Scholl, R. (2003). Leadership overview. Kingston: University of Rhode Island. Retrieved from http://www.uri.edu/research/lrc/scholl/webnotes/Leadership.htm

Schwarz, R. (2002). *The skilled facilitator: A comprehensive resource for consultants, facilitators, manager, trainers, and coaches.* San Francisco, CA: Jossey-Bass.

Yalom, I., & Leszcz, M. (2005). *The theory and practice of group psychotherapy* (5th ed.). New York, NY: Basic Books.

Training DVDs

Group Work

See a number of group work videos from Microtraining Associates/Alexander Street Press (available at www.emicrotraining.com/index.php?cPath=22_82_35):

Afrocentric Approaches to Group Work: I Am Because We Are (S. Pack-Brown, L. Whittington-Clark, & M. Parker, 2002)

Ethnic Sharing: Valuing Diversity (J. Giordano, 1992)

Group Microskills: Encountering Diversity (L. Banez, A. Ivey, & M. Ivey, 2002)

Psychotherapy Group Leadership

Group Therapy: A Live Demonstration with Yalom and Leszcz. (n.d.). American Group Psychotherapy Association. Retrieved from http://member.agpa.org/static content/staticpages/product_info.cfm?SKU=YALOMDVD11_IND&PRODUCT_

For a number of group videos, go to www.psychotherapy.net/learning-centers/ approach/group-therapy.

Counseling Group Leadership

The following are available at asgw.org/asgw_training_dvds.htm:

Group Counseling for Children: A Multicultural Approach (S. Bauman & S. Steen, 2009)

Group Counseling with *Adolescents* (S. Bauman & S. Steen, 2012)

Group Counseling in the Here and Now (P. Carroll, 1985)

Developmental Aspects of Group Counseling (R. Stockton, 1995)

The Bauman and Steen video focused on adolescents also can be found online at www.youtube.com/watch?v=JOpdhvCBZ28.

Group counseling: Strategies and Skills (E. E. Jacobs, R. L. L. Masson, R. L. Harvill, & C. J. Schimmel).

Evolution of a Group: Student Video and Workbook (G. Corey, M. Corey, & R. Haynes, 2000)

Group Counseling: Process and Technique. Fall, K. (n.d.). Microtraining.

Gazda on Groups: Group Counseling. Gazda, G. M. (1992). Microtraining.

Psychoeducation Group Leadership

Leading Groups with Adolescents. DeLucia-Waack, J., & Segrist, A. (2006). Retrieved from http://asgw.org/asgw_training_dvds.htm

Talking Troubles: A Teen Problem Solving Program. Tellerman, J. S. (1998). Verona, Wisconsin: Attainment Co., Inc.

Psychoeducation Group Demonstration: A Career Development Group for International Students. Conyne, R., & Wilson, R. (1999). North Amherst, MA: Microtraining Associates, Inc.

Task Group Leadership

Task Group Demonstration: Learning through Discussion. Conyne, R., & Wilson, R. (1999). North Amherst, MA: Microtraining Associates, Inc.

GENERAL RESOURCES

In addition to training videos, a variety of other resources (books, monographs, training curricula, training opportunities, reference lists, manuals, etc.) can be found on the websites of the Association for Specialists in Group Work (www.asgw.org) and the American Group Psychotherapy Association (www.agpa.org).

For instance, if you are interested in a list of many of the books published in the group area, see agpa.org/pubs/Booklist.htm.

The compendium *Exercises in Group Work* (Kraus, 2003) is particularly useful.

CHAPTER 6

GROUP WORK THEORIES

There is nothing so practical as a good theory.
—Kurt Lewin (1951, p. 169)

INTRODUCTION ●

Having a Theory Is a Very Good Thing

Why is having a theory so recommended? Isn't a theory kind of superfluous in daily practice where the really important goal is to get things done well and—all too often—quickly?

Well, yes, we are judged as professionals and as group leaders by our capacity to do good work and to be efficient in doing so. To help others, to behave professionally and ethically, to deliver on time, and to be a trusted colleague are all examples of how we may be evaluated. No argument there.

But there are lots and lots of "moving parts" involved with professional practice as a group leader. As we have seen, group work is dynamic, and it constantly generates new and changing conditions to be addressed. It certainly helps to have strategic theories, models, and constructs at one's disposal to help guide practice. Gerald Corey (2012) has likened practicing group work leadership without a theoretical base behind it as flying without a flight plan.

At a broader level, it also is helpful, if not essential, to possess the overarching map supplied by theory to serve as a North Star orienting system. For many, group development theory provides such a focal point, while for some, it may be theory derived from personality development. In any case, why is theory so useful? Theory provides a conceptual system comprised of interlacing principles and assumptions that can be drawn from to make sense of situations being faced and a source of guidance for actions taken.

You are never alone if you carry around in your head a theory that works for you. This is where having a theory is a very good thing, indeed—as Lewin (1951) indicated, "there is nothing so practical."

Turn to Case Illustration 6-1 to consider what theory might mean to you personally.

Case Illustration 6–1: Your "Every Day" Theory

*The **object** of this learning exercise is to gain an appreciation for one's personal theory.*

Background

There are many definitions of theory. I defined it at the beginning of this chapter and portrayed it as a kind of "North Star orienting system":

Theory provides a conceptual system comprised of interlacing principles and assumptions that can be drawn from to make sense of situations being faced and to be a source of guidance for actions taken.

Whether we are aware or not, we operate—at least in part—based on informal theories we've developed over time. For instance, one of mine is a kind of practical theory of living: "I tend to feel good and get more accomplished each day, in general, when I can build in time for writing, exercise with my dog, and spending time with my family." I don't have any solid empirical data to support this so-called theory, but it is time-tested over decades, and I believe it to be true. And its elements reflect considerable research about healthy living: It's beneficial to exercise physically, do something you value, have social support.

Look for the interlacing principles and assumptions in the theory (time writing, exercise with dog, time with family), and how these actions tend to lead me to feeling good and getting things accomplished.

Personal Application

Well, what about you? What kind of practical theories might you have evolved over time? Think about it, you no doubt have some.

(Continued)

1. Briefly summarize one personal theory: _____

   _____

   _____

2. Identify "interlacing principles or assumptions": _____

   _____

   _____

3. Describe personal benefits or outcomes: _____

   _____

   _____

CHAPTER OBJECTIVES

As a result of reading this chapter you will be able to

- Point out the value of theories
- Argue that existing theories in group work, although useful, fall short of what is needed
- Discuss theories associated with group work types:
  - Group counseling and group psychotherapy
  - Task groups
  - Psychoeducation groups
- Discuss six transtheoretical orientations:
  - Contextual (systemic, ecological, multicultural)
  - Interpersonal (including online and social media formats)
  - Interactive
  - Interpersonal neurobiology
  - Process (developmental, dynamic, positive, and cohesive climate)
  - Purpose (healing, enhancing, empowering—prevention, social justice— or producing)
- Provide guidance for developing an overarching theory of group work. (The transtheoretical orientations may well be the key ingredients to developing an overarching theory of group work.) Suggest how to evolve a personal theory of group work

Existing Theories Fall Short of What Is Needed

Most existing theory in group work is an outgrowth of the theory of individual counseling and therapy. Group work theory needs to more fully support the concept of *group*: interpersonal, interactive, and interdependent. It also needs to become more fully harmonious with initiatives to empower people and systems (Conyne, 2004). These two assumptions suggest that a different kind of group work theory needs to emerge or be synthesized from existing theories, one that clearly is synchronous with the concept of group and that connects with societal issues of concern.

Therefore, I believe that group work leaders and those in training need to become familiar with a *full range* of group work leadership theory. A full range of group work leadership theories includes what I term "traditional counseling and helping theories," such as person centered or cognitive-behavioral, and others. These theories have emerged from personality theory and individual counseling, and they have been adapted, where possible, for use with groups. It also includes theory-supporting task groups and psychoeducation groups. Finally, a full range of theory might also include trans-theoretical orientations that are quite sensitive to the concept of group and aligned with missions aimed at human and societal betterment.

Students in graduate professional helping programs are probably already quite aware of the traditional theories from the subject matter of such courses as Theories of Personality, or Theories in Counseling and Psychotherapy. Students in undergraduate programs, such as human services, also will recognize the reliance of helping-oriented courses on this kind of individually based approach. I signify these theories as being traditional for two reasons. These theories are historically and presently dominant in the helping professions, and they emanate from the Western worldview that cherishes the uniqueness of the individual (Morris & Robinson, 1996). The other theories and orientations may be ones you are less familiar with, and I will try to assist you with those.

A Need for Theories Particularly Congruent With Groups

As I have hinted already, one should use caution when considering group work theory. As Donigian and Hulse-Killacky (1999) put it (retaining their words that were placed in italics): "Historically, most group therapy models grew out of individual psychotherapy . . . Therefore, we need to be careful not to confuse *theories of individual therapy,* which are applied to group therapy, with *theories of group therapy*" (p. 1).

Polcin (1991) previously had suggested that counselors rely too heavily on the applications of individual treatment theories to group work. When an individual treatment theoretical perspective dominates, Polcin warned that critical events and experiences that attend group work can be ignored, such as group development, leadership, membership, cohesion, critical incidents, and interaction variables.

In addition, counseling professionals "must be willing to redefine traditional counseling models and roles in order to serve diverse groups" (Holcomb-McCoy, 2007, p. 17). Ratts points out that the counseling profession has too easily accepted the status quo regarding counseling theories. In a *Counseling Today* article on the future of counseling (Shallcross, 2012), Ratts goes on to explain:

> We have developed what I refer to as an "additive approach" to helping that does not fully address the needs of culturally diverse clients. An additive approach to counseling is when we integrate multicultural and social justice into predominant counseling theories and ways of practicing without changing the core structure of an existing theory or practice. (p. 37)

There is a groundswell of agreement building with this sort of viewpoint, one with which I agree. Here is what Herlihy (in Shallcross, 2012) had to say in the same *Counseling Today* article:

> Our profession will need to move away from existing theories that focus on individuals, couples, and families and instead embrace systemic theories that address social ills and foster healing on global level . . . if counselors acquiesce to this status quo, we will contribute to the demise of our profession. (p. 34)

While attempts have been made to adapt theories that are derived primarily from personality theory and individual counseling to more closely reflect group phenomena (see, for example, Corey, 2012; Gladding, 2011b), those adaptations are not enough. As Duba (again, in Shallcross, 2012) observed, "In terms of theories, systemic, wellness-based theories in practice is crucial . . . it is time to begin applying these theoretical models within a systemic context" (pp. 41–42).

Figure 6-1 depicts generally desirable aspects of group with qualities that may be less desirable. Group theory reflecting these desirable qualities is preferred.

Now try out the first learning exercise of this chapter, which builds on Figure 6-1.

Figure 6.1   Desirable Group Qualities Theory Might Reflect

Accessing theories that are synchronous with the generally desirable interpersonal, interdependent, interactive, contextual, and collaborative qualities of a group is important.

Some Desirable Modal Group Qualities	*Some Generally Less Desirable Group Qualities*
Interpersonal	Solo
Interdependent	Isolated
Interactive	Internal
Collaborative	Working alone
Contextual	Apart from, separated

Learning Exercise 6–1: Illustrate Group Qualities

The **object** of this learning exercise is to creatively express dominant qualities of a group that are (a) desirable and (b) less desirable.

So, let's get creative! Ready?

Essentially, what you are trying to illustrate are pictures of a more "positive" and of a more "negative" group.

1. Take out a blank piece of paper. If you have any colored pens, pencils, paint, or crayons, break those out, too.

2. Look at the two columns of group qualities presented in Figure 6–1. Your assignment is to create a drawing or figure (or whatever comes to you) that captures the essence of the qualities (10 minutes):

   a. In Column 1 (*more desirable* group qualities)
   b. In Column 2 (*less desirable* group qualities)

3. Describe in writing what you have created (5 minutes).

4. Show your products to a colleague or friend and discuss (20 minutes):

(Continued)

> a. How did you illustrate desirable group qualities?
> b. How did you illustrate less desirable group qualities?
> c. What would it feel like to be in one group or the other?
> d. Finally, how does a group leader try to foster desirable group qualities?

No Overarching Theory of Group Work Exists

Group work enjoys no overarching conceptual framework (Bemak & Conyne, 2004; Conyne & Bemak, 2004a, 2004b). That this is the case is due to many factors. For one reason, group work stretches over a wide territory that includes the four group work types, and this poses a challenge. Moreover, counseling leaders over the decades have locked the profession, however unwittingly, into the narrow confines of an individual, remedial box that has served to limit the creation of theories that are responsive to group qualities and to changing needs and conditions.

However, on the positive side, there are theories, or at least models and orientations (one step short of theory) existing in each of the group work types. As well, I have identified six transtheoretical orientations that hold promise because they connect well with groups and with the larger issues of modern society.

GROUP WORK THEORY SOURCES: THE CURRENT STATUS ●

In this section on sources of group work theory, I summarize examples pertaining to group counseling and group psychotherapy, and then to task and psychoeducation groups. I also highlight aspects of transtheoretical orientations that can be used in conjunction with other theories and may represent key elements in developing a more comprehensive theory of group work.

Group Counseling and Group Psychotherapy Theories

There is a rich literature addressing theories of group counseling and theories of group psychotherapy. These theories connect most strongly with personality theories, which have been translated to individual counseling and later were adapted to group counseling and psychotherapy.

Examples of theoretical approaches include psychoanalytic, Adlerian, psychodrama, existential, person centered, gestalt, transactional analysis, cognitive-behavioral, reality, and solution focused. They range across affective (feeling), cognitive (thinking), combined (thinking, acting, and doing), and behavioral (doing) domains of human functioning. In addition, they accent intrapersonal or interpersonal processes.

Following are brief summaries of a sampling of these theories selected for their representation from the domains of human functioning (heaviest on the affective domain, where the theories are most frequently represented) mentioned earlier: (a) *feeling:* psychoanalytic, person centered, and gestalt examples; (b) *thinking:* existential example; (c) *thinking, acting, and doing:* Rational-Emotive Behavioral Therapy (REBT) example; and (d) *behaving:* multimodal therapy with the BASIC I.D. illustration. Covered are a general definition and a snapshot of goals, leader interventions, and member behavior expected. For a broader coverage of information about group theories, I refer you to other sources (Corey, 2012; Gladding, 2011b; Yalom & Leszcz, 2005); additional, and more specific, sources are listed for you as we move onward in examining particular theoretical orientations.

Affective domain Example 1: Psychoanalytic theory. This orientation emerged early with the work of Sigmund Freud, and it was applied first to a group format by Alexander Wolf (1963) in the mid-1930s. It is a depth theory, seeking to help group clients to plum their histories in order to reexperience early formative influences and events that serve to still impact present behaviors. A key to psychoanalytic approach is the identification of insight into these causes of dysfunction that can then mobilize corrective emotional experiences in the group.

The *group leader/therapist* in this orientation generally avoids an active and directive role in the group, preferring to create an open environment into which group members are invited to contribute (Rutan, Stone, & Shay, 2007). Members are supported in expressing feelings, material from their past that remains salient in their lives, as well as from their unconscious. Following group therapist leads, they make interpretations and share insights about others and may become helpers. Leaders draw from a range of techniques that are provided in order to obviate the unconscious and to occasion insight. These may include free association, analysis of resistance and transference, interpretation, and dream analysis. The focus of the group tends toward being intrapersonal but also can be interpersonal, as in Yalom's model.

Affective domain Example 2: Person-centered theory. Developed by Carl Rogers, this approach has occupied a valuable position in counseling history and in group counseling and therapy. Person-centered theory values trusting the inner resources and potential of clients, their capability to be self-directive, and the key contribution of therapeutic group conditions to member growth and change. Person-centered approaches were mainstays of the group explosion in the late 1960s and early 1970s in the form of basic encounter groups, which involved little or no structure, a here-and-now focus, and were intended as a kind of group therapy for everyone. The goals of these groups were to create a climate of trust and safety where members could take the lead in experiencing the group process, their own participation in it, and that of other members. Through this involvement and openness to their experience, growth would unfold.

Group leaders/facilitators in this process "trust the process," choosing to offer little structure or direction. They attend closely to others, provide warmth and empathy, and communicate acceptance, respect, and understanding. Facilitators avoid using exercises, games, or other structured interventions in favor of trying to provide an authentic presence and to develop a trusting working environment. Members are empowered to proceed within this climate of acceptance, trust, and openness to experience that is created and maintained.

Affective domain example 3: Gestalt theory. This theoretical orientation is based on an assumption that people bring their "unfinished business" to the group, which then forms the raw material for working in the group. Goals are to increase self-awareness in the here-and-now of the group experience, to highlight the "figure" (most important and pressing issues) from the "ground" (background and generally less urgent and important matters), and to promote integration of polarities that may exist (e.g., between feeling strong or weak).

In gestalt groups, members are encouraged to closely attend to ongoing experiencing in the group so they can drop or complete unfinished business and integrate competing sides of themselves. *Group leaders* can be active in this stance, drawing from their present experiencing of themselves, the members, or the group. They also tend to appropriately use experiments and structured experiences (e.g., "go-round"; "empty chair technique") to highlight and intensify relevant experiential issues in the group. Gestalt theory in groups is associated most closely with Fritz Perls, and others have contributed significantly to its development (e.g., Feder, 2006; Polster & Polster, 1990).

See Learning Exercise 6–2 that provides an opportunity to clarify a feeling-oriented response to a group member.

Thinking domain example: Existential theory. This theoretical orientation represents a philosophy perhaps more than it does a group theory. This philosophy

Learning Exercise 6–2: Antwan's Heart Races: Feelings

*The **object** of this learning exercise is to advance your ability to provide empathic statements that might be appropriate in a group situation.*
Context

It's the first session of a psychoeducation group. The group leader has asked each of the nine members to participate in a "go-round," taking 1 minute or so to do it.

Antwan waited until last to go. As the others spoke, he really didn't get more than a word or two. He was entirely caught up in his own anxiety about speaking. "Why," he yelled in his own ears, "*why* is this happening all over again?" Antwan could hear, and feel, his heart thump, thump, thump in his chest. He tried hard to quiet its booming (he thought) noise by planning each and every word of what he would say when his turn came.

He finally heard the leader saying, "Antwan, can you go now?"
Action

1. Imagine you could have a moment with Antwan, helping him to get ready for his introduction. Draw from your understanding of a theoretical approach from the Feelings domain. What might you do to assist Antwan?

2. Write two possible feeling-oriented statements, and then, compare your statements with those of a partner (5 minutes):

   a. Feeling-oriented Statement #1: _____

   _____

   b. Feeling-oriented Statement #2: _____

   _____

3. Join with another student to discuss and compare your statements (15 minutes).

is concerned with the meaning of life and what living as a human being is all about. Therefore, the choices that people make in their life and the meaning they derive from their experience and those choices are considered to be essential. Concepts of *umwelt*, *mitwelt*, and *eigenwelt* each capture a distinct part of one's existential experience. Umwelt refers to being-in-the-world, especially its biological and physical elements. Mitwelt refers to being-with-others, the relational, social, and cultural elements of personal existence. Eigenwelt refers to one's relationship with and experiencing of the self, or the self-in-existence. Important existential theorists include Rollo May (1961), Viktor Frankl (1962, 2000), and J. F. T. Bugenthal (1965).

Goals of existential groups are to develop therapeutic conditions aimed at helping members to confront and explore their humanity and purpose in life, to heighten their self-awareness, to encounter themselves and each other in the group, and for them to assume increased personal responsibility for choices they make and their consequences. *The group leader's* emphasis is not on use of structure or techniques but on authenticity in the here-and-now of the group and, through that, helping members to increase awareness, choice making, responsibility, and meaning.

Case Illustration 6–2 and Learning Exercise 6–3 address a central theme of an existential approach, life predicaments, and choice surrounding them.

Case Illustration 6–2: Dilemma

The **object** of this case illustration is to present an example of an existential condition.

Samantha pondered Phil's predicament. She was amazed he could be so forthright in the group so quickly. "I could never do that," she admitted to herself. "It seems like we just got started with group." But there he was, wrestling as he is with whether to end his marriage or to find ways to move on in a different way, wondering if he still loves his wife, worrying about his kids, his job, all their futures. "What a struggle," Sam thought. "I wonder what I would do in his situation? How will he make this choice? Can I be of any help here?"

Learning Exercise 6–3: Your Dilemmas

The **object** of this learning exercise is to examine how you handled an existential challenge in your own life and what you learned from this experience.

(Continued)

(Continued)

Context

Think about it yourself. Phil seems to be facing a major life challenge. We all face existential challenges as we live our lives.

What kind of existential challenges have you faced? How have you dealt with them? What meaning have you derived?

In this exercise, do the following:

1. Choose one challenge and describe it:

   _____

   _____

   _____

2. Describe how you dealt with that challenge. What did you do?

   _____

   _____

   _____

3. Finally, what did you learn from that experience? What might you be able to apply in the future?

   _____

   _____

   _____

Thinking-acting-doing domain example: Rational-Emotive Behavior Therapy (REBT) theory. In this theoretical orientation, how people feel and what they do are mediated by how they interpret their experience. Albert Ellis postulated that how people feel about something and how they act result from what they tell themselves about a situation or activating event. Feelings and actions arise indirectly, in this perspective, based on thoughts about an event. The A-B-C model of human interaction captures this sequence, where "A" stands for the activating event, "B" for beliefs about the event, and "C" for consequences (feelings, actions) resulting from the beliefs, not directly from the event or situation itself. If the beliefs or internal thinking are "crooked" or maladaptive (such as "I must always succeed—no matter what!"), then the consequences to the activating event may well be maladaptive in some way. Two additional steps were added to the A-B-C approach: "D," standing for how a person can dispute faulty beliefs to produce "E," which stands for effects that are adaptive. If persons can learn to think more rationally, then their feelings and behavior can be straightened out and become more effective, appropriate, and satisfying.

Ellis (2011) viewed REBT as being very applicable to group therapy, such that it often is the preferred approach. In a group, the REBT approach is applied to help members assess how their thinking patterns affect their behavior. General and specific goals are set to help direct actions taken in the group as members learn to replace ineffective behaviors with new effective ones based on more rational thinking.

Leaders in these groups function as *educators*. They directly explain, demonstrate, provide feedback, and structure learning experiences aimed at positively modifying thinking patterns to produce behavior change. Both cognitive and behavioral techniques are used. Cognitive ones might include homework, learning how to dispute faulty thinking, and lecturettes on coping styles. Behavioral techniques might include skills training, giving and getting specific feedback related to thinking and skills, and role-playing in the group. Members are led to practice new skills and approaches in the group and to apply learning through use of assigned homework. The group members are expected to actively participate, to assess their thought patterns, to practice new ways of thinking and doing both in the group and outside it.

Case Illustration 6–3 shows one way a group leader might present a skill to be practice and how it might be tied to internal thoughts.

Case Illustration 6–3: "Here's What I'd Like You To Do"

*The **object** of this case illustration is to show one way a group leader might provide a set of instructions for practicing a skill being learned, while also considering how thoughts and behaviors might be associated.*

So now that I've outlined what *responding* is, let's see if we can apply it.

Here's what I'd like you to do. Pair up with another group member. We'll have a speaker, let's call that person "A," and a listener (Person "B"), and the listener will practice responding. Person "A" chooses any mildly personal topic about which you have some feeling (e.g., this might be related to coming into group today, or an event that happened in class yesterday), and talk about it for 2 minutes. Person "B" listens closely and then takes 30 seconds to respond. When you

(Continued)

(Continued)

listen, remember to face the talker, maintain eye contact, provide some indications that you are following (for example, a simple "uh huh" or a head nod). Then, when responding, try beginning with this statement: "What I hear you saying is that _____[fill in content] and that you feel _____[try capturing the feeling accompanying the content]." Conclude with something like, "Am I getting it right?"

Then we will gather together as a group to discuss what we observed and see what we have learned. One of the things I will ask all of you is to identify and share what you were *thinking* as you were speaking or listening and responding. What were you telling yourselves? This will help get to how our thoughts connect with our behaviors. Okay, any questions?

Behaving domain, multimodal therapy BASIC I.D. example. Behavioral theory supports a variety of group approaches. These include psychoeducation groups carrying a particular theme (such as communication), social skills training, stress management, multimodal therapy, and mindfulness and acceptance-based groups. In all these behavioral approaches to group, the emphasis on systematic and precise specification sets them apart from the approaches of other theories. Careful behavioral assessment leads to concrete goal setting, to design of a systematic treatment plan, to concrete implementation steps, and finally to objective evaluation (Corey, 2009).

Group leaders design and deliver concrete, time-limited interventions aimed at solving problems and teaching new skills in group members. Leaders are active instructors who encourage group members to learn, practice, and apply skills. Procedures used include goal setting, modeling, practice, feedback, coaching, behavioral rehearsal, relaxation, meditation, and homework.

The BASIC I.D. of Arnold Lazarus (e.g., 2008), is a multimodal approach that includes attention to **b**ehavior, **a**ffect, **s**ensation, **i**magery, **c**ognition, interpersonal relationships, and **d**rugs/biology. It is based on social learning and cognitive theory but draws from a range of theories, as you can surmise from the range of modes contained. Group leaders may find the multimodal areas included in this theory to be useful during group sessions and especially helpful at the planning stage of their group.

A developing theory that draws from the *sensations* mode of the BASIC I.D. approach is Mindfulness-Based Stress Reduction (MBSR). This approach takes place in an 8- to 10-week group program (Kabat-Zinn, 1994). Incorporating meditation, relaxation, yoga techniques, and homework within an overall group approach, as MBSR does, can provide a unique and valuable experience for many group members.

Now, in Learning Exercise 6–4, let's turn to a behavioral technique that emphasizes sensing, relaxation.

Learning Exercise 6–4: Relaxing . . .

*The **object** of this learning exercise is to practice and experience a behavioral approach that can be used in groups.*

1. Pair up.

2. Take turns, 20 minutes for each round (take-your-time)

   a. Round 1: Person A gives the instructions, while Person B follows them.
   b. Round 2: Person B gives the instructions, while Person A follows them.

"Okay, now, let's start as we usually do with a relaxation exercise. I'll dim the lights. Just get comfortable in your seat, telling yourself your two-word calming message. It might be something like 'calm and serene,' or something really simple like 'in' and 'out.' Take a deep breath, count to four, and then release it, again for a count of four. Let's repeat this a few times. As you take in your breath, think of first word in your calming message; as you release your breath, then think of the second word . . . Now, let's scan your body starting with the crown of your head all the way to the soles of your feet. Notice any tension, breathe out and release that tension . . ."

3. Process your experiences (10 minutes)

   a. What was it like to give instructions?
   b. What was it like to follow them? What did you experience?

Task Group and Psychoeducation Group Theory and Models

By contrast with the variety of group counseling and group psychotherapy theories, contributions to theories of task groups and psychoeducation groups are less direct and well defined. Therefore, these two group work types will be considered together, beginning first with task groups.

Task group theory. Theoretical contributions to task groups come from many sources, including the developmental perspective (e.g., Brabender, 2011; Brabender & Fallon, 2009; Wheelan, 2005), social psychology perspective (e.g., Schmuck & Schmuck, 2001), group dynamics (e.g., Forsyth, 2009), process consultation (e.g., Kormanski, 2001; Reddy, 1994; Schein, 1998), team building/development (e.g., Bradford, Gibb, & Benne, 1964; Cummings & Worley, 2008; Hackman, 2002), and performance models (Conyne, Rapin, & Rand, 1997; Schwarz, 2002; Weisbord, 1978).

Social psychology perspective. This perspective informs task groups in several ways (Schmuck & Schmuck, 2001), viewing them as (a) *systems,* where the group is a living system of interrelated parts; (b) possessing both *informal and formal* characteristics, where the more formal structure and procedures of the group are supplemented by the more informal peer and social patterns of behavior that develop; (c) containing *emotional aspects,* the feelings that emerge within and among group members; (d) affecting members' *views of themselves,* where group events and experiences can foster or detract from self-esteem and self-concept; (e) providing *motivation* where affiliation, achievement, and striving for power can be mediated by the social context of the group; (f) affecting *intellectual and motor performance,* which can be influenced by group competition and support; and (g) contributing to *cooperative learning,* where individual member goals can become linked together to benefit all while accomplishing targeted goals.

Process consultation. This form of consultation (Schein, 1969, 1998) is concerned with facilitating the human interrelationships and process events occurring within a work unit. It pays attention and attempts to activate the group member maintenance/human relations roles, along with the task roles you just read about earlier. The process consultant functions as a *facilitator of human processes* in a task or work group. As Reddy (1994) described *group* process consultation, it is "the reasoned and intentional interventions by the consultant, into the ongoing events and dynamics of a group with the purpose of helping that group effectively attain its agreed-upon objectives" (p. 8). Kormanski (2001) identifies critical skills for group process consultants as including active listening, reflecting, linking, summarizing, interpreting, blocking, disclosing self, and suggesting.

Team building/development. As Kormanski (1999) noted, "all teams are groups; however, the reverse may not be true" (p. 6). In this perspective, a group is understood as a collection of people who gather but may not have defined or be interested in seeking specific goals that are necessary to be reached through coordinated enterprise. A group could be five employees who meet occasionally at the end of the week for a drink. A team, however, consists of people who consistently gather together with a purpose that is met through the members pooling together their resources intentionally to satisfy that purpose in such a way as to hold each other and the group liable. Thus, in this view, a team possesses goals, commitment, interdependence, and accountability. (It should be noted that other definitions of a group also contain these ingredients.)

Team development is concerned with advancing the effectiveness and efficiency of a group (team) in its pursuit of personal and organizational objectives (Solomon, 1977). Team leaders apply their knowledge about group dynamics as they assess team situations (such as conflict or avoidance of risk taking) and member needs in order to make process interventions that are timely and effective (Kormanski, 1999).

But it's not all about the leader in a team, either, just as it isn't only the leader who determines an effective therapy group. Hackman's research (2011) indicates that the most powerful leader behavior is to create the conditions that allow members to become effective participants in and managers of the group, which accounts for about 60% of the variation of how a team will perform. Other key factors relate to helping the team get off and running well at its beginning (about 30% of the variance), and then following up with ongoing support and coaching (about 10%).

Performance models. Conceptions of how performance occurs in task groups and in organizations inform task group leadership. Three examples follow.

Weisbord (1978) suggested that six coordinated processes are involved in organizational functioning: (a) *purposes* (what are we trying to do?), (b) *structure* (how is work divided up?), (c) *rewards* (is there an incentive to do this work?), (d) *helpful mechanisms* (do we coordinate our efforts well?), (d) *relationships* (how do we communicate and manage conflict?), and (e) *leadership* (how are all these processes kept in balance?). These six processes are influenced by the outside environment.

Schwarz (2002) indicated that task group effectiveness is dependent on the interactions among group *context* (e.g., supportive culture), *group structure* (e.g., clearly defined roles), and *group process* (e.g., problem solving). In his perspective, three overall criteria for effective groups include that the products delivered meet or exceed performance standards, the processes and structures of the group facilitate performance, and involvement in the group advances the personal growth and well-being of its members.

Conyne, Rapin, and Rand's (1997) model for leading task groups is anchored by the processes that are used by the task group to produce performance outcomes of practices, procedures, products, or people. The model includes attending to the *context* surrounding the group (e.g., performance expectations, resources), along with the premise that "task group leaders must choose from a range of possible intervention options and that informed leader choice is a critical action" (p. 121). These intervention choices include the *type* of the intervention (problem solving or group process), the *level* of leader intervention (individual, interpersonal, group, or organizational), and the *function* of the leader intervention (caring, meaning, motivating, or managing).

Case Illustration 6–4 addresses the role of context. It is an important influencing factor in all group work types, including task groups.

Case Illustration 6–4: Context

*The **object** of this case illustration is to emphasize the importance of context in task groups.*

You've read many reports in the popular press where the (usually) outraged subject of a story maintains not only his or her innocence but may exclaim, "It was all taken out of context!" Indeed, context can be all important, including in all types of group work.

A task group always exists and functions within a larger system. Typically, it is part of an organization or a community, such as the weekly staff meeting within a mental health center. The nature and quality of any single meeting is to some degree reflective of outside events. Examples might include budget cuts announced by the state, or a recent rash of suicides occurring in the community.

The task group leader, or any consultant to such a group, needs to be aware of such contextual events and influences. Any meeting needs to be informed by the group context and be responsive to it.

Let us now turn to psychoeducational groups.

Psychoeducational group theory. This approach is based on learning and education theories and principles, and on general experiential and team-based learning.

Learning and education theories and principles include social learning (e.g., Bandura, 1997; Brown, 1998); cognitive, affective, and psychomotor educational taxonomies (e.g., Bloom, 1956); educational philosophy (e.g. Dewey, 1938, 1966; Harrow, 1972; Krathwohl, Bloom, & Masia, 1973); problem solving (e.g., Davis, 1973); and operant conditioning (Skinner, 1974).

Experiential and team-based learning include experiential learning (e.g., Brown, 2011; Kolb, 1984); interpersonal relations (e.g., Schutz, 1958;

Sullivan, 1953); small-group processes (e.g., Napier & Gershenfeld, 2004; Schmuck & Schmuck 2001); and team-based learning (e.g., Kormanski, 1991, 1999; Michaelsen, Knight, & Fink, 2002).

Learning and education theories and principles. "The principal thrust of psychoeducational groups is learning" (Brown, 1998, p. 15). New information is learned, new skills are developed or existing ones are sharpened, more effective ways to communicate with others are explored, and figuring out how to apply a problem-solving model to everyday life is mastered—these all exemplify the place of learning in these kinds of groups. Learning and educational theories, such as operant conditioning and social learning, support these efforts.

Psychoeducation groups depend on basic *learning principles,* such as motivation, active participation, transfer of learning, and retention. Group leaders also are informed by *instructional principles* that stem from these principles and serve to guide the group's plan, implementation, and evaluation. These principles of instruction have been identified by Brown (1998) as including clear goals, member readiness, motivation, active engagement, whole–part organization, comprehension, and practice. Benjamin Bloom's (1956) taxonomy of educational objectives in the cognitive domain illustrates a progression of goals that can be reflected in psychoeducation groups: from knowledge, to comprehension, to application, to analysis, to synthesis, and to evaluation. To this mix of learning principles must be added knowledge and skill in group facilitation where the power of group dynamics is harnessed, for groups do not provide adequate learning milieus without attention to member thoughts, feelings, and interactions.

Experiential and team-based learning. Experiential learning fuels psychoeducation groups and also learning that occurs in teams, such as problem-based learning (e.g., Duch, Groh, & Allen, 2001) and other educational team-based learning approaches (Michaelsen et al., 2002). These approaches all rely on interpersonal and small group processes whose power source is direct personal experience coupled with its processing. Learning generated from this kind of engagement influences and guides action (Johnson & Johnson, 2008).

David Kolb's (1984) experiential learning theory includes a four-stage learning cycle and four learning styles. The four-stage learning cycle is predicated on the theory that immediate or concrete experience provides a basis for observations and reflections, from which abstract concepts are extracted that can be actively tested for effectiveness. In shorthand, this cycle involves *experiencing, reflecting, thinking,* and *acting.*

An experiential learning model applied to groups and teams (Jones & Pfeiffer, 1980) is similar and contains the following stages: (a) *experiencing,* where group members participate in a structured exercise, which they experience; (b) *publishing,* where group members share their experience and observations of it with others in the group; (c) *processing,* the pivotal step in experiential learning, where group members examine and make sense of their common experience; (d) *generalizing,* where learning generated from processing in the group is transformed to generalizable principles; and (e) *applying,* where these broad principles are put to use in specific real world situations, which actually is the main purpose of experiential groups.

In Figure 6-2, see one example of an experiential learning cycle (Greenaway, 2012), drawn from Pfeiffer and Jones (1983).

Figure 6.2   Experiential Learning Cycle: One Example

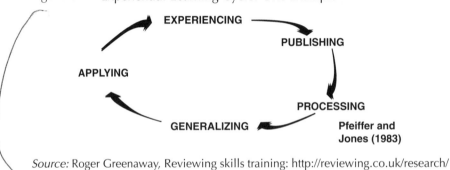

Source: Roger Greenaway, Reviewing skills training: http://reviewing.co.uk/research/learning.cycles.htm

● IDENTIFYING SIX TRANSTHEORETICAL ORIENTATIONS IN GROUP WORK: CONTEXTUAL, INTERPERSONAL, INTERACTIVE, INTERPERSONAL NEUROBIOLOGY, PROCESS, AND PURPOSIVE

Transtheoretical orientations span existing theories and can contribute to them. A well-known example is the well-researched Transtheoretical Model of Behavioral Change (e.g., Prochaska & DiClemente, 2005), which is briefly discussed under Prevention in the following. This model contains progressive stages of pre-contemplation (not ready to take on a change project), contemplation (getting ready), preparation (ready), action, maintenance, and termination. These stages can be applied within existing theories of counseling and psychotherapy.

I have identified six transtheoretical orientations that apply to group work. These orientations deserve discussion, consideration, and research. They hold the potential of being used in conjunction with existing theories within group work, and they serve to amplify the scope and application of these other theories. Moreover, these transtheoretical orientations seem to support the concept of group, and they address societal issues of high concern. *But not only are these transtheoretical orientations to be discussed helpful or additive. I believe they may well be the key ingredients to a maturing overarching theory of group work.*

See Figure 6-3 for these orientations.

Figure 6.3   Six Transtheoretical Orientations for Group Work

CONTEXT

(Systemic, Ecological, Multicultural)

INTERPERSONAL

INTERACTIVE

INTERPERSONAL NEUROBIOLOGY

PROCESS

(Developmental, Dynamic, Positive, and Cohesive Climate)

PURPOSIVE

(Healing, Enhancing, Empowering [Prevention, Social Justice], Producing)

Contextual Orientation

A contextual orientation situates people in relation to each other and varying levels of their environment. It is the opposite of an individual, independent perspective in which people are seen situated apart from each other and their environment. Three prime examples of a contextual orientation in mental health are systemic, ecological, and multicultural.

Systemic (e.g., Agazarian, 2004; Agazarian & Gantt, 2005; Arrow, McGrath, & Berdahl, 2000; Donigian & Hulse-Killacky, 1999; Wheelan, 2005). A systemic orientation in psychology and the social sciences first took root with work of the biologist, Ludwig von Bertalanffy (1956, 1968). He suggested that biological organisms needed to be understood in relationship to larger systems (and their subsystems) and that they existed in an open system of mutual influence and permeation. Think of the process of photosynthesis as a plant interacts in an open system with sunlight, oxygen, and carbon dioxide. This linked set of relationships can be viewed as input-transformation-output, with renewed input processes recycling.

The systems-centered approach to group work is said to apply to all forms of groups. It views a group as existing within a hierarchy of other core systems. An individual is a core system, who is a part of a group core system, which is a part of a larger core system such as an organization, and so it goes. Thus, a group member and the group are interdependent systems, each exerting mutual influence on the other. The group leader helps members to focus on systems-centered culture and norms throughout the life of the group.

Ecological (e.g., Bemak & Chung, 2004; Bemak & Conyne, 2004; Bronfenbrenner, 1979; Conyne & Bemak, 2004a, b; Conyne & Cook, 2004; Conyne, Crowell, & Newmeyer, 2008; Conyne & Mazza, 2007; Cook, 2012; Lewin, 1936). The ecological orientation was set into being by Kurt Lewin (1936) when he suggested that human behavior results from the interaction of people with their environment, that is B = f(PxE). Thus, we live in a reciprocal relationship with those around us and in reference to various levels of our environment. This interactive and contextualized view of functioning was followed up by Urie Bronfenbrenner (1979), who from the microsystem (direct, face-to-face contact, such as a family) through the macrosytem (institutional, global), much as in the systemic perspective just described.

Ecological counseling is one approach that has emerged from the ecological orientation. It is defined as "contextualized help-giving that is dependent on the meaning clients derive from their environmental interactions, yielding an improved ecological concordance" (Conyne & Cook, 2004, p. 6). Related to a systems perspective, ecological counseling sets a person within a nested set of mutually influencing systems. In this view, "a group is . . . a complex, living, open and interactive social system" (Conyne & Bemak, 2004b, p. 9).

Ecological counseling is guided by a set of 14 such underlying principles that positively reinforce a contextual person x environment interacting system (Conyne & Cook, 2004). In ecological group work, six of these concepts are theorized to be particularly salient (Conyne et al., 2008):

a. *Context:* Group and external factors influencing members and the group

b. *Interconnection:* Frequency and the quality of member-to-member relationships

c. *Collaboration:* Linking and functioning together to accomplish personal, interpersonal, or task-related goals

d. *Social system maintenance:* Creation and continuation of a group culture characterized by clarity and integrity of expectations, norms, rules, and other patterns of interaction

e. *Meaning making:* Draw significance and value from group experiences

f. *Sustainability:* Transferring learning from the group to outside the group in the "real world"

One of the important aspects of ecological group work is to attend to how group members and the group itself are affected by economic, political, and demographic trends.

Multicultural (Association for Specialists in Group Work [ASGW], 1998; DeLucia-Waack, 2011; DeLucia-Waack & Donigian, 2004; Frew & Spiegler, 2012; Ivey, D'Andrea, & Ivey, 2012; Lee, 2012; Merchant, 2006; Pedersen, 1991; Sue & Sue, 2008). As globalization accelerates, the world in which we all live is becoming ever more diverse. Attitudes about this range of diversity have begun to change, as well. American society, for instance, for a long time was referred to as a "melting pot," where immigrants of different backgrounds, ethnicities, races, and cultures would eventually blend together in unity, much as cheeses might blend together when heated for a fondue. That metaphor has given way to others, such as viewing the demographic range of American society as a bouquet of flowers, or as a tossed salad, a mosaic, or a kaleidoscope (Halstead, 2007). In these metaphors, differences are accentuated and honored.

Diversity and multiculturalism represent desirable impulses in society, a condition which the counseling profession—and group work—has endorsed. Organized methods for addressing diversity and multiculturalism in counseling have emerged, and we previously looked at some of this material in Chapter 2.

With regard to one such approach, Ivey et al. (2012) indicate that multicultural counseling and therapy (MCT) "recognizes the value of traditional methods of helping *as long as they are employed in a culturally meaningful and culturally sensitive fashion* [italics original]" (p. 677). As well, MCT begins the process of counseling by assessing how clients construct meaning in the world, and it stresses an egalitarian, nonhierarchical counselor-client relationship. As a part of this perspective, it is argued that all counseling must be reframed as multicultural counseling (Arredondo, 1994) and that multiculturalism is inherent in all group work (DeLucia-Waack, 1996).

Interpersonal Orientation

One at a time, individuals compose a group, not to overstate the obvious. At times, a group leader working with one individual at a time in a group is advisable and even necessary. As a general rule, however, maintaining this stance would miss vital ingredients of what a group is all about.

A large part of what defines a group, instead of a collection of individual persons (think the audience at a lecture), are relationships—the interpersonal connections among people that develop—and the degree of interdependence these interpersonal connections spawn. Taking the lead from the poet, John Donne (1624), "no man [*sic*] is an island entire of itself; every man is a piece of the continent, a part of the main."

In general, the social context is where human connectedness, interpersonal support, and positive relationships are forged, and these processes are strongly associated with mental health. A group affords a unique social context for building these kinds of interpersonal connections and then for group leaders to draw from them to help members to grow, develop, change, and produce. Many theorists have captured this perspective (e.g., Bugenthal, 1965; Maslow, 1970; Schutz, 1966; Sullivan, 1953; Yalom & Leszcz, 2005).

Online and social media format. Traditionally and typically the social context of the group is a face-to-face experience, sometimes referred to now as *offline* experience. This is how group work generally occurs and is the focus of all textbooks and training programs. Yet, as we know, there is an explosion in online interpersonal and interactive social contexts, with social media and online technologies of a bewildering variety (bewildering, that is, to many older folks!). These cyberspace settings for computer-based interaction are available to connect people across the world, if necessary, and engage them in discussion and interaction. This, indeed, is an interpersonal and interactive (see the next section) process, albeit not conducted in person and in the same space.

And, of course, these different technological approaches can work effectively in promoting connection, sharing, and interaction. Here is just one example. Having worked now with military personnel in Iraq and Afghanistan and their family members back home, I have witnessed how Skype and other related video and voice technologies can help service men and women and their family members continue communicating, allowing for contact and connection over the thousands of miles of distance. This process is extended to businesses and other collections of people who also need to communicate in real time.

Videoconferencing and electronic blackboards are technological variations allowing users also to directly communicate for a range of purposes, including conducting meetings and in teaching and learning experiences. Synchronous online support groups using downloaded Internet software permit members to connect simultaneously in a graphical space where they can interact verbally and be "seen" using icons (Page, 2004, 2011). And these are just beginning points for online technologies geared to promote group connection and interaction. I have no doubt that you can easily identify other technologies that serve these purposes, too.

In the midst of all this innovation, it is critically important for research and quality assurance to test, validate, and support effective and ethically appropriate approaches, as well as for what works to make its way into teaching and training programs.

Note that Chapter 8 also addresses this general topic of online and social media interpersonal interaction.

Interactive Orientation

Yalom's theory of group psychotherapy is based not only on an interpersonal (and existential) orientation but also on an interactive one. So, too, is the interactive group approach to counseling and psychotherapy described by Kline (2003). As Yalom and Leszcz (2005) emphasized (italics retained), "*The interactional focus is the engine of group therapy*" (p. xvi), a declaration that also is in keeping with the experiential and team-based learning approach discussed earlier with psychoeducation groups.

Interpersonal interaction of members in the here-and-now is the raw material of all group work. A primary way for members to progress in groups is through vicariously observing and actively participating with others, engaging in behaviors such as interpersonal feedback. As they make contact, both nonverbally and with words and actions, members become exposed to other ways of being and doing that may lie outside their own experience. Many of the therapeutic factors identified by Yalom (1975), such as universality, instillation of hope and certainly interpersonal learning, are outgrowths of member-to-member interaction.

Interpersonal Neurobiology Orientation

Neurobiology is the interdisciplinary study of the comprehensive nervous system. Interpersonal neurobiology (IPNB; Siegel, 1999, 2010) specifies this study upon how interpersonal relationships shape the brain. This is a burgeoning and complex area of study, based on the ideas that "human beings are hard-wired to connect with one another throughout life" (Badenock & Cox, 2010, p. 463) and that "the brain is profoundly social and highly plastic, malleable, and pliable throughout one's lifespan" (Flores, 2010, p. 562).

IPNB suggests that group psychotherapy is a social brain treatment for which we are hardwired (Flores, 2010). Some would insist that group therapy is the most finely targeted type of treatment available for improving social functioning and remediating social dysfunction (Denninger, 2010).

This brain-based approach to group work underscores the value of interpersonal connections in strengthening the prefrontal cortex of the brain. A complicated process, it involves establishing the group as a safe environment for interpersonal engagement, and stimulating neuronal activation and growth ("SNAG": Siegel, 2010, p. 484), an approach consistent with the neuroscience axiom "neurons that fire together, wire together" (Hebb, 1949; Siegel, 2010, p. 484). As is being learned (Seung, 2013), the *connectome* (the totality of connections of neurons in nervous system) is malleable and open to being shaped by ongoing experiences. This shaping occurs through the "four *R*s" of reweighting, reconnecting, rewiring, and regeneration. The primary task of the group leader from the IPNB perspective is to nurture and guide this interpersonal activity in order to free the natural drive toward integration (Siegel, 2010). *Therefore, the goal is not only to foster corrective emotional experiences in group but to cause changes in the neural pathways of group members through the stimulation and repetition of new behaviors* (Ferguson, 2010). When considered through the lens of interpersonal neurobiology, group work holds the capacity to change behavior and brain functioning.

Neuroscience, neurobiology, and IPNB in particular hold much promise and excitement for group leadership and this exciting area of study and application literally is in its infancy. As pointed out by Schermer (2010), it may be time to reexamine group therapist style, technique, and training because of what is becoming understood about the social brain.

The emerging work of Ivey (2012), for example, based on Walsh's (2011) conception of *Therapeutic Life Changes* (TLC), stems from research showing that three quarters of health costs are related to lifestyle (Matthews, 2011). The TLC approach includes a range of evidence-based approaches that can bolster brain functioning (e.g., social relationships, exercise, stress management, nutrition and diet, relaxation), which strongly influences health and mental health; many of these approaches include a social component, which can be mediated through and accentuated by psychoeducational group work.

I admit to being a neophyte in this whole new and exciting area of IPNB, but evidence is accruing to warrant support and additional exploration; see Ratey and Hagerman (2008), and the masterful special issue of the *International Journal of Group Psychotherapy* on neurobiology and building interpersonal systems that was coedited by Gantt and Cox (2010).

Process Orientation

Developmental. Similar to the life stages of other living systems, whether these be butterflies or humans, studies and observations of many groups indicate that they, too, pass through identifiable stages of development. In general, if a group continues over time, it can be expected to evolve from a simpler to a more complex unit. A mark of this progression is that group members and the leader(s) collaborate to produce a positive working culture and climate that allows members to become less dependent on structure and leadership, and to discover in one another a collective capacity for interdependence and action. The group leader's primary role is to build a positive working climate with members that will serve to unleash growth forces both within members, between them, and as expressed in the group itself.

Not all theorists agree on the conception of group development you just read. Different positions about this developmental process are held: even whether it occurs in the first place, follows a life cycle consistent with my general description, or proceeds in fits and starts. Many examples of group development theory exist (see Brabender, 2011; Brabender & Fallon, 2009; Wheelan, 2005; and Chapter 5 of this book for more detail).

Best practice in groups asks that group leaders adopt a developmental perspective. It provides a map for understanding and predicting patterns of interaction, and it offers a source of guidance for group leaders as they confront their work. As an example, one might hold a developmental perspective beginning with a group being formed, then it may progress to an initial stage of dependence and a need for orientation, followed by a transition stage of confronting and managing control and power, to a working stage where a positive climate fosters opportunities for growth and productivity, and finally, to an ending stage where members consolidate their learning, give thought to its application outside the group, and say good-bye to each other. Such a schema (which I just fabricated; again see Chapter 5 for some actual cases) can be used by a group leader to plan the overall group, individual group sessions, to guide interventions, and to design evaluation. A group development perspective (and adopted model) helps leaders sort and make sense of group phenomena, which otherwise sometimes can seem excessively challenging.

Group dynamics. Group dynamics are "the actions, processes, forces, and changes occurring over time that affect and influence the group, its members, and leader." (See Chapter 3 for elaboration.) Group development is one important aspect of group dynamics. Others include task (such as initiator, summarizer, and timekeeper) and maintenance roles (such as encourager, harmonizer, and gatekeeper).

Group process also is a key part of overall group dynamics. It can be defined as "the experiencing by group participants of influential group dynamics as they occur separately and in combination over a group's development" (Chapter 3). An important consideration in group process is the attention given to content (what is being discussed) and process (how it is being discussed) in a group and how these dimensions can be appropriately balanced to yield engaging and meaningful group interaction among group members.

All group dynamics are important in all types of groups. It's the relative emphasis that matters in relation to other factors such as goals, and stage of group development.

Positive and cohesive climate. Of course, what leaders of groups do is important. Their execution of knowledge, attitude, values, and skills contribute directly to an effective group. But, regardless of group work type, the ability of group leaders to collaborate with group members to create a positive and cohesive climate is most essential. Group leaders do this by creating strong bonds, promoting healthy interaction, developing facilitative conditions, facilitating a sense of belonging and identity with the group, and working through conflict and disagreements therapeutically. It is through the dynamic of a positive working climate that member growth, change, and productivity emerge.

Purposive Orientation

Healing. Often a purpose of group counseling and group psychotherapy is to help members to remediate concerns, which may be experienced along a range of dysfunction from mild to severe. The outcome sought is to heal, to get better, to learn, and once again approximate a state of well-being.

Enhancing. In other cases, groups are offered to help members' lives become even more satisfying and fulfilling. These are developmental purposes, where enhancement of existing assets is sought—to become more self-aware, to develop additional skills at communicating, and so on. Some counseling groups and many psychoeducation groups are oriented in this direction.

Empowering: Prevention and social justice. Empowerment in counseling (McWhirter, 1994) is concerned with helping people, groups, organizations, or communities that presently are marginalized and without power to gain strength. Empowerment can occur by people becoming more aware of (a) how power dynamics affect them, (b) how they can gain increased control over their lives without infringing or hurting others, and (c) how they can actively support the empowerment of others in their environment.

Prevention and social justice are initiatives in counseling and mental health aimed at empowerment. Each contains a variety of methods for building strength in people and systems and for positively altering environmental properties and processes so that persons and groups can realize improved qualities of life.

Prevention (Clanton Harpine, 2011; Clanton Harpine, 2013; Conyne, 2004; Conyne, 2012; Conyne & Clanton Harpine, 2010; Conyne & Horne, 2001; Conyne & Horne, 2013; Hage & Romano, 2010; Hage & Romano, 2013; Vera, 2012; Waldo, Schwartz, Horne, & Cote, 2011). Prevention in mental health and the use of group methods to reach prevention goals are gaining increased attention. Prevention practice includes the collaborative design and delivery of strengths-based health promotion and environmental improvement strategies. These strategies frequently are included together within organized prevention programs that are conducted prior to dysfunction becoming entrenched within members of a targeted population. These programs typically are designed to promote protective factors present in a context (e.g., existing interpersonal strengths or supportive procedures within a setting) while reducing risk factors (e.g., high levels of stressors coupled with limited support). Program examples include developing resilience through a group-based parent training program (Borden, Schultz, Herman, & Brooks, 2010) and a group-based program to address bullying in the schools by increasing teacher competencies (Bell, Raczynski, & Horne, 2010).

Hage and Romano (2013) have identified theoretical models that support preventive practice. These include (a) Transtheoretical Model of Behavior Change (TTM; e.g., Prochaska & DiClemente, 2005; Prochaska, Johnson, & Lee, 2009), which I referred to briefly earlier in this chapter; (b) Theory of Reasoned Action and Planned Behavior (TRA/PB; e.g., Ajzen, 1991); (c) Positive Psychology (e.g., Seligman, Steen, Park, & Peterson, 2005); and (d) Social Justice (e.g., Albee, 2005). They point out that the first two models are considered theories in the traditional understanding of theory, while the latter two are broader-based perspectives that may inform prevention work.

TTM is a progressive process involving vague thoughts about a possibility for change (Pre-contemplation) through becoming increasingly more concrete and focused about specifying (Contemplation), planning (Preparation), implementing (Taking Action), and maintaining the behavioral change project, for example, an effort to lose weight. The last stage in the progression is Termination.

TRA/PB addresses the most relevant and important attitudes and beliefs that motivate people to either continue present behaviors or to adopt new and more health-promoting behaviors. In this theory, behaviors are influenced by intentions to change them. Think of becoming a better listener, for instance. In turn, these behavioral intentions (becoming a better listener in our example) are influenced by attitudes about the behavior in question, the amount of control persons seeking to change perceive they actually have over said behavior, and the viewpoints of others who are important about the behavior.

Positive Psychology (e.g., Linley, Joseph, Harrington, & Wood, 2006; Seligman et al., 2005) is a fast-growing theoretical, research, and applied approach to improved health that is very compatible with prevention. It is predicated on identifying and cultivating existing strengths and protective factors in persons and institutions. It is concerned with advancing well-being and resilience as means for not only recovering from deficits but importantly for optimizing functioning. Identifying and then enhancing character strengths and virtues (Peterson & Seligman, 2004)—wisdom and knowledge, courage, humanity, justice, temperance, and transcendence—represent one major set of assumptions in positive psychology.

Social Justice (e.g., Albee, 2005; Hage, Mason, & Kim, 2011; Kenny, Horne, Orpinas, & Reese, 2009; McWhirter, 1998; Prilleltensky, 1997; Rawls, 1971; Singh & Salazar, 2011; Vera & Kenny, in press; Vera & Speight, 2003). Sharing much with multicultural counseling and with prevention, social justice group work (Hage et al., 2011) focuses on identifying and understanding issues and challenges connected with oppression, privilege, and social inequities (Anderson, 2007; Smith & Shin, 2009). See Chapter 2 for previous discussion.

Social justice is concerned with social, historical, political, and cultural contexts that shape and are shaped by human endeavors. More specifically, it seeks to reduce, eliminate, or forestall conditions of social injustice, the reproduction of inequity, and how such conditions influence the mental health and well-being of communities.

Group workers explore and discuss how privilege and oppressive systems influence leaders and members' lives (ASGW, 2012), but they also have an opportunity through their group work to take action at the systems level. At a group level, leaders can strive to increase access to groups for all members of a community, thus working toward equity and equal access to services. Group workers can partner with target populations to help ensure that the format, location, and concepts of the group fit the cultural context of the group members.

Group workers can help clients negotiate systems, such as access to health care or housing opportunities. When group workers encounter systemic barriers in their professional work, they develop plans for confronting them (Toporek, Lewis, & Crethar, 2009). Possible actions could include serving on a local, state, or national committee that is working to address injustices.

As a way to help group workers to actualize social justice in their groups, Ratts, Anthony, and Santos (2010) created a developmental framework, the *Dimensions of Social Justice Model.* This model is influenced by a group worker's comfort and expertise with issues pertaining to social justice. I draw from Conyne and Diedrich's (2013) discussion of the model.

The Ratts et al. (2010) model includes five dimensions: (a) *Naiveté,* where cultural variables are not considered, with group development and ongoing interaction approached as typical and normal; (b) *Multicultural Integration,* where leaders and members seek to understand each other within a cultural context, including how culture influences their thinking about problems, conflict, and the relationships among members; (c) *Liberatory Critical Consciousness,* where a kind of "cognitive and emotional awakening" occurs (Ratts et al., p. 164), and members begin to understand that their lives emerge from and are informed by deeper historical, social and political origins. Here, group leaders can help members become aware of the roles that homophobia, sexism, ageism and other oppressive forces and social injustices may play in their lives. Next are (d) *Empowerment,* where members start to recognize that knowledge and awareness are insufficient by themselves for change to occur and that self-advocacy skills are required to alter corrosive environmental factors, and (e) *Social Justice Advocacy,* where group members learn that self-advocacy can be supplemented by broader advocacy efforts aimed at combining with others to work for systemic change. In each dimension, group leaders maintain a responsibility to teach members about social justice, self-awareness, and system change.

Social justice endorses both social change and strengthening the well-being of individuals, families, groups, and society as necessary means toward human betterment. In this perspective, it is theorized that mental health problems and promotion can no longer be considered apart from social conditions (Nelson & Prilleltensky, 2005), which suggests that group work and other counseling interventions must take into account political, socioeconomic, and demographic trends in modern society when designing therapy models and curricula (Bemak & Chung, 2004). Another theoretical assumption of social justice group work is that its principles apply to internal group dynamics, as well as to external applications. Harmful societal processes, such as social power and privilege, can be replicated within the group, which group leaders need to be aware of and attempt to protect against within an overall change model (McNair-Semands, 2007; Roysircar, 2008).

Producing. It is important to keep in mind that a group is vehicle—a means—that is being used to realize certain goals. All group work is aimed at helping members to become more productive in some way. Benefits realized may be tied to gains in personal and interpersonal growth and development (as in counseling and therapy groups), in new skills (as in psychoeducation groups), or in accomplishing tangible goals or products (as in task/work groups). Keeping your "eyes on the prize" in group work leadership means being sure that the group experience is authentically geared to reach the goals set for it: personal, interpersonal, or task related.

● TOWARD AN OVERARCHING THEORY OF GROUP WORK

There is a gathering nexus of thought emerging, some of which I've reported in this chapter, that the status quo of group theory is insufficient to meet the dynamically changing demographics of our society or to best represent the very concept of "group" itself. Some critics think that theories based on a Western model of individual personality, adapted as they have been to better fit both the group context and the growing diversity of society, fall short of what is needed. I must say that I agree with these critics.

Which begs the question, then, "What is needed?"

Three large needs exist, in my view, each of which is beginning to be addressed by scholars: (a) a comprehensive theory of group work, one that spans the breadth of group work types, to augment the separate theories that exist currently; (b) this overarching theory needs to be grounded in the concept of "group," rather than of the "individual"; and (c) this inclusive theory needs to embrace diversity and cultural variety. The transtheoretical orientations you've read about in this chapter would seem to hold much promise for reshaping theory in group work.

Now take some time to reflect on relationships between the transtheoretical orientations and traditional group counseling and psychotherapy theories. (See Learning Exercise 6-5.)

Continue examining the transtheoretical orientations, this time in relation to both task and psychoeducation groups. (See Learning Exercise 6-6.)

● YOUR PERSONAL THEORY IN ACTION

I hope that, as you read about and weigh examples of various theoretical approaches and of the theoretical perspectives, you will gradually begin to

Learning Exercise 6–5:
Outline an Oral Presentation: Part 1

*The **object** of this learning exercise is to help you to more completely understand the traditional theories applied to group work.*

The course assignment for next week is to turn in an outline of the key points in the traditional theories applied to group work, which are listed in Figure 6–3.

Imagine you own six pairs of eyeglasses, one of each transtheoretical orientation. Put on each pair of eyeglasses, one at a time. As you peer through the lenses each time, write down the *major points* you see as you look through the examples of *ONE* of the *traditional group counseling and psychotherapy theories* that are listed. Use the schema below to assist you.

Traditional Theory Examples
Gestalt   Existential   BASIC I.D.   REBT

Lenses

Contextual_____

Interpersonal_____

Interactive _____

Interpersonal Neurobiology _____

Developmental_____

Purposive_____

Learning Exercise 6–6:
Outline an Oral Presentation: Part 2

*The **object** of this learning exercise is to help you more completely understand the transtheoretical orientations to group work.*

The course assignment for next week extends the assignment. This time, you are to turn in an outline of the key points in the transtheoretical orientations for group work, which are listed in Figure 6–3.

(Continued)

(Continued)

Again, imagine you own six pairs of eyeglasses, one of each trans-theoretical orientation. Put on each pair of eyeglasses, one at a time. As you peer through the lenses each time, write down the *major points* you see as you look at task and at psychoeducation groups. Use the schema below to assist you.

	Task Groups	Psychoeducation Groups
Lenses		
Contextual		
Interpersonal		
Interactive		
Interpersonal Neurobiology		
Developmental		
Purposive		

work on developing your own personal theory in action that is informed by and effectively integrates aspects of other theories within your own personal value system. It is not just a good idea that you develop such a theoretical orientation. It is necessary for you to do so, as many scholars have urged (e.g., Corey, 2012; Corey, Corey, & Corey, 2010; Gladding, 2011b).

Your personal theory will take time to evolve. At its best, it will mesh coherently with your personality and values. It also needs to fit the group members you work with and the kind of group work you provide. There is no need to rush it along, but there is benefit in keeping the agenda for its development alive, tucked away somewhere on a back burner as you read, think, try out ideas, and generally become deeper involved in the overall process of professional identity development. As it crystallizes, your personal theory will serve as a touchstone, a guide to shape and sustain your practice, and to lead you through the troubled waters we sometimes encounter in our work as group leaders. A theory should not be compartmentalized as a set of interesting, but lofty, statements that are divorced from reality. No, a theory holds considerable practical value and utility, just as Kurt Lewin (1951) indicated in the introductory quotation in this chapter.

As you move ahead to develop your own personal theory in action, therefore, I encourage you to consider *several* theoretical sources to inform you. I encourage you to access other texts that may concentrate more thoroughly on theories and models corresponding to each of the group work types. The material in this chapter serves as a kind of general sample of those theories. Please refer to the sources I have provided for each group work type for more information about particular theories and models.

As well, as I pointed out earlier, it is important for you to give at least equal attention to your own values, attitudes, interests, and competencies. These theories should include, but not be limited to, individual counseling theory adapted to groups and certainly incorporate attention to theories and conceptual models associated with task and psychoeducation groups, as well as to transtheoretical models. Your "customized" theory of group work should connect with your personality, group member needs, and the type of group work you are providing. (See Learning Exercise 6-7.)

Learning Exercise 6–7: Outline and Share Your Developing Personal Theory of Group Work

*The **object** of this learning exercise is to outline and then share your developing personal theory of group work.*

In this chapter, you have considered a range of traditional and transtheoretical theories of group work. The importance of adopting or, most likely, adapting aspects of these theories for your personal use also was emphasized. This learning exercise provides you with this opportunity.

Here is what I invite you to do:

1. Identify five points that have most appealed to you from your reading of group theory. There is no need to worry about how everything fits together. Just identify what you seem to like and what might be potentially useful (10 minutes):

   Point 1: _____

   Point 2: _____

   Point 3: _____

   Point 4: _____

   Point 5: _____

   (Continued)

(Continued)

2. In a personal theory, it is important to integrate with existing theories your values, attitudes, interests, and competencies. Highlight salient aspects of these areas (10 minutes):

Your values: _____

_____

Your attitudes: _____

_____

Your interests: _____

_____

Your competencies: _____

_____

3. Summarize in a paragraph how the material you presented in Question 1 (theories) and Question 2 (personal domains) might fit together (15 minutes):

_____

_____

_____

_____

_____

_____

4. Pair up. Each person take 10 minutes to share what you developed.

● GROUP WORK KEYSTONES

- A theory provides a framework of interlacing factors that can be drawn from to help understand situations and to guide action.
- Existing theories in group work have been adapted to fit groups from personality theory and individual counseling and psychotherapy.
- Examples of traditional theories of *group counseling and psychotherapy, task groups,* and *psychoeducation groups* were covered.

- There is a need to develop a more comprehensive theory of group work, having the capacity to overarch all group work types or to be used in conjunction with existing theories.
- Six transtheoretical orientations that apply to group work were identified. *Not only are these transtheoretical orientations helpful or additive; they may well be the key ingredients to a maturing overarching theory of group work.*
- You were encouraged to begin evolving your own personal theory of group work.

RECOMMENDED RESOURCES

Agazarian, Y. (2004). *Systems-centered therapy for groups.* London, England: Karnac Books.

Brown, N. (2005). Psychoeducational groups. In S. Wheelan (Ed.), *The handbook of group research and practice* (pp. 511–529). Thousand Oaks, CA: Sage.

Conyne, R., & Clanton Harpine, E. Prevention groups: Evidence-based approaches to advance the field [Special issue]. *Group Dynamics: Theory, Research, and Practice*, 193–280.

Conyne, R., Crowell, J., & Newmeyer, M. (2008). *Group techniques: How to use them more purposefully.* Upper Saddle River, NJ: Pearson.

Conyne, R., Rapin, L., & Rand, J. (1997). A model for leading task groups. In H. Forester-Miller & J. Kottler (Eds.), *Issues and challenges for group practitioners* (pp. 117–130). Denver, CO: Love.

Corey, G. (2012). *Theory and practice of group counseling* (8th ed.). Pacific Grove, CA: Brooks/Cole.

DeLucia-Waack, J., & Donigian, J. (2004). *The practice of multicultural group work: Visions and perspectives from the field.* Pacific Grove, CA: Wadsworth.

Ellis, A. (2011). Rational emotive behavior therapy. In R. Corsini & D. Wedding (Eds.), *Current psychotherapies* (9th ed., pp. 196–234). Belmont, CA: Brooks/Cole, Cengage Learning.

Feder, B. (2006). *Gestalt group therapy: A practical guide.* Metairie/New Orleans, LA: Gestalt Institute Press.

Frankl, V. (1962, 2000). *Man's search for meaning: An introduction to logotherapy.* New York, NY: Beacon.

Gantt, S., & Cox, P. (2010). Neurobiology and building interpersonal systems: Groups, couples, and beyond [Special issue]. *International Journal of Group Psychotherapy, 60*, 453–604.

Gladding, S. (2011). *Groups: A counseling specialty* (6th ed.). Upper Saddle River, NJ: Pearson

Hackman, R. (2002). *Leading teams: Setting the stage for great performances.* Boston, MA: Harvard Business Review Press.

Hage, S., Mason, M., & Kim, J. (2011). A social justice approach to group counseling. In R. Conyne (Ed.), *The Oxford handbook of group counseling* (pp. 102–117). New York, NY: Oxford University Press. doi: 10.1037/a0020736

Ivey, A., D'Andrea, M., & Ivey, M. B. (2011). *Theories of counseling and psychotherapy: A multicultural perspective*. Thousand Oaks, CA: Sage.

Kolb, D. (1984). *Experience as the source of learning and development*. Englewood Cliffs, NJ: Prentice Hall.

Kormanski, C. (1991). Using theory as a foundation for group training designs. *Journal for Specialists in Group Work, 16*, 215–222.

Lazarus, A. (2008). Multimodal therapy. In R. J. Corsini & D. Wedding (Eds.), *Current psychotherapies* (8th ed., pp. 368–401). Belmont, CA: Brooks/Cole.

Lewin, K. (1951). *Field theory in social science*. New York, NY: Harper.

Peterson, C., & Seligman, M. (2004). *Character strengths and virtues: A handbook and classification*. New York, NY: Oxford University Press.

Polster, M., & Polster, E. (1990). Gestalt therapy. In J. Zeig & W. Munion (Eds.), *What is psychotherapy? Contemporary perspectives* (pp. 103–107). San Francisco, CA: Jossey-Bass.

Prochaska, J. O., Johnson, S., & Lee, P. (2009). The transtheoretical model of behavior change. In S. A. Shumaker, J. K. Ockene, & K. A. Riekert (Eds.), *The handbook of behavior change* (3rd ed., pp. 59–83). New York, NY: Springer.

Ratts, M., Anthony, L., & Santos, K. N. (2010). The Dimensions of Social Justice Model: Transforming traditional group work into a socially just framework. *Journal for Specialists in Group Work, 35*, 160–168. doi: 10.1080/01933921003705974

Rogers, C. (1967). The process of the basic encounter group. In J. F. T. Bugenthal (Ed.), *Challenges of humanistic psychology*. New York, NY: McGraw-Hill.

Rutan, S., Stone, W., & Shay, J. (2007). *Psychodynamic group psychotherapy* (4th ed.). New York, NY: Guilford Press.

Schein, E. (1998). *Process consultation revisited: Building the helping relationship*. Boston, MA: Addison-Wesley Longman.

Schwarz, R. (2002). *The skilled facilitator: A comprehensive resource for consultants, facilitators, manager, trainers, and coaches*. San Francisco, CA: Jossey-Bass.

Sullivan, H. S. (1953). *The interpersonal theory of psychiatry*. New York, NY: Norton.

Wheelan, S. (2004). Groups in the workplace. In J. DeLucia-Waack, D. Gerrity, C. Kalodner, & M. Riva (Eds.), *Group handbook of group counseling and psychotherapy* (pp. 401–413). Thousand Oaks, CA: Sage.

Wolf, A. (1963). The psychoanalysis of groups. In M. Rosenbaum & M. Berger (Eds.), *Group psychotherapy and group function* (pp. 273–327). New York, NY: Basic Books.

CHAPTER 7

GROUP LEADER STYLES AND FUNCTIONS

If your actions inspire others to dream more, learn more, do more and become more, you are a leader.

— John Quincy Adams, 6th U.S. President

INTRODUCTION ●

As the introductory quotation indicates, leadership *actions* can inspire growth in others. Having considered what leadership and group work leadership is, it's time to examine the foundational elements supporting group leadership, what I term, its *building blocks*. An excellent beginning point for considering building blocks in group leadership is with your own experience with group leadership and with observing it being done. This is how we begin this chapter.

CHAPTER OBJECTIVES

As a result of reading this chapter you will be able to

- Identify the foundational elements, or *building blocks*, of group leadership through examining:
- Leader functions

- Leader styles and types
- Leader competencies (knowledge and skills)

● LOOKING AT PERSONAL EXPERIENCE WITH GROUP LEADERSHIP

I remember my first group leading experience very well—and with a few shudders, too. It was a part of my practicum, with a small group of undergraduates. This group, and several others, was organized within a much large course in "helping skills."

Read about my first group leading experience in Case Illustration 7-1.

Case Illustration 7-1:
Bob's First Group Leading Experience

This group occurred a long time ago, during the late 1960s (I know, I know . . .), when group training was in its absolute infancy. I was then a doctoral student in Purdue University's counseling program, which was early on giving attention to group counseling (thanks to counseling Professors Richard Diedrich, Allan Dye, and Al Segrist, and also to Richard Levin in clinical psychology).

I had studied the limited scholarly sources available then, which was fascinating stuff, and quite different from the dominant counseling literature of the time. Some examples included sources drawn from (a) T-groups (Bradford, Gibb, & Benne, 1964, (b) the encounter group movement (Burton, 1969), (c) small-group dynamics (Cartwright & Zander, 1968; Hare, Borgatta, & Bales, 1965; Thelen, 1954), and (d) the microscopic professional literature existing in group counseling and psychotherapy (Gazda, 1968).

This was before the time of Yalom's first edition of the *Theory and Practice of Group Psychotherapy* (1975) and the wider and impressive stream of group work professional literature that began to flow with increasing force over the ensuing decades, perhaps best exemplified in the counseling profession by the continuous production over the years by Gerald and of Gerald and Marianne Corey in group counseling and group techniques.

It also was before group work training, practice, and research had begun to evolve. At the time, it was largely uncertain either how to

(Continued)

train future group leaders or how a group leader was supposed to translate the limited knowledge base available into practice. In fact, as I have mentioned before, the dominant group work leadership method was tied to spontaneity and a fairly unplanned way to be in the group. As for me, I had supplemented my graduate school education in group counseling with training I'd been encouraged by my professors to seek through the National Training Laboratories (NTL), conducted both at the NTL "holy land" in Bethel, Maine, and at its Midwestern Group Human Relations locations. As well, my Purdue program conducted periodic weekend T-group workshops for faculty and students.

Back to my first group leading experience. I was very green, with this group leading experience occurring before I had trucked off to Bethel for training, for instance. I remember sitting in the circle looking around at each of the student group members, my heart racing, as I said to myself, "Be calm. At least appear like you know something!" What I did is what I still often do as a matter of good practice (I hope) and also when I get into a pinch in group: I relied on group process. I knew enough to begin by talking some about general goals for the helping skills group and to invite group members to introduce themselves in a "go-round." I remember asking them to discuss one of the helping skills presented earlier in the week during the instructional part of the class, and then asking some open-ended questions; I think I was wanting to engage the members, however ugly and clumsy my attempts were. I also recall, quite happily, surviving the first session, to live another day and be able to move on toward the next week's session. *I remember a strong feeling of relief.*

Now I'm wondering about your group experience and especially a first group leading experience you already may have had. Take a look at Learning Exercise 7-1.

WHAT DO GROUP LEADERS DO? ●

Recall, in Chapter 1, we discussed how ubiquitous groups are in our culture. If you are like most of us, you've been involved with a lot of groups in your life, something that you may have become more aware of through the "Take

Learning Exercise 7–1:
Your First Group Leading Experience

*The **object** of this learning exercise is to assist you to explore one of your group experiences (formal or informal) to identify important learning about group work.*

I wrote about my first group leading experience that occurred when I was a graduate student. I wonder if you have had such a first experience? Or, maybe that one still awaits you. Otherwise, looking back over the course of your life experience, it is likely you have served in a group leadership role of some kind, perhaps in high school or college.

In any case, identify your first such group leading experience (even if it was not in a typical group counseling or group work capacity) and let that be the focus of the next four questions:

1. What was your experience like? Describe as much of it as possible.

2. What was your leadership role?

3. How did it go?

4. What did you learn?

a Life Sample" learning exercise in Chapter 1. Some of those group experiences may have been generally positive, while others may not have been. Learning Exercise 7-2 asks you to think about what you have noticed group leaders doing by scanning your own experience.

Be mindful of your own group leadership and membership experience as we turn now to exploring some of the major activities of group work leaders. Covered will be group work leader building blocks: (a) functions, (b) styles and types, and (c) competencies. These are the major classes of actions for all group work leaders. We examine the more advanced topics of group leader methods and strategies in Chapter 8.

Group Leader Functions and Styles

One of the classic studies in group history was the large study of encounter groups conducted by Lieberman, Yalom, and Miles (1973). This study was

---

Learning Exercise 7–2:
What Did the Group Leaders Do?

The **object** of this learning exercise is to identify positive and negative aspects of group leaders.

Take a moment to once again scroll back in time, considering some of the many leader-led groups you've been a part of in your life as a member. For instance, when I tried doing this, I immediately remembered the Cub Scout pack I was part of (my mother was the Den Mother/group leader!)—now that's going way back in time—as well as some recent ones, such as the many program faculty meetings I led and a psychoeducational group of soldiers I coled when I was on a work assignment overseas at a U.S. Army post.

What do you come up with through your scroll?

Now I want you to focus specifically on two of those groups, one that you remember as being generally a positive experience and the other that generally was a negative one. In each case, focus on the leadership of the group and consider the following questions:

1. *How did the group leader contribute to the nature of the experience?*

   In the generally positive group:
   In the generally negative group:

2. *What specifically did the leader do?*

   In the generally positive group:
   In the generally negative group:

3. *What do you conclude from your analysis?*

---

conducted with 210 Stanford University students enrolled in an experimental course called Race and Prejudice, during the latter 1960s, so you will want to keep that context in mind. As well, it is timely to observe that research in this important area of group leader functions and styles urgently needs updating; see Bauman (2011) for several useful recommendations, one of which is to be able to more concretely define these two essential aspects of group leadership and then to apply innovative research technologies.

Returning to the Lieberman et al. (1973) study, students were assigned to 18 groups for 30 hours of participation and a control group. The treatment groups were associated with 10 different types of encounter groups. Thumbnail descriptions of those orientations are (a) *T-group,* with attention to interpersonal and group-as-a-whole issues; (b) *gestalt therapy,* attending to body-mind connections and often using "hot seat" techniques; (c) *transactional analysis,* with parent–child–adult analysis in, not necessarily, with the group; (d) *Esalen electic,* which was highly experiential with an emphasis on both doing and experiencing; (e) *personal growth,* a "Western style T-group," with more emphasis on intra- and interpersonal dynamics; (f) *Synanon,* including expression of anger; (g) *psychodrama,* with emphasis on both role playing and psychodrama; (h) *marathon,* a high-intensity, time-extended approach; (i) *psychoanalytically oriented,* with attention to personal history; and (j) *encounter tapes,* the one instance where no human leadership was provided but where structured experiences were mediated though leaderless audio tapes. All group leaders used in the study were specifically chosen for their extensive group leading experience in the type of group they led and for the high level of esteem in which they were held by peers.

A number of important results were produced from this large study. One major outcome, which already had been suggested with regard to individual psychotherapy (e.g., Fiedler, 1950), and later refined by other scholars (Hubble, Duncan, & Miller, 1999; Wampold, 2001, 2010), was the theoretical stance followed by therapists that showed little association with client outcome. More important, for example, were the "common factors" characterizing the helping encounter, such as the quality of the working alliance and adherence to a therapeutic regimen. Similarly, with regard to group work leadership and member outcomes, study results indicated that it did not matter much if the leader followed one particular theoretical orientation or another. Rather, these results pointed to what group leaders did and how they did it to make the difference.

I highlight two sets of findings from Lieberman et al. (1973) and related studies, which are especially relevant for our present examination of what group work leaders do. These are (a) group leadership functions and (b) group leader styles and types.

Group leader functions. The functions that group work leaders perform can be thought of in different ways. For instance, Cohen, Ettin, and Fidler (1998) discussed what they termed generic work-group functions of leadership and their application to group psychotherapy. These generic functions include *nurturance* (e.g., provision of empathy), *protection* (e.g., ensuring a safe and confidential space), and *representation* (e.g., providing meaning making and healing). Lieberman, Yalom, and Miles' (1973) *empirically derived functions.* Perhaps the most well-known research of the practical issues of group leadership was conducted by Lieberman et al. (1973), which

I briefly discussed earlier. Among other findings, four major *group leader functions* were identified: (a) emotional stimulation (ES), (b) caring (C), (c) meaning attribution (MA), and (d) executive function (EF). These functions emerged from a factor analysis of 27 leader variables covering leader behavior (e.g., support, intrusive modeling), style (e.g., teacher, social engineer), focus (group, interpersonal, intrapersonal), and symbol (e.g., charisma, technical), accounting for 74% of the variance. The researchers claimed that the four functions "may constitute an empirically derived taxonomy for examining leadership in all forms of groups aimed at personal change, be they therapy or personal growth groups" (p. 235).

Now for some caveats to consider. As with all studies, this one is time and place bound. It was conducted in the late 1960s with college students at Stanford. This was a unique period and place in our history, marked by a high degree of experimentation in personal behavior and in environmental changes. Keep this particular context in mind as you consider the study's results.

Note that an empirical study by Tinsley, Roth, and Lease (1989) of group leadership styles failed to confirm these four functions, but it used a different methodology. Major findings of that study suggested that (a) group leader style can be viewed as being cognitive, affective, behavioral, or connected with nonverbal exercises; (b) group leader personal qualities emphasize nurturant attractiveness or charismatic expertness; and (c) group leader objectives revolve around group functioning and personal functioning. You may want to locate this study to see how it was conducted and to learn more about its findings, which generally are in agreement with those of Lieberman et al. (1973).

Another point for you to keep in mind is that the findings of the two studies mentioned do not necessarily extend to task groups. These studies focused on groups for personal growth and change.

So, returning to the Lieberman et al. (1973) study, as you read about the four leader functions and, later, about the six types of group leadership they form, I encourage you also to think about how they might best be used. Waldo (1985), for instance, indentified certain conditions to take into account, including the stage of a group's development, the expressed concerns of group members, the focus of the group, and the theoretical orientation of the group leader. Polcin (1991) suggested that the functions also might be used differentially according to the specific needs and the functional capacity of the group members, and the characteristics of the group or clinical setting. *These are sound points emphasizing, in general, the importance of these four functions (and any other group leader action) to be respectful of the group context.*

The four group leadership functions that emerged are described next.

Emotional stimulation (ES). This function involves catalytic group leader behaviors, where the leader challenges, confronts, exhorts, and can be intrusive. The intent is to stimulate, to instigate, to stir up, to activate processes and people. Emotional stimulation emphasizes release of member emotions through leader demonstration. The leader is a risk taker, one who is actively involved with edging members to express themselves emotionally and directly in the group.

Caring (C). This function involves warm, supportive, and encouraging group leader behaviors. Group leaders high on this function are perceived as being open and kind, warm and supportive, understanding and genuine. They would rank high on the Rogerian conditions you know about from person-centered counseling. These leaders occupy the opposite pole from using technical, expert-based efficiency.

Meaning attribution (MA). This function involves cognitizing behavior, where the group leader helps members to understand their experience, to translate experiencing into learning. Leaders using meaning attribution explain, clarify, interpret, and they provide cognitive frameworks to guide how to go about the process of change and learning. Meaning attribution is the "naming" function of leader behaviors, where member behavior and feelings are transmuted into personal meaning (personal meaning attribution), or in terms of learning about the group itself (group meaning attribution).

Executive function (EF). This function involves the group leader in managing the group as a social system, serving as a kind of orchestra conductor or movie director. Executive functioning includes such group leader behaviors as setting rules and limits, managing time, blocking, sequencing, pacing, suggesting ways to move forward, and introducing structured exercises. Use of this function does not tap into making interpretations or catalyzing, or making strong emotional connections with members. Its emphasis is on managing the group and its members.

Figure 7–1 summarizes some leader behaviors associated with each of these functions. The following Learning Exercise 7-3 permits you to do some self assessment of group leadership functions.

Lieberman and Golant (2002) and meaningful group processes. Following up on the Lieberman et al. (1973) project, these researchers studied group leader behaviors as perceived by cancer patients in support groups that were led professionally. Five dimensions of group leadership were identified that were very similar, over, to those of the Lieberman et al. (1973) study we have been focusing on (a) *evoke-stimulate,* similar to the emotional stimulation function; (b) *executive-management,* similar to executive function; (c) *meaning attribution;* (d) *support-caring,* similar to the caring function;

Figure 7.1   Group Leader Functions and Some Sample Behaviors

Emotional Stimulation	Caring	Meaning Attribution	Executive Function
Challenging Confronting Releasing strong emotion Intrusive modeling Catalyzing interaction	Accepting Understanding Supporting Modeling warmth Developing intimate relationships	Reflecting Interpreting Explaining Labeling Linking	Gatekeeping Setting standards Giving directions Blocking Directing traffic

Learning Exercise 7–3:
A Group Leadership Functions Activity

This learning exercise was adapted from Conyne (1975).
Objects

1. To explore four basic leadership functions of group leaders

2. To study the relationship between leadership functions and general interpersonal style

Group Size
   An unlimited number of groups of three to five members each
Time Required
   Adjustable, 1 hour to 2 hours

Materials

1. A copy of the following for each participant: Group Leadership Functions Scale, Group Leadership Functions Interpretation Sheet, and Group Leadership Functions Situations Sheet

2. Pencils

Physical Setting
   A room large enough to allow subgroups to engage in simultaneous, undistracted discussions

(Continued)

(Continued)

Process

1. The facilitator discusses the objectives of the experience (5 minutes).

2. The Group Leadership Functions Scale is completed by all participants. The facilitator directs the scoring of the scale by distributing the Group Leadership Functions Interpretation Sheet and answering any questions (5 minutes).

3. The facilitator discusses the four leadership functions (10 minutes).

4. The facilitator obtains group score tallies by asking for a show of hands for high, medium, and low scores on each subscale (5 minutes).

5. The facilitator leads a discussion of the group norms (5 minutes).

6. Groups of three to five are formed. The Group Leadership Functions Situations Sheet is distributed and each group is asked to choose one situation on which to focus.

7. Group members apply the guidelines to the selected case situation (15 minutes).

8. The facilitator directs a discussion of reactions and learning in the activity. Particular attention is given to the relationship between group leadership functions and general interpersonal style (15 minutes).

Variations

1. Depending on the time available, each group can be assigned one or more situations to role-play, each illustrating one of the group leadership functions.

2. Persons with similar or dissimilar profiles can be paired to discuss the possible problems that they may encounter when acting as coleaders.

Group Leadership Functions Questionnaire

Instructions: Respond to each of the following items with respect to your general and actual interpersonal behavior effectiveness. Consider the entire 1 to 7 scale for each item.

(Continued)

Choose or do both: As the leader of a *therapeutic* group, I . . .

	Very Low		Moderate			Very High	
1. reveal my feelings to others	1	2	3	4	5	6	7
2. show understanding of others	1	2	3	4	5	6	7
3. clarify others' feelings	1	2	3	4	5	6	7
4. suggest or set limits	1	2	3	4	5	6	7
5. offer my friendship to others	1	2	3	4	5	6	7
6. challenge others' behavior	1	2	3	4	5	6	7
7. conceptualize ideas	1	2	3	4	5	6	7
8. elicit others' reactions	1	2	3	4	5	6	7
9. manage my time and that of others	1	2	3	4	5	6	7
10. confront others	1	2	3	4	5	6	7
11. interpret others' statements	1	2	3	4	5	6	7
12. praise others	1	2	3	4	5	6	7
13. accept others	1	2	3	4	5	6	7
14. encourage or urge others	1	2	3	4	5	6	7
15. manage activities involving others	1	2	3	4	5	6	7
16. explain situations involving others	1	2	3	4	5	6	7
17. participate actively with others	1	2	3	4	5	6	7
18. question others	1	2	3	4	5	6	7
19. give emotionally to others	1	2	3	4	5	6	7

(Continued)

(Continued)

	Very Low		Moderate			Very High	
20. summarize others' statements	1	2	3	4	5	6	7
21. suggest procedures	1	2	3	4	5	6	7
22. am genuine with others	1	2	3	4	5	6	7
23. take risks with others	1	2	3	4	5	6	7
24. translate behavior to ideas	1	2	3	4	5	6	7
25. develop close relationships with others	1	2	3	4	5	6	7
26. deal with decision making	1	2	3	4	5	6	7
27. help others understand their experience	1	2	3	4	5	6	7
28. inspire others	1	2	3	4	5	6	7

Leader Functions

Emotional Stimulation (ES): Challenging, confronting, intrusive leadership, catalytic
Caring (C): Warm, supportive, personal relationships
Meaning Attribution (MA): Translating feelings and behavior into ideas
Executive Function (EF): "Movie director," sets limits, pacing, sequencing, keeps time

Scoring

ES: Items 1 + 6 + 10 + 14 + 17 + 23 + 28 = _____
C: Items 2 + 5 + 12 + 13 + 19 + 22 + 25 = _____
MA: Items 3 + 7 + 11 + 16 + 20 + 24 + 27 = _____
EF: Items 4 + 8 + 9 + 15 + 18 + 21 + 26 = _____

Score Inerpretation

High: More than 41
Medium: 15–41
Low: Less than 15

(Continued)

Group Leadership Functions Situations

Recurring Problem Situations in Groups

1. *Silent member:* The group has been meeting weekly for 8 weeks. You have been observing that one of the nine members is not actively participating. In fact, she might be termed a "silent member." The general trust level among members appears high, and the group members seem to be functioning well. What leadership functions might you use?

2. *Hidden agendas:* The group has met twice. The first session was characterized by uncomfortable feelings, tentative behavior, and uncertainty. The second session felt dull, listless, and blocked. You hypothesize that some issues are unmet, unattended to, but present (hidden agendas). What leadership functions might you use?

3. *Termination:* The group has met for 10 sessions, and 2 more are scheduled before termination. The prospect of ending seems to be affecting the current behavior of all the members, as evidenced by retreating and withdrawing. What leadership functions might you use?

4. *Aggressive member:* During the first three group sessions, a member has consistently interrupted in aggressive hostile ways. He has been highly verbal and demanding, while also being extremely critical and judgmental of others, including you. What leadership functions might you use?

5. *Power and control:* The first six sessions of the group have resulted in a power distribution among the members that to you seems unbalanced and dysfunctional. You wonder whether other members share these observations and reactions. What leadership functions might you use?

Guidelines for Each Example:

1. Assume that you are cofacilitating a therapeutic group (e.g., counseling, psychoeducation, therapy) or another group aimed at personal and interpersonal growth or change.

2. Try to "flesh out" each situational example in your group so that you can relate to it from a common perspective.

3. Write your own responses to the situations.

4. When all members of your subgroup have finished, share these responses, considering alternatives.

and (e) *use of self,* to participate as a member in the here-and-now using self-disclosure. These researchers found that the leadership functions contributing most to positive outcomes were executive-management and meaning attribution. In a later study, this time involving online groups, Lieberman (2008) replicated these findings.

Perhaps of more importance, both of these studies suggested that *meaningful experiences in the group,* such as support and disclosure that may be generated, mediated between group leader skills and outcomes. That is, it may be that a group leader's effect on participant outcomes may be more indirect than direct, tending to occur through positive processes that are generated within the group. This possibility seems consistent with other research attesting to the value of group leaders working with members to create mechanisms for change (e.g., therapeutic factors, therapeutic alliance) and key processes, such as positive group climate (Kivlighan et al., 2011; Marmarosh & Van Horn, 2011; McClendon & Burlingame, 2011; Harel, Shechtman, & Cutrona, 2011). Shechtman and Toren (2009) examined the effects of leader behavior on processes and outcomes, finding in their group counseling study with 205 master's-level students in counseling, psychology and continuing education programs that meaning attribution and support were leader functions most affecting group process and outcome variables.

Other group leader functions. Others have analyzed what group leaders do, resulting in varying functions. The work of Cohen et al. (1998) was cited earlier. For another example, take a look at those from Trotzer (2006): (a) promoting interaction, (b) facilitating interaction, (c) initiating interaction, (d) guiding interaction, (e) intervening, (f) rules keeping, (g) consolidating, (h) enhancing communication, (i) resolving conflicts, and (j) mobilizing group resources. I describe the first four of these functions next; the remaining ones are addressed later when we discuss group leader skills.

Promoting, facilitating, initiating, and guiding interaction. A productive group is dependent on the presence of positive and active member participation. Another way to say this is that the action of a group is found in its interaction. Therefore, group leaders need to be fixed on productive member interaction and on how to develop and sustain it.

When group leaders *promote and facilitate* interaction, they work with members to establish positive therapeutic conditions and a safe and challenging working climate. They tend to de-emphasize their own central position in the group, choosing instead to maximize the visibility and stature of members. They foster exchanges among members and positively reinforce their continuation, such that strong bonds develop amid a network of connections. They are inclusive, respectful of differences, and seek to empower members.

When group leaders *initiate* interaction, they stimulate member involvement by introducing structured exercises aimed at getting members actively involved, by concretely inviting members to engage, and by modeling desired behaviors for members to consider trying. This function is an active one, similar to the emotional stimulation function of Lieberman et al. (1973) discussed earlier and geared toward group leaders reaching out to members to actively engage them in group activities.

When group leaders *guide* interaction, they are helping to "keep the train on track." This function is similar to the executive function of Lieberman et al. (1973), discussed earlier. They question, draw out, set tone, stop action, and otherwise help to actively shape positive member interaction.

Group leader styles. Fiedler's (e.g., 1996) contingency model of leadership posits that success depends on matching a leader's personal characteristics and motivational style with the demands of the group situation. This conception of leadership particularizes the general ecological model suggested by Lewin (1936): Behavior is a function of Persons interacting with the Environment, or B = f(PXE). With regard to group work, while the characteristics of both the group leader and group members (e.g., personality and life history) and the group environment (e.g., group climate and contextual issues, such as support of the agency sponsoring the group) are important, it is their *interaction* and resulting effects that matter most (Bemak & Conyne, 2004; Conyne & Cook, 2004; Cook, 2012).

Three approaches to leadership styles are summarized in this section: (a) autocrat, democrat, laissez-faire; (b) task versus relationships; and (c) leadership types.

Autocrat, democrat, laissez-faire. As you learned in Chapter 5, one way of understanding leadership styles is found in the degree to which a leader behaves *autocratically, democratically,* or in a *laissez-faire* manner (Lewin, Lippitt, & White, 1939). In the autocratic style, a group leader tends toward controlling the action, making decisions, and setting rules. A democratic style finds a leader tending to equalize relationships, share power and influences, and value collaboration with members. In a laissez-faire style, a leader tends to allow members freedom to participate and make decisions, without providing guidance.

Tasks vs. personal relationships. Another group leadership style is connected with how strongly a leader emphasizes tasks or relationships in the group (e.g., Lord, 1977, in Forsyth, 2009, p. 252). As we have seen, a leader with a task style tends toward being goal directed, with a focus on work. A leader with a relationships style tends toward providing personal and interpersonal support, places a high value on relationships among members, and elevates group maintenance.

An effective group leader style requires an appropriate balancing of these two dimensions that alter in relation to different situations in the group. That is, group leaders need to be able to assist group members to handle effectively the tasks that emerge, such as clarifying responsibilities and planning action steps; they also must be able to assist the personal and interpersonal interactions in the group, such as by listening and reducing conflict.

The *Leadership Grid* (Blake & Mouton, 1982) identifies five different leadership styles, each of which is dependent on the degree to which a leader is concerned with people versus results. They suggest that the best leaders score high on both of these dimensions; that is, their leadership behavior equally values people and product.

In a related approach, the *Situational Leadership* model (Hersey, Blanchard, & Johnson, 2001) also views leadership through the lens of relationship and task dimensions. In this approach, leaders match combinations of directive and supportive behaviors with the developing maturity level of the group. Four leadership styles emerge: (a) directing style (high directive, low supportive) appropriate early in a group's development; (b) coaching style (high directive, high supportive) appropriate when a group is beginning to gel; (c) supporting style (high supportive, low directive), appropriate when a group is maturing in its functioning; and (d) delegating style (low supportive, low directive), appropriate for a mature group that is largely able to function relying on its own resources. Therefore, what developmental stage the group finds itself in (e.g., beginning, middle, and end—just to keep it simple) sets a context for how much attention might be placed on tasks and how much on personal relations. More about group development will be presented in the next chapter.

Group leader types. I spend more space examining the six types of leadership that were identified by Lieberman et al. (1973) in the landmark study I have been referencing. Recall reading about the four leadership functions of emotional stimulation (ES), caring (C), meaning attribution (MA), and executive function (EF) that emerged from this study and what you took away from Learning Exercise 5–3. Further statistical analysis of these four functions produced a typology of six uniquely different leader types. Each type is composed of clusters of functions, which I describe next.

Type A: Energizers. Energizers are most clearly indicated by a style that is high in intense emotional stimulation. They also tend to include moderate to high amounts of executive function and caring. These leaders were viewed as being the most charismatic.

Type B: Providers. Providers are high in caring and in meaning attribution with moderate use of emotional stimulation and executive function. These leaders provide frameworks for change within a supportive and caring style.

Type C: Social engineers. These group leaders exhibited high amounts of group-oriented meaning attribution along with a moderate amount of caring and low emotional stimulation. The amount of executive function showed varied from low to high. They are focused primarily on the group and how members relate to its social system.

Type D: Impersonals. These group leaders demonstrated moderately high emotional stimulation with low amounts of caring, executive function, and meaning attribution. They were described as being "distant, aggressive stimulators" (Lieberman et al., 1973, p. 244).

Type E: Laissez-Faires. These group leaders showed elevation only on meaning attribution, which ranged from moderate to high. They tended to be generalists who provided some understanding of how members learn but with no discernible support from the other leadership functions; thus, these leaders did not offer support, did not stimulate, and did not guide.

Type F: Managers. These group leaders notched very high scores on executive function with low amounts of the other functions, leading observers to label the style as "Top Sergeant" (p. 244).

How did these different group leader types fare in terms of producing positive outcomes (learning, change) while keeping negative ones (dropouts, casualties) to a minimum? The *Provider* type generated the largest overall yields with the least harmful results. *The Social Engineers* produced positive learning with low negative outcomes. *Energizers* produced some high learners and many moderate changers, but also a high number of drop outs and casualties. The *Impersonal, Laissez-faire,* and *Manager* types trailed far behind. The *Manager* type clearly was the poorest performing style, with no high learners or moderate changers, and with some negative outcomes.

This research study suggests that group leaders who demonstrate continual caring for members while helping them to make meaning of their experience in the group possess key aspects of the "right stuff" of good group leadership. These functions, when accompanied by the capacity to manage the group well and to stir members to become actively engaged, cluster to yield the Provider leader type. There is enough energy generated within a properly managed group environment, all suffused with caring and helping members to learn from their experience.

Learning Exercise 7–4 will assist your understanding of leader types.

Learning Exercise 7–5 asks you to self-assess, which is a very important ongoing activity for group workers.

Group Leader Competencies

Now that we have considered the functions and styles of group leaders, let's drill down a bit deeper to think about group leader core competencies. These core competencies establish a common platform of proficiency.

Learning Exercise 7–4:
Avi's Test: Match Functions With Types

The **object** of this learning exercise is to help you connect group leader functions with group leader styles.

1. Avi is taking a test in his Group Work Introduction course. See if you can correctly answer the matching questions he was asked by drawing lines connecting leader *functions* (Column A items) with group leader *types* (Column B items):

Column A (Functions)	Column B (Types)
High emotional stimulation	Social Engineers
High executive function	Providers
"Distant and aggressive"	Energizers
High caring and meaning attribution	Managers
Low caring, meaning attribution, executive function	Laissez-Faires
High meaning attribution (group-oriented)	Impersonals

2. Compare your pairings with another student and confirm the correct answers.

Learning Exercise 7–5:
Assessing the "Provider" Type and Yourself

The **object** of this learning exercise is to better understand what leader functions comprise the Provider type and then to self-assess.

You've read that the Provider is the group leader type most clearly associated with group member positive outcomes while minimizing negative ones.

1. Indicate the pattern of leader functions associated with a Provider type.

2. Self-assess: Analyze where you stand presently in relation to the Provider type.

(Continued)

3. How might you try to strengthen your "Provider orientation"?

4. Use the following layout to complete this exercise:

List the pattern of Provider functions.
Self-assess yourself in relation to the Provider pattern (circle one):
OK   Needs Improving

Describe what seems to be working and what may need to be further developed:
(Note that other leader types—for example, Social Engineer, Energizer—also are associated with certain positive benefits for members. The point here is not to try to force yourself into the Provider type but to recognize that its pattern of functions clearly is worth emulating).

Erected upon that platform are the more advanced structures of group leader functions and styles, just discussed, and then methods and strategies, which are taken up in the next chapter.

The relationships among core competencies, functions, styles, methods, and strategies look like the following, as Figure 7–2:

Figure 7.2   Core Competencies, Functions, Types, Methods, Strategies, and Techniques

*The **object** of the content in this figure is to show the progression of key elements of group work leadership, beginning with core competencies.*

STRATEGIES & TECHNIQUES
METHODS
TYPES
FUNCTIONS
CORE COMPETENCIES

What, then, are the core knowledge and skills that leaders of all kinds of groups need to possess? Let's begin by taking a look at Learning Exercise 7-6. Especially note the opportunity for giving and getting feedback.

Learning Exercise 7–6: Tom's Group Visits yalOMMM, the Group Guru With Feedback

*The **object** of this learning exercise is to identify core group work skills and to give and get feedback.*

Tom knew deep down in his bones that he wanted to be a professional helper, either a counselor, a psychologist, a social worker . . . More than that, he felt a calling to help people through groups. He loved all kinds of groups and, in fact, had even been a member of three different counseling groups in the last 2 years. In many ways, Tom saw himself as a seeker, one who had a voracious appetite to learn about himself, others, and the whole wide world.

He supposed that's why he was right now climbing Mt. Grouperama, the highest and most sacred spot on earth devoted to group work. Of course, he was climbing with a small group, not alone, and everyone was super excited about reaching the summit, where—if they were very fortunate—they could have an audience with the revered "Group Guru," known cryptically as yalOMMM.

Finally arriving at the peak, Tom's small group was led to yalOMMM, who was sitting in a group circle of members. As the designated group spokesperson, Tom asked, "yalOMMM, what are the mysteries of outstanding group leadership?"

"Why," yalOMMM quickly replied, directly and simply, "There are no mysteries, my good man. All group leaders must have basic *skills*— at the least. It's up to you to find them."

Maybe too cryptic, you say? Well, try filling in what the guru did not. What kinds of basic skills do you think are necessary for all group leaders?

1. List five such core skills below.

2. Assess your competency presently with each skill using the 5-point scale provided (where "1" = Lacking, "2" = Pretty good, "3" = Average, "4" = Above Average, and "5" = Excellent)

3. Compare and discuss the skills and your self-assessment with another student or reader

4. Request feedback from the other person:

    a. How accurate is my self assessment of each skill?
    b. What might I do to further develop?

(Continued)

1. **SKILL AREAS**   2. **SELF ASSESSMENT**

a. _____   1 2 3 4 5
b. _____   1 2 3 4 5
c. _____   1 2 3 4 5
d. _____   1 2 3 4 5
e. _____   1 2 3 4 5

3. **Assess and compare:** Compare your list with another person. Note and discuss any similarities and differences.

4. **Request feedback** from the other person.

    a. ASK: "How accurate is my self-assessment of each skill?"
    b. ASK: "What might I do to further develop each skill?"

Various lists of core group leading skills and competencies have been developed. I draw from two sources: (a) the *Core Group Work Skills Inventory—Importance and Confidence (CGWSI-IC;* Wilson, Newmeyer, Rapin, & Conyne, 2007) and (b) *Basic skills for group leaders,* as suggested by Jacobs, Masson, Harvill, and Schimmel (2012).

Core Group Work Skills: The *Core Group Work Skills Inventory-Importance and Confidence (CGWSI-IC).*The *CGWSI-IC* contains 27 items, each of which describes a behavior that pertains to group member or group leader effectiveness.The inventory is intended to be a content valid measure of how respondents view the ASGW core group work knowledge and skill competencies, the degree to which they think the competencies are important, and how confident respondents are in their ability to apply them.This inventory and a description of its development and psychometric properties can be viewed at the ASGW website (www.asgw.org), with further explanation found at Wilson and Newmeyer (2008).

Core group work knowledge and skills contained in the *CGWSI-IC* are the following:

1. Evidences ethical practice in group membership or leadership

2. Evidences best practice in group membership or leadership

3. Evidences diversity competent practice in group membership or leadership

4. Develops a plan for group leadership activities

5. Seeks good fit between group plans and group member's life context

6. Gives feedback to group members

7. Requests feedback from group members

8. Works cooperatively with a coleader

9. Identifies group process

10. Works collaboratively with group members

11. Encourages participation of group members

12. Responds empathically to group member behavior

13. Responds empathically to group process themes

14. Keeps a group on task

15. Requests information from group members

16. Requests disclosure of opinions and feelings from group members

17. Provides information to group members

18. Discloses opinions and feelings to group members

19. Assesses group functioning

20. Identifies personal characteristics of individual members of the group

21. Develops hypotheses about the behavior of group members

22. Develops overarching purpose and sets goals/objectives for the group, as well as method for determining outcomes

23. Employs contextual factors in interpreting individual and group behavior

24. Conducts evaluation of one's leadership style

25. Engages in self-evaluation of personally selected performance goals

26. Contributes to evaluation activities during group processing

27. Provides appropriate self-disclosure

Note that these knowledge and skills are not "owned" by group leaders. Many of them also are appropriate for use by group members. This observation highlights one of the unique features of group work: It's an endeavor where the designated group leader(s) and the group members *work together* to solve problems and create change.

Let's take just one of the skills, #6, "Gives feedback to group members," as an example. Stephanie, who's been a member of the therapy group for 3 months, has been noticing that another member, Jose, consistently avoids eye contact with other group members. She decides to act on her observation and says to him, "Jose, can I say something to you?" (Jose nods yes.) "Okay," she says, "I've noticed over our many sessions that you usually don't look at us, you look down at the floor most often. I wonder what's goin' on?" Now, the group leader might have provided this feedback, as well, but sometimes group members can engage with others in ways that can be even more effective than leaders. Peer influence is not to be underestimated, for good or ill, but when employed appropriately it can be positive and powerful. And, to repeat, most of these group leading core competencies (with some exceptions, such as those in Items 4, 5, 8, 22, and 24) are available for appropriate use by group leaders and group members, alike.

Learning Exercise 7–7 gives you the chance to apply two of the core group work competencies.

Learning Exercise 7–7:
Using Group Work Core Competencies

Object: To develop an understanding of using CGWSI-IC competencies in group practice.
Instructions

1. Refer to the example on page 199 where one group member, Stephanie, gives feedback to another group member, Jose, demonstrating CGWSI-IC #6.

2. Develop a similar case scenario that illustrates a group leader keeping a group on task (CGWSI-IC #14). In your case, provide background on the type of group, any relevant history from previous group sessions, and dialogue.

3. After developing your scenario, compare with a partner. Some questions to consider discussing with your partner: How effectively did the leader handle the situation? Would it be appropriate if a group *member* had responded instead of the group leader? Why or why not? What are some other ways the group leader could have kept the group on task?

(Continued)

(Continued)

4. Develop another case scenario that illustrates a group member providing appropriate self-disclosure (CGWSI-IC #27). In your case, provide background on the type of group, any relevant history from previous group sessions, and dialogue.

5. After developing your scenario, compare with a partner. Some questions to consider discussing with your partner: How appropriate was the member's disclosure? Would it be appropriate if a group *leader* had similarly self-disclosed instead of the group member? Why or why not?

Item 14: *Keeps a group on task,* by a group *leader.*
Item 27: *Provides appropriate self-disclosure,* by a group *member.*
When you are done, spend 10 minutes discussing your work with a partner.

Another perspective: Basic skills for group leaders. Group work authors (e.g., Corey, 2012; Gladding, 2011b; Jacobs et al., 2012) have been examining and writing about group leading skills and strategies for decades. As a sample, I draw primarily from how Jacobs et al. enumerate what they term "basic skills for group leaders." As they put it, some of these skills are common human relations skills, while others become developed through specialized training.

These *basic skills for group leaders,* with a brief definition for each, follow.

Active listening: Listening to all aspects of a group member's message and communicating that you are following

Reflecting: Communicating content and affect you are receiving from a group member's message

Clarifying and questioning: Checking with a group member to be sure you are getting it right

Linking: Connecting the nugget of different members' messages or a key aspect of where those messages may vary

Summarizing: Pulling together a theme occurring in a group discussion

Mini-lecturing and information giving: Presenting timely information to members in an interesting, relevant, and engaging way

Encouraging and supporting: Inspiring hope in members by modeling optimism and supporting their efforts to interact and connect with others

Tone setting: Promoting a positive group climate through its physical and psychological environment

Modeling and self-disclosure: Demonstrating qualities to be emulated (such as trustworthiness) and sharing personal information appropriately

Using eyes: Scanning for nonverbal cues, drawing out members, encouraging members to look directly at other members, and cutting off interactions that are not working

Using voice: Helping to set the tone, energize, or pace the group

Using energy: Conveying enthusiasm and high interest in members and the group

Identifying allies: Learning which members might be especially helpful and cooperative

Multicultural understanding: All leader behavior needs to be mediated by multicultural sensitivity because cultural differences can strongly affect group participation.

As I mentioned earlier, other exemplary compilations of group leading skills have been presented by Corey (2012), Gladding (2011b), and Trotzer (2006). Each has its own special merits, and I refer you to those sources. Trotzer, for instance, helpfully organizes group leadership skills within three large categories: (a) *action skills* (e.g., self-disclosure, confronting), (b) *reaction skills* (e.g., active listening and reflecting), and (c) *interaction skills* (e.g., linking and blocking).

The chapter content emphasizing foundation elements of group leadership, or its building blocks—the functions, styles, and competencies we have considered—may seem a bit bewildering, at first. I'm hopeful, as in all chapters, the case illustrations and learning exercises contained will help you to better organize and make sense of the information. Rest assured, as you practice delivering these action steps and receive feedback about your work you will develop the confidence and competence you need to become a good group leader—one whose actions, recalling the words of President

J. Q. Adams that opened this chapter, "inspire others to dream more, learn more, do more, and become more."

● GROUP WORK KEYSTONES

- Functions, styles, and competencies were identified as the *building blocks* of group leadership. These elements are the primary modes for delivering group leadership and for how group leaders can promote learning, growth, and change.
- Leadership studies (e.g., Lewin et al., 1939) contribute to understandings of group work leadership.
- Four group leader functions, each comprised of skills, were described.
- Group leader styles have been defined in different ways, including (but not limited to) attention to task or to personal relations; autocratic, democratic, or laissez-faire orientation; and leader types.

RECOMMENDED RESOURCES

Bauman, S. (2011). Group leader styles and functions. In R. Conyne (Ed.), *The Oxford handbook of group counseling* (pp. 325–345). New York, NY: Oxford University Press.

Blake, R., & Mouton, J. (1982). How to choose a leadership style. *Training and Development Journal, 36,* 39–46.

Fiedler, F. (1996). Research on leadership selection and training: One view of the future. *Administrative Science Quarterly, 41,* 241–250.

Hersey, P., & Blanchard, K., & Johnson, D. (2001). *Management of organizational behavior: Leading human resources* (8th ed.). Upper Saddle River, NJ: Prentice Hall.

Lieberman, M., Yalom, I., & Miles, M. (1973). *Encounter groups: First facts.* New York, NY: Basic Books.

Tinsley, H., Roth, J., & Lease, S. (1989). *Journal of Counseling Psychology, 36,* 48–53.

Wilson, F. R., Newmeyer, M., Rapin, L., & Conyne, R. (2007). *Core Group Work Skills Inventory-Importance and Confidence (CGWSI-IC).* Alexandria, VA: Association for Specialists in Group Work.

Wilson, F. R., & Newmeyer, M. (2008). A standards-based inventory for assessing perceived importance of a confidence in using ASGW's core group work skills. *Journal for Specialists in Group Work, 33,* 270–289. doi: 10.1080/01933920802196146

CHAPTER 8

GROUP WORK METHODS, STRATEGIES, AND TECHNIQUES

The more you know about where you're going, the closer you are to being there.

—Craig (1978)

Thinking is easy, acting is difficult, and to put one's thoughts into action is the most difficult thing in the world.

—J. W. von Goethe

INTRODUCTION ●

This chapter considers methods involved in group work leadership. It builds on the preceding chapter that focused on the building blocks supporting group leadership: its core competencies, leader functions, and leader styles. *Methods* in group work leadership represent blueprints for action, consistent with Dorothy Craig's quote above. They are the application ideas guiding action. *Strategies and techniques* are action tools that are used to implement plans for action, as Goethe's quote above suggests. Strategies and techniques are used to focus on thoughts and feelings, on interpersonal and group interaction, and on group processes; they also are used to accentuate thoughts and feelings and to provide opportunities for learning and its transfer outside the group. We examine these areas in this chapter.

CHAPTER OBJECTIVES

As a result of reading this chapter you will be able to

- Better understand group work methods, strategies, and techniques
- Highlight 10 examples of generic methods in group work leadership
- Identify and discuss five strategies and techniques
- Get guided experience in further developing your group skills
- Conclude by referencing a number of useful group work resources

● GROUP LEADER *METHODS:* BLUEPRINTS GUIDING ACTION

In many ways, methods are consistent with *best practices,* which you read about in Chapter 2, and with major aspects of the general definition of group leadership itself that you considered in Chapter 5. (Note: You may want to refer to those chapters for a refresher.) The *methods* of group work leadership depend on those building blocks, but they are more complex and overarching. If competencies, for instance, might be thought of as representing one type of building block, then methods represent *blueprints for action* that provide guidance for use. Examples include protecting group members and promoting safety, energizing and involving group members, and assisting group members to make sense of their experience (Morran, Stockton, & Whittingham, 2004). These intentional blueprints, however, are neither carved in stone nor written in sand. While firmly held, they are subject to reasonable adaptation, responsive to changing circumstances.

Ten Examples of Methods

What might be some examples of generic methods in group work leadership? These are considered to be *generic* because they tend to cut across most theoretical approaches and accommodate a wide variety of groups.

Take a look at the list of 10 examples of generic methods that I have culled from the professional literature and that are summarized in Figure 8–1. These include the following: (a) draw from one's personhood; (b) consider context; (c) be intentional; (d) be creative and spontaneous; (e) be guided by a group development framework; (f) facilitate connection and interaction; (g) build cohesion; (h) create and use therapeutic factors; (i) endorse diversity, multiculturalism, and social justice; and (j) draw from and appropriately adapt evidence-based practice when possible.

Figure 8–1   List of 10 Examples of Generic Methods

a. Draw from one's "personhood" as a group leader.

b. Ground group leadership in context.

c. Be intentional.

d. Be creative and spontaneous.

e. Be guided by a group development framework.

g. Facilitate connection and interaction among members.

h. Build cohesion.

i. Create and use therapeutic factors.

j. Endorse diversity, multiculturalism, and social justice.

k. Draw from and appropriately adapt evidence-based approaches when possible.

Other examples of generic methods could be listed (e.g., to collaborate with members). You might have some personal "favorites" as well, because what methods are adopted reflects, in part, one's personal theory and approach to group work leadership. A method I especially value, for instance, is the importance of processing experiences and events that occur in a group.

Draw from one's own "personhood" as a group leader (Corey, Corey, & Corey, 2010; Trotzer, 2011). According to Trotzer (2011), *personhood* is the "thread that connects and weaves together personal development and professional development in the fabric of professional practice" (p. 302). And, as Corey et al. (2010) put it, "In our view, the counselor as a person is one of the most significant variables influencing the group's success or failure" (p. 30). Theory, methods, competencies, strategies, and techniques (and supervision) all play a vital role in the training and practice of a group work leader. Yet who you are as a person—combined with who you are as a person with others—may be the single most important ingredient. See Learning Exercise 8-1.

Learning Exercise 8–1: What's the Big Deal About Personhood, Anyway?

*The **object** of the learning experience is to deepen your understanding of what is sometimes referred to as the "personhood" of a group leader.*

(Continued)

(Continued)

You're out socializing with a good friend who happens to be getting his doctorate in physics. He's explaining, for what must be the sixth time, the essential thesis of his research in some aspect of quantum theory. Not that you are clueless, but it really does seem to be quite complicated; "essential" is how your friend puts it.

Well, okay, maybe so.

The conversation lags for a while, and then he says, "I've been trying to explain something really important in physics to you, but let's turn it. You talk a lot about groups and all that. So, what's the essential part of being a good group leader, or whatever you may call it?"

Hmmm, you think to yourself, good question. You've come to believe that it's the so-called personhood of the group leader that stands out, among many other factors. But talking about that seems *so* trivial, especially in light of the quantum theory presentation.

But, is it? What's the big deal about personhood, anyway?

Try this:

1. Put your understanding of what is meant by the personhood of a group leader in your own words. Try to capture its essential nature. Write what you might say about the personhood of the group work leader below:

   _____

   _____

   _____

2. Team up with a partner. Ask your partner to bring some disbelief about the idea that personhood could be important in group work leadership. See if you might be able to shift his or her ideas.

Some aspects of personhood. You already know from reading about best practices (Chapter 2) that it is very important for a group leader to be self-aware of values, attitudes, interests, personality, interpersonal impact, and other characteristics. Why is this so? Because, in a very real way, *you and the kinds of relationships you are able to create and sustain,* even more than what you know, or the skills and techniques you have mastered, are your primary instrument of change in a group. Who you are—trustworthy or not;

caring or not; challenging or not, and so on—sets the stage for what you do and how you do it.

Next are just three (of many) separate personhood characteristics (Corey et al., 2010; Trotzer, 2006) that can be significant: presence, flexibility, and openness.

Presence. Consider sitting by yourself in a restaurant waiting for your order. Across the way enters two people, seemingly a happy couple, holding hands while laughing and talking as they approach their table. They sit. All of a sudden, it seems, they stop conversing or gazing at each other. Rather, they both quickly grasp what appears to be their smart phones and begin texting vigorously. This parallel texting continues after your meal arrives and until you are asked by the server about dessert. You know this, because you're amazed by the fact that, although they came in together, they seem not be present to one another but to be totally engaged in texting. Sadly (in my judgment), this kind of occurrence is not rare.

Now, don't turn on me. I recognize the value that social media contributes, with just one way being the connective capacity they can provide. However, we may be distancing ourselves without knowing it from *being present in the moment* through how we sometimes overuse the many social media that are available, especially when we choose attending to them over the person sitting across the table with us.

For group leaders, being present in the moment is critically important. Being observant of others, listening for obvious and subtle messages both verbal and nonverbal, being "tuned into" one's own affect. In these and many more ways, presence is invaluable.

Flexibility. You've heard of the maxim "My way or the highway." You've also heard of, maybe even known some, people who can be inexorably wishy-washy. To be flexible is to inhabit neither of those poles. Rather, it is to be able to assess situations and to adaptively adjust a course of planned action, if warranted, to best fit the present circumstance while providing the greatest opportunity for an effective and ethical outcome. Group leaders need to be principled, to enter sessions with a possible plan of action, but to be "field dependent," too. That is, they need to develop a capacity to scan the group environment and "read" it, integrating the information obtained with previous intentions to yield productive next steps. Group leaders do not force their way, nor do they simply go along with whatever anyone desires. They collaborate and adjust as needed to produce desirable ends in healthy ways.

Openness. Group leaders are not closed to themselves, to others, or to ideas. To the contrary, they are both sharing and receptive. That is, group leaders disclose sufficient and appropriate information about themselves to allow others to sense them as being both genuine and real, not as technical automatons who go through some set of prescribed motions. As well, they are genuinely inviting of others in the group to be themselves. They accept and respect others and listen carefully to what they have to say. This open stance, to themselves and to group members, promotes involvement and impetus for growth and change.

Ground group leadership in context (Bemak & Conyne, 2004; Stern, 1970). Any organism exists nestled within a series of influential contexts. Unless in the rare case of a hermit, most people live in relation to others and often within a larger community. A community is situated within successively larger rings of influence, such as a city, a state, and a nation. So it is with a group. A group is set within an organization or a community. It evolves according to rules and regulations that have been prescribed or have developed. Individual members interact with one another under the guidance of a group leader in order to gain desired outcomes that can be applied outside the group, with families, friends, or colleagues.

Moreover, the nature of a context is that it is a place of reciprocal influence. Group members influence one another, the physical setting of a group affects what can get accomplished (e.g., the temperature is too hot, too cold) and it, in turn, is impacted by members (e.g., chairs get moved), rules and norms guide behavior and are altered by behavior, the group evolves a healing culture (or fails to do so), network-based communication develops. Levels of influence interact mutually.

Group leaders who appreciate the contextual nature of the group can harness more of its potential power. In reality, this power can be found in the interdependence, interactions, and transactions occurring within and between levels: individuals with each other, subgroups with the whole group, using the group as a fulcrum for individual change and growth (and vice versa), transferring learning from the group to the outside, or bringing inputs from outside to the group.

Figure 8-2 depicts interdependence of group members, which is one aspect of context. Group leaders who concertedly try to help members become connected with one another contribute to growth opportunities.

Figure 8.2   A Context of Interconnection in Group

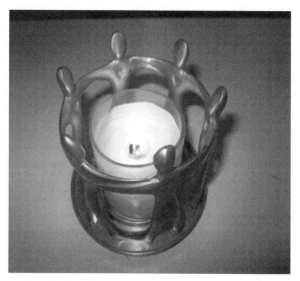

Source: Photograph by R. Conyne.

Be intentional (Cohen & Smith, 1976; Conyne, Crowell, & Newmeyer, 2008; Ivey, Ivey, & Zalaquett, 2009). When discussing the best practice of planning in Chapter 2, I mentioned that spontaneity in group leadership was a source of pride during the early years of group leading. I'm talking here about the 1960s into the early 1970s. This was due to two factors. First, the tenor of the times, its overarching context, if you will, lauded freedom, experiencing, and open personal expression. This was, after all, the time of "peace, love, and understanding," when encounter groups sprung up throughout our culture. Second, research and theory development in group work leadership lagged behind practice by many leagues. Group leaders were largely learning by doing in the meantime.

My reference to spontaneity in group leadership, tied to the time period I mentioned, takes on a particular meaning, closer to "flying by the seat of your pants." Absent supportive theory and research, and prior to the spread of training programs in group work, leaders were literally on their own, doing what came naturally.

Spontaneity, intuition, and creativity (see the following discussion) remain key methods in today's group leader's repertoire. However, research and theory development have shown over the ensuing decades that it also is necessary for *intentionality* to be added.

Intentionality in group work leadership is a complex method. First, groups need to be planned carefully. Except in certain unique circumstances, perhaps during a time of crisis, they should not "just happen." Context, member needs, goals, supportive theory, group developmental stage, methods, activities, anticipated outcomes, and more need to be carefully considered. Second, leaders need to consider and choose interventions during group sessions with care, becoming adept at weighing anticipated advantages and disadvantages of alternatives in real time. Third, how the group is proceeding over time, its process, needs to be evaluated, with information that is produced, are used to continue what is working and to modify what is not. Fourth, what members are gaining (or failing to achieve), their outcomes, also needs to be assessed. Fifth, careful processing of experience needs to be engaged in by members and by leaders; in the latter case, ongoing supervision is necessary and important.

Learning Exercise 8–2 provides a glimpse into the method of intentionality.

Learning Exercise 8–2: Weighing Group Leader Intervention Choices

The **object** of the learning exercise is to explore intentionality in group leader interventions by experimenting with a choice.

It's early in the sixth session of a 12-session counseling group. You notice that Tabitha, a member who has so far in the group presented as being quite timid and unreactive, uncharacteristically begins to fidget some in her seat and to wring her hands. Usually appearing to follow along conversations nonverbally by holding eye gaze, you observe that she now is either looking around the room, eyes darting, or avoiding looking at other members.

"What is causing Tabitha's change of behavior?" you wonder. Is it the subject of conversation, where Joe has been disclosing about his problems with women? Maybe this is touching off something in Tabitha's life history or present life circumstances? Did something unfortunate happen to her during the week that she is now suddenly recalling? Does she have something urgent that she needs to bring up in the group? Or wishes to avoid bringing up? What else could explain this?

"In any case, what should I do, if anything?" you ask yourself. Might I let it go for now, observing what evolves? Should I divert the discussion from

(Continued)

Joe to Tabitha, to give her room to say anything she needs to say? Might I try to catch her attention nonverbally by use of my eyes, to let her know I am aware something is going on, but not putting her on the spot? Might I look for a transition point to offer a group-level intervention, asking if anyone else in the group has any comments on Joe's situation, thus providing an open invitation that would include Tabitha but not single her out? Should I just speak directly to her, saying something like, "I notice, Tabitha, that you seem to be squirming a bit in your seat and I'm wondering if you might have something you would like to share with us?" What else?

Here is where you come in, remembering the method of intentionality. Given the preceding scenario,

1. Identify a possible cause for Tabitha's behavior.

2. Provide a supportive rationale.

3. Identify a possible leader intervention tied to the cause you identified, writing exactly how you would say it here: _____

_____

4. Provide a supportive rationale for your choice.

_____

Be creative and spontaneous (Gladding, 2011a, 2011c). You've just finished reading about the values of intentionality in group. But if everything in a group were done with intentionality as the sole method, a dull group likely would result, one that is tightly constructed and administered, but which wrenches out the creative spark. So, intentionality needs to be counterbalanced appropriately by spontaneity and the creative impulse. Spontaneity can energize action, while creativity invites novel and potentially useful results.

Recently, I toured the Cincinnati Museum of Art, and I was drawn to two particular abstract pieces and the commentaries that accompanied them, the latter of which follows:

"If a man [*sic*] is satisfied only with what he sees physically and cannot imagine creatively, he will stagnate."

—Ashile Gorky, comments in relation to his abstract painting *Virgina Landscape* (1944)

"Depth in a pictorial plastic sense is not created by arrangement of objects one after another towards a vanishing point, but on the contrary by the creation of forces of push and pull."

—Hans Hoffman, comments in relation to his painting *Toward Crepuscule* (1963)

While the two quotations I've just cited about creativity are drawn from the unique world of abstract art, I am fascinated by them because they also connect with group work leadership. As in the Gorky quote, if group leaders see and hear only what is before them, much is lost. What is unsaid, for instance, and what that could mean. Patterns of comments might not be sensed. Asking *why* might not happen. Imagining new possibilities would be impossible. Viewing other physical arrangements for the group, such as breaking into dyads or a trying an in-group, out-group configuration for a while might not occur. The Hoffman quote leads us in another valuable direction for group work leadership. It was in the "forces of push and pull" that Hoffman found artistic creativity. Likewise, for group leaders, similar kinds of forceful dynamics—the ebb and flow of group dynamics, such as closeness and distance or of energy and silence, occurring over time—generate the "right stuff" from which creative ideas can spring.

As Gladding (2011a) points out, creativity and spontaneity are closely related. Spontaneity is a state of mind, a readiness to act creatively (cited by Kipper, 2006). Spontaneity also can be understood as an energy source or an intrinsic motivation that stimulates the process of creating.

Models for using creativity in group work are emerging as its importance becomes better understood. For instance, Gladding (1997, 2011c) has adapted from Eberle (1971) the *SCAMPER* model to group counseling. The letters stand for (a) **S**ubstitute, (b) **C**ombine, (c) **A**dapt/Alter, (d) **M**odify, (e) **P**ut to other uses, (f) **E**liminate, and (g) **R**earrange/**R**everse. See the references cited for detailed descriptions.

Two brief illustrations may give you a sense of how this model can be used. The "S" in *SCAMPER,* standing for substitute, captures the importance of being open to trying something else. What else is possible to do? Who else could be involved? Could other materials or equipment be used? Alternatives emerge all the time, all around us. For instance, watches now are becoming accessories for many, with the function of timekeeping being satisfied through the ubiquitous smartphone. In a group, we might ask if a member could communicate her anger in some other way than holding it in: "How else could you express it?" The *C* in *SCAMPER* stands for combine. For good or ill, many people today are multitasking, combining different functions simultaneously. Sometimes that can work, as in listening to soft music while writing or reading; other times it may be stress producing or, in fact, illegal (think texting while driving). In a group, an art project might be introduced where members create a project, such as a collage, together—thus, merging product with process. Each letter in the model provides an action that can be taken. The acronym itself suggests a sense of fun and playfulness, besides being quite easy to recall.

See Learning Exercise 8–3 for a dose of playfulness.

Learning Exercise 8–3: Walk With a Book on Your Heads

*The **object** of this learning exercise is to help you consider your thinking about the use of a creative exercise such as this in group work.*

Long ago, in a place far away, I was coleading a personal growth group. My coleader was being visited by a friend who was an actor in a noted repertory theater. With permission of the group members and with my support, he invited his friend to a group session in order "to add some creative juices." I recall that we thought the group was a bit stiff, tight.

He did just that.

After joining the session and observing for half an hour or so, the guest asked us all if we would like to try an experiment that might help to loosen us up and ignite our creative sides more. All agreed. He explained that sometimes actors are asked to experiment with what at first might seem to be extraneous and usually uncomfortable activities as a way to facilitate their spontaneity and creativity. With that thought as background, he introduced an activity where each of us, one at a time, would place the dictionary he had brought with him on top of our head and then walk a straight line he had drawn across the room and back while the others would feel free to comment on the passage. Weird, huh?

Team up with another person and discuss these questions (20 minutes):

1. What do you imagine might have occurred?

2. How might the "dictionary walkers" have felt and reacted?

3. What kinds of comments were offered by other group members?

4. What were the effects, in general, and on spontaneity and creativity specifically?

5. How do you think you might have responded had you been a group member?

6. Could you envision introducing any such activity in one of the groups you might lead? Explain to each other your thoughts about this.

Maybe you found the illustration you just read a bit extreme, or perhaps, you really liked it. In any case, one does not have to be in any way extreme to engender spontaneity and creativity. Gladding (2011a) provides an example, which I adapt in Learning Exercise 8–4.

Learning Exercise 8–4: Use of Language: "Yes, but"; "Yes, and"

*The **object** of this learning exercise is to explore the use of "yes, but" and of "yes, and" in a group.*

Group member, Sue:	"I really would like to learn meditation."
Group member, Wayne:	"Yeah, that might be nice for you, but I know you as a complete extrovert, so it would be quite impossible for you to become meditative."
Group member, Phyllis:	"I have a different take on this, Wayne. I offer to Sue a different thought to try: Yes, that would be nice for you, and I would like to encourage you to look into this as a way to perhaps counterbalance your tendency to be outgoing. Can you think of some ways to get started?"

———————

What is going on here?

1. Suppose you are Sue. Indicate your likely response to Wayne's comment.

   ———————————————————————————

2. Write how you imagine you'd respond to what Phyllis said.

   ———————————————————————————

3. This example highlighted the use of "yes, *but*" and of "yes, *and*." Who used which?

   Phyllis: ————————————————————————

   Wayne: ————————————————————————

Be guided by a group development framework (Brabender, 2011). As I discussed in Chapters 3 and 4 that dealt broadly with group dynamics and more specifically with group development (you may want to refer to those discussions), group dynamics change throughout a group's life requiring group leaders to sensitively shift and balance their attention and leader style. Leaders who have adopted or modified one of the many group development frameworks available possess a predictive method that increases their potential for anticipating and managing these dynamics more effectively than if they were guided by no such framework.

As a quick review (Conyne et al., 2008), in the beginning of a group, there generally is a need for becoming oriented, learning about goals, and beginning to establish both trust and a way of working. There often is a transitional period next, in which various issues are clarified related to power, control, and how decision making will occur. If successfully accomplished, then the group may proceed toward its middle and productive stage, where information and data are shared, members can give and get feedback, and they are able collaborate on processes of learning and change. As the group moves toward its conclusion, learning needs to be consolidated, members may need to tidy up loose ends and say good-bye, and they are encouraged to both draw meaning from their experience and make plans for how to apply what they have gained.

As you also know, no one group actually proceeds just in this way! Activities within a group ebb and flow can recycle, or in some cases, a group may literally leap over a stage—or never get out of one. There are no guarantees. At the same time, experience has shown that having a predictive map in mind to be used in planning, performing, and processing a group can be of great assistance.

Learning Exercise 8-5 serves as a checkup for you.

Learning Exercise 8–5: Match Up Stages With Activities

The **object** of this learning exercise is to help consolidate your learning about group developmental stages by connecting each one with the correct set of activities.

1. Draw lines between each group developmental stage in Column A and the correct anticipated activities in Column B.

Column A (Stages)	Column B (Activities)
Beginning	information sharing, problem solving, action
Transitioning	orienting, rule establishment, clarifying goals
Middle	evaluating, transferring learning, meaning
End	testing, conflict resolution, control

Facilitate connection and interaction among members (Corey, 2012; Kline, 2003;Yalom & Leszcz, 2005). Group work is an *interactive* and interpersonal process that is conducted to help members learn, grow, change, and become more productive. Member-to-member connections, communication, and relationships—in short, interaction—are the fundamental key to unlocking the potential that exists within individual members, relationships between and among members, and the group itself.Trotzer (2006) captured this interactive method by the terms promoting interaction, facilitating interaction, initiating interaction, and guiding interaction.

Group leaders, therefore, generally need to employ methods that emphasize interactive potential.Their continual frame of reference *should* (I dislike and usually find ways to avoid using the word *should*, but in this case I use it deliberately) revolve around the following question:"How can I consciously foster positive connections among group members so they can form relationships allowing them to interact?" The goal is not to focus on individuals one at a time, except in certain circumstances where that may be demanded. Rather, the goal is *to connect* members with each other so they can interact and learn from each other.

Two figures follow. Figure 8–3 illustrates an old and outdated telephone operator who controls all phone calls and where all the action goes through her. She serves literally as a telephone switchboard operator. Group leaders can also operate this way, where all action goes through them. Members speak to them, not to each other, unless the operator/group leader decides to connect them. Sometimes, as I mentioned, this method is needed; for instance, when leader expertise is called for in a period of high emotional intensity. Generally, though, it has been overtaken by the second method, described next.

Figure 8–4 shows a network where all parts are interconnected. A group functioning like a network enables all members to directly access all other members. Now they can initiate conversations directly, interacting actively to learn, exchange information, provide support and challenge, and whatever else might be needed. I've left the designated leader out of this figure not because he or she is unimportant but to emphasize the collateral networking. In fact, the leader is critically important in facilitating the creation and maintenance of such a network:These do not occur easily and require considerable skill to execute.

Pictorially, you can see the desired configuration representing how group leaders might position themselves with group members. The desired picture is the group as a kind of "web of life" (Capra, 1996) that I referred to in Chapter 1. But, how does one get there? What can be done? See Learning Exercise 8–6.

Figure 8.3   Switchboard Method Supporting Group Leadership: A Relic?

Source: Reprinted with permission from *Encyclopædia Britannica,* © 2012 by Encyclopædia Britannica, Inc.

Figure 8.4   Network Method Supporting Group Leadership: A "Web of Life"

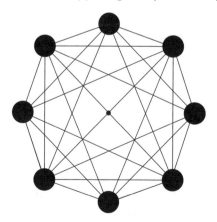

Source: Reprinted with permission from http://evolutionarymedia.com.

Learning Exercise 8–6: Activating the "Web of Life" in Group

The **object** of this learning exercise is to form a group, identify ways that the "web of life" (interconnection among participants) can be fostered, and then discuss how your group has operated.

1. Form your own small group of five to seven people.

2. Discuss for 30 minutes the two figures contained in this section: (a) switchboard method and (b) network method.

3. Give specific attention to how a network method—the so-called web of life—could be activated. See if your group can identify five steps a group leader could take. List those five ways on your sheet:

a. _____

b. _____

c. _____

d. _____

e. _____

4. Now, after your group has finished listing, examine your group's functioning. Discuss to what extent was a "web of life" present? A switchboard?

Online and social media groups. Before leaving this discussion of interaction and connection, I would be remiss by not including social media and online approaches, both of which are essential vehicles for millions today. I touched on this area previously in Chapter 6.

Online approaches have been the subject of special issues of scholarly journals, including the *Journal for Specialists in Group Work* (2003) and *Group Dynamics* (2002). Marty Jencius's *Counseling Today* column, "The Digital Psyway," organizes information that is contemporary and thoughtful about all things digital, with a counseling connection. Examples of topics discussed include microblogging, wikis and blogs, online counseling, and virtual worlds.

Page (2011) provides a rich discussion of some of the wide range of online possibilities available. She reports that in one Google search she completed on August 27, 2009, some 225,000 sites were identified. Now, a few years later, it would not be surprising for the number to have dramatically increased.

Page (2011) sorted the first 100 sites from the Google search mentioned, yielding sites that emphasized (a) general factors, containing many groups; (b) the Internet to recruit group members; (c) social networking, such as Facebook and Twitter; (d) communities based on geography; (e) health and/or medical issues; (f) mental health issues; (g) parenting; (h) politics; (i) ecology; (j) business and enterprise; (k) teaching and/or academics; and (l) specifically focused interests.

The potential for using online and social media to form and facilitate effective support, mental health, and educational groups exists, and programs are underway. Page (2011) reports some examples, and Shallcross (2012) provides an issue-oriented discussion of various applications, as well as challenges that need to be addressed.

Special care needs to be exercised when using online and social media vehicles to assist group work. For instance, just two of many ethical concerns revolve around informed consent and the often ambiguous personal and professional boundaries that can emerge in online discussions. It is very easy to make unintentional mistakes in these non-face-to-face venues. False assumptions can be made that others we are communicating with share our viewpoints. One could easily slip into an online classroom discussion related to people and systems, for example, one's political value that people "need to take care of their own business and not rely on government handouts"—especially in the midst of a heated election campaign cycle. And such a comment could just as easily trigger an intense negative reaction that could thoroughly derail thoughtful intercourse, if not careful. I've seen this occur myself in Blackboard (an e-learning system) discussions where typically rational and responsible students suddenly become confrontational without boundaries. Because there may be limited or even no accountability in some forms of social media that could accompany group work, people can forget normal rules of engagement or simply feel empowered to express themselves in ways they probably never would consider doing offline, in the full presence of others.

Despite the concerns, the online environment is playing a significant role in connecting people and in promoting their interaction. In fact, online communication is becoming a standard form of social interaction for millions around the world, and it is becoming more prevalent as an educational and therapeutic modality, too. Of course, the need and opportunity for research in all phases of online and social media groups is obvious, as is continued attention to the ethics of their applications in groups. And, in the end, "Cyberspace . . . is just another behavior setting where group members come together for interaction, influence, and action" (Forsyth, 2009, p. 456).

Build cohesion (Marmarosh & Van Horn, 2011; Yalom & Leszcz, 2005). As Yalom (1970) observed decades ago, cohesiveness is "the group therapy analogue to the relationship in individual therapy" (Yalom & Leszcz, 2005, p. 53). It is a nettlesome construct to define, associated as it seems to be with positive bonding, esprit de corps, therapeutic alliance, group climate, and with other therapeutic factors, such as universality. However, one summative way to think of cohesion is that it's the attractiveness of a group to its members. Important by itself, cohesion also serves as a precondition for other therapeutic factors. So an important method for group work leaders to prioritize is to continually search for effective ways to build cohesion among members and of the group to its members.

How can group leaders encourage the development of cohesion in their groups? Burlingame, Fuhriman, and Johnson (2001) identified six empirically supported principles. These are (a) conduct pre-group preparation; (b) provide early clarity about general goals and procedures; (c) model here-and-now interaction, guide effective interpersonal feedback, supply moderate control; (d) focus on relationship building and time feedback to fit developmental progress in the group; (e) provide a positive presence as the leader, being open, genuine, and empathic; and (f) facilitate the mutual emotional expression of members, cultivating empathy, and helping to draw meaning from disclosure. See Figure 8–5 and suggestions for conducting pre-group preparation.

Figure 8–5   Suggestions for Conducting Pre-Group Preparation

Pre-group preparation is highly recommended for counseling and psychotherapy groups. It fosters the development of cohesion among members and generally sets the tone and environment for positive group participation. Following are some key steps in pre-group participation.

Describe general group purpose.

Indicate general group goals.

Outline general expectations of group members.

Describe rules and procedures, such as confidentiality.

Identify possible gains to be made through participating.

Elicit member expectations.

Keep homogeneity in mind through balanced gender.

Be sensitive to issues surrounding race, culture, and gender.

Screen out those for whom this group might not "fit."

Create and use therapeutic factors (Kivlighan, 2011; Yalom & Leszcz, 2005). Research and practice have shown that the primary function of the group leader is to create a therapeutically effective group culture, rather than focusing on changing individuals in the group. As Yalom and Leszcz (2005) described it, "if it is the group members who, in their interaction, set into motion the many therapeutic factors then it is the group therapist's task to create a group culture maximally conductive to effective group interaction" (pp. 120–121). A highway billboard might read: *FIRST THINGS FIRST: GROUP LEADERS ARE CULTURE BUILDERS.*

As with other group constructs, group culture is not easily defined. A simplistic, but useful, way to think about it is that group culture is akin to the *personality* of a group. A group can be experienced as warm or cold, happy or sad, active or passive, positive or negative, safe or threatening, and so on.

Group leaders build a culture in many ways. You just read about the value of pre-group preparation in promoting cohesion. In turn, cohesion is one of several *therapeutic factors* (see Chapter 4 for a discussion) that have been shown to be critically important in the creation and maintenance of a positive group culture.

So, how do positive group cultures get created and maintained? Turn to Learning Exercise 8–7 to focus your attention on this question.

Learning Exercise 8–7: Some Ways to Establish a Positive Group Culture

*The **object** of this learning exercise is to identify how a group work leader might help generate a positive group climate.*

1. Form a small group of any size.

2. Review the list of therapeutic factors following:

List of Therapeutic Factors (refer to Chapter 5 for a discussion of these factors)

Instill hope

Universality

Impart information

Altruism

(Continued)

(Continued)

Corrective recapitulation of the primary family group

Developing socializing techniques

Imitative behavior

Interpersonal learning

Group cohesiveness

Existential factors

3. Agree on three therapeutic factors to address and list them below (20 minutes):

   a. _____

   b. _____

   c. _____

4. Brainstorm and list two ways for each factor that a group leader could promote a positive group culture (20 minutes):

   Therapeutic Factor #1: _____

   Way 1: _____

   Way 2: _____

   Therapeutic Factor #2: _____

   Way 1: _____

   Way 2: _____

   Therapeutic Factor #3: _____

   Way 1: _____

   Way 2: _____

5. Discuss what you learned through this learning exercise (10 minutes).

Endorse diversity, multiculturalism, and social justice (Association for Specialists in Group Work [ASGW], 2012; DeLucia-Waack, 2011; Hage, Mason & Kim, 2011). Consistent with a competency principle (I-4) drawn from *The Association for Specialists in Group Work Multicultural and Social Justice Competency Principles for Group Workers* (2012) document, group leaders are encouraged—at the least—to "seek to understand the extent to which general group leadership skills and functions may be appropriate or inappropriate for group work facilitation with multicultural group members" (p. 4). Likewise, as presented in Hage et al. (2011), "counselors have a responsibility, personally and collectively, to pursue justice at the collective level so that wellness may flourish at all levels" (Prilleletensky, Dokecki, Frieden, & Wang, 2007, p. 28). Group leading needs to be a contextually and culturally relevant method, as well as one that can be employed when needed to push for needed societal change.

It needs to be emphasized that group work embracing diversity, multiculturalism, and social justice must begin with *the personhood of the group leader.* Negative values, biases, and assumptions about other people hold no place in group work. It is essential that practitioners be first of all aware and sensitive to their own multicultural identity, as well as that of group members. This takes study, commitment, and prioritizing over time. Issues of ethnicity, race, age, socioeconomic class, sexual orientation, religion, spirituality, gender identity and expression all are impacted by experiences and life histories (ASGW, 2012).

American society is becoming increasingly multicultural and diverse, a direction that is fully in accord with the helping professions. Groups we form and lead need to be reflective of that phenomenon, whenever the opportunity presents itself. Attending to the needs and values of diverse groups allows for representative, vibrant, dynamic, and empowered groups, but it can also contribute positively to society overall.

It is important for group leaders to understand that psychological and emotional problems emerge in context, and they generally do not exist independent of surrounding circumstances. As pointed out by Prilleltensky (1999), these problems "are connected to people's social support, employment status, housing conditions, history of discrimination, and overall personal and political power. Promoting complete health means promoting social justice for there cannot be health in the absence of justice" (p. 106). Social justice involves identifying ways to take action related to various social justice issues and locations group members experience (Singh & Salazar, 2011).

In the interest of fairness, I also should point out that the areas of multiculturalism and social constructionism in the counseling profession can engender controversy. As but one example, Hansen (2005) raised issue with what he termed the "de-emphasis of inner subjective experiences in the counseling profession" in favor of collective interpretations and other forces, a point that stimulated reaction and discussion (e.g., Hansen, 2010; Rudes & Guterman, 2007). On a daily basis, the conservative wing of the popular press in the United States has a field day criticizing multiculturalism and diversity (others would be quick to point out the obverse occurring with the liberal wing). A recent posting by the conservative columnist George Will (2012), contained a discussion of one university adding a diversity requirement for graduation to cultivate a "student's understanding of her or his identity." Having already pointed out that the same university had recently cut a master's program in electrical and computer engineering and some courses in German, French, Spanish, and English literature, one observer commented, "So, rather than study computer science and Cervantes, students can study their identities—themselves. Diversity, it turns out, is simply a code word for narcissism" (Will, 2012). Ouch, such a comment treads heavily on hallowed counseling profession ground, where self-knowledge and respect for others are preeminent values.

Learning Exercise 8–8: Good Luck, Mr. Phelps

The **objects** of this learning exercise are to

    a. advance one's understanding of how systems and communities can be included within a definition of "client" and

    b. suggest implications of this broadened definition for group work practice.

"Your assignment, should you choose to accept it, Mr. Phelps" (a continuing line from the original *Mission Impossible* television show) is to draft a 1-page paper addressing the topic presented earlier.

Follow these steps:

1. Access the document, *ASGW Multicultural and Social Justice Competency Principles for Group Workers* (2012) and refer to Section III, Social Advocacy, Item #13, which expands the concept of "client" to include systems and communities when examining change.

2. To assist your task, read more about social justice advocacy for group workers, such as the Hage, Mason, and Kim (2011) source cited in this text.

3. Consider how to conceptualize "client"; you might find useful a seminal journal article by Morrill, Oetting, and Hurst (1974) on the variety of ways counseling methods, targets, and purposes can interact.

4. Draw from appropriate sources and integrate with your own thinking a coherent response to the question posed in a 1-page paper.

5. These papers can be presented and discussed in class in an upcoming session.

"Good luck, Mr. Phelps."

Draw from and appropriately adapt group work advantages and associated evidence-based approaches (Barlow, 2011; Jacobs, Masson, Harvill, & Schimmel, 2012). You will recall from Chapter 1 the discussion about group work being effective, in general. For some circumstances and with some populations, it is even better than individual counseling. The research that has been accumulated on this topic is quite clear, and we all should rejoice in documenting something that many of us knew from our own experiences was possible.

Advantages of group work. In addition to the key fact that group work is effective, many additional reasons exist for using a group approach (Jacobs et al., 2012). Groups are efficient ways to provide help. After all, one group work leader can reasonably manage the interactions of up to 12 members, and sometimes more. Compare that ratio with the traditional individual counseling model of 1:1. Groups allow for therapeutic factors, such as universality (i.e., it is reassuring to realize that you are not the only one with such issues) to develop and take root. Groups are environments in which members can experiment with behavior change, with trying out new approaches. They provide the opportunity for giving and getting feedback on behavior. Properly managed, they are a safe space where self-disclosure is possible without the fear of reprisal. They provide a milieu in which members can observe and learn from each other, as well as from the group leader. Multiple group members mean that a rich array of resources and experiences are brought to the group, allowing for amplified learning opportunities. Members with different abilities, demographic characteristics, cultural backgrounds, and experiences add appreciably to the richness that diversity affords. Finally, participating with others in an ongoing group experience provides continuous opportunities for mutual responsibility and accountability for what occurs.

Because groups are effective and afford many unique advantages, though, does not mean that any one group format can be generalized across all situations. As Barlow (2011, p. 228) reminds us by quoting Villemaire (2002, p. 237), "we need to hold a "constant and continuing faith in the pursuit of knowledge while acknowledging human contextuality." Group leaders need to keep in mind that tested and proven programs, strategies, and techniques—that is, those for which there is evidence—can inform their work. At the same time, it usually is necessary to adjust what works to fit more closely the existing situation and population (without sufficiently altering the core elements or processes), because contexts differ. There still is much not known or verified by scientific evidence, and there are many circumstances in group work where reliance on careful planning, thoughtful professional behavior, and creative impulse point to a better, or often the only, way.

● GROUP LEADER STRATEGIES AND TECHNIQUES: ACTION TOOLS OF THE TRADE

Strategies and techniques in group work leadership provide the tools for translating methods into action. While methods may be thought of as blueprints that guide action, strategies and techniques are the action *tools of the trade* (Newmeyer, 2011). While certainly being tools for action, strategies and techniques resist clear definition, and they are difficult to differentiate. Corey, Corey, Callanan, and Russell (2003), for instance, suggest that techniques can amount to virtually anything that a group leader does. They then proceed to highlight explicit purposes of techniques, aimed at focusing attention, augmenting emotion, practicing behavior, and facilitating insight.

Considered together, *strategies and techniques are the action tools that are used by group leaders—and sometimes by group members—to focus attention on thoughts and feelings, on interpersonal and group interaction, and on group processes; they also are used to accentuate thoughts and feelings, and to provide opportunities for learning and its transfer outside the group.* Newmeyer (2011), following up earlier work by Conyne et al. (2008), organizes 40 strategies and techniques by group developmental stage (e.g., beginning stage: Using "I" terms; middle stage: physiogram; and end stage: follow-up session). Jacobs et al. (2012) have produced seven editions of their text dealing with group leader strategies and skills, describing in detail such approaches as using rounds and dyads, various kinds of structured activities and exercises, focusing on ongoing experiences, processing activities, and using selective group leader skills such as cutting off and drawing out interaction.

● FIVE SELECTED STRATEGIES AND TECHNIQUES IN GROUP LEADERSHIP

To review, group leader action draws from
- Core competencies, functions, and styles—the building blocks that support everything else
- Methods: Blueprints for guiding action, which are larger intentions, such as facilitating connection and interaction among members
- Strategies and Techniques: Action tools of the trade that focus attention on thoughts and feelings, on interpersonal and group interaction, and on group processes; they also are used to accentuate thoughts and feelings, and to provide opportunities for learning and its transfer outside the group.

This section centers on strategies and techniques, with much of the material stimulated by the work of Jacobs et al. (2012). Five categories of strategies will be highlighted: (a) focusing; (b) shifting interaction; (c) preplanned, structured exercises; (d) intuitive experiments; and (e) psychoeducation lecturettes. A variety of more specific strategies and techniques are contained within each of these categories.

Focusing

Focus, according to Jacobs et al. (2012) refers to what is happening in a group. It can emphasize (a) a topic of conversation, such as the weather or trust in the group; (b) an activity taking place, such as a go-round or a guided fantasy exercise; or (c) a person, such as a conflict or goal.

In any group session, a focus or a number of foci occur naturally as a consequence of member involvement. Group leaders also can, and should, use the focus as an explicit strategy by establishing, holding, or shifting the focus.

In all types of groups a leader needs to facilitate an appropriate match between the focus underway and the group's purpose. For instance, in counseling, psychotherapy, and psychoeducation groups the general focus intended is toward increased depth of disclosure and connection. In task groups, the leader generally is interested in promoting a focus toward increased productivity. See Case Illustration 8–1.

Case Illustration 8–1: Establish, Hold, and Shift the Focus: Sample Group Leader Strategies and Techniques

*The **object** in this case illustration is to provide examples of strategies and techniques in modifying the focus of group interaction through establishing, holding, and shifting the focus.*

To *Establish* the focus

Strategy: "For the next 15 minutes, let's see if we can pay attention to our breathing."

Technique: Introduce a deep breathing exercise.

Strategy: "Brainstorming can be a useful approach. Let's take a closer look at it."

Technique: Hand out a definition of brainstorming and how to use it.

(Continued)

(Continued)

To *Hold* the focus

Strategy: "Continuing to discuss this topic for a while longer might be helpful for us."

Technique: Weigh costs and benefits before making statement.

Strategy: "Bill, are you wanting some more feedback at this point?"

Technique: Check in with the affected member.

To *Shift* the focus

Strategy: "We've been talking about next steps for some time now; I'm wondering if we might be at a point where we can begin moving on them, taking some action?"

Technique: Shift from talking only to doing, but checking it out first.

Strategy: "Mark, I notice as you are speaking that you are bobbing your left leg up and down . . . I wonder if you might shift your focus to your left leg . . . what are you trying to say with it?"

Technique: Shift from verbal to nonverbal attention.

Shifting Interaction by Loosening and by Tightening

Borrowing from a perspective on organizational leadership, one way of viewing human interaction is that it can vary along a dimension anchored at one end by "Tight" and at the other end by "Loose" (Sage, Zaidman, Amichaie-Hamburger, Te'eni, & Schwartz, 2002). When it is tight, then all portals are battened down, people are closed and locked up, tucked in and, feeling they are protected from invasion of some sort, all risk is dampened. When human interaction is loose, then everything hangs out, boundaries are limited to nonexistent, maximal output occurs, a constant state of "TMI" ("too much information") is in effect, and—in extreme cases—chaos may fill the room, or be at its door step.

Two important group leader strategies can be of assistance with managing interaction that occupies too much of the space at either end of the tight-loose dimension. In groups characterized by, or experiencing some problems with, tightness, then the strategy of *drawing out* (see Case Illustration 8-2) might be useful. In groups tilted the other way, the strategy of *cutting off* (see Case Illustration 8-3 and Learning Exercise 8-9) might be of value (Jacobs et al., 2012).

Case Illustration 8–2: *Drawing Out* Strategy, With Techniques

*The **object** in this case illustration is to present examples of strategies and techniques in drawing out group interaction.*

Strategy: "As I gaze around the group, I notice most of you are silent and looking away from one another. I'm wondering what that might be all about? Anyone want to take a stab at that?"

Technique: Use of eyes, making a group observation, asking an open-ended question of the group, inviting anyone to comment.

Strategy: "Things seem a bit slower in our session tonight. I'm curious about why that may be and bet that each of you may have some ideas about that.

Technique: Make the rounds, starting with a member who may be highly likely to have a comment.

Case Illustration 8–3: *Cutting Off* Strategy, With Techniques

*The **object** in this case illustration is to demonstrate techniques that might be used with the leader strategy, cutting off.*

The group members arrive for the session and—for whatever reasons—have high energy. They interact actively, laughing, telling jokes and stories. This goes on for nearly 10 minutes with no apparent awareness that group start up is overdue. The group leader simply has been watching, listening, and waiting to find out what will happen. "Will they self-regulate, she asks herself silently?"

Finally, when it appears they will not, she decides to intervene by gently cutting off continued social chatter, with an intention to divert to something more meaningful (from her perspective):

Strategy: She needs to stand up to get their attention and then sit down. She is moving to cut off the continued discussion.

Technique: "Wow, what energy!" she begins. "I've been wondering where this was going to go and it seems it would just continue . . . so I am moved to ask you to comment on it. What's going on? How do you want to proceed?"

Learning Exercise 8–9: Role Playing *Cutting Off* as a Strategy?

*The **object** of this learning exercise is to draw conclusions about the group work leader strategy of "cutting off."*

Let me ask you: What do you think of this kind of intervention? Cutting off interaction can be one of the more important leader strategies, but it can be sensitive to pull off without hurting people's feelings sometimes.

1. Discuss with another student your thoughts about cutting off.

2. What are your thoughts about the way it was done in the case illustration?

3. Would you have proceeded differently? How?

4. Role-play a group interaction in which you both take a turn to try this strategy.

Pre-Planned, Structured Exercises

As a group evolves, it tends naturally to evolve its own character and structure. However, it also is possible for group leaders to introduce pre-planned, structured exercises into a group, and this frequently is done.

What is an exercise? "When the leader directs the behaviors, discussion, or attention of the group members by using a specific activity, it is an exercise" (Jacobs et al., 2012, p. 219). Exercises that are well constructed, fit the developmental stage and purpose of the group, and are introduced and processed effectively can be helpful in promoting learning. Exercises that do not fit these criteria and/or that are overused in relation to time devoted to unstructured activity may be ineffective and, worse, harmful.

Structured exercises generally can be most useful in the beginning and ending stages of a group, again, if not overused (Corey, 2012; Jacobs et al., 2012). In the beginning, a structured exercise such as pairing up to introduce one's partner, can assist with lowering anxiety and in facilitating the sharing of low-intensity personal information. Toward closing of a session or of the entire group, a structured exercise such as "reflecting in the rear-view mirror," can prove to be helpful.

Yalom and Leszcz (2005) indicate that the most important point to remember when thinking of using structured exercises is the "degree, accent, and purpose associated with them" (p. 474). For instance, it is an error to use structured exercises as a filler for silence, or certainly, it is a grievous mistake to fill any session with a series of structured exercises. Why? In the first case, exercises are not intended to be rescuers or to serve as a quick way to accomplish goals. In the second, exercises should never dominate but, when used, should only highlight or facilitate processes; room always is needed for open interaction and for processing the meaning of experiences.

Research (Stockton, Rohde, & Haughey, 1992; Yalom & Leszcz, 2005) has shown that leaders can receive favorable ratings when using structured exercises. Members may tend to associate their use as a sign of leader competency. However, caveat emptor, once again. Overuse is to be avoided.

An issue usually arises about leader participation in structured exercises. That is, should leaders include themselves or not? Yalom and Leszcz (2005) discuss the group leader role as ranging from a "model-setting participant," on one hand, to a "technical expert," on the other. In the former, leaders tend to become involved similar to how they would like or expect group members to function; so, if an exercise is introduced, the leader might be likely to complete it, too, unless other conditions preclude that from occurring (e.g., the leader needs to be free to observe and monitor the others). In the technical expert role, though, leaders tend to maintain a more distant relationship with members. When structured exercises are introduced, this role suggests the leader might refrain from directly participating.

What are some examples of types of structured exercises? See Figure 8–6 (adapted from Jacobs et al., 2012):

Figure 8–6   A List of Some Types of Structured Exercises

Movement exercises

Dyads and triads

Rounds

Written exercises

Feedback exercises

Physical space exercises

Group-decision exercises

Using creative props

Arts, crafts, and music

Common reading exercises

Source: Adapted from Jacobs et al. (2012).

See Case Illustration 8-4 for an example of a structured exercise.

Case Illustration 8–4: Using the "Life Line" Exercise

*The **object** of this case illustration is to provide an example of a classical structured exercise in group.*

In the small group, the group leader suggests (Note: There are different versions of these instructions and they can be modified to fit the circumstances of the group) the following:

"We've been talking about where we are in our lives, how we are living our lives today.

I'd like to introduce a structured exercise for you to participate in that will help focus your lives and will also help place where you are today in context. Here's how this goes:

I'm passing around a blank piece of paper and a pencil. On the paper, I ask you to draw a horizontal line and to mark it at the left end with "Childhood" and at the right end with "Today." The line in the middle is for you to divide up and label with significant life events that have occurred for you along the way. Write those in (for example, "1999 my Dad died" or "2003 I got into college"), and then, we will draw from your work to share with one another in the group. Any questions?"

Intuitive Experiments

The previous class of structured exercises follows a plan for their use. The class of exercises now considered is not planned in advance. Rather, they emerge on the spot. They are intuitively derived, born out of a creative process, and can be thought of as experiments.

In fact, a group can be thought of as an experimental (and ethical) interpersonal laboratory. A group is a special place where members can try out novel behaviors and styles and learn useful information about themselves by doing so.

In some introductory exercises occurring in a first group session or in a workshop, for example, members might be asked to strip away their personal identifiers when meeting and becoming known initially to others. "Name, rank, and serial number" are all removed. The fact that George is a plumber or an oral surgeon is not revealed. In fact, "George," becomes—for a while—let's say, "Herman," and other members get to know him without the benefit, or the curse, of his typical identifiers.

Why might this experiment be tried? Because sometimes people peg others by virtue of those very personal identifiers. If I know you are a PhD, or rather that you went to prison for 2 years, these personal descriptors may strongly influence how I view you right from the start. By stripping away her or his personal identifiers such labeling is minimized, and members are presented with the opportunity to get to know others on the basis of how they are in the present moment.

In other cases, intuitive experiments may be introduced as a group session is in progress. A leader senses that a member is blocking affect surrounding his mother, for instance, or that in a task group the members may seem reluctant to take any risks. The leader may introduce an exercise, activity, or experiment then, as a way to facilitate movement. In the first situation, the member may be asked to role-play a discussion with his mother. In the second, the group may be asked to brainstorm a set of possibilities. The idea for change, the experiment, is born on the spot; it is an intuitive creation of the group leader that emerges from and responds to the group situation as it is occurring.

Needless to say, such a group leader strategy is appropriate for use *only* by very experienced practitioners. Having said that, the intuitive experiment is a clear example of how creativity can be employed in group leadership.

Psychoeducation Lecturettes

This strategy falls under one of the therapeutic factors called, *imparting information.* Yalom and Leszcz (2005) include under this factor "didactic instruction about mental health, mental illness, and general psychodynamics given by the therapists as well as advice, suggestions, or direct guidance from either the therapist or other group members" (pp. 8–9).

There is remarkable early precedence for imparting information to a group. Dr. Joseph Pratt in 1905 presented inspirational lectures to his patients after he had formed them into a group on how to deal with tuberculosis. In the 1920s and 1930s at the Boston Dispensary, he began placing less emphasis on disease, focusing more on emotions and their effect on neurosis; the group became for him the focal point of therapy (Blatner, 2007). In a second famous case, Dr. Maxwell Jones in the 1940s would lecture 3 hours a week to his patients about the nervous system's connection with psychiatric symptoms and dysfunction (Yalom & Leszcz, 2005).

Psychoeducation lecturettes are short instructional presentations given by the leader to group members, either planned or offered spontaneously, on a topic relevant to the members and to the group. One class of groups, often associated with prevention, is termed "psychoeducation groups." In these groups, the intent is to forestall the emergence of maladaptation in members. One of the approaches is to help members develop, or strengthen already existing, coping skills. Lecturettes may be provided on such coping skills topics as stress management, communication skills, problem-solving steps, and others. Psychoeducation lecturettes also are sometimes a part of other types of groups in addition to those focusing on prevention.

As research has shown (Conyne & Clanton Harpine, 2010; Conyne & Horne, 2001; Yalom & Leszcz, 2005), however, for psychoeducation lecturettes that are presented within a group session, it is important that they be couched within opportunities for member interaction, discussion, application, and processing. There is little to gain by overemphasizing the presentation of content without the balancing of process yielded through connection with member engagement and sense making. See Learning Exercise 8–10.

Learning Exercise 8–10: Content and Process in Psychoeducation Lecturettes

*The **object** of this learning exercise is draw your focus to the importance of balancing content and process in psychoeducation (and all) groups.*

How might you envision balancing content and process in a psychoeducation lecturette?

Try working with the following scenario:

You are leading a psychoeducation group in which a present theme is "coping with life stress." You decide to begin the next session (number 3 of 10 two-hour sessions) with a 5-minute psychoeducation lecturette on "stress and how to manage it." You appreciate the importance of including in the presentation, or of following it, opportunities for members to engage actively with the topic and to connect with its meaning for their lives.

1. List two ways to include member discussion within the session (process) (10 minutes).

   a. _____

   b. _____

2. Outline the main elements of your presentation (content) (20 minutes).

3. Discuss the content and process approach with a partner. Usually, we all can improve our work. Ask for feedback about ways to improve what you have developed so far (20 minutes).

GROUP WORK KEYSTONES ●

- Group leading methods, strategies, and techniques were highlighted and contrasted in this chapter.
- There is considerable value for group work leaders to be able to draw both from intentionality and from spontaneity in their interventions.
- A "network" metaphor fits group work leadership very well.
- Perhaps the most important task of group leaders is to be the builder, with group members, of a positive culture.

RECOMMENDED RESOURCES

Burlingame, G., Fuhriman, A., & Johnson, J. (2001). Cohesion in group psychotherapy. *Psychotherapy, 38*, 373-379.

Corey, G., Corey, M., Callanan, P., & Russell, J. M. (2003). *Group techniques* (3rd ed.). Pacific Grove, CA: Brooks/Cole.

DeLucia-Waack, J. (2011). Diversity in groups. In R. Conyne (Ed.), *The Oxford handbook of group counseling* (pp. 83-101). New York, NY: Oxford University Press.

Gladding, S. (2011). Creativity and spontaneity in groups. In R. Conyne (Ed.), *The Oxford handbook of group counseling* (pp. 383-398). New York, NY: Oxford University Press.

Jacobs, E., Masson, R., Harvill, R., & Schimmel, C. (2012). *Group counseling: Strategies and skills* (7th ed.). Belmont, CA: Brooks/Cole.

Kivlighan, D. M., Jr. (2011). Individual and group perceptions of therapeutic factors and session evaluation: An actor-partner interdependence analysis. *Group Dynamics: Theory, Research, and Practice, 15*, 147-160.

Morrill, W., Oetting, E., & Hurst, J. (1974). Dimensions of counselor functioning. *Personnel and Guidance Journal, 52*, 354-359.

Newmeyer, M. (2011). Group techniques. In R. Conyne (Ed.), *The Oxford handbook of group counseling* (pp. 307-324). New York, NY: Oxford University Press.

Page, B. (2011). Online groups. In R. Conyne (Ed.), *The Oxford handbook of group counseling* (pp. 520-533). New York, NY: Oxford University Press.

Singh, A., & Salazar, C. (Eds.). (2011). *Social justice in group work: Practical interventions.* New York, NY: Routledge.

Trotzer, J. (2011). Personhood of the leader. In R. Conyne (Ed.), *The Oxford handbook of group counseling* (pp. 287-306). New York, NY: Oxford University Press.

SECTION III

MEANING, ACTION, AND PROFESSIONAL IDENTITY IN GROUP WORK

Section III is concerned with three central aspects of group work: meaning (Chapter 9), action (Chapter 10), and professional identity development (Chapters 9 and 10). The Epilogue provides an opportunity for me to highlight key facets of the book and focus comments on processing, professional identity, and passion.

Chapter 9 is concerned with group workers helping members to identify large life lessons from their work in group, which they can apply to their ongoing life "in the real world": *big, life principles we carve out of the crucible of our experience, whether positive or negative, which we can then use to more effectively cope with similar situations we may face in the future.* Two types of processing are highlighted to assist with meaning attribution: (a) within session, where leaders help members translate experience into cognition and application, and (b) between session, where leaders themselves focus on what they are learning, in order to improve present practice in this group and future practice in other groups. The Deep Processing Model is presented as also holding considerable attention for enhancing personal development, self-care, and professional identity of group leaders.

Chapter 10 specifically focuses on *examples of group interaction* drawn from each of the four types of group work, although all this book's chapters devote considerable attention to practice examples through case illustrations and learning exercises. The examples in this chapter are organized around a conception of choice making, enhancing strengths, and turning potential failures into adequacies and even successes. The Purposeful Group Techniques Model is presented as a helpful tool to assist progress.

The Epilogue provides an opportunity for me to comment on some aspects of the text. Particular attention is given to the value of *processing and learning from experience* and both to improving practice and to enhancing one's professional identity. Finally, I encourage you to be open to your experience, process it, seek formal learning opportunities, scan your everyday environment for how groups are at work, join professional associations of group work, and more. My wish for you is that you may discover your passion for group work.

CHAPTER 9

REFLECTING IN AND ON GROUP WORK PRACTICE

We should every night call ourselves to an account: What infirmity have I mastered today? What passions opposed? What temptation resisted? What virtue acquired? Our vices will abort of themselves if they be brought every day to the shrift.

—Seneca

The quotation, above, by the Roman philosopher Seneca stems from the first century C.E. You may recall that Yalom (1975) referred to a similar process in group as a "self-reflective loop" (p. 123), where an event or experience is then examined for lessons learned.

This chapter is devoted to looking back for lessons learned coming, as it does in our sequence, immediately following attention to group leader functions, styles, methods, strategies, and techniques—all of which focused on how to engage members directly in the group experience.

But, alas, direct engagement is just not enough. In groups, we must also learn from what emerges from direct experience, to draw meaning from it. In this way, we can continuously improve our leadership of specific groups with which we are working. We also need to understand the value of taking perspective—that is, reflecting on our group practice in terms of overall effectiveness and in light of our own development as a person and a group leader.

239

CHAPTER OBJECTIVES

As a result of reading this chapter you will be able to

- Address reflecting *in* group practice, one group at a time
- Understand the importance of lessons learned in group work
- Implement within- and between-session processing
- Understand the importance of scheduling processing
- Understand how to reflect *on* group practice by taking a long-range perspective
- Implement the Deep Processing Model (Conyne, 1999)
- Understand the importance of personal, professional, and ethical development and professional practice and accountability
- Self-care

● REFLECTING *IN* GROUP WORK PRACTICE: FOCUSING ON ONE GROUP AT A TIME

Lessons Learned

What is a lesson learned? A classic view is to ask people toward the end of their long lives about such lessons. For instance, Pillemer's (2012) book, *30 Lessons for Living,* details 30 such gems (e.g., avoid major regrets, discover work you love) culled from research conducted with 1200 older people as part of the Cornell University Legacy Project. More than a few popular songs have addressed this specific question, including one by Alicia Keys (Mayer, 2008), who examined a heartbreak and finally concluded, "Yes, I was burned but I call it a lesson learned."

Another example of lessons learned emerges from the experience of darker times of the Oklahoma City Thunder professional hockey team, when losing was more frequent than winning. Their coach, Scott Brooks, saw it this way during that time: "We're not losing games. We're learning how to win games" (Brooks, 2012).

Lessons learned, then, are big, life principles we carve out of the crucible of our experience, whether positive or negative, which we can then use to more effectively cope with similar situations we may face in the future. In dealing with difficult experiences, they enable us to learn from our experiences and our mistakes and to be resilient rather than to fall apart. As in the Alicia Keys song, the experience may involve heartache. Or in the hockey quotation, continual losing. I can imagine that you are able to relate to these kinds of lessons learned in your own life.

What might some examples of difficult situations for group leaders be, do you think? See Case Illustration 9–1.

Case Illustration 9–1: Some Difficult and Enjoyable Situations in Group Leading

*The **object** of this case illustration is to contribute to improving your capacity to better handle difficult situation in group work leadership and to appreciate it when things go well.*

First, I provide an example of a difficult situation for a group leader. Then, I ask you to try doing the same.

Challenge to leader's authority, competency, and self-concept:

The group leader tells his supervisor, "And then she said directly to me in the group, '*I* could do this leading thing *so* much better than you, you don't seem to have *any* idea of what to do! You're a loser!' I don't have to tell you, but I was absolutely crushed."

Situations such as this one can be very difficult for group leaders to handle, as you might expect. As you lead groups, indeed as you function as a helper, you will experience such moments; it just sort of goes with the territory.

Now, I provide a positive and enjoyable situation for a group leader.

Praising a leader's behavior:

The group leader tells her supervisor, "And then he said directly to me in the group that he found my ability to listen to everyone and to provide really warm support were—his words, now, not mine—fantastic!"

Well, fortunately, group leaders also sometimes receive kudos from members—and that can feel really good!

Lessons learned can hold both immediate and long-term significance. They can be immediately applicable in the current group, as well as in the longer term. Refer to the attack on leader authority, competency, and self-concept that you just read. How might that group leader have felt in the situation? Thought? Done? In the midst of all the possible anguish, might there be a positive life lesson that could emerge? What might it be? As well, group work leaders can be praised and supported, too. I had a long-term client once who, in her final session, said the most important thing she had learned was "It's important to accept the good." Simple but, at the same time, quite profound. Now, take a look at Learning Exercise 9–1.

Learning Exercise 9–1: A Possible Life Lesson From the Difficult Group Leading Situation

*The **object** of this learning exercise is to enhance empathy and skill in working with challenging situations in a group.*

Now let's return to the difficult leader situation in Case Illustration 9–1. Indicate your best guesses

How might that group leader have felt in the situation? _____

What might he or she have thought? _____

Done? _____

_____

How about *you*? Put yourself in that situation. Now try responding to the same questions, this time, because it's about you, being more informed:

How might *you* have felt in the situation? _____

_____

What might *you* have thought? _____

Done? _____

_____

In the midst of all the possible anguish, might there be a positive life lesson that could emerge? What might it be for you?

Consider another instance, involving a confrontation between two members. When examined, it could suggest that expression of high emotion may not always equal quality and that conditions of empathy and respect also need to be present. The group members involved may then be able to apply this learning in other situations that may occur in the group. Moreover, if wise, a group leader can derive longer term lessons from this reviewed incident, lessons that can contribute to his or her personal and professional identity development. "As a professional group leader, I will never forget the importance of empathy and respect in helping intense group interactions become valuable and meaningful," offers an example of a lesson learned that can be carried forward.

Not everyone agrees, however, that reflecting on life experience is a good or even a necessary activity. Following the death on April 7, 2012, of the formidable newscaster Mike Wallace, the public media devoted considerable attention to Mr. Wallace's career and life. Many clips of his famous interviews of celebrities, politicians, gangsters, sports heroes, and everyday people were shown on television, every one of them illustrating his brilliance and tenacity as an interviewer.

One interview, this time with him as the subject, stands out for me. In this one, being interviewed by his longtime CBS colleague and friend Morley Safer about his impending retirement, Mike was asked if he felt it was time to maybe pack it in and reflect. This kind of question is, of course, an archetypal bid for reflective meaning. Wallace scoffed at the very idea, literally sneering: "Give me a break! *Reflect?* Reflect about *what?*" (*Face the Nation*, 2012).

Give some additional thought now to reflecting, before we delve into the topic in this chapter, by working with Learning Exercise 9-2.

Learning Exercise 9–2: Are you a Seneca or a Wallace?

The **object** of this learning exercise is to help readers identify their orientation to reflecting and processing and how it might connect with group work leadership.

As you consider the different approaches attributed to Seneca to Mike Wallace as they relate to reflection and processing, which comes closest to your general position?

1. Circle one: Seneca   Wallace   In Between

   Please explain your choice: _____

   _____

2. How does your thinking apply to group work leadership? _____

   _____

I hope you find yourself being more Seneca than Wallace, in this case, because reflecting on experience is a vital part of group leadership. Direct experience in groups is essential for meeting goals and producing learning, growth, and change, as we have seen. But you also have read that direct experience in groups, as important and necessary as it is, is insufficient by itself for realizing desired outcomes. That is, interacting actively, connecting, and engaging with one another in positive ways needs to be complemented by processes that lead members to reflect on their experience—to process it—in a guided effort to translate the raw stuff of experience into meaningful life lessons. Think of a shorthand way of expressing this: *Meaningful Life Lessons = Direct Experience/Reflecting.*

Moreover, reflective practice, what I refer to increasingly in this chapter as *processing*, is a best practice, as an Association for Specialists in Group Work (ASGW) Guideline (C-2) indicates:

> *Reflective practice:* Group workers attend to opportunities to synthesize theory and practice and to incorporate learning outcomes into ongoing groups. Group workers attend to session dynamics of members and their interactions and also attend to the relationship between session dynamics and leader values, cognition and affect. (ASGW, 2007, p. 117)

Reflective Practice, or Processing, Between and Within Group Sessions

In Chapter 2, a review of the *ASGW Best Practice Guidelines* indicated that group work practice involves cyclical phases of planning, performing, and processing. This third phase, processing, is a unique term that is reserved to represent "reflecting" in group work. So, to *process* in group work is to *reflect,* with the intention of drawing meaning from experience. Processing can occur both *within* sessions and *between* sessions.

Within-session processing. Group leaders and members together need to create group conditions that promote direct interpersonal experiences and opportunities to review especially salient experiences for their meaning and future application (Bridbord, 2002; Cohen & Smith, 1976; Conyne, 1997a; DeLucia-Waack, 1997; Glass & Benshoff, 1999; Kees & Jacobs, 1990; Lieberman, Yalom, & Miles, 1973; Newmeyer, 2011; Stockton, Morran, & Nitza, 2000; Trotzer, 2011; Ward & Lichy, 2004; Yalom, 1975). This form of processing is known as *within-session* processing.

Within-session processing emerged out of happenstance, in 1946, at the beginning of the National Training Laboratories (NTL) and of T-groups in Bethel, Maine (Benne, 1964). The training leaders were a Who's Who of behavioral scientists and educators, including Ronald Lippitt, Kenneth

Benne, and Leland Bradford, and of noted social psychology researchers, including Kurt Lewin.

Three training groups (T-groups) were operating, each with research observers. There was no plan for analysis of here-and-now events and for involvement of group members in examining the behavioral observations that researchers were gathering of the groups. Benne discusses how Lewin decided to hold evening meetings of the training and research staff so that observations being gathered about leader and member behavior in the groups might be shared and discussed.

Some participants walking by on a summer evening happened to overhear one of these discussions through an open window. They were amazed by what they heard, these discussions about them and how they were behaving in the groups! The next day, they asked if they might be able to attend these evening sessions, which was approved, with the staff having no preconceived expectation of what might occur. In fact, Benne (1964) indicates that "Actually, the open discussion of their own behavior and its observed consequences had an electric effect both on the participants and on the training leaders" (p. 83). What had been a private staff analysis and discussion was now a shared one. Within-session processing had been born.

Ward and Lichy (2004) provide a helpful summary of a number of within-session processing approaches and how to use them effectively. They list 18 recommendations for group processing, including these three: (a) Processing is a critically important part of modern group work; (b) effective processing addresses both the content (the "what") of group interaction as well its process (the "how"); (c) effective group processing involves, where appropriate, the shared responsibility and participation of group leader(s) with members. The authors also summarize a range of group processing approaches and models, including those of Cohen and Smith (1976), Glass and Benshoff (1999), and Stockton, Morran and Nitza (2000). These approaches explicate Yalom's conception of processing as illuminating an important group event or experience so that it becomes understandable and subject to learning and application.

Stockton et al. (2000) suggest that within-session processing be managed in four steps: (a) identify a critical incident, (b) examine the event and member reactions, (c) derive meaning and self-understanding from the event, and (d) apply new understanding toward personal change. In Glass and Benshoff's (1999) PARS (*P*rocess, *A*ctivity, *R*elationship, and *S*elf) model, three steps are included: (a) reflect on what occurred, (b) understand the meaning behind it, and (c) apply the meaning to member behavior outside the group. Conyne's (1997a) Grid model for processing experiences in groups involves examining an identified experience or event using three dimensions: (a) the level of focus ("I," "You," or "Us"), (b) the content (*what*), and (c) the process (*how*). In all of these approaches, you can notice the attention on group events, an arcing back to learn from it, and a looking ahead to apply learning that was gained (see Case Illustration 9–2).

Case Illustration 9–2: Arcing Back, Looking Forward

*The **object** of this case illustration is to demonstrate the importance of sometimes reaching back and also moving forward in group.*

About halfway through the eighth session, Adrian offers the following, probably appearing to most in the group (well, certainly to the leader, Alice) to come out of the blue:

"I'm feeling dog tired right now, really was okay coming into group today, though. I'll be honest, I don't have the least bit of interest in anything you've just said, Tim, and that really goes for all of it today. Not other days, but today. And don't rush in to help me, either. Just let me be. Just let me be. I'm okay, I think, just maybe worn out with all the drama."

The Arc:

Alice decides not to let it go, while also respecting Adrian and his request. She sees this disclosure as important and does not know its origins. She risks reaching out to Adrian:

"Adrian, I know you asked for no help, and to just let you be. I want to respect that and you, although I'm finding myself wondering what may have happened, what's going on. But I'm just going to respect your request and say that the door is open, you know, for you to come through it when you are ready, and I will be glad then to be one of the ones welcoming you back."

Looking forward:

Alice thought about this incident a lot as she reviewed the group. She decided, at least for now, that what she did was useful, but that remains to be seen in subsequent sessions. She took away this learning: "Let it be" can be an appropriate request. Respect and honor it; invite future involvement. But don't push if not wanted.

Within-session processing can occur in three ways, by leaders (a) pausing the action, (b) scheduling at the session's end, or (c) using both ways. When leaders pause action for in-session processing they take advantage of immediacy as a learning device. Something has just occurred that seems significant, and the leader senses that examining it *right-then-and-there* might potentially yield valuable learning, insight, or meaning. The obvious advantage in pausing the action is that key events and experiences can be captured for processing. The disadvantage is that the ongoing flow of inter-action is disturbed. See Case Illustration 9–3.

Case Illustration 9–3: Pausing the Action

*The **object** of this case illustration is to demonstrate how at times it can be valuable for a group work leader to seek some space in the interaction—to request a pause in it—to allow time for reflection.*

Suzanne ends her statement about her struggle with a personal reluctance to stay involved with the group: " . . . and so, I'm not sure if I really want to go ahead with it or not."

The group leader says, "I wonder if this might be a good time to stop for a moment and review where we are, to take a step back and see what has been going on and then what we might be able to learn from it.

"Suzanne, I'd like to invite you to begin because you're closest to it all. Looking back over the last several minutes, can you share how you've gotten to this point and what it means?"

When group work leaders schedule processing to occur at the end of a session, they choose to allow interaction to complete itself without inter-ruption by processing; saving it for the end provides the opportunity to address the entire session for its meaning. The advantage of this approach is that members are able to consider for processing the material from the entire session; as well, the opportunity exists for a complete session to be summarized and integrated. Another advantage is that processing becomes an additional topic and does not interrupt the ongoing course of interaction. A disadvantage of holding processing until a session's end is that significant events and experiences are not caught at the moment of their occurrence, possibly diminishing the intensity of learning. See Case Illustration 9–4.

Finally, leaders may select both approaches to use in a session, if the com-bination fits the circumstances. All advantages inherent in the previous two approaches can be gained. A disadvantage might be that a disproportionate time could be spent on processing, as opposed to direct interaction.

Between-session processing. In all professional pursuits, practitioners can continuously improve. In fact, continuing education is required in most, if not all, professions and preparation and review are routine.

Case Illustration 9–4: At the End of a Session

*The **object** of this case illustration is to show one way that within session processing can occur.*

About 10 minutes remain in the session. As is expected, the leader turns the discussion toward processing:

"Well, I notice we are moving quickly now toward the end of our session for today. As usual, then, it's time for us to take a look back at what's been occurring and identifying any bigger learning that may have arisen.

"So, I'll open this up for anyone to begin . . ."

Music and sports are two domains that provide clear illustrations of how essential preparation and review are. These are processes occurring outside of actual performance, as you recall.

If you've ever been a member of a choir, chorus, band, or other musical group or played a team sport, such as basketball, baseball, or soccer, you are very aware of the time and effort spent on training, preparation, practice, rehearsal, and review of performance. Even if you have not personally been involved in such activities, you most likely know from observational experience how much preparation and review are involved. Game plans, musical scores, practicing plays, use of videotape for review, and long practice and rehearsal sessions are prototypically part of the life of a musician or an athlete. For the conductor or the coach, managing and directing these procedures is a major responsibility, as is spending long hours in review of one's own performance as a way to personally achieve at higher levels, and to assist the team and its members do the same.

Similar attention to preparation and review outside of performance itself also is an important feature of group work leadership. This activity is known as *between-session processing,* and it is a best practice (Guideline C-1):

Group workers process the workings of the group with themselves, group members, supervisors or other colleagues, as appropriate. This may include assessing progress on group and member goals, leader behaviors and techniques, group dynamics and interventions, developing understanding and acceptance of meaning. Processing may occur both within sessions and before and after each session, at time of termination, and later follow up, as appropriate. (ASGW, 2007, p. 117)

Therefore, group leaders are encouraged to conduct processing of their leadership between sessions. It can be accomplished by a leader independently, with a coleader, or in supervision (Riva, 2011). Approaches used in within-session processing, such as the one suggested by Stockton et al. (2000), also can be applied in between sessions.

A model very appropriate for between-session processing is termed, *deep processing* (Conyne, 1999; Conyne et al., 2008; Rapin & Conyne, 2006). Deep processing, to be described later in this chapter, provides a means for translating experience to meaning, as do other approaches. In addition, it can assist in developing leadership expertise over time (Trotzer, 2011) and for accentuating personal and professional identity and development.

Benefits accruing from between-session processing are obvious. First and foremost, this form of processing can directly improve practice. Reflective examination of troublesome group events, or of those that have gone well, can illuminate the processes involved allowing leaders to identify what works and what does not with the potential existing for developing useful follow-up applications in the present group. Meaning extracted allows for the emergence of potentially generalizable principles (Conyne, 1997b) that can be of service in future group situations.

Moreover, between-session processing can be a tool for personal and professional identity development, a point to be considered in more detail later in this chapter. It provides a structured and intentional opportunity for examining and enhancing one's development as a professional.

There are virtually no downsides to between-session processing.

Guarding against nudging out processing during sessions. Processing is frequently overlooked by group leaders in favor of direct experience. But, if processing is so important in group work, why do leaders often omit it during group sessions (Riva, Wachtel, & Butcher, 2000; Riva, Wachtel, & Lasky, 2004)? When push comes to shove during a group session, especially when the session seems to be flowing well, the tendency for leaders to stop the action and ask for processing decreases; in a very real sense, they want the good times to roll on without interruption. When a session is going poorly, conversely, some leaders are unlikely to pause for processing out of fear that member comments could be hurtful or from a reluctance to put members on the spot. Finally, leaders can simply allow time to cut short an opportunity for processing, particularly if it had been planned for the end of a session. Whatever the reasons for omitting processing from a session, this oversight inevitably is associated with shallow progress and limited learning for group members and leaders alike. Again, why is this is so? It is because it is out of the analysis of direct experience, employing the self-reflective loop, that learning occurs most efficaciously.

Guarding against omitting between-session processing. Similar tendencies to minimize or even avoid processing can and often do occur with its between-session form. Other duties and responsibilities call, so does relaxation, and understandably so. Tempus fugit indeed is a contemporary dynamic with which we all must deal. The effect of these forces on between-session processing is that for many leaders it becomes difficult to schedule time for it to occur and to be able to maintain that schedule (Conyne, Wilson, & Ward, 1997).

Because of the importance of processing for effective group leading, therefore, wise group leaders need to be mindful of the tendency for external (and some internal) forces to nudge processing out. They are encouraged to work concertedly to keep it an integral part of group sessions and to consistently schedule it into life outside the group. See Learning Exercise 9–3.

Learning Exercise 9–3:
Schedule Coleader Between-Session Processing

*The **object** of this learning exercise is to try out a way to schedule group leader processing between sessions and to identify learning.*

As Phil and Gigi planned their upcoming staff training group, they moved to the question of assuring quality. They knew about between-session processing from their study of best practices. While they both felt committed to making their group as effective as possible, and valued the concept of processing their work, actually scheduling a regular meeting time seemed burdensome. Was it really necessary?

Here's where you come in.

Select a partner. Role-play being Phil and Gigi in the above situation.

The desired outcome is for you to find a workable way to set a between-session processing meeting following each group meeting. Yet, as you can see, there is reluctance. See if you can work through that.

When done (allot 10 minutes to this discussion), process your interaction.

- What did you learn?
- What could you potentially apply?

REFLECTING *ON* GROUP ●
WORK PRACTICE: TAKING PERSPECTIVE

I assume that most readers of this volume and the series of volumes of which it is a part are drawn from the counseling profession. At the same time, there are a number of readers who share an interest and even a specialization in group work and who are affiliated with a related profession, such as clinical psychology or social work.

Some of the commonalities across these helping professions are the unshakable value assigned to client welfare, to the quality of practice, and to the personal and professional well-being of practitioners. The common ethic surrounding client welfare is no doubt clearly understood as a priority among priorities. The importance placed on quality of practice, in this case of group work, is an obviously important factor. An emphasis placed on the health and well-being of practitioners in the profession, however, is only beginning to be realized as an imperative concern.

The term *group work practice*, as I use it here, is intended to include the delivery of group work by those who deliver it. That is, it embraces both the practice itself as well as the practitioner. So there is a vital and dynamic link existing between the healthiness of group leaders and their ability to execute leadership responsibilities effectively.

In the pages of this chapter, "Reflecting *in* Group Practice," you read about how group leaders can be reflective in their work with particular groups through such means as within- and between-group processing. In addition, it is necessary for group leaders to engage in reflecting more broadly on their work as leaders, that is, to take perspective of themselves and their work. In so doing, they can continuously assess their professional identity, development, satisfaction, and well-being and how these factors relate to their overall effectiveness as group leaders. Reflecting *on* group practice is the way I refer to that approach.

The Deep Processing Model (Conyne, 1999): Toward Personal and Professional Development

This model of between-session processing drills downward. It asks group leaders to engage in a series of examinations leading to concrete application possibilities for the current group being led. Beyond that, the model is aimed at identifying potential generalizable action strategies, while facilitating personal, professional, and ethical development. See Figure 9-1.

Figure 9.1   Steps in the Deep Processing Model

Step 1: TRANSPOSE/RECORD

Objective observation and recording

Step 2: REFLECT

Subjective awareness

Step 3: DISCOVER

Integration

Step 4: APPLY

Evaluated action

Step 5: EVOLVE

Derivation of substantive principles

Step 1: Transpose/Record. When using this model, leaders are guided to begin their review of a previous group session by taking close note of the concrete events that occurred and making a record of them without any manipulation or hypothesizing. The intent in this step is to objectively and pragmatically record or take note of the specific happenings of interest in the session, without any attempt whatsoever at interpreting them. That is, transposing means to specifically convert concrete observations made during the session or meeting to written form in order to better retain the observations. In doing so, subjective elements related to affect or theorizing are stripped away—only the objective data remains (at least as much as possible).

In shorthand, in this step, the group leader describes and records (transposes) exactly what happened in the session's incident, without elaborating hypothesizing, or interpreting.

Step 2: Reflect. Where Step 1 is restricted to objective description, this step is centered on subjective awareness. Here, the group leader is asked to identify her or his own thoughts, feelings, sensations, awareness, and values as they relate to the incident described in Step 1.

In shorthand, in this step, the group leader describes his or her awareness of the selected event(s) captured in Step 1.

Step 3: Discover. Now it's time to go to the extant research, the relevant professional literature base having bearing on the incident being considered. What is happening now when using the Deep Processing Model is that knowledge and evidence from external professional sources is being integrated with the objective (Step 1) and subjective (Step 2) information produced earlier. For example, this external information might be a theory, data from a study, reviewing a group development model, or interventions that have been shown to work.

In shorthand, in this step, the group leader integrates external sources of information with both objective and subjective information.

Step 4: Apply. This step is concerned with asking the question, "What can be done in my current group?" A leader asks how progressing through the previous three steps (the integration of objective, subjective, and external information) relates to the challenges being faced in this group right now? What can be done?

Various strategies are considered, weighed for potential effectiveness, and eventually one strategy (with a Plan A, there always needs to be a Plan B) is selected to try in the next session. This is an evaluated action kind of approach.

In shorthand, in this step, the group leader evaluates action possibilities emerging from the integration of objective, subjective, and external information and selects at least one for a tryout in the next session.

Step 5: Evolve. In this final step of the model, the leader is asked to turn attention to a broader perspective, exceeding the question of what might best be done in the current group. Instead, here the leader is asked to take perspective, focusing on issues connected with potential generalizable action strategies, with personal and professional identity and development, and with best practice and ethical issues.

Example questions that a group leader might confront during Step 5 are "What am I learning that might rise to the level of a substantive principle that can be generalized to other situations I may face in the future?" "What am I learning about myself as a person and as a group leader?" "How am I progressing?" "What do I need to do?" "How is my level of wellness?" "Am I taking proper care of myself?" and "How am I evolving as an ethical group leader?"

Step 5 may not always produce results. After all, big principles, such as those looked for here, tend to come gradually. But concentrating on this step consistently serves the purpose of evolving movement gradually and inextricably toward these big principles, making them that much more likely to be found.

In shorthand, in this step, the group leader takes a broader perspective, searching for substantive principles about his or her level of functioning, about leading groups that may be generalizable to other situations, and about general issues of personal, professional, and ethical identity and development.

Self-Care

A key aspect of professional development is personal development. How happy and satisfied one is in life affects—and is affected by—everything else. One's overall wellness status across the major domains of life (physical, emotional, spiritual, work, leisure, family, friends, overall balance) is a critically important gauge of quality of life.

A tenet of the counseling profession rests on a foundation of wellness for counselors in training and for counseling professionals (Ramey & Leibert, 2011). For group work leaders and those who are preparing to assume that role, attending to one's level of wellness is essential. The American Counseling Association Task Force on Counselor Wellness and Impairment has produced a variety of helpful resources on self-care (American Counseling Association [ACA], 2010b). As well, ACA and other professional helping associations have included impairment within their codes.

Counseling, in general, and group leading, in particular, can be highly stressful as well as rewarding. As we have seen, the group situation is replete with challenges. It is a complex social milieu with constantly changing dynamics. The group work leader's responsibilities are nearly always demanding, due to the multiplicity of shifting interaction patterns and to the ambiguities and subtleties that often are at play. Even the joys of group leading—and there can be many—can be source of stress for, as we know, positive events in life also can stretch personal resources.

For these, and many other reasons, group leaders and those in training need to find ways to take care of themselves. The Deep Processing Model discussed above has built into it the capacity to attend to matters of self-care, especially at its Step 5, "Evolve." While this provides one means for self-assessment related to caring for oneself, group leaders might well find a variety of ways.

By self-care I do not mean self-indulgence. Indeed, this is not a narcissistic endeavor, but one attuned to self-preservation and self-efficacy. Belonging to a cadre of helpers, counselors and group leaders want to be helpful to others and, in many ways, doing so explicates a deep-seated personal need, as well as a professional prerogative.

Yet, too much giving without nurturing oneself along the way may jeopardize one's health and effectiveness. Without appropriate self-replenishment, it is possible to continually erode one's resources on an eventual road to depletion and burnout, where productivity is reduced considerably and one can end up feeling helpless, hopeless, cynical, and resentful, with nothing left to give (Norcross & Guy, 2007). The ACA and other related associations, such as the American Psychological Association and the National Association of Social Workers, have incorporated into their ethical codes guidance related to "impairment" (e.g., ACA, 2005, A.11b), *the situation when a counselor or therapist needs to refrain from providing professional services and instead must seek help.*

An antidote and preventive tool to this trek toward emptiness is *self-care*: "Allowing yourself to be a human being with needs to be respected" (Adams, 2010, p. 2). If you believe that what you do as a group leader is important, then it behooves you to nurture yourself so you can continue to do it well.

One way to monitor how you are doing with taking care of yourself is to periodically self-assess. Refer to Learning Exercise 9–4 that contains one way to accomplish this goal.

Learning Exercise 9–4: Excerpts From *Assessing Self-Care Assessment Worksheet*

The **object** of this learning exercise is to assess strategies for self-care and to select specific ones to personally implement.

After completing the full assessment, choose one item from each area that you will actively work to improve.

Using the scale below, rate the following areas in terms of frequency: 5 = Frequently, 4 = Occasionally, 3 = Rarely, 2 = Never, 1 = It never occurred to me

Physical Self-Care

___ Eat regularly (e.g., breakfast, lunch, and dinner)

___ Exercise

___ Get medical care when needed

___ Take time off when needed

___ Dance, swim, walk, run, play sports, sing, or do some other physical activity that is fun

___ Get enough sleep

___ Take vacations

(Continued)

(Continued)

___ Make time away from telephones

___ Other:

Psychological Self-Care

___ Make time for self-reflection

___ Write in a journal

___ Read literature that is unrelated to work

___ Decrease stress in your life

___ Notice your inner experience—listen to your thoughts, judgments, beliefs, attitudes, and feelings

___ Practice receiving from others

___ Be curious

___ Other:

Emotional Self-Care

___ Stay in contact with important people in your life

___ Give yourself affirmations, praise yourself

___ Reread favorite books, re-view favorite movies

___ Identify comforting activities, objects, people, relationships, places, and seek them out

___ Find things that make you laugh

___ Other:

Spiritual Self-Care

___ Make time for reflection

___ Find a spiritual connection or community

___ Be open to inspiration

___ Be aware of nonmaterial aspects of life

___ Try at times not to be in charge or the expert

___ Identify what in meaningful to you and notice its place in your life

(Continued)

___ Meditate

___ Sing

___ Spend time with children

___ Contribute to causes in which you believe

___ Read inspirational literature (talks, music, etc.)

___ Other:

Workplace or Professional Self-Care

___ Take a break during the workday (e.g., lunch)

___ Make quiet time to complete tasks

___ Identify projects or tasks that are exciting and rewarding

___ Balance your caseload so that no one day or part of a day is "too much"

___ Negotiate for your needs (benefits, pay raise)

___ Have a peer support group

___ Other:

Balance

___ Strive for balance within your work-life and workday

___ Strive for balance among work, family, relationships, play, and rest

Source: Adapted from *Transforming the Pain: A Workbook on Vicarious Traumatization,* Saakvitne, Pearlman, & Staff of TSI/CAAP (1996).

Meditation as one self-care tool. Self-care strategies can be applied to address each of the domains I mentioned earlier. For instance, including a program of healthy nutrition and regular exercise can yield improvements in the physical domain and others. I want to briefly address just one way to nurture oneself: mindful meditation. A recently reported study (Gray, 2012) indicated that just a few hours of meditation training, involving intense focus and concentration, may improve one's brain functioning, leading to improved self-control, mood, stress, and immunity response. Incidentally, as I have been practicing yoga over the last year, I have found not only improved flexibility and balance resulting (physical domain) but also an elevation of what I would call "quietness" in my life. Now, for any group leader being able to find periods of quietude would be a welcomed balance to the intensity found in group leadership.

Professional Practice and Accountability

As with any other professional practice, group work is held accountable. *Is there evidence that it works* is an essential question asked by many audiences, including potential group members, agencies considering including groups in their service repertoire, funding sources of mental health and educational organizations, and third-party insurance carriers.

The good news is that group does work, as I reported in Chapter 4. For instance, group counseling and psychotherapy has been documented as an important intervention for psychologists and other practitioners based on its evidence of effectiveness and other factors (Leszcz & Kobos, 2008). Generally, it has been found through experience and empirical research to be at least as effective as individual therapy in promoting client change while offering additional efficiencies and cost benefits in some cases (see Barlow, 2011; McRoberts, Burlingame, & Hoag, 1998; and the wide range of other supportive sources cited in Conyne, 2012).

Group leaders can draw from the accrued knowledge base supporting group work effectiveness to bolster their work. It is incumbent on them to stay current with the relevant professional literature. For instance, in the field of group work they will need to regularly read such journals as *Group Dynamics: Theory, Research and Practice* (the official journal of the Society of Group Psychology and Group Psychotherapy of the American Psychological Association) and the *Journal for Specialists in Group Work* (the official journal of the Association for Specialists in Group Work, a division of the American Counseling Association). They can take care, whenever possible, to set their own groups within an appropriate research design (Stockton & Morran, 2011) that might allow them to better understand their practice and to communicate about it with others. At the least, when unable to execute a research design (which may be often), they can and should conduct program evaluations (Conyne, 2010) of the processes and outcomes of their groups, drawing from both quantitative and from qualitative approaches (Rubel & Okech, 2011).

Competent group work leaders are accountable professionals. They follow best practice and ethical guidelines, stay current in the field, process and evaluate their groups, and practice appropriate self-care.

GROUP WORK KEYSTONES

- Reflecting is an important practice for group work leaders and members.
- Reflecting in group work is expressed through processing, whether that be conducted within a group sessions or between them.
- To address reflecting *in* group practice, one group at a time, considerable attention was given to processing both within sessions and between sessions. Various ways to conduct processing were discussed, and the importance of scheduling between-session processing time was emphasized.
- Reflecting *on* group practice means to take a longer range perspective, in addition to focusing on a specific group currently being led. It is an effort to improve overall professional practice, one's own leadership efficacy, and is relevant for facilitating self-care.
- Self-care was emphasized as a critically important process for group leaders to build into their daily lives. Appropriate nurturing of self can buffer excessive stress that group leadership situations can produce over time.
- Accountability is an important part of group leadership. Evidence was cited attesting to the general effectiveness of group work and various strategies were suggested for how group leaders can accentuate accountability in their practice.

RECOMMENDED RESOURCES

American Counseling Association. (2005). *Code of ethics and standards of practice.* Alexandria, VA: Author. Retrieved from http://www.counseling.org/Resources/CodeOfEthics/TP/Home/CT2.aspx

Bridbord, K. (2002). Processing activities to facilitate the transfer of learning outside of group. In J. DeLucia-Waack, K. Bridbord, & J. Kleiner (Eds.), *Group work experts share their favorite activities: A guide to choosing, planning, conducting, and processing* (pp. 15–25). Alexandria, VA: Association for Specialists in Group Work.

Conyne, R. (1999). *Failures in group work: How we can learn from our mistakes.* Thousand Oaks, CA: Sage.

DeLucia-Waack, J. (1997). The importance of processing activities, exercises, and events to group work practitioners. *Journal for Specialists in Group Work, 22,* 82–84.

Glass, J., & Benshoff, J. (1999). PARS: A processing model for beginning group leaders. *Journal for Specialists in Group Work, 24,* 15–26.

Kees, N., & Jacobs, E. (1990). Conducting more effective groups: How to select and process group exercises. *Journal for Specialists in Group Work, 15,* 21–30.

Leszcz, M., & Kobos, J. (2008). Evidence-based group psychotherapy: Using AGPA's practice guidelines to enhance clinical effectiveness. *Journal of Clinical Psychology, 64*, 1238–1260.

Norcross, J., & Guy, J. (2007). *Leaving it at the office: A guide to psychotherapist self-care*. New York, NY: Guilford Press.

Riva, M., Wachtel, M., & Butcher, G. (2000, March). *Understanding group co-therapy relationships: A developmental approach*. Paper presented at the American Counseling Association Annual Convention, Washington, DC.

Riva, M., Wachtel, M., & Lasky, G. (2004). Effective leadership in group counseling and psychotherapy. In J. DeLucia-Waack, D. Gerrity, C. Kalodner, & M. Riva (Eds.), *Handbook of group counseling and psychotherapy* (pp. 37–48). Thousand Oaks, CA: Sage.

Rubel, D., & Okech, J. Qualitative research approaches and group counseling. In R. Conyne (Ed.), *The Oxford handbook of group counseling* (pp. 260–286). New York, NY: Oxford University Press.

Stockton, R., Morran, D. K., & Nitza, A. (2000). Processing group events: A conceptual map for leaders. *Journal for Specialists in Group Work, 25*, 343–355.

Ward, D., & Lichy, M. (2004). The effective use of processing in groups. In J. DeLucia-Waack, D. Gerrity, C. Kalodner, & M. Riva (Eds.), *Handbook of group counseling and psychotherapy* (pp. 104–119). Thousand Oaks, CA: Sage.

CHAPTER 10

SELECTING EFFECTIVE INTERVENTIONS

A guy gets into a cab in New York City and asks the cab driver, "How do I get to Carnegie Hall?" and the cab driver replies, "Practice, practice, practice."

—Attributed to Youngman

There are no mistakes, no coincidences. All events are blessings given to us to learn from.

—Elisabeth Kubler-Ross

INTRODUCTION ●

How do professionals and those in training apply their group work leading competencies to effectively and appropriately lead groups, whether they be task, psychoeducation, counseling, or therapy in scope? What are the roles of practice and processing in group work leadership? How can group work leaders learn from errors and mistakes? How are alternatives, choices, and consequences involved? How can leaders select interventions that *best fit* the situations they face, that stand the best chance to be effective? These are some of the important questions addressed in this chapter.

We examine some specific interactions among members and leaders and involve you at critical decision points. Practical situations drawn from each of the four group work types are presented. Intervention possibilities are considered, guided by a set of progressive steps group leaders may follow in their own practice. Analysis of choices is provided, yielding selections that are examined for their consequences.

In a sense, this is a culminating chapter of the book. It builds on all the case illustrations and learning exercises you've encountered in previous chapters. Chapter contents provide you with applications that will be useful and meaningful for you in your development as a professional helper and, more particularly, a group work leader.

CHAPTER OBJECTIVES

As a result of reading this chapter you will be able to

- Address the role of practice and processing in group work leadership
- Note the value of learning from errors, mistakes, and failures
- Become acquainted with the *Purposeful Group Techniques Model (PGTM)*
- Review a *critical incident* approach
- Examine interaction samples from four types of group work: task, psycho-education, counseling, and psychotherapy
- Highlight salient *choice points* and related leader behavior
- Examine how group leaders can arrive at selecting effective interventions
- Underscore the importance of professional judgment in selecting group leader interventions

● THE ROLE OF PRACTICE AND PROCESSING IN ACCOMPLISHED GROUP LEADERSHIP

Let's begin by asking an important question that has been kind of bouncing around and through the previous book chapters: "How does one become an accomplished group work leader?"

Here is where I should rush out all the old bromides. You know, take the right courses, get the right training, learn the right knowledge and skills, connect them with who you are as a person, and then once you have those under control—voilá—You're a good group work leader! The previous book chapters have dealt with all those elements, and more.

Well . . . maybe, that can do it, but I don't think so. There is nothing simple or instantaneous about becoming a good group work leader. Sure, knowledge, skills, and personal characteristics are of vital importance, but the critical essence of it all is contained in the phrase *once you have those under control.*

Becoming proficient as a group leader exceeds the simple execution of knowledge + skill + personal characteristics, even though those are fundamental. No, it's more than that. Two other elements are needed, for getting things under control. These additional elements forge knowledge, skills, and personal characteristics, on the one hand, and then age them like a fine wine, on the other. They are

(a) *intense practice* in being a group member and leader, which can yield both successes and failures

(b) *processing,* including supervision, to help make sense of practice and experience, yielding learning principles that can be applied in group leadership. Processing, with its within- and between-session forms, was a focus of Chapter 9. The two chapter-opening quotes address those very points.

Practice: Providing Opportunities to Learn From Successes and Failures

Importance of practice. Malcolm Gladwell (2002) in his book *The Tipping Point* indicates that it takes 10,000 hours of practice to create an expert. One way of calculating that number of hours is 20 hours a week for 10 years. Unmistakably, becoming an expert group leader involves a staggering amount of effort and dedication. He also said in another book, *Outliers* (Gladwell, 2008, p. 42) that "Practice isn't the thing you do once you're good. It's the thing you do that makes you good."

Preparation standards, with CACREP as the example. Standards addressing the preparation of professional helpers help to guide and monitor the development of new professionals. In Chapter 2, you read about Council for the Accreditation of Counseling and Related Educational Programs (CACREP) accreditation requirements and related training standards of Association for Specialists in Group Work (ASGW). I pointed out my view that the CACREP standards are deficient with regard to preparing students to be adequate group leaders.

To review, the CACREP standards speak to practice in group work by addressing *direct experience, practicum,* and *internship.* The standard for direct experience requires that students participate directly in a small group activity approved by the program for a minimum of 10 clock hours over the course of one academic term. The practicum experience standard requires at least 40 direct service clock hours and specifies no attention to group work. The internship experience standard is somewhat improved, requiring at least 240 direct service clock hours "including experience leading groups." One wonders, though: Would 10 clock hours of experience leading groups in internship satisfy the requirement? How about 1 hour? Not nearly enough.

I imagine Gladwell would agree, while recognizing that a graduate training program can do only so much in helping students move along toward accumulating the 10,000 practice hours he claims are needed to become experts. If nothing else, the apparent gap in group work clock hours between what a student can attain at graduation from a counseling program and what is needed to attain expert status suggests the need for considerable postgraduate specialized continuing education, supervised practice, and/ or additional formalized training in group work. In addition, it is my view that the group work preparation situation would be improved by CACREP shoring up its direct experience requirements in group work to a level suggested by the ASGW in its training standards (ASGW, 2000). You may want to refer to the relevant discussion in Chapter 2 as a reminder.

Mistakes and failures. Within one's training program and then as a graduate, if you are really trying, you will enjoy successes and also make innumerable mistakes. Realizing success is an obvious benefit that is immediately recognizable. Being able to help a group member achieve a long-standing desire to express himself or herself unambiguously for maybe the first time, for instance, can bring a strong sense of satisfaction. It's the mistakes side of the equation that I want to focus on, one that may not be quite so obvious as a source of value.

You will make mistakes, errors, blunders, slip-ups, gaffes, missteps, bloopers and experience failures. Not that there's anything wrong with that. In fact, contrary to what many would think, there is a whole lot that can be right about it. Burkeman (2012), for example, in a treatise that challenges some of the basic tenets of positive psychology, suggests that accepting our failures and learning how to cope with and even enjoy uncertainty are better routes to becoming truly happy. After all, as Kottler and Blau (1989) pointed out about counselors and therapists, we all are "imperfect therapists" just as we all are flawed humans.

Our first task in dealing with mistakes and failures is to accept our limitations and the reality that we will make mistakes and that sometimes we will fail. Our second task is to place these eventualities in a perspective from which we can learn.

In an interview summarized in the *Newsweek* column "My Favorite Mistake" (Stern, 2012), the actress Maggie Gyllenhaal related a painful incident involved with messing up her lines while shooting a movie. Stressed out by all kinds of things to do from her personal life and under the demands of a full day of complicated shooting, she had nonetheless finished the day feeling fine about how things had gone, only for her producer to ask if she might need someone to assist with mastering her lines. Gyllenhaal declined the offer, only to wind up bursting into uncontrollable tears back in her makeup trailer.

The writer and star of the film, Emma Thompson, provided a balancing vantage point. She pointed out to Gyllenhaal that she was only recently married, had a 2-year-old, and had been shooting the movie on location for 4 months. It was only natural, she suggested, that lines would be flubbed occasionally and that is certainly OK; however, Thompson also said, "And you didn't know your lines that well today" (Stern, 2012, p. 56). What was Thompson's contribution? As would a good mentor, she helped to put the whole event into a more manageable perspective, being both empathic and supportive, while pointing out that some more work did need to be done on the lines.

Here's another everyday example, this one from my life. I can get lost in a bathtub, if I'm not paying close attention, which—often—I'm not, nearly always thinking about projects and other things as I move about my day. One time, I drove to the airport to pick up a job candidate who was to be interviewed for a university position in my department over a couple of strenuous days. I parked in one of the interlinked (mark, confusing) airport parking garages and went to fetch him. Having picked him up, we now exited the airport, talking away, with the next step being to get in my car and return to the university to begin the interviewing process. Simple enough, right?

But I could not, for the life of me, find my car! Now, this is embarrassing, especially at a time when everyone is interested in making positive impressions. We circled around, the candidate and I, in and out of a couple of the connected garages. I enlisted him in the search, having described my car (thank goodness for that), and we prowled together, finally to literally stumble across it about half an hour later. I laughed it off with him, hoping he'd buy my story of "just trying to show you my error-prone way is really very human, after all." Well, in the end, did he accept the job offer? Yes! In spite of my bungling around.

I've adopted two strategies to help me cope with my proclivity to get turned around when my mind is elsewhere: The first is to laugh when this occurs and certainly to not berate myself. In fact, I sometimes autosuggest that in getting lost I provide yet another opportunity for self-discovery—in the existential sense, as well as literally. I admit having to continually work at this one. The second, which I tend to quite naturally use when traveling in a new and foreign environment, is to actually pay attention, to look for sign posts, and to actively place them in recall. In other words, I have found ways to turn mistakes into adequacies.

Group work leaders can turn their mistakes and failures into learning opportunities, too. That's the main point I emphasize in my book *Failures in Group Work: How We Can Learn from Our Mistakes* (Conyne, 1999). Sometimes during long periods of a monologue in group, especially when one member is going on and on and on, I catch myself drifting, losing contact with the present, lost somewhere in another place. Usually, it has to do with something I need to get done later in the day, like an upcoming lecture that ekes its way into my consciousness and takes over for a while. Yes, I can catch myself, which certainly is beneficial. But the elapsed time, when I am away from the here-and-now, is not. It's a mistake, really, something that I need to learn from and prevent in the future.

Processing: Converting Experience and Practice Into Meaning

As you read in the preceding chapter, processing enables group members and leaders to learn from their experience and to draw meaning from all the practice in which they must engage. It was Socrates who is credited with the bold assertion that the "unexamined life is not worth living." Not even partially, for him. Do you know of someone who may be nearly allergic to self-examination? Who may, for instance, charge through life like a "bull in a china shop"? Or, less dramatically, may simply "keep on keeping on," the "same ole, same ole"; you may sometimes have used these kinds of phrases yourself from time to time. These sayings capture in short hand the mundane routine of life, where little seems to happen or matter, or where whatever does occur (for certainly events do occur) are not noticed or appraised. Or, in the opposite case, sometimes so much is transpiring with such intensity and rapidity that it may be challenging to find the time and energy to slow down, to take a breath, to take a look, and reflect on the value and significance of these events.

Purposeful Group Techniques Model (PGTM). Group leaders need to attend to and learn from the ongoing group experience, warts and all, while drawing from it to select well-suited interventions. The Deep Processing Model (Conyne, 1999) we examined in Chapter 9 provides one method that is used by group leaders for drawing meaning from experience. A second one, which will inform leader intervention choices in the cases that are considered later in this chapter, is the *Purposeful Group Techniques Model* (Conyne, Crowell, & Newmeyer, 2008; Newmeyer, 2011). The PGTM relies on the importance of generating action alternatives in a group situation and then learning how to arrive at reasoned choices for action. See Figure 10–1 that describes the steps of the model.

Critical incidents. Cohen and Smith (1976) developed an approach to training in growth groups and in group leadership that is based on critical incidents. The PGTM draws from the critical incident approach. Others have

Figure 10.1   The Purposeful Group Techniques Model (PGTM)

> Step 1: Identify
>
> Step 2: Analyze
>
> Step 3: Review
>
> Step 4: Select
>
> Step 5: Implement and Evaluate

Identify: Group type (task, psychoeducational, counseling, psychotherapy)

Developmental stage of the group (e.g., beginning, middle, end)

Best practice area involved (planning, performing, processing)

Analyze: Group situation analysis; Ecological concepts may be of value (e.g., context, degree of interconnection).

Review: Possible strategies and techniques available

Select: Appropriateness, adequacy, effectiveness, efficiency, side effects

Implement and evaluate: How well did it work?

applied this approach to therapy groups (Donigian & Hulse-Killacky, 1999) and to counseling groups (Tyson, Perusse, & Whitledge, 2004). I draw from the critical incident approach in this chapter.

A *critical incident* refers to a group situation that demands of the group leader an explicit opinion, decision, or action. A *choice point* is always involved, where alternatives are considered, weighed, and selected—with a *best fit* intended (Cohen & Smith, 1976). By "best fit," I mean that the intervention selected meshes most closely with important aspects of the presenting situation, with the capabilities of the group leader to deliver it well, and affords the highest potential for effectiveness.

For instance, a leader may consider making an individual-level versus a group-level intervention. Furthermore, he or she may think in terms of responding to feelings or to thoughts. Many considerations factor into a best fit decision: context, culture, group's developmental stage, and others. One of the features of choice possibilities is that the alternative selected and applied takes the group in one direction, while a second or a third alternative would lead the group in other directions.

These choice points have received attention outside of group work, of course. You probably are familiar with Robert Frost's (1916) classic poem "The Road Not Taken." Confronted with two roads in the wood, the traveler takes one of them, the one less traveled, which is reported to have "made all the difference." The reader assumes that is a positive difference, but who knows? And recall, the title of the poem addresses the road *not* taken, rather than the one chosen. One wonders what might have occurred if the other road had been traveled instead?

The movie *Sliding Doors* (Intermedia Films, 1998) also deftly presents the critical incident choice. After Helen (played by Gwyneth Paltrow) is fired unexpectedly, she dejectedly heads back down to the Underground to return to her London flat. But as she runs down the stairs to catch the train that is about to depart the station, the narrative of her life is split off, with the movie playing out in two parallel versions. In one scenario, Helen catches the train, and in the second, she misses it. Throughout the rest of the film, the viewer discovers what would have happened in each scenario, and the results are dramatically different.

Choices have consequences. We choose the best that we can at a moment in time, given what we know and what we think the odds are. Or, maybe not so much thinking enters in; we just react, quite impulsively, trusting our gut. In any case, we are put on one path, not the other. A door opens, another closes, for a while or perhaps permanently. We learn. We rejoice or we move on, hopefully wiser for the experience.

Before we begin examining some group interactions in terms of choices made and not made—and their consequences—please take a look at Learning Exercise 10-1.

Learning Exercise 10–1: Personal "Sliding Doors"

*The **object** of this learning exercise is to increase awareness of life choices made, with implications for group work.*

All of us have faced innumerable choices in life. One of mine involved purchasing, largely on impulse, a plot of land in the boonies of northern Ontario. Why? I dunno! Not very elegant, but it has turned out to be a pivotal action. That remote spit of land now anchors our family cottage, and it is a true beacon not only for my life, but for those of my wife and two children as well. If we were unable to spend part of our summers there, every summer since I made that spontaneous purchase 40 years ago now, we would feel bereft.

In other critical incidents in which I invested more analysis, I selected one college to attend instead of others, chose to remain in a job rather than to accept another offer, and on a long bicycle ride

(Continued)

decided to divert to a route around eastern Lake Michigan (a much longer way) rather than taking the more direct path.

Well, how about you? What sliding doors have you experienced? Complete these steps:

1. Identify one example of a personal or professional sliding door in your life.

   _____

   _____

2. Describe the options that presented themselves so that you could have chosen *this* way or *that* way. . . .

   _____

   _____

3. Indicate which way you chose: _____

4. What benefits came your way; what was lost or gained? _____

   _____

   _____

5. How does your sliding door experience connect with group work?

   _____

   _____

LEADER CHOICES IN GROUP: THOSE MADE, THOSE NOT MADE ●

For the remainder of the chapter, you will be able to consider case situations illustrating interventions made by group leaders and those they could have made. A case is presented from four types of group work (ASGW, 2000): a task group, psychoeducation group, counseling group, and a psychotherapy group. Although the cases are based on actual occurrences, all information provided has been otherwise fabricated and/or disguised so as to bear no direct relationship to any past or existing situation with which I have been involved.

The inspiration for these cases can be found in two of my earlier books, *Failures in Group Work,* which I mentioned earlier (Conyne, 1999), and

How Personal Growth and Task Groups Work (Conyne, 1989). Both of those sources contain several examples of groups in action, along with analysis.

The 10-step format is followed in this chapter employs a *choice-point* approach and engages you at select moments. It also connects essential aspects of theories discussed in Chapter 6 with the four case examples presented.

- *Group interaction will be examined from a task, psychoeducaton, counseling, and psychotherapy group.*
- *Each case will begin with a context, or background.*
- *Interaction will converge on what appears to be a choice point facing the leader.*
- ***You will be asked for your input.***
- *Two possible intervention choices (of course, there could be more than two), with rationale, will be presented, connected with theories.*
- *A decision will be reached, to pursue Option A or Option B (drawing from the PGTM).*
- *Interaction will continue following leader Choice A.*
- *Interaction will continue following leader Choice B.*
- *Consequences will be identified.*
- ***You will be asked for your overall comments.***

● INTERVENTION SELECTION CASES FROM FOUR GROUP WORK TYPES

Task Group Illustration: Student Representative at the Weekly Faculty Meeting

You've gotten an eyeful, an earful, and more in your role as elected student representative at the weekly faculty meeting. It's amazing to you that faculty sometimes can act so badly when they are together in this meeting, as opposed to how they are in class or just hanging around the office area.

As you, the reader, ponder the following case illustration dealing with this task group, you might put yourself into the role as the student rep., knowing that sometimes Dr. Fulbright, the chair, occasionally asks you for your views and that you are supposed to report back to the other students. If nothing else, you think, being involved in this way probably is a valuable experience.

Context. Dr. Fulbright wakes up with a start. "Damn," he said to himself, seething, "it's another faculty meeting day!"

Harmon Fulbright chairs the English Department at Chase, a position he somewhat reluctantly accepted 3 years ago. This happened the way it often does in the academy. Fulbright enjoys hugely positive student ratings for his teaching—his Chaucer course crams the gallery. His seventh book, which earned him the prestigious James Falan Duval Award, cemented his place in the firmament among American university authors. The community tutoring and mentoring program he established with Helen Fulsom, the counseling center director, continues to bolster the academic performance of many young ethnic and racial minority students. Finally, Harmon is a likeable guy in spite of all his successes, not stuffy at all like some of his English colleagues and certainly not full of himself, which seems to cover most of the rest of them—anyway, that's the word on the student grapevine, he's told.

And so, for all the above reasons, he was drafted to serve as chair, a position he did not really want. As I said, this is not unlike how it can happen; a popular and successful faculty member gets "bumped up" (many would see it as being "bumped down") to chair. "If he's so good at these things, meaning teaching and the like, then the distorted logic goes, he'll certainly be good at being chair."

It frequently doesn't work out that way.

Once in his role, Fulbright found the demands generally doable, as much as could be so given the 600 undergraduate majors, 15 faculty, 40 graduate students, and shrinking budget he was asked to oversee. Three bones of contention gnawed at him, though. First, he found it necessary to reduce his own teaching load, then he had to turn over codirecting the tutoring and mentoring project to a young colleague, and third, he found that he absolutely detested running the weekly faculty meetings.

Amazing how quickly those weekly faculty meetings came around; it felt more like every other day to him! You know how that can be, what one loves and yearns for can take forever to arrive while what one would like never to be involved with again constantly buts in for attention.

As he dressed for work, he noticed he had slipped into counting the ways that these faculty meetings bugged him:

No one wanted to be there.

When there, probably half attended to other tasks.

The other half seemed either bored or contentious.

Getting them to agree on anything at all was next to hopeless.

Tom Self, he of the huge ego, just rubs me the wrong way.

Thank goodness for Maria Joseph, the one bright light in the whole group.

But, the student rep., oh my, this is embarrassing . . .

He knew there was more, but enough, it's off to the U.

As for you, the student representative, you had been advised by your predecessor that the best approach to take is to "lay low and simply observe." It was not part of the role to provide any input, unless to the chair, who sometimes would indirectly ask for some ideas during the week (but never in the meeting). The meeting, you had decided, was not a time to try to change things, even if it looked like change was needed. Not your role. Yep, just be there, observe, and try to learn for the future. Who knows, some day you might be a faculty member in such meetings, too!

Interaction. He gets up from his desk; it's 1:00, time for the dreaded faculty meeting. He enters the room to find, as usual, just Maria present. "Ahh, my old reliable," he thinks, as he greets her warmly.

Gradually, over the next 10 minutes, the others filter in, most carrying their smart phones and other materials to be used for burrowing. He notices no contact with one another is made, each faculty member seems in his or her own protective bubble, concerned only with what's going on inside of it.

"Good afternoon, all," begins Dr. Fulbright. And they're off.

A few head nods, and Maria says, "Hello, Harmon; hi, everyone." No response.

Fulbright scans the room and sees people seated in various locations in the room, many already starting to open their troves, some checking cell phones. "Well, at least the student rep. seems alert," he thought to himself.

It suddenly occurs to him—why didn't he think of this before—that getting a big table in here (assuming the department could afford it) might be a helpful step. It could provide some center point to sit around, at least.

"OK, the main item on the agenda today is the summer teaching schedule. You'll remember last week I passed out last summer's plan to refer to as a guide. Since then—no one will want to hear this one—dear 'Old Freddie' (the dean everyone loves to hate) passed down a 10% cut, said it's across the university."

At this point, heads popped up. At least he was getting their attention.

"What?" demanded the predictably self-protective Self. "Here we go again; we just shouldn't stand for it! I know one thing for sure; in no way will *my* courses be cut!"

"Oh, drop it, Self," spit out Dr. Banyon, the only one who ever would dare to take on Self. "Try thinking about the rest of us for a change; it's high time you did that."

"Wow," worried Fulbright, "this could get out of hand."

"I never trusted Old Freddie from the start of his reign," allowed Johnson, always a suspicious sort whose main job in the department seemed to be to throw darts at administrators. "Probably making the whole thing up just to tinker with us."

"Maybe so, but how about looking at it this way," suggested Maria, as she caught the eyes of everyone. "We know things definitely are tight here and everywhere. Let's see if we might hold off a bit until we get some more information about what's being asked of us."

"OK, I'll buy into that—for now. Harmon, what's up?" asked Self, somewhat ominously.

Choice Point A and B: Your suggestions. Chairperson Fulbright is confronted by a group member, Tom Self, one way in which a choice point can arise. What might he do? Now, take a look at Learning Exercise 10-2.

Learning Exercise 10–2:
Your Thoughts for Chairperson Fulbright

*The **object** of this learning exercise is to explore how to select effective interventions in group work leadership.*

1. Put yourself in the observing student's role.

2. Draw from your knowledge of group work leadership.

3. Describe two possible leader interventions that you might have suggested, if you had been asked.

4. Provide a rationale for each one.

Suggested leader Intervention A:

_____

_____

Rationale for A:

_____

_____

Suggested leader Intervention B:

_____

_____

Rationale for B:

_____

_____

Possible Choice A:

"Thanks for asking, Tom, for helping us move forward. And, you too, Maria. If we can stay focused on what is being asked of us and how we might best be able to respond, I think that would be very helpful."

Rationale for Choice A:

Supporting positive contributions, especially from a member whose track record tends to be negative, can provide impetus for continued contributions not only by that member but also by others. This rationale connects with the person-centered theoretical approach, where affect plays a critically important role, and with the interpersonal orientation, where forming connection among members is vitally important.

Possible Choice B:

"You know, we can mistrust Old Freddie all we want, and we can resist, but that's not the way to go, believe me. We need to get serious here and get the job done."

Rationale for Choice B:

Focusing the group on the task at hand can help clarify and prioritize energies. This emphasis connects with the purposive theoretical orientation and with the task dimension of human relations models.

Choice made. In this hostile group context that is characterized by disconnectedness and resistance, one strategy a leader can employ is to search for positive contributions that arise and then to reinforce them. This is especially the case when the source is an unlikely one, such as found here with Tom Self. The leader needs to avoid defensiveness on his own part and find ways to reach out and foster greater connection among others. The unexpressed idea Harmon had about getting a table into the room, for instance, might be a change to discuss with the faculty, as both the discussion about connection and the introduction of the table could promote connection.

Of the two leader intervention possibilities provided, Choice A would seem to provide the greater opportunity for supporting and connecting. Choice B is very task focused, is somewhat defensively put, and does not capture the supportive, connective theme.

Continued Interaction, Choice A

"Thanks for asking, Tom, for helping us move forward. And, you too, Maria. If we can stay focused on what is being asked of us and how we might best be able to respond, I think that would be very helpful."

"Banyon, you got to me some," said Tom, looking at Dr. Banyon. "I guess maybe I deserved that."

"Well, moving on as best we can is the thing, really," replied Banyon. "But I appreciate your willingness."

"This is a tough nut to crack, always, Summer school courses," offered Harmon. "But I like the way right now we are beginning to move on it."

Continued Interaction, Choice B (Had this choice been selected)

"You know, we can mistrust Old Freddie all we want, and we can resist, but that's not the way to go. We need to get serious here and get the job done."

"Yeah, maybe so, but I wish you wouldn't push, push us, Harmon," said Banyon. "Makes me want to leave the room, actually."

"Now you're finally with *me!*" chimed in Johnson. "Doesn't matter who's in power, and I even like Harmon, but they're all the same, trying to shove stuff down our throats."

"Every year it seems we take it in the neck for Summer school; this is serious business, it's how I put bread on the table, and to cut a class would be losing $10,000 for my family!" added Williams, who always could be counted on to complain about lack of money.

Consequences. Choice A was followed by some productive interaction. Choice B was followed by diversion. If Choice B could be viewed as a possible emerging mistake, what can be learned from it? If Dr. Fulbright asked your opinion about how to handle the faculty group, what might you advise him? How might he try responding to elicit more positive interaction? How might he be able to turn around a mistake so that this faculty meeting—which he so much dreads now—might become more satisfying and effective?

Psychoeducation Group Illustration: Lifestyle and Healthy Functioning Group

Context. Frederica and William are offering this psychoeducation group as part of their internship, which was set in the community college near their university. This was a new venture for this internship as no groups previously had been delivered at the college. However, there was a 5-year history of interns providing individual counseling there. Being developing mental health providers who were providing a new service within this environment, Frederica and William felt a lot of pressure to succeed.

Consistent with their training about psychoeducation groups, they had created a detailed group plan composed of six weekly 1.5-hour sessions. This plan included guiding theoretical framework, group goals, methods, session-by-session activities, coleader responsibilities, and process monitoring. Because this group was to emphasize education and wellness, prospective group members were not screened. In fact, the eight group members self-selected to participate in this group to satisfy a requirement for their college course in human growth and development. Many of the students in the course are interested in pursuing a career in mental health.

The focus of this group addresses the relationship between lifestyle choices and healthy functioning. It is based research indicating that 75% of behavior is accounted for by the lifestyle choices people make.

Each group session includes a content module derived from the work on Therapeutic Life Changes (TLC) described by Walsh (2011) and Ivey (2012). These modules focused on exercise (Session 1), nutrition (Session 2), stress management (Session 3), positive thinking (Session 4), service to others (Session 5), and social interaction (Session 6).

From their training, the coleaders understand the importance of blending attention to the content contained in each module with involving group members interactively and with providing opportunities for members to process their learning—but they are quite anxious about their capacity to do that effectively. They were hopeful that they would be able to activate the plan within each group session to promote interaction and to provide time for processing of experience. In addition, they were comforted by the time they planned to spend together each week processing the group's (and their own) progress, and they looked forward to support they anticipated receiving through the weekly intern supervision sessions back at the university.

The group interaction excerpt to be examined is drawn from Session 4 (of six).

Interaction. Frederica began the session: "Well, it's good to be back with you and ready to move on. Today we will take a look at how positive thinking can be helpful in maintain a healthy way of being."

As she said that, though, she suddenly realized that the group was smaller today, and for the first time. Attendance had been 100%. "Hmm," she thought to herself, "Jaime and Bethany are missing so far today; wonder why."

Choice Point A and B: Your suggestions. What might the group leaders do? And why? See Learning Exercise 10–3.

Learning Exercise 10–3: Your Thoughts for Frederica and William: What Might They Do?

The **object** of this learning exercise is to explore how to select effective interventions in group work leadership.

1. Put yourself in either of the coleader's role.

2. Draw from your knowledge of group work leadership.

3. Describe two possible leader interventions that you might have tried.

4. Provide a rationale for each one.

Suggested leader Intervention A:

_____

_____

Rationale for A:

_____

_____

Suggested leader Intervention B:

_____

_____

Rationale for B:

_____

Possible Choice A:

She looked across the circle at William, who seemed preoccupied with getting together the materials for the upcoming group exercise. So, not really knowing what to do, Frederica quickly decided to move on.

"You know, how we view our life situation has been shown through research to affect how we feel about it and then how we behave. Here's an example. Say you are facing a midterm exam in one of your courses. Although you've prepared for it, attended all the classes, and had done the best you could to be ready, the nagging thought keeps running through your mind that you just don't get it, that the exam will be incredibly hard, and that you no doubt will do poorly. Well, as I mentioned, research has shown that this kind of negative thinking can contribute to actually depressing your performance on the exam, acting like a self-fulfilling prophecy."

Now William adds, "Yes, and the reverse can occur, too, and it is a far better stance to be taking in life. Remember, Frederica mentioned that you had prepared and gotten ready for that exam—still you were nagging at yourself, sort of tripping yourself up even before taking the exam. By contrast, research suggests that if you take the exact opposite approach in your thinking—that is, an approach lodged in positive thinking, in optimism about your ability and readiness to do well—you may very well improve your opportunity to succeed."

Rationale for Choice A:

The coleaders have a well-conceived and designed plan, and they stick to it. It seems to have been working so far.

Possible Choice B:

Noticing that two members were absent, Frederica checks in with the group this way: "I'm glad to see all of you back today. But before we pick up with taking a look at how positive thinking can help us with our overall functioning, I'm noticing that Bethany and Jaime are not yet here ..." Looking around the group as she says, "Is it okay with all of you if we hold off for a couple of more minutes to give them a chance to arrive?"

The others nod yes.

Rationale for Choice B:

Frederica remembers recent supervision discussions she and William participated in at the university about the inherent value of process in a group and how that can be particularly difficult to maintain in a psychoeducation group such as theirs. The tendency in such groups can be to press on with the planned content, thereby neglecting or short shifting process. She also recalled reading in Yalom how process and reflecting on it powers the group. Therefore, she wanted to be sure that attention is paid to both content (in this session, on positive thinking) and on process (in this situation, the absence of two group members). She decides to prioritize process at this moment and then to pick up with the content later.

Choice made. There is a guiding principle in group work leadership: *Process takes precedence over content*. When a choice presents itself, as in this scenario, all things being equal (which they never really are, so judgment also is required), prioritizing attention to process typically is the better way. Therefore, in this case, Choice B may be preferred.

Continued Interaction, Choice A (Had this choice been selected)

Frederica and William continue for another 5 minutes to describe salient aspects of positive thinking, and then William begins to introduce the first exercise.

"So, let's see if we can begin to apply some positive thinking approaches to our own lives. As we have been doing in the first three sessions, let's now move to an exercise, where we pair up. This time, though, be sure to choose a person you haven't yet connected with in the group, OK? Everyone game?" he asks the group members, looking around.

There seemed to be some hesitancy, really, for the first time. No one moved to select an exercise partner, as they had done before with no delay and with apparent excitement. "Hmm," mused William, "I wonder what's going on?" He decided to ask.

"I can't help but notice that, for the first time, no one seems to want to begin. Can I ask for some comment on this?"

Silence.

Frederica follows up: "Yeah, this is kind of new for us. That's okay," she said reassuringly. "Don't hold back," she added as she scanned the group, inviting comment with her eyes, "just let's maybe talk about what might be going on now . . ."

Sam offers, "Let me step out some here; it feels like some bit of risk; I dunno. But, OK, here goes. I couldn't help but wonder where Bethany and Jaime are, they've never missed—well, ya know, no one has—but it seemed like you two [he looks at the coleaders] didn't notice or didn't care [his voice rises]. You're just gonna sail right ahead, anyway. I didn't like that and just don't feel ready to begin."

Janeka picks up where Sam left off. "I agree with ya, Sam, and I'm wondering more about this. I'll just come out and say it. I wonder if Jaime and Bethany were white, if this same thing would have happened? I mean, I've gotten the feeling all along, from examples and the stuff we're covering, ya know—about good nutrition, exercise, and the rest—I don't know, it just has seemed to be a bit outside my experience in life as an African American. What am I sayin' here, not sure." Janeka drops off, now feeling somewhat overexposed.

William and Frederica feel attacked. Never intending to leave out any members or their culture, they were reeling now internally. Frederica calms herself and gets back to what she knows to be important now, the value of attending to process and how members are thinking and feeling.

"Oh, my," she begins, "I'm *so* sorry to have given the impression that we're being exclusive. We don't at all mean to be . . . but, I want to thank you for being so candid. Let's set aside our plan for today, what do you think, and spend some more time on how we're all thinking and feeling about what's going on in the group . . ."

"Anyone else?" she asks, probing for more discussion from members about how the group is going so far and, particularly, about the possibility of preferential treatment and cultural exclusion.

Continued Interaction, Choice B

"Good, let's just pause then for a moment. You might want to take a look at your notes, or maybe chat with a neighbor, or just relax," Frederica says.

After pausing for a couple of minutes, it appears that Jaime and Bethany are not going to appear for this session.

William begins. "We think it's really important to spend some time on the fact that two of our members are not here this week. Not to talk about them in their absence, that is never a good idea. But, I'm wondering if we might just set aside our subject for today, at least for a bit, and maybe offer some thoughts about what it's like to have some members not here with us, which also might give us a chance to talk about how the group's going so far . . ."

Frederica: "Yes, and also how the group is going for each of you; we haven't really given that question as much attention as we perhaps should or could. We want this group to be meaningful to everyone, from all backgrounds and situations, so let's see how we're doin', OK? Who'd like to begin?" she says, looking around the room.

Sam steps in right away: "Thanks for doing this; I mean, I've been sort of wondering if we might have more of a chance to 'just talk,' if ya know what I mean? I mean, learning about these healthy ways of living is great, and all, but I've been also wanting some to learn more about each of us, or how we are doing with these different ideas, like exercise, and such."

Janeka follows, saying, "Yeah, me, too." Looking at Sam, she adds, "And maybe just another thought. [Janeka takes a deep breath, holds it, and blows it out.] It may just be some sort of fluke, I don't know, but I'm wondering about the ones who didn't come today and why? I know, not to talk about them when they're not here, I don't mean to do that. But, being an African American, maybe, that's it, I just can't help but wonder if the two of them—I mean, Jaime and Bethany—who are also minorities—may not be getting so much out of the group? Hey! That's probably just *crazy* thinkin' on my part, but I can't help wondering, so I'll just throw it out there."

Other members add their thoughts as they explore their experience in the group. They get to the value of positive thinking, but indirectly, not through the lesson plan that was prepared: at the end of the session, the coleaders observe that the group discussion about how things were going reflected a positive approach to their functioning together, giving them the opportunity to correct what may be needed and to continue what is functioning well.

Consequences. You might see how the discussion of process occurs much more organically in Choice B because the leaders recognize the need for attending to process issues and invite their discussion. They are exercising excellent leader skills in doing so, and activating the principle of "process precedes content." The path followed in Choice A illustrates one way that a process choice is not taken, instead moving ahead with the predeveloped plan without directly considering the absence of two members. Avoiding that consideration inadvertently communicated to members a disregard for members and even raised issue about the possibility that the coleaders may be expressly excluding those who are multiculturally diverse. Fortunately, in this case, the situation was correctable due to how William inquired openly about what seemed to be the reluctance of members to move ahead with the prescribed exercise. His question, "I can't help but notice that, for the first time, no one seems to want to begin. Can I ask for some comment on this?" acknowledged an ongoing issue, and it took some risk in asking it. Frederica supported it further and in such a way as to encourage member response. Interaction following seems positive and represents what may have been both a useful recovery permitting an opportunity for everyone to learn.

Counseling Group Illustration: Stress Management During Deployment Group

Context. Susan Johnson, a master's level counselor, provides consultation to military personnel and their families located on U.S. military bases or posts. She sometimes is able to lead counseling groups that have been organized by the Services Readiness Center dealing with concerns of spouses or partners of active duty service members. Issues being faced typically revolve around different aspects of deployment—getting ready for it, during the months of separation itself, and the reintegration processes involved when the service-man or -woman returns home. A constant theme running through these deployment phases is management of stress. The members of this group have identified themselves to the center as experiencing some challenges and difficulties with managing their end of the deployment and are looking for some help. Susan's individual interviews with them confirmed this assessment, while indicating that all members seemed appropriate for this group, which is to be centered on stress management during deployment.

This is the first meeting (of six planned) of a group consisting of eight partners of soldiers who have been deployed to Afghanistan for the last 3 months, with 9 more to go. It will be the third such group she's been honored to lead. Feedback about the previous two groups was quite positive, although one concern had to do with privacy.

Interaction. Susan begins by welcoming everyone to the group:

"It's so good to see everyone again," she starts warmly, looking and smiling supportively at each member.

"You recall the informed consent statement I discussed with you during our interview, just to remind you of that. As you also know, our group will be centered around the kinds of stress you may be experiencing during your partner's time away during this deployment and how you all are coping here back home. Believe me, there will be no Power Point presentations in this group [a little levity here, and to everyone's relief, too, because these typically are part of most presentations in the military], but we will interact openly, without much prestructure from me. I will try to facilitate our discussions and seek to help you learn from each other. How does that sound so far?"

She didn't expect much at this point and was planning to move next to ask members to go round the circle introducing themselves to one another as she begins to build a climate of trust and connection.

To her mild surprise, though, a member (Joyce) says, "Yes, well, I wonder if I might ask a question before we get too much into it?" as she looks at you.

"Of course," Susan responds.

Joyce says, "I've never been one to hold back much [here, you try to recall you individual interview with her for any clues, but come up short], and only have become more outspoken during the last couple of months Barry has been away. Maybe it's a sign of stress, maybe not; don't know for sure. But there are a couple of things I'm wondering about. [You notice some others are beginning to shift a little in their seats.] Somebody told me they were in one of your groups before and that there wasn't much information they learned, that it was mostly talking together, listening to one another. That's kind of what you just said, too. I don't know about *you* [she looks around the group] but, for *me*, I gotta be honest with you, for me I really need some information about deployments, I mean this is the first one we've been through, and I'm not sure how to handle so much of this, you know, with the kids and all and the money issues [she pauses for a moment] . . . and I've been feeling kind of under the weather for a week or so [now there is much more shifting in chairs and you, too, are beginning to feel a bit uncomfortable] and it's just that I'm afraid by coming here every week that maybe I won't get much out of it and my time—well, I know all our time—is so short with so many things to do and not nearly enough time to do them that I am feeling so rushed and pushed . . . I don't know, it might be I just miss Barry too much and with few friends, having just moved here 4 months ago and all." (NOTE: Joyce continues for another 3 minutes before stopping.)

Choice Point A and B: Your suggestions. What might the group leader do? And why? See Learning Exercise 10-4.

Learning Exercise 10–4: How to Address Monopolizing?

The **object** of this learning exercise is to develop ways group leaders might constructively address one problem in groups: monopolizing behavior.

1. Put yourself in the group leader's shoes.

2. Draw from your knowledge of group work leadership.

3. Suggest two possible leader interventions for managing monopolizing.

4. Provide a rationale for each one.

Leader Intervention A:

_____

_____

Rationale for A:

_____

_____

(Continued)

(Continued)

Leader Intervention B:

_____

_____

Rationale for B:

_____

_____

Possible Choice A:

Actually, Choice A already has been made. It is to do nothing. It is important to realize that doing nothing is an active choice. In such a situation, the leader (a) intentionally allows the member to continue to learn more about her and to demonstrate my respect for her, and also to provide others with the opportunity to interject, or the leader (b) may become entangled, caught up with indecision, and is unable to produce an intervention.

Rationale for Choice A:

Let's assume this leader, Susan, is intentionally permitting Joyce to finish her "question," as a way to demonstrate respect for her and to allow her to become known to others. This choice connects with the parts of gestalt and person-centered theory that highlight acceptance and respect of members, along trusting the essence of the group.

Possible Choice B:

Picking up with a portion of Joyce's comment:

That's kind of what you just said, too. I don't know about you [she looks around the group] but, for me, I gotta be honest with you, for me I really need some information about deployments, I mean this is the first one we've been through, and I'm not sure how to handle so much of this, you know, with the kids and all and the money issues [she pauses for a moment] . . . and

At this point, Susan intervenes with a comment: "Joyce, I wonder if I can slip in here quickly for a moment and make a comment?" (The leader pauses and looks at Joyce for validation, before continuing.)

Joyce says, "Oh, sure, yes."

"OK, thanks. I think the point you are raising about learning and getting information in the group is important . . . can we all chime in about this? As for me, I just want to clarify that I think the best thing that could happen is for us to share how we're doing with one another and to learn about what works from each other but that I also will have some points to make, too.

"Well, let's see, how do the rest of you view this? What would you like to be happening? And, after that, Joyce let's get back to you, all right?"

Rationale for Choice B:

Group development theories generally posit that it is important in the beginning stage of a group to take care that everyone gets an opportunity to become involved in some way. This possibility is reduced when any member begins to command what might become an excessive amount of time, in a sense, monopolizing attention. The group leader in this situation was beginning to get the sense (including noting the increased wriggling in chairs by other members as Joyce continued speaking) that Joyce was just getting warmed up. If allowed to continue, then, others might become disenchanted. As well, Joyce had brought up an important topic for consideration and discussion by all members, and the leader chose to refocus group interaction around it.

Choice made. As I pointed out, the choice was made by the leader to refrain from actively intervening, allowing the process to proceed unencumbered.

Continued Interaction, Choice A

"*. . . I don't know it might be I just miss Barry too much and with few friends, having just moved here 4 months ago and all.*" (NOTE: Joyce continues for another 3 minutes before stopping.)

Joyce spoke without interruption for 6 minutes in total. Upon stopping, there is a brief silence while most members shuffle a bit, and the group leader picks up the conversation.

"There's a lot going on for you, Joyce. I wonder."

At this point, Sandra, another group member, jumps in: "Gosh, [addressing the group leader] I hope you're not going to keep talking with . . . Joyce, is it? I mean, the rest of us have just been sittin' here for the longest time while she—and I don't mean any disrespect at all, at all, to you, Joyce—just, well, went on and on, and on some more."

Joyce jumps in, with some hurt in her voice: "Well, now, that isn't at all what I meant to do. I'm just wanting to get straight what we're doing and also I guess I do have lots on my mind, too."

Another member, Treminda, enters the conversation: "But so do we all, I suppose, I mean at least that's the case for me. But if there's no room to talk, then it's just no good. And I don't know if I want to keep coming back for something like that."

The group leader comes back into the conversation: "Let's see if we might be able to back-track here some and see just where we are . . ."

Continued Interaction, Choice B (Had this choice been selected)

"Well, let's see, how do the rest of you view this? What would you like to be happening? And after that, Joyce, let's get back to you, all right?"

Sandra says, "I'm glad this is coming up early. I'm not sure about it, I've never been in a group like this before, but I think the plan sounds good. I know I really don't want to have anyone talking *at* me; yeah, being able to be more social seems good."

Treminda adds, "I agree with that and, you know, I just don't get any time to be around very many others during the week, so I'm looking forward to it. But I wanna learn how to handle what I'm going through better, much better!"

The group leader, Susan says "Anyone else?" (Gazing around the group, nonverbal behavior suggests the others seem to concur.) "OK, so, back to you, Joyce. Maybe we can have a blend of some time where we can connect together—that support can be very helpful—and where we can share information about what works to help deal with the stress you all are feeling, how does that sound?"

Joyce and the others seem to be settling in . . .

Consequences. Choice A, to allow the speaker to continue, may have been too liberal. Especially in the beginning of a group, it runs the risk of disenfranchising other members, not giving them the opportunity to connect. Some struggle occurs, with the possibility of at least one member thinking about not coming back. If Choice A could be viewed as a possible emerging mistake, what can be learned from it? What might be learned and applied at the start of future groups?

Choice B found the group leader intervening early. Members seemed to rally around this point, appreciating the opportunity raised to provide their views on directions for the group. Susan also was careful to return to Joyce, not leaving her outside looking in, and she responded to all of that well.

Psychotherapy Group Illustration: Struggling With Lifestyle and Family

Context. Arianna relocated temporarily a year ago on a student visa from Italy to the United States to accept a postdoc in biochemistry research at a major university in the Bay Area. She grew up in a small commune in Lazio district of Italy but graduated from college and then graduate school from two universities in Rome. Her family (Note: in the traditional Italian culture, "La familiglia e tutto," meaning *your family is your life*) meant the world to her. However, her experiences in Rome and now on the West Coast of the United States exposed her to much that is in conflict with her family values and culture.

As most of her fellow students were doing, she had placed her religious practice on hold (oh, my, if father ever found out I'm not attending Mass, she often thought, guiltily), found occasional use of pot with friends to be fun, and had become so embroiled in her research and with the lure of Bay Area attractions that her communications with family had fallen off. She also was becoming increasingly aware that another reason accounted for fewer phone calls back home—what was so important to her now, her work and her relationship with Tanya, especially the latter, could never be acceptable to her family. These are things that nag at her every day, but she carries them deep in her heart, never having shared them with her family—of course—or really with anyone else, except her partner.

She had met Tanya early in her move to California. Tanya was a doctoral student in feminist archeology, with a focus on Etruscan culture. Although American, Tanya was very familiar with the general area of Arianna's childhood years, centered as it is in a virtual hotbed of Etruscan history and active archeological digs; she spent two summers on research projects in the area and fell in love with the place and the general culture.

The two of them began hanging out at first because of their overlapping interest and experience. Over the first 6 months of Arianna's stay at the university, the nature of their relationship deepened as it evolved from shared interest, to fondness and admiration, and now to love.

They had become a couple. In the Bay Area, being a gay couple was acceptable and not unusual, and that felt good to both of them. However, for Arianna a storm brewed inside her due to the competing forces of what seemed genuine and right, on one hand, and what she knew was fully unacceptable to her strong Italian family. She too often felt riddled through with shame and guilt, such that she could become immobilized with anxiety, torn up about what she found herself preferring and needing and the scorn she knew would descend upon her should her family ever learn how she was living her life.

Supported by Tanya, she decided to join a therapy group. She felt a need to talk with some others whom she did not know, guided by a professional, and maybe get some help with the conflict she carried around all the time. She debated about a group aligned with the gay community or one that was unaffiliated with any one lifestyle. She decided to seek out a group recommended by one of their friends, one that is run through a local branch of the mental health center. As she thought about it, she began to realize she is not yet comfortable—would she ever be, she wondered—with identifying publicly as a gay person, in a gay relationship.

Although being generally social, if not gregarious (after all, she would cheerfully chide people, "I *am* Italian!"), she anticipated it being difficult to open up in the group about what was troubling her, but realized this was something she could most likely benefit from if she tried. Five weeks into the 14-week therapy group experience, we come to the following interaction.

Interaction. Rhonda, the group leader says, "You know, we've heard from just about everyone now to some degree, but maybe not so much from you, Arianna." Rhonda casts her gaze toward her. "I've certainly felt your presence and involvement but now just want to check with you about if you're getting what you need from the group here. Not wanting to put you on a hot spot, but I wonder—how are things going for you in here?"

Arianna gulps, suddenly overwhelmed by so much internal turbulence that did not want to come out. She sure she was blushing that red that seemed so characteristic of people in her family when they might be feeling pushed or vulnerable in some way. She feels locked up, too, not sure of what to say or how to say it. "It's one thing to ruminate about things, but it's something else to 'proclaim' them," she thinks.

Rhonda, sensing her to be caught, follows up, saying "Hmm, seems like you may be kind of struggling with something, Arianna. You know, that's not at all unusual; actually, it often is a sign of something important going on. Again, not wanting to push you, may I ask what is the nature of your struggle, maybe what is competing with what?"

"I'm usually more open," Arianna starts. "I don't know, I think I'm not knowing where to go, how much to let out, *what* to let out, even." She pauses, gathering some of her scattered thoughts and feelings. "Maybe part of it's my family—you know, big, strong, very traditional Italian family from back home and what they expect of me—part of it might be not feeling all that comfortable in sharing anyway. I know I *need* to let some things out . . ."

Arianna's voice suddenly begins to shake some now and tears start to well up, almost like a dam could be on the verge of breaking. She clearly shows she is struggling with something deep, something that she may be considering sharing with the group. She knows full well what it is, churning as she is with her love for Tanya but torn about revealing it here, or anywhere. Yet, she, thinks, "But why not here? Tanya encouraged me to come, to talk, to reach out . . ."

At that point, another member, Gus, barges into the conversation.

Gus (intensely) says, "Ya know, I just don't get it. With me, you're [he looks intently at Rhonda] right on my case always, demanding I talk, I spill my guts. With *her* [he jabs his thumb aggressively at Arianna] you pussyfoot around: like 'pretty please,' 'don't wanna push you,' and all that bull. Come on, girl [he demands of Arianna], get on with it or get off it!"

The room temperature suddenly ratcheted up a 100 degrees or so, or so it seemed. "Leave it to Gus," thought Rhonda, "the anger he brings seems to just explode." As she is considering what to do next another group member, Ashley, who is struggling mightily with self-worth and assertion issues, tentatively takes the floor.

Ashley (shakily) sighs softly, "Oh my, I'm feeling *real* bad right now. I hate the anger and strife. I just can't stand it; it's so much like my family. It makes me just want to cry, or to just leave, really!"

Rhonda, the group leader, considers her choices.

Choice Point A and B: Your suggestions. What might the group leader do? And why? Take a look at Learning Exercise 10-5.

Learning Exercise 10–5: Your Thoughts for How Rhonda Might Intervene

*The **object** of this learning exercise is to explore how to select effective interventions in group work leadership.*

1. Put yourself in either of the group leader's role.

2. Draw from your knowledge of group work leadership.

(Continued)

(Continued)

3. Describe two possible leader interventions that you might have tried.

4. Provide a rationale for each one.

Suggested leader Intervention A:

_____

_____

Rationale for A:

_____

_____

Suggested leader Intervention B:

_____

_____

Rationale for B:

_____

_____

Possible Choice A:

Rhonda says, "Ashley, I can see and hear the pain in you, how much of what you experience as strife and conflict in here shakes you, even reminding you of family situations. And I want us to be able to support you in these moments, so that you can have the opportunity here—in this safer kind of place—to be able to hang in there and walk through it to the other side . . . do you understand what I'm trying to say?" she asks, looking at Ashley. "And anyone else, where are you on this?"

Ashley, head bowed, nods slightly.

Maria, another group member, adds "Maybe I can come in here, just to add that I'm feeling so supportive of Ashley."

Rhonda interrupts: "I wonder, Maria, if you can say that directly to Ashley?"

Maria says, "Oh, yeah, sorry. Let me try this again. I mean to say, Ashley, that I'm with you on this; you can count on me here, that's all. But I hope it means something to you, too, can be helpful."

Rhonda asks, "Anyone else want to comment, and then maybe, Ashley, we can come back to you."

Rationale for Choice A:

In this approach, the group leader decides to continue a focus on the most recent therapeutic issue, assigning action priority to addressing the fragility she senses in Ashley's emotional state. She also seeks to invite other members to become involved, which Maria does, and to promote the direct expression of communication by asking Maria to speak to Ashley and not about her.

At the same time, Rhonda no doubt is aware that other important therapeutic issues are on the table. What are the other issues? See Learning Exercise 10-6.

Learning Exercise 10–6: Other Therapeutic Issues in the Group

*The **object** of this learning exercise is to identify and describe what other important therapeutic issues are underway in the group.*

1. Identify any other issues you find occurring in the group:

    a. _____

    b. _____

    c. _____

2. Describe each one: What makes each an "issue"?

    a. _____

    b. _____

    c. _____

Possible Choice B:

Rhonda: "You know," she starts in a soothing voice, projecting calm, "this might just be a really good time to take a pause in the action for just a moment." We've got some important things going on in here. I'm thinking of Ashley's deep concern, the anger Gus seems to be feeling, and back to Arianna what I sense she is struggling with . . . do you recall all these?" she asks the group, looking around the circle.

Most nod in agreement.

Rhonda says, "These all are important and deserve our attention. So, I am grappling a little bit right now, wanting us to address everyone's concern. Let's all take a deep breath and step back for a moment ..."

Rhonda continues: "Okay, good, ya know, I want to ask Ashley and also Gus if we can hold off a little while there and maybe go back to Arianna and what she seems to be struggling with, would that work?"

Gus answers, "I don't really care; 'do your own thing' is what I like to say!"

Rhonda responds, saying, "I'll take that as a yes, Gus, but remember we will come back to you. ... Ashley, where are you on this?"

Ashley (a delay, as she seems to be searching for the right words), then offers gently, "Thank you for asking. I'd just as soon move back to Arianna; anyway, she was first."

Rhonda says, "Okay, thank you, Ashley; we'll return to you then. So I wonder, now, Arianna, can we come back to your concern, with what you seem to be jostling with. Can we be of help?"

Rationale for Choice B:

In selecting this intervention approach, Rhonda seeks to redirect the flow of interaction back to the original source of concern—Arianna's struggle with something—that got cut off, in a way, when Gus jumped in, followed by Ashley's unsettledness. While any of these matters is important, Rhonda believes that Arianna cannot be abandoned, that she is finally beginning to take a risk in opening up. To leave her behind and pick up on another's concern, even though legitimate, would be a disservice to Arianna at this point and even serve to close her down. So, she chose to go back to her and give her the opportunity to proceed.

Simultaneously, Rhonda communicates to both Gus and Ashley that the issues they bring are important, they will not be put aside over the longer term, and she seeks their support for returning to Arianna. Doing so underscores respect for them and, by extension, all group members, and it provides a clear map about how to proceed.

Choice made. Both choices have merit, and there could have been other legitimate possibilities, too. For instance, Rhonda may have decided to work with Gus on his interruption. She might also have used a group-level intervention, asking the members in an open-ended question, after Ashley spoke: "I'm wondering what you all are thinking and feeling right now ..." Perhaps you identified some other alternatives in Learning Exercise 10-5.

The existence of group leader intervention alternatives illustrates how there often is no one best choice. Rather, what is selected is done so intentionally to fit the context, the issues and how they are interpreted and weighed by the group leader, best practices, and leader and member resources. In all cases, professional judgment is at the forefront.

In this instance, Rhonda selects intervention Choice B. She prioritizes Arianna's situation. It came first and was in process when Gus fairly summarily interjected his objection. The group leader wants Arianna to take her opportunity to express herself in the group and does not want to leave her hanging.

Continued Interaction, Choice A (Had this choice been selected)

Rhonda asks "Anyone else want to comment, and then maybe, Ashley, we can come back to you."

Andre, another group member, says to Ashley: "I was afraid you were going to walk, no kidding! I'm glad you're here, but I'm worrying about you, too. What's up? I wanna know, if that's all right."

Brittany, another group member, says to Rhonda: "I sometimes feel the same way in here, I have to admit it. I can get scared when stuff gets hot."

Rhonda asks "Anyone else?" She pauses. "Okay, you know, Ashley, it seems you have some support here from at least Marie and Andre, and then in listening to Brittany, I get the sense that you are not alone in sometimes becoming afraid. I wonder how you see this?"

And the group interaction proceeds to focus on Ashley for the next 20 minutes.

Continued Interaction, Choice B

Rhonda says, "Okay, thank you, Ashley, we'll return to you then. So I wonder, now, Arianna, can we come back to your concern, with what you seem to be jostling with. Can we be of help?"

Arianna says, "I guess I'm glad you came back; I've been kind of working myself up to letting you know some of what's going on with me, but—damn it, it's hard! [Once again, she begins to choke up.] I've been hiding from everyone, well, nearly everyone, a main part of my life now and my family in Italy—my God, they would shoot me—if they knew. [The words were spilling out faster now, with more energy.] I came here to this country to study and, oh, that's great, very hard, but great, anyway. I like it here, the Bay Area is so beautiful and Napa—which we love to go to—reminds me of home. Wait, did I say 'we'? I did, didn't I! Okay [and a smile begins to form on her lips, just a little], I might as well come out with it. Yeah, that's it, I need to 'come out'! So, I'll try it here. [She takes a deep breath, then looks around the group, where all the members, even Gus, seem transfixed.] I have a partner, a woman, I think I'm in love. She's who I was referring to about us going to Napa. We're living together, we're happy—she even suggested I join the group! But I'm miserable, too. It's so right and it's so wrong; well, wrong for my family, I'm sure, I know them all too well about stuff like this. Anything that goes against the church and they are *so* traditional and *so* wonderful at the same time." (She stops, unsure about where to go with this.)

Rhonda says, "Wow, I can feel the air whooshing out, Arianna. You've not been breathing about this for a long time now. Good for you! How does it feel to have shared this very important information about you with us just now?"

Arianna begins to laugh and cry at the same time: "Very emotional, *obviously,*" she emphasizes, "but—I think—relieved, too."

Arianna experiences a reduction of internal pressure about letting this out to the group, but she also feels deeply conflicted about how to resolve being gay with her family. But she now has a supportive forum for exploring this struggle and does so as the group proceeds.

Consequences. Exploring alternatives for group work leaders to intervene—in each of the four group work types we have considered—demonstrates the importance of intentionality in arriving at selections that best fit the circumstances and the uncompromising importance of using good professional judgment. Moreover, it demonstrates that choosing one intervention can lead to one set of possibilities, while selecting another alternative can lead to a different set of occurrences.

These points can be easily seen in this last case. Two viable group leader interventions were considered by Rhonda. Choosing Alternative A would take the group down the path of focusing on Ashley, while selecting Alternative B (for which she opted) led to a continuing focus on Arianna.

Group work is a means for helping people and systems. Those who are honored to lead groups are at the helm of a powerful resource and set of dynamics that, when guided properly, can contribute substantially to health, well-being, and productivity. The interventions that leaders select need to be carefully considered, drawing from good professional judgment. See Learning Exercise 10–7.

● GROUP WORK KEYSTONES

- This chapter focused on how practice and processing assist group leaders to develop their craft by integrating knowledge, skills, and personal characteristics.

Learning Exercise 10–7: Your Concluding Comments

The **object** of this final learning exercise is to provide you with an open space for integrating and expressing your understanding of group work leadership.
Overall,

1. What is your main "takeaway" about group work leadership?

2. What have you learned about yourself as a group work leader?

3. Indicate any future plans you may have about group work leadership.

- The importance of learning not only from successes but from mistakes and failures was emphasized.
- The chapter's inclusion of case situations illustrating portions of a task group, a psychoeducation group, a counseling group, and a psychotherapy group provide readers with concrete opportunities to become engaged in group leader intervention choices.
- Choice points within critical incidents were presented as providing important pivotal directions for action by group leaders.
- Good professional judgment undergirds the selection of proper group leader interventions.

RECOMMENDED RESOURCES

Burkeman, O. (2012). *The antidote: Happiness for people who can't stand positive thinking*. Edinburgh, Scotland: Canongate Books, Ltd.

Cohen, A., & Smith, R. D. (1976). *The critical incident in growth groups: Theory and technique*. La Jolla, CA: University Associates.

Conyne, R., Crowell, J., & Newmeyer, M. (2008). *Group techniques: How to use them more purposefully*. Upper Saddle River, NJ: Pearson.

Donigian, J., & Hulse-Killacky, D. (1999). *Critical incidents in group therapy* (2nd ed.). Belmont, CA: Brooks/Cole.

Kottler, J., & Blau, D. (1989). *The imperfect therapist: Learning from failure in therapeutic experience*. San Francisco, CA: Jossey-Bass.

Tyson, L., Perusse, R., & Whitledge, J. (Eds.). (2004). *Critical incidents in group counseling*. Alexandria, VA: American Counseling Association.

EPILOGUE

From the Author's Chair

We should not look back unless it is to derive useful lessons from past errors and for the purpose of profiting by dearly bought experience.
—George Washington, First President
of the United States

INTRODUCTION

"From the Author's Chair" is a special feature of this book series. In the following, we ask Bob Conyne to comment on his book.

OBJECTIVES

After reading this epilogue you will be able to

- Understand better the author's perspective about group work
- Understand what the author considers to be key aspects of the book
- Identify some challenges and supports for your developing professional identity

Why do we have to know this?

All helping professionals need to not only know about group work but also to be able to conduct it. This is so not because accreditation pushes in this direction, but that's a factor, of course. Even more so, it's because working with people in groups provides *therapeutic* benefits—in personally oriented groups, such as psychoeducation, counseling, and psychotherapy—and *production* benefits—in task and work groups—that supersede any other helping approach. Group work is a comprehensive and unique service delivery method for helpers. Not to mention, of course, that we are all together in this thing called life, reflecting the concept of *universality*—one of the therapeutic factors discussed by Yalom—and group captures this phenomenon beautifully.

There is a matchless power in groups. This power needs to be harnessed for good but also to be heeded to prevent bad things from happening, such as coerciveness, or "groupthink" (which is allowing oneself to be swayed by the power of others' arguments for the sake of harmony). Counselors and other helping professionals who lead groups, if well trained to do so, can collaborate with their members to produce remarkable growth and change. These are some of the reasons why I think practitioners need to be able to be group workers.

What is professional identity, and how will the material presented in this text help in the formation of my own identity?

Professional identity is an important construct, and it is essential that professionals and those in training develop a clear one that fits their situation. I think it's unfortunate that it also has become for many a hot-button issue. It isn't for me.

What I'm interested in is not whether a student or professional can pass any kind of litmus test for belonging within a particular profession. Here, I refer to holding all the credentials (e.g., license, accreditation, professional association) in the "correct" profession, although I certainly agree that proper education, training, and supervision in the "right" areas are all essential.

Rather, I'm concerned with whether a professional or student in training possesses the proper competencies, values, personal characteristics, and ethics to be turned loose upon the world of helping. While I'm fully aware that many of my trusted colleagues and friends in the profession will disagree with me (perhaps including the editors of this series), I believe that the unique profession one identifies with (e.g., counselor educa-tion, psychology, and social work) is of far less consequence than are the values, ethics, and competencies of the professional. There is so much more that these professions hold in common than not; choosing to emphasize any perceived differences over the commonalities, I think, takes us down a wrong road. And I think we can get there through different ways and routes.

In some ways I believe it would do us far more justice if we were to blend our existing professions, as opposed to erecting barriers separating them, to yield a common helping profession. Doing so would be far less confusing to the public, the government, educational institutions, third-party payers—everyone.

Now having upset probably two thirds of the readers, let me move on to expand on what I think is truly important about professional identity, which I hinted at earlier. That is, if I'm considering joining an advertised group offered by, let's say, Counselor Martinez, I want to know that Ms. Martinez is qualified, is competent, is governed by ethics and best practices, functions well as a person, will be someone I can trust and respect, will help me and other members by avoiding doing wrong things, and will promote our health and well-being as well as her own. I would want her to be a positive person who looks for the good in group members, while having the ability to help us to move forward progressively. I would not much care if she identifies with ACA or APA, or AASWG or AGPA, or is a licensed psychologist as opposed to a licensed coun-selor, or social worker. It is adherence to ethical standards and best practices positive personal characteristics, and professional competence that would mat-ter to me. And so, that's my take on professional identity—not to get caught up in the political but to keep focused on the identity issues that really matter.

Out of all the information presented—what "keystone" would you highlight as essential to the practice of group work?

As I have done with each chapter, I supplied a quotation at the start of this epilogue. George Washington is credited with many sayings (how about #2 of 110 from his *Rules of Civility & Decent Behavior in Company and Conversation* (Internet Archive, 2011): "When in Company, put not your Hands to any Part of the Body, not usually Discovered"; all right, a little sus-pect, maybe, but at least good for a laugh (and, I believe, mental health pro-fessionals—as everyone—all can benefit by laughing more). But the George Washington quote I presented at the beginning of this interview captures a *keystone* of this book that stands out for me:

Reflection is aimed at making sense of direct experience in the group. This "sense making" can yield *lessons learned,* which I defined in Chapter 9 as "*big, life principles we carve out of the crucible of our experience, whether positive or negative, which we can then use to more effectively cope with similar situations we may face in the future.*"

Why do I value this particular keystone so highly? Looking back with purpose to learn lessons that can be applied to improve future group leading should become a routine practice for group workers and those in training. As I've pointed out, direct here-and-now experience in group is both necessary and critically important, but it's deficient by itself to power and direct learning and positive change. Reflection on the experience is needed to complete the process. It is through reflecting, or processing, that we acquire the lessons needed to move us forward productively.

For group leaders, I also pointed out that this kind of focused looking back, often in the form of between-session processing or in supervision, provides the stimulus needed for not only identifying how to best proceed with the current group being led; importantly, it also establishes conditions under which leaders can test and evolve both their future practice and their continued professional identity development. This kind of reflection on experience permits meaning to be derived about the group, its members, and about oneself as a leader—and there can be nothing more consequential than that.

Finally, I think professionals who develop the habit of ongoing reflecting on their practice—whether that be teaching, research, service delivery, or service to others or the community—gain something special to contribute to the profession, as well. These are the professionals who tend to make a significantly positive difference in their work. Moreover, they are apt to be the ones who are most involved in their profession, attending conferences, making presentations, serving on task forces, running for office, both keeping abreast of professional developments and helping to shape them, too.

As you wrote this text, did you find something that was especially exciting to you?

Yes, I've become excited about the field of neuroscience and, more particularly, work emerging in interpersonal neurobiology (IPNB) that Siegel has been in the forefront of. I found the special issue of the *International Journal of Group Psychotherapy* I mentioned in Chapter 6 on this topic (coedited by Susan Gantt and Paul Cox) to be full of wonderfully innovative research, with implications for practice emerging. The idea of a social brain and how group psychotherapy and other group approaches can directly stimulate brain activity leading to improved interpersonal functioning is entirely fascinating to me.

I guess I find the contents of Chapter 6 in their entirety to be intriguing. Kind of "out there," I suppose. The six transtheoretical orientations I described hold lots of potential for theory development in group work leadership. As I stressed, I believe we very much need to loosen our theoretical ties to individual counseling models in favor of transtheoretical ones that emphasize interconnections. I'm hopeful readers may become interested in this direction and help to flesh it out.

What would you suggest a young counselor or other mental health worker, in formation, read/do/experience or reflect upon next in the process of that formation?

You know, here I am addressing *my* version of professional identity formation, not what I see as the more politically motivated one.

Young helpers who are interested in becoming good group leaders need to find their passion in it. As I mentioned in earlier chapters, in my experience as a professor training future professional helpers, I found no more highly ardent practitioners than those who lead groups and, for whatever reasons, found a love and passion in it.

How does one get there? No one way, nothing guaranteed. I have worked with many students, for instance, who came into my introductory group work class strongly feeling a discomfort with groups and that they would hate the class and detest group work, besides. An appreciable number of them somehow made radical transformations, from being highly resistant to becoming very eager for more experience. What happened? I think that somehow they allowed themselves to be open to experience, to try it out, to see where it takes them, and to reflect along the way. These are the sorts of students who would come to me toward the end of the course and ask if there were other ways they could continue their learning, if they had any opportunities beyond course work, for instance, or a research project. Nearly anything that connected with group work. They had permitted themselves to "be bitten" by the group work bug, never more to be the same.

I think that so-called group work bug bites through the feeling one can get when participating in a group that moves into a phase of sailing along, where members are connecting, information and energy are flowing, and members are showing gains. When future group leaders can experience this for themselves through their own participation as a member in a group, they will be on to something very valuable, and it's likely they, too, will be bitten. As well, for some reason I am almost always inspired by reading group literature, by seeing in print how the small group can motivate and change people.

Studying with professors who themselves not only know their stuff but who really care about group work and passing on its culture to others is invaluable. Find such professors and programs.

Join professional associations that are dedicated to group work. Within American Counseling Association, the Association for Specialists in Group Work can't be recommended highly enough. The Society for Group Psychology and Group Psychotherapy of American Psychological Association is wonderful. The American Group Psychotherapy Association provides fantastic learning opportunities. The Association for the Advancement of Social Work with Groups, which I know less about than the others, also provides great opportunities. These group work professional associations provide a culture, people, and programs that can inspire, direct, and nurture young professionals. Become involved.

Look around you. See where and how groups in your everyday life are at play. Study how they work. Learn from them. Add what you learn from these everyday groups with what you learn from directed academic study. I have a favorite personal tale that is so important for me that I elevated it to a principle: the "Ruby and Oren Principle." I've written about it in various sources. This principle exemplifies how looking around at "everyday groups" can be of value.

You see, Ruby and Oren were older neighbors of ours, older by 60 years or so, when my wife Lynn and I were in our mid-20s. They had lots of wisdom. But they would play weekly card games, I came to understand, something that I—an anti-card playing kind of guy—could not grasp. One Sunday, Oren told me he and Ruby had missed Saturday's card playing—just the third time in 35 years, he said (I'm thinking, "Amazing, I wonder why this could be?"), due to the severe ice storm that prohibited driving out into the country to visit the friends who were hosting that week's card game. So, here it was again, this card playing—and from such a person of wisdom, too. So, this time I asked Oren, "What do you and Ruby find so involving about playing cards, week after week, for 35 years?" So, what do you suppose this man of wisdom said? "Why, Bob, it's not the card playing that keeps us coming back, it's the people, our longtime friends. We gripe and moan, talk about the weather, even talk some about ourselves—that's why we do it, I guess."

And now you see why Oren was the person with wisdom. I instantly understood. It was people, connections, social support that fueled their fire for more card playing. It could have been doing just about anything that would allow them the excuse of gathering each and every Saturday to commune.

What's the lesson for group work from that ordinary, everyday experience? Groups, at their heart, help people to commune, to be in touch, to connect, and through those kinds of processes to aid participants in their lives.

So, for the students and new professionals who may be interested in group work (or even, right now, think you may not be), get out there. Be open to your experience. Process it. Read. Select, if it's not too late, a training program and professors who know their business with groups and who care about passing their essence on. Observe your daily life for how groups are at work. Join relevant professional associations and become actively involved. Work on creating your own personal theory of group work leadership that honors and is based on existing and emerging theory but is integrated within your personal values and personality.

Expand your professional identity to include "group worker."

Here's to you—and to good groups,

Bob Conyne

Learning Exercise Epilogue-1: Where Are You? Where Do You Want to Go?

So, now you've finished this book on group work. Congratulations, I hope you found it interesting and of value!

Permit me two concluding questions:

1. Where are you in your own development as a group worker? Where do you hope to be?

_____

_____

_____

_____

_____

2. I've mentioned at various points in the text that group work is a unique service delivery method.

   Identify what about group work makes it unique:

_____

_____

_____

_____

_____

● GROUP WORK KEYSTONES

- Group work is important to learn about because it is a unique and essential part of a helping professional's role, geared to help others in ways that other methods cannot.
- Reading this book can contribute to one's professional identity because it provides ways group workers can use to review and learn from their experience, both to improve their practice and to evolve their development and identity as helping professionals. Chapter 9 especially addresses this point.
- There is a strong need for theory development and practice based on interpersonal and connective models, being much less bound to individual counseling ones.
- Interpersonal neurobiology (INPB) is an emerging line of research with implications for group work leadership that are only beginning to be glimpsed.
- If they don't watch out, young professionals and students are susceptible to catching the bug of group work! I hope you are at risk for being bitten, as this is one "infection" that would be healthy. Be open to your experience, process it, seek formal learning opportunities, scan your everyday environment for how groups are at work, join professional associations of group work, and more. My wish for you is that you may discover your passion for group work.

REFERENCES

Adams, S. A. (2010, September 27). Counselor self-care [American Counseling Association Web log]. Retrieved from http://my.counseling.org/2010/09/27/counselor-self-care/

Agazarian, Y. (1997). *Systems-centered therapy for groups.* New York, NY: Guilford Press.

Agazarian, Y. (2004). *Systems-centered therapy for groups.* London, England: Karnac Books.

Agazarian, Y., & Gantt, S. (2005). The systems perspective. In S. Wheelan (Ed.), *The handbook of group research and practice* (pp. 187–200). Thousand Oaks, CA: Sage.

Ajzen, I. (1991). The theory of planned behavior. *Organizational Behavior and Human Decision Processes, 50,* 179–211.

Albee, G. W. (2005). Call to revolution in the prevention of emotional disorders. *Ethical Human Psychology and Psychiatry, 7,* 37–44.

American Association for Social Work with Groups. (2010). *Standards for social work practice with groups* (2nd ed.). Retrieved from http://www.aaswg.org/files/AASWG_Standards_for_Social_Work_Practice_with_Groups.pdf

American Counseling Association. (2005). *ACA code of ethics.* Retrieved from http://counseling.org/Resources/CodeOfEthics/TP/Home/CT2.aspxuthor

American Counseling Association. (2010a). *Licensure and certification.* Alexandria, VA: Author. Retrieved from http://www.counseling.org/counselors/LicensureAndCert.aspx

American Counseling Association (2010b). *ACA's taskforce on counselor wellness and impairment.* Retrieved from http://www.counseling.org/wellness_taskforce/PDF/ACA_taskforce_assessment.pdf

American Group Psychotherapy Association. (2007). *Practice guidelines for group psychotherapy.* New York, NY: Author. Retrieved from http://agpa.org/guidelines/AGPA%20Practice%20Guidelines%202007-PDF.pdf

American Group Psychotherapy Association. (2012). Publications: Group psychotherapy book list. Retrieved from http://www.agpa.org/pubs/Booklist.htm

American Group Psychotherapy Association. (n.d.). Group works! Evidence on the effectiveness of group therapy. Retrieved from http://agpa.org/efficacy-brochure.htm

American Psychological Association. (2011, November 23). About accredited doctoral programs in professional psychology. Retrieved from http://www.apa.org/ed/ accreditation/programs/accred-professional.aspx

Anderson, D. (2007). Multicultural group work: A force for developing and healing. *Journal for Specialists in Group Work, 32,* 224-244.

Armstrong, S., & Berg, R. (2005). Demonstrating group process using 12 Angry Men. *Journal for Specialists in Group Work, 30,* 135-144. doi: 10.1080/ 01933920590925986

Arredondo, P. (1994). Multicultural training: A response. *The Counseling Psychologist, 22,* 308-314.

Arredondo, P., & Perez, P. (2003). Expanding multicultural competencies through social justice leadership. *The Counseling Psychologist, 31,* 282-289.

Arrow, H., McGrath, J., & Berdahl, J. (2000). *Small groups as systems: Formation, coordination, development, and adaptation.* Thousand Oaks, CA: Sage.

Association for the Advancement of Social Work with Groups. (2006). *Standards for social work practice with groups.* Alexandria, VA: Author. Retrieved from http://www.aaswg.org/files/AASWG_Standards_for_Social_Work_Practice_ with_Groups.pdf

Association for Specialists in Group Work. (1983). *ASGW professional standards for group counseling.* Alexandria, VA: Author.

Association for Specialists in Group Work. (1991). *Professional standards for the training of group workers.* Alexandria, VA: Author. Retrieved from http://asgw. org/pdf/training_standards.pdf

Association for Specialists in Group Work. (1998). *Association for Specialists in Group Work principles for diversity-competent group workers.* Alexandria, VA: Author. Retrieved from http://asgw.org/pdf/Principles_for_Diversity.pdf

Association for Specialists in Group Work. (1998, 2007). *Association for Specialists in Group Work best practice guidelines.* Alexandria, VA: Author. Retrieved from http://asgw.org/pdf/Best_Practices.pdf

Association for Specialists in Group Work. (2000). *Professional standards for the training of group workers.* Alexandria, VA: Author. Retrieved from www.asgw .org/training_standards.htm

Association for Specialists in Group Work. (2012). *Multicultural and social justice competency principles for group workers.* Retrieved from http://asgw.org/pdf/ ASGW_MC_SJ_Priniciples_Final_ASGW.pdf

Badenoch, B., & Cox, P. (2010). Integrating interpersonal neurology with group psychotherapy. *International Journal of Group Psychotherapy, 60,* 462-482.

Bales, R. F. (1950). *Interaction process analysis.* Cambridge, MA: Addison-Wesley.

Bales, R. F. (1999). *Social interaction systems: Theory and measurement.* New Brunswick, NJ: Transaction.

Bandura, A. (1997). *Self-efficacy: The exercise of control.* New York, NY: Freeman.

Barlow, S. (2004). A strategic three-year plan to teach beginning, intermediate, and advanced group skills. *Journal for Specialists in Group Work, 29,* 113–126. doi: 10.1080/01933920490275600

Barlow, S. (2011). Evidence bases for group practice. In R. Conyne (Ed.), *The Oxford handbook of group counseling* (pp. 207–230). New York, NY: Oxford University Press.

Barlow, S., Burlingame, G., & Fuhriman, A. (2000). Therapeutic applications of groups: From Pratt's "Thought Control Classes" to modern group psychotherapy. *Group Dynamics: Theory, Research, and Practice, 4,* 115–134.

Barlow, S., Fuhriman, A., & Burlingame, G. (2004). The history of group counseling and psychotherapy. In J. DeLucia-Waack, D. Gerrity, C. Kalodner, & M. Riva (Eds.), *Handbook of group counseling and psychotherapy* (pp. 3–22). Thousand Oaks, CA: Sage.

Barlow, S., Fuhriman, A., & Burlingame, G. (2005). The history of group practice: A century of knowledge. In S. Wheelan (Ed.), *Handbook of group research and practice* (pp. 39–64). Thousand Oaks, CA: Sage.

Bass, B. (1995). The meaning of leadership. In J. T. Wren (Ed.), *The leader's companion* (pp. 37–38). New York, NY: Free Press.

Bauman, S. (2009). Group work in the economic downturn. *Journal for Specialists in Group Work, 34,* 97–100.

Bauman, S. (2011). Group leader styles and functions. In R. Conyne (Ed.), *The Oxford handbook of group counseling* (pp. 325–345). New York, NY: Oxford University Press.

Bauman, S., & Waldo, M. (1998). Improving the goals and process (GAP) matrix for groups: Incorporating feedback from the field. *Journal for Specialists in Group Work, 23,* 215–224.

Beck, A. (1974). Phases in the development of structure in therapy and encounter groups. In D. Wexsler & L. Rice (Eds.), Innovations in client centered therapy (pp. 421–462). New York, NY: Wiley InterScience.

Bell, C., Raczynski, K., & Horne, A. (2010). Bully busters abbreviated: Evaluation of a group-based intervention and prevention program. *Group Dynamics: Theory, Research, and Practice, 14,* 257–267. doi: 10.1037/a0020596

Bemak, F., & Chung, R. C. (2004). Teaching multicultural group counseling: Perspectives for a new era. *Journal for Specialists in Group Work, 29,* 31–42. doi: 10.1080/01933920490275349

Bemak, F., & Conyne, R. (2004). Ecological group work. In R. Conyne & E. Cook (Eds.), *Ecological counseling: An innovative approach to conceptualizing person-environment interaction* (pp. 195–217). Alexandria, VA: American Counseling Association.

Benne, K. (1964). History of the T-group in the laboratory setting. In L. Bradford, J. Gibb, & K. Benne (Eds.), *T-group theory and the laboratory method* (pp. 80–135). New York, NY: Wiley.

Benne, K., & Sheats, P. (1948). Functional roles of group members. *Journal of Social Issues, 4*, 2.

Bennis, W., & Nanus, B. (1997). *Leaders: Strategies for taking charge* (2nd ed.). New York, NY: HarperCollins.

Bernard, H., & McKenzie, K. R. (Eds.). (1994). *Basics of group psychotherapy.* New York, NY: Guilford.

Bertcher, H., & Maple, F. (1977). *Creating groups.* Beverly Hills, CA: Sage.

Bieschke, K., Matthews, C., Wade, J., & Pricken, P. (1998). Evaluation of the process observer method: Group leader, member, and observer perspectives. *Journal for Specialists in Group Work, 23*, 50-65.

Bion, W. (1961). *Experience in groups* (2nd ed.). New York, NY: Basic Books.

Blake, R., & Mouton, J. (1982). How to choose a leadership style. *Training and Development Journal, 36*, 39-46.

Blatner, A. (2007). A historical chronology of group psychotherapy and psychodrama. Retrieved from www.blatner.com/adam/pdntbk/hxgrprx.htm

Bloom, B. (1956). *Taxonomy of educational objectives. Handbook I: Cognitive domain.* New York, NY: David McKay.

Bobby, C. (2009). Accreditation. In American Counseling Association (Ed.), *The ACA encyclopedia of counseling* (p. 2). Alexandria, VA: American Counseling Association.

Borden, L., Schultz, T., Herman, K., & Brooks, C. (2010). The Incredible Years Parent Training Program: Promoting resilience through evidence-based prevention groups. *Group Dynamics: Theory, Research, and Practice, 14*, 230-241. doi: 1089-2699/10.1037/a0020322

Brabender, V. (2011). Group development. In R. Conyne (Ed.), *The Oxford handbook of group counseling* (pp. 182-204). New York, NY: Oxford University Press.

Brabender, V., & Fallon, A. (2009). *Group development in practice: Guidance for clinicians and researchers on stages and dynamics of change.* Washington, DC: American Psychological Association.

Bradford, L., Gibb, J., & Benne, K. (Eds.). (1964). *T-group theory and laboratory method.* New York, NY: Wiley.

Bridbord, K. (2002). Processing activities to facilitate the transfer of learning outside of group. In J. DeLucia-Waack, K. Bridbord, & J. Kleiner (Eds.), *Group work experts share their favorite activities: A guide to choosing, planning, conducting, and processing* (pp. 15-25). Alexandria, VA: Association for Specialists in Group Work.

Bridbord, K., & DeLucia-Waack, J. (2011). Personality, leadership style, and theoretical orientation as predictors of group co-leadership satisfaction. *Journal for Specialists in Group Work, 36*, 202-221. doi: 10.1080/1933922.578117

Brinson, J., & Lee, C. (1997). Culturally responsive group leadership: An integrative model for experienced practitioners. In H. Forester-Miller & J. Kottler (Eds.), *Issues and challenges for group practitioners* (pp. 43-56). Denver, CO: Love.

Bronfenbrenner, U. (1979). *The ecology of human development.* Cambridge, MA: Harvard University Press.

Brooks, S. (2012). Thunder coach Scott Brown says early losses all part of learning to win. Retrieved from http://www.washingtontimes.com/news/2012/jun/7/brooks-says-early-losses-all-part-of-learning-to-w/

Brown, N. (1998). *Psychoeducational groups.* Philadelphia, PA: Accelerated Development.

Brown, N. (2005). Psychoeducational groups. In S. Wheelan (Ed.), *The handbook of group research and practice* (pp. 511–529). Thousand Oaks, CA: Sage.

Brown, N. (2009). Group work dynamics: Content and process. In American Counseling Association (Ed.), *The ACA encyclopedia of counseling* (pp. 229–230). Alexandria, VA: American Counseling Association.

Brown, N. (2011). Group leadership teaching and training: Methods and issues. In R. Conyne (Ed.), *The Oxford handbook of group counseling* (pp. 346–369). New York, NY: Oxford University Press.

Bugenthal, J. F. T. (1965). *The search for authenticity.* New York, NY: Holt, Rinehart and Winston.

Burkeman, O. (2012). *The antidote: Happiness for people who can't stand positive thinking.* Edinburgh, Scotland: Canongate Books, Ltd.

Burlingame, G., Fuhriman, A., & Johnson, J. (2001). Cohesion in group psychotherapy. *Psychotherapy, 38,* 373–379.

Burlingame, G., Fuhriman, A., & Johnson, J. (2004). Process and outcome in group psychotherapy: A perspective. In J. DeLucia-Waack, D. Gerrity, C. Kalodner, & M. Riva (Eds.), *Handbook of group counseling and psychotherapy* (pp. 49–61). Thousand Oaks, CA: Sage.

Burnes, T., & Ross, K. (2010). Applying social justice to oppression and marginalization in group process: Interventions and strategies for group counselors. *Journal for Specialists in Group Work, 35,* 163–176. doi: 10.1080/01933921003706014

Burton, A. (Ed.). (1969). *Encounter.* San Francisco, CA: Jossey-Bass.

Capra, F. (1996). *The web of life: A new scientific understanding of living systems.* New York, NY: Anchor Books.

Cartwright, D., & Zander, A. (Eds.). (1968). *Group dynamics: Research and theory.* New York, NY: Harper & Row.

Chen, M-w, & Rybak, C. (2004). *Group leadership skills: Interpersonal process in group counseling and therapy.* Belmont, CA: Brooks/Cole.

Clanton Harpine, E. (2011). *Group-centered prevention programs for at-risk students.* New York, NY: Springer. doi: 10.1007/978-1-4419-7248-4

Clanton Harpine, E. (2013). Prevention groups. In R. Conyne & A. Horne (Eds.), *Prevention practice kit: Action guides for mental health professionals.* Thousand Oaks, CA: Sage.

Cohen, S., & Bailey, D. (1997). What makes teams work: Group effectiveness research from the shop floor to the executive suite. *Journal of Management, 23,* 239–290.

Cohen, A., & Smith, R. D. (1976). *The critical incident in growth groups: Theory and technique.* La Jolla, CA: University Associates.

Cohen, S., & Bailey, D. (1997). What makes teams work: Group effectiveness research from the shop floor to the executive suite. *Journal of Management, 23,* 239-290.

Cohen, B., Ettin, M., & Fidler, J. (1998). Conceptions of leadership: The "analytic stance" of the group psychotherapist. *Group Dynamics: Theory, Research, and Practice, 2,* 118-131.

Conyne, R. (1975). In J. Jones & J. Pfeiffer (Eds.), *The 1975 annual handbook for group facilitators* (pp. 63-68). La Jolla, CA: University Associates.

Conyne, R. (1989). *How personal growth and task groups work.* Newbury Park, CA: Sage.

Conyne, R. (1996). The Association for Specialists in Group Work Training Standards: Some consideration and suggestions for training. *Journal for Specialists in Group Work, 21,* 155-162.

Conyne, R. (1997a). A developing framework for processing experiences and events in group work. *Journal for Specialists in Group Work, 22,* 167-174.

Conyne, R. (1997b). Group work ideas I have made aphoristic (for me). *Journal for Specialists in Group Work, 22,* 149-156.

Conyne, R. (1998a). Personal experience and meaning in group work leadership: The views of experts. *Journal for Specialists in Group Work, 23,* 245-256.

Conyne, R. (1998b). What to look for in groups: Helping trainees become more sensitive to multicultural issues. *Journal for Specialists in Group Work, 23,* 22-32. doi: 10.1080/01933929808411379

Conyne, R. (1999). *Failures in group work: How we can learn from our mistakes.* Thousand Oaks, CA: Sage.

Conyne, R. (2003). Group work issues: Past, present, and future. *Journal for Specialists in Group Work, 28,* 291-298.

Conyne, R. (2004). *Preventive counseling: Helping people to become empowered in systems and settings.* New York, NY: Brunner-Routledge.

Conyne, R. (2010). *Prevention program development and evaluation: An incidence-reduction, culturally relevant approach.* Thousand Oaks, CA: Sage.

Conyne, R. (Ed.). (2011). Group counseling. *The Oxford handbook of group counseling.* New York, NY: Oxford University Press.

Conyne, R. (2012). Group counseling. In E. Altmaier & J. C. Hansen (Eds.), *The Oxford handbook of counseling psychology* (pp. 611-646). New York, NY: Oxford University Press.

Conyne, R., & Bemak, F. (2004a). Preface: Special issue on teaching group work. *Journal for Specialists in Group Work, 29,* 3. doi: 10.1080/01933920490275295

Conyne, R., & Bemak, F. (2004b). Teaching group work from an ecological perspective. *Journal for Specialists in Group Work, 29,* 7-18. doi: 10.1080/01933920490275312

Conyne, R., & Bemak, F. (2005). *Journeys to professional excellence: Lessons from leading counselor educators and practitioners.* Alexandria, VA: American Counseling Association.

Conyne, R., & Clanton Harpine, E. (2010). Prevention groups: Evidence-based approaches to advance the field [Special issue]. *Group Dynamics: Theory, Research, and Practice* (pp. 193–280).

Conyne, R., & Cook, E. P. (Eds.). (2004). *Ecological counseling: An innovative approach to conceptualizing person-environment interaction.* Alexandria, VA: American Counseling Association.

Conyne, R., Crowell, J., & Newmeyer, M. (2008). *Group techniques: How to use them more purposefully.* Upper Saddle River, NJ: Pearson.

Conyne, R., & Diedrich, L. (2013). What is group work? In R. Conyne (Ed.), *Group Work Practice Kit.* Thousand Oaks, CA: Sage.

Conyne, R., Dye, H. A., Kline, W., Morran, D. K., Ward, D., & Wilson, F. R. (1992). Context for revising the ASGW training standards. *Journal for Specialists in Group Work, 17,* 10–11.

Conyne, R., & Horne, A. (2001). The use of groups for prevention. [Special issue]. *Journal for Specialists in Group Work, 26,* 205–292.

Conyne, R., & Mazza, J. (2007). Ecological group work applied to schools. *Journal for Specialists in Group Work, 32,* 19–30. doi: 10.1080/01933920600977499

Conyne, R., Rapin, L., & Rand, J. (1997). A model for leading task groups. In H. Forester-Miller & J. Kottler (Eds.), *Issues and challenges for group practitioners* (pp. 117–130). Denver, CO: Love.

Conyne, R., Tang, M., & Watson, A. (2001). Exploring diversity in therapeutic groups. In E. Welfel & R. E. Ingersoll (Eds.), *The mental health desk reference* (pp. 358–364). New York, NY: Wiley.

Conyne, R., & Wilson, F. R. (1998). Toward a standards-based classification of group work offerings. *Journal for Specialists in Group Work, 23,* 177–184.

Conyne, R., Wilson, F. R., Kline, W., Morran, D., & Ward, D. (1993). Training group workers: Implications of the new ASGW training standards for training and practice. *Journal for Specialists in Group Work, 18,* 11–23.

Conyne, R., Wilson, F. R., & Ward, D. (1997). *Comprehensive group work: What is means and how to teach it.* Alexandria, VA: American Counseling Association.

Cook, E. (Ed.). (2012). *Understanding people in context: The ecological perspective in counseling.* Alexandria, VA: American Counseling Association.

Corey, G. (2009). *Theory and practice of counseling and psychotherapy* (8th ed.). Pacific Grove, CA: Brooks/Cole.

Corey, G. (2012). *Theory and practice of group counseling* (8th ed.). Pacific Grove, CA: Brooks/Cole.

Corey, G., Corey, M., Callanan, P., & Russell, J. M. (2003). *Group techniques* (3rd ed.). Pacific Grove, CA: Brooks/Cole.

Corey, M., Corey, G., & Corey, C. (2010). *Groups: Process and practice* (8th ed.). Pacific Grove, CA: Brooks/Cole.

Council for the Accreditation of Counseling and Related Educational Programs. (2009). *2009 standards.* Alexandria, VA: Author.

Council on Social Work Education. (2008). *Educational policy and accreditation standards.* Retrieved from http://www.cswe.org/Accreditation/2008EPAS Description.aspxork

Craig, D. (1978). *HIP pocket guide to planning & evaluation*. Austin, TX: Learning Concepts.

Cummings, T., & Worley, C. (2008). *Organization development & change* (8th ed.). Florence, KY: Cengage Learning.

Davis, G. (1973). *Problem solving: Theory and practice.* New York, NY: Basic Books.

DeLucia-Waack, J. (1996). Multiculturalism in inherent in all group work. *Journal for Specialists in Group Work, 21,* 218-223.

DeLucia-Waack, J. (1997). The importance of processing activities, exercises, and events to group work practitioners. *Journal for Specialists in Group Work, 22,* 82-84.

DeLucia-Waack, J. (1998). Grouping our groups: What works? *Journal for Specialists in Group Work, 23,* 117-118.

DeLucia-Waack, J. (2001). Mentoring future group workers [Editorial]. *Journal for Specialists in Group Work, 26,* 107-110.

DeLucia-Waack, J. (2006a). *Leading psychoeducational groups for children and adolescents.* Thousand Oaks, CA: Sage.

DeLucia-Waack, J. (2006b). Multiculturalism is inherent in all group work [Editorial]. *Journal for Specialists in Group Work, 21,* 218-223.

DeLucia-Waack, J. (2011). Diversity in groups. In R. Conyne (Ed.), *Oxford handbook of group counseling* (pp. 83-101). New York, NY: Oxford University Press.

DeLucia-Waack, J., & Donigian, J. (2004). *The practice of multicultural group work: Visions and perspectives from the field.* Pacific Grove, CA: Wadsworth.

DeLucia-Waack, J., Gerrity, D., Kalodner, C., & Riva, M. (Eds.). (2004). *Group handbook of group counseling and psychotherapy.* Thousand Oaks, CA: Sage.

Denninger, J. (2010). Group and the social brain: Speeding toward a neurobiological understanding of group psychotherapy. *International Journal of Group Psychotherapy, 60,* 595-604.

Dewey, J. (1938). *Experience and education.* New York, NY: Collier.

Dewey, J. (1966). *Democracy and education.* New York, NY: Free Press.

Dies, R. (1994). Therapist variables in group psychotherapy research. In A. Fuhriman & G. Burlingame (Eds.), *Handbook of group psychotherapy* (pp. 114-154). New York, NY: Wiley.

Donigian, J., & Hulse-Killacky, D. (1999). *Critical incidents in group therapy* (2nd ed.). Belmont, CA: Brooks/Cole.

Donne, J. (1624). Meditation XVII. In A. Raspa (Ed., 1987), *Introduction to devotions upon emergent occasions.* New York, NY: Oxford University Press.

Duch, B., Groh, S., & Allen, D. (Eds.). (2001). *The power of problem-based learning.* Sterling, VA: Stylus.

Dye, H. A. (1996). Foreword: Four perspectives on the training and education of group leaders. *Journal for Specialists in Group Work, 21,* 15.

Eberle, R. (1971). *Scamper games for imagination development.* Bel Air, CA: DOK.

Ellerbee, L. (1986). *And so it goes: Adventures in television.* New York, NY: Putnam.

Ellis, A. (2011). Rational emotive behavior therapy. In R. Corsini & D. Wedding (Eds.), *Current psychotherapies* (9th ed., pp. 196-234). Belmont, CA: Brooks/Cole, Cengage Learning.

Face the Nation. (April 8, 2012). Remembering Mike Wallace: 1918–2012. Retrieved from http://www.cbsnews.com/8301-3460_162-57410999/remembering-mike-wallace-1918-2012/

Faherty, J. (2012, September 28). Camaraderie creates success: Theories about whey the Reds are doing so well this year abound among fans. *The Cincinnati Enquirer*, pp. A-1, A-13.

Fatout, M., & Rose, S. (1995). *Task groups in the social services.* Thousand Oaks, CA: Sage.

Feder, B. (2006). *Gestalt group therapy: A practical guide.* Metairie/New Orleans, LA: Gestalt Institute Press.

Ferguson, D. (2010). Introducing couples to group therapy: Pursuing passion through the neo-cortex. *International Journal of Group Psychotherapy*, 60, 572–594.

Fiedler, F. (1950). A comparison of therapeutic relationships in psychoanalytic, nondirective, and Adlerian therapy. *Journal of Consulting Psychology*, 14, 436–445.

Fiedler, F. (1996). Research on leadership selection and training: One view of the future. *Administrative Science Quarterly*, 41, 241–250.

Flores, P. (2010). Group psychotherapy and neuro-plasticity: An Attachment Theory perspective. *International Journal of Group Psychotherapy*, 60, 546–571.

Forsyth, D. (2009). *Group dynamics* (5th ed.). Belmont, CA: Wadsworth.

Forsyth, D. (2011). The nature and significance of groups. In R. Conyne (Ed.), *The Oxford handbook of group counseling* (pp. 19–35). New York, NY: Oxford University Press.

Frankl, V. (1962, 2000). *Man's search for meaning: An introduction to logotherapy.* New York, NY: Beacon.

Frew, J., & Spiegler, M. (2012). Contemporary psychotherapies for a diverse world. New York, NY: Routledge.

Frost, R. (1916). The road not taken. *Mountain interval.* New York, NY: Henry Holt & Co.

Fujishin, R. (2001). *Creating effective groups: The art of small group communication.* San Francisco, CA: Acada.

Furr, S. (2000). Structuring the group experience: A format for designing psychoeducational groups. *Journal for Specialists in Group Work*, 25, 29–49.

Gantt, S., & Cox, P. (Special issue editors). (2010). Neurobiology and building interpersonal systems: Groups, couples, and beyond. *International Journal of Group Psychotherapy*, 60, 453–609.

Gazda, G. (Ed.). (1968). *Basic approaches to group psychotherapy and group counseling.* Springfield, IL: Charles C Thomas.

Gersick, C. (1988). Time and transition in work teams: Toward a new model of group development. *Academy of Management Journal*, 31, 9–41.

Gladding, S. (1997). The creative arts in groups. In H. Forester-Miller & J. Kottler (Eds.), *Issues and challenges for group practitioners* (pp. 81–99). Denver, CO: Love.

Gladding, S. (2011a). Creativity and spontaneity in groups. In R. Conyne (Ed.), *The Oxford handbook of group counseling* (pp. 383–398). New York, NY: Oxford University Press.

Gladding, S. (2011b). *Groups: A counseling specialty* (6th ed.). Upper Saddle River, NJ: Prentice Hall.

Gladding, S. (2011c). *The creative arts in counseling* (4th ed.). Alexandria, VA: American Counseling Association.

Gladwell, M. (2002). *The Tipping Point: How little things can make a big difference.* New York, NY: Back Bay Books.

Gladwell, M. (2008). *Outliers: The story of successes.* New York, NY: Little, Brown & Company.

Glass, J., & Benshoff, J. (1999). PARS: A processing model for beginning group leaders. *Journal for Specialists in Group Work, 24,* 15–26.

Goodman, M. (1995). From the outgoing president: A blue print for the future (or my personal wish list). *The Group Psychologist, 5,* 2.

Gorski, P. (1995–2012). *Critical multicultural pavilion awareness activities: An EdChange project.* Retrieved from http://www.edchange.org/multicultural/activityarch.html

Gray, B. (2012, June 12). Mindful meditation tied to healthy brain change: Study. Retrieved from http://healthyliving.msn.com/health-wellness/mindful-meditation-tied-to-healthy-brain-changes-study-1

Greenaway, R. (2012). Reviewing skills training. Retrieved from http://reviewing.co.uk/research/learning.cycles.htm

group dynamics. (n.d.). *Collins English dictionary—Complete & unabridged 10th edition.* Retrieved January 19, 2013, from *Dictionary.com* website http://dictionary.reference.com/browse/group dynamics

Hackman, R. (2002). *Leading teams: Setting the stage for great performances.* Boston, MA: Harvard Business Review Press.

Hackman, R. (2011, June 7). Six common misperceptions about teamwork. *HBR Blog Network.* Retrieved from http://blogs.hbr.org/cs/2011/06/six_common_misperceptions_abou.html

Hage, S., Mason, M., & Kim, J. (2011). A social justice approach to group counseling. In R. Conyne (Ed.), *The Oxford handbook of group counseling* (pp. 102–117). New York, NY: Oxford University Press.

Hage, S., & Romano, J. (2010). History of prevention and prevention groups: Legacy for the 21st century. *Group Dynamics: Theory, Research, and Practice, 14,* 199–210. doi: 10.1037/a0020736

Hage, S., & Romano, J. (2013). Best practices in prevention. In R. Conyne & A. Horne (Eds.), *Prevention practice kit: Action guides for mental health professionals.* Thousand Oaks, CA: Sage.

Halstead, J. M. (2007). Education in the era of globalization. *Philosophy and Education, 16,* 147–160. doi: 10.1007/9781-1-4020-5945-2_8

Hansen, J. (2005). The devaluation of inner subjective experience by the counseling profession: A plea to reclaim the essence of the profession. *Journal of Counseling & Development, 83,* 406–415.

Hansen, J. (2010). Inner subjective experiences and social constructivism: A response to Rudes and Guterman (2007). *Journal of Counseling & Development, 88,* 210–213.

Hanson, P. (1972). What to look for in groups: An observation guide. In J. Pfeiffer & J. Jones (Eds.), *The 1972 annual handbook of group facilitators* (pp. 21-24). San Diego, CA: Pfeiffer.

Hare, A. P., Borgatta, E., & Bales, R. F. (Eds.). (1965). *Small groups: Studies in social interaction.* New York, NY: Knopf.

Harel, Y., Shechtman, Z., & Cotrona, C. (2011). Individual and group process variables that affect social support in counseling groups. *Group Dynamics: Theory, Research, and Practice, 15,* 297-310. doi: 10.1037/a0025058

Harrow, A. (1972). *A taxonomy of psychomotor domain: A guide for developing behavioral objectives.* New York, NY: David McKay.

Hebb, D. O. (1949). *The organization of behavior: A neuropsychological theory.* New York, NY: Wiley.

Herr, E. (2004). The context of American life today. In R. Conyne & E. Cook (Eds.), *Ecological counseling: An innovative approach to conceptualizing person-environment interaction* (pp. 37-66). Alexandria, VA: American Counseling Association.

Hersey, P., & Blanchard, K., & Johnson, D. (2001). *Management of organizational behavior: Leading human resources* (8th ed.). Upper Saddle River, NJ: Prentice Hall.

Hill, W. F. (1965). *HIM: Hill Interaction Matrix.* University of Southern California: Youth Studies Center.

Hill, W. F. (1969). *Learning thru discussion: Guide for leaders and members of discussion groups.* Beverly Hills, CA: Sage.

Holcomb-McCoy, C. (2007). *School counseling to close the achievement gap: A social justice framework for success.* Thousand Oaks, CA: Corwin.

Hubble, M., Duncan, B., & Miller, S. (1999). *The heart and soul of change: What works in therapy.* Washington, DC: American Psychological Association.

Hulse-Killacky, D. (1996). Using the classroom as a group to integrate knowledge, skills, and supervised practice. *Journal for Specialists in Group Work, 21,* 163-168.

Hulse-Killacky, D., Killacky, J., & Donigian, J. (2001). *Making task groups work in your world.* Upper Saddle River, NJ: Merrill Prentice Hall.

Internet Archive. (2011). *George Washington's rules of civility & decent behavior in company and conversation.* Retrieved from http://www.archive.org/details/georgewashington00unse

Ivey, A. (2012). Therapeutic Lifestyle Changes (TLC): Increasing daily Neurogenesis and the "Take Rate" for maintenance of new neurons and neural connections (AKA "Use it or Lose it!). Unpublished manuscript.

Ivey, A., D'Andrea, M., & Ivey, M. B. (2012). *Theories of counseling and psychotherapy: A multicultural perspective.* Thousand Oaks, CA: Sage.

Ivey, A., Ivey, M. B., & Zalequett, C. (2009). *Intentional interviewing: Facilitating client development in a multicultural society* (7th ed.). Pacific Grove, CA: Brooks/Cole.

Jacobs, E., Masson, R., Harvill, R., & Schimmel, C. (2012). *Group counseling: Strategies and skills* (7th ed.). Belmont, CA: Brooks/Cole.

Johnson, D., & Johnson, F. (2008). *Joining together: Group theory and group skills* (10th ed.). Upper Saddle River, NJ: Pearson.

Jones, J. (1973). A model of group development. In J. Pfeiffer, & J. Jones (Eds.), *The 1973 annual handbook for group facilitators* (pp. 127-129). La Jolla, CA: University Associates.

Jones, J., & Pfeiffer, W. (1980). Introduction to the structured experience, adapted. *The 1980 annual handbook for group facilitators.* San Diego, CA: Pfeiffer & Co.

Journal for Specialists in Group Work. (1981). Special issue on issues in the training of group workers. *Journal for Specialists in Group Work, 6,* 123-182.

Journal for Specialists in Group Work. (1996). Special issue on training. *Journal for Specialists in Group Work, 21,* 151-180.

Journal for Specialists in Group Work. (2004). Special issue on teaching group work. *Journal for Specialists in Group Work, 29,* 1-148.

Kabat-Zinn, J. (1994). *Wherever you go there you are: Mindfulness meditation in everyday life.* New York, NY: Hyperion.

Kees, N., & Jacobs, E. (1990). Conducting more effective groups: How to select and process group exercises. *Journal for Specialists in Group Work, 15,* 21-30.

Kenny, M., Horne, A., Orpinas, P., & Reese, L. (2009). *Realizing social justice: The challenge of preventive interventions.* Washington, DC: American Psychological Association.

Kipper, D. (2006). The canon of spontaneity-creativity revisited: The effect of empirical findings. *Journal of Group Psychotherapy, Psychodrama, & Sociometry, 59,* 117-125.

Kitchener, K. S. (1984). Intuition, critical evaluation and ethical principles: The foundation for ethical decisions in counseling psychology. *The Counseling Psychologist, 12,* 43-55.

Kivlighan, D. M., Jr. (2011). Individual and group perceptions of therapeutic factors and session evaluation: An actor-partner interdependence analysis. *Group Dynamics: Theory, Research, and Practice, 15,* 147-160.

Kivlighan, D. M., Jr., & Holmes, S. (2004). The importance of therapeutic factors: A typology of therapeutic factors studies. In J. DeLucia-Waack, D. Gerrity, C. Kalodner, & M. Riva (Eds.), *Handbook of group counseling and psychotherapy* (pp. 23-48). Thousand Oaks, CA: Sage.

Kivlighan, D. M., Miles, J., & Paquin, J. (2011). Therapeutic factors in group counseling: Asking new questions. In R. Conyne (Ed.), *The Oxford handbook of group counseling* (pp. 121-136). New York, NY: Oxford University Press.

Kline, W. (2003). *Interactive group counseling and therapy.* Upper Saddle River, NJ: Merrill.

Koch, G., & Dollarhide, C. T. (2000). Using a popular film in counselor education: *Good Will Hunting* as a teaching tool. *Counselor Education and Supervision, 39,* 203-210.

Kolb, D. (1984). *Experience as the source of learning and development.* Englewood Cliffs, NJ: Prentice Hall.

Kormanski, C. (1991). Using theory as a foundation for group training designs. *Journal for Specialists in Group Work, 16,* 215-222.

Kormanski, C. (1999). *The team: Explorations in group process.* Denver, CO: Love.

Kormanski, C. (2001). From group leader to process consultant. In H. Forester-Miller & J. Kottler (Eds.), *Issues and challenges for group practitioners* (pp. 133-164). Denver, CO: Love.

Kozlowski, S., & Ilgen, D. (2006). Enhancing the effectiveness of work groups and teams. *Psychological Science in the Public Interest, 7,* 77-124.

Kottler, J. (1981). The development of guidelines for training group leaders: A synergistic, 10-model. *Journal for Specialists in Group Work, 6,* 125-129.

Kottler, J., & Blau, D. (1989). *The imperfect therapist: Learning from failure in therapeutic experience.* San Francisco, CA: Jossey-Bass.

Krathwohl, D., Bloom, B., & Masia, B. (1973). *Taxonomy of educational objectives, the classification of educational goals. Handbook II: Affective domain.* New York, NY: David McKay.

Kraus, K. (2003). *Exercises in group work.* Upper Saddle River, NJ: Pearson.

Kraus, K., & Hulse-Killacky, D. (1996). Balancing process and content in groups: A metaphor. *Journal for Specialists in Group Work, 21,* 90-93.

Kubler-Ross, E. (2012). Quoteworld. Retrieved from http://quoteworld.org/quotes/7961

Larson, C., & LaFasto, F. (1989). *Team work: What must go right/what can go wrong.* Newbury Park, CA: Sage.

Lazarus, A. (2008). Multimodal therapy. In R. J. Corsini & D. Wedding (Eds.), *Current psychotherapies* (8th ed., pp. 368–401). Belmont, CA: Brooks/Cole.

Leddick, G. (2011). The history of group counseling. In R. Conyne (Ed.), *The Oxford handbook of group counseling* (pp. 52-60). New York, NY: Oxford University Press.

Lee, C. (Ed.). (2012). *Multicultural issues in counseling: New approaches to diversity* (4th ed.). Alexandria, VA: American Counseling Association.

Leszcz, M., & Kobos, J. (2008). Evidence-based group psychotherapy: Using AGPA's practice guidelines to enhance clinical effectiveness. *Journal of Clinical Psychology: In session, 64,* 1238-1260.

Lewin, K. (1936). *Principles of topological psychology.* New York, NY: McGraw-Hill.

Lewin, K. (1951). *Field theory in social science.* New York, NY: Harper.

Lewin, K., Lippitt, R., & White, R. K. (1939). Patterns of aggressive behavior in experimentally created social climates. *Journal of Social Psychology, 10,* 271-279.

Lieberman, M. (2008). Effects of disease and leader type on moderators in online support groups. *Computer in Human Behavior, 24,* 2446-2455. doi: 10.1016/j.chb.2008.02.018

Lieberman, M., & Golant, M. (2002). Leader behaviors as perceived by cancer patients in professionally directed support groups and outcomes. *Group Dynamics: Theory, Research, and Practice, 6,* 267-276.

Lieberman, M., Yalom, I., & Miles, M. (1973). *Encounter groups: First facts.* New York, NY: Basic Books.

Linley, P., Joseph, S., Harrington, S., & Wood, A. (2006). Positive psychology: Past, present, and (possible) future. *The Journal of Positive Psychology, 1*, 3-16.

Lord, R. (1977). Functional leadership behavior: Measurement and relation to social power and leadership perceptions. *Administrative Science Quarterly, 22*, 114-133.

Luke, M., & Hackney, H. (2007). Group coleadership: A critical review. *Counselor Education and Supervision, 46*, 280-293.

Mackenzie, K. (1997). Clinical applications of group development ideas. *Group Dynamics: Theory, Research, and Practice, 1*, 26-34.

Mackenzie, K., & Livesley, W. (1983). A developmental model for brief therapy. In R. Dies & K. MacKenzie (Eds.), *Advances in group psychotherapy: Integrating theory and research* (pp. 101-135). Madison, CT: International Universities Press.

MacKenzie, K., Dies, R., Coche, E., Rutan, S., & Stone, W. (1987). An analysis of APGA Institute groups. *International Journal of Group Psychotherapy, 37*, 55-74.

Marmarosh, C., & Van Horn, S. (2011). Cohesion in counseling and psychotherapy groups. In R. Conyne (Ed.), *The Oxford handbook of group counseling* (pp. 137-163). New York, NY: Oxford University Press.

Maslow, A. (1970). *Motivation and personality* (2nd ed.). New York, NY: Harper & Row.

Master's in Psychology and Counseling Accreditation Council. (2011, June 6). *Accreditation manual*. Retrieved from http://www.mpcacsite.org/mpac/

Mathieu, J., Maynard, M. T., Rapp, T., & Gilson, L. (2008). Team effectiveness 1997-2007: A review of recent advancements and a glimpse into the future. *Journal of Management, 34*, 410-476.

Matthews, A. (2011, December 12). U.S. health care's future. *Wall Street Journal,* 4 B4.

May, R. (1961). *Existential psychology*. New York, NY: Random House.

Mayer, J. (Writer and producer). (2008). Lesson learned [Recorded by A. Keys]. On As I am. J Records: Sony Music Entertainment.

McClendon, D. T., & Burlingame, G. (2011). Group climate: Construct in search of clarity. In R. Conyne (Ed.), *The Oxford handbook of group counseling* (pp. 164-181). New York, NY: Oxford University Press.

McNair-Semands, R. (2007). Attending to the spirit of social justice as an ethic approach in group therapy. *International Journal of Group Psychotherapy, 57*, 61-66.

McRoberts, C., Burlingame, G., & Hoag, M. (1998). Comparative efficacy of individual and group psychotherapy: A meta-analytic perspective. *Group Dynamics: Theory, Research, and Practice, 2*, 101-117.

McWhirter, E. H. (1994). *Counseling for empowerment*. Alexandria, VA: American Counseling Association.

McWhirter, E. H. (1998). Emancipatory communitarian psychology. *American Psychologist, 53*, 322-323.

Merchant, N. (2006). Multicultural and diversity-competent group work. In J. Trotzer, *The counselor and the group: Integrating theory, training, and practice* (4th ed., pp. 319–350). New York, NY: Routledge.

Merchant, N. (2009). Types of diversity-related groups. In C. Salazar (Ed.), *Group work experts share their favorite multicultural activities: A guide to diversity-competent choosing, planning, conducting, and processing* (pp. 13–24). Alexandria, VA: Association for Specialists in Group Work.

Michaelsen, L., Knight, A., & Fink, L. D. (2002). *Team-based learning: A transformative use of small groups.* Westport, CT: Praeger.

Morran, D. K., Stockton, R., & Whittingham, M. (2004). Effective leader interventions for counseling and psychotherapy groups. In J. DeLucia-Waack, D. Gerrity, C. Kalodner, & M. Riva (Eds.), *Handbook of group counseling and psychotherapy* (pp. 91–103). Thousand Oaks, CA: Sage.

Morrill, W., Oetting, E., & Hurst, J. (1974). Dimensions of counselor functioning. *Personnel and Guidance Journal, 52,* 354–359.

Morris, J., & Robinson, D. (1996). A review of multicultural counseling. *Journal of Humanistic Counseling, 35,* 50–60. doi: 10.1002/j.2164-4683.1996.tb00352.x

Napier, R., & Gershenfeld, M. (2004). (7th ed.). *Groups: Theory and experience.* Boston, MA: Houghton Mifflin.

Nelson, G., & Prilleletensky, I. (Eds.). (2005). *Community psychology: In pursuit of liberation and well-being.* New York, NY: Palgrave Macmillan.

Newmeyer, M. (2011). Group techniques. In R. Conyne (Ed.), *The Oxford handbook of group counseling* (pp. 307–324). New York, NY: Oxford University Press.

Norcross, J., & Guy, J. (2007). *Leaving it at the office: A guide to psychotherapist self-care.* New York, NY: Guilford Press.

Ogrodniczuk, J., & Piper, W. (2003). The effect of group climate on outcome in two forms of short-term group therapy. *Group Dynamics: Theory, Research, and Practice, 7,* 64–76. doi: 10.1037/1089-2699.7.1.64

Okech, J. E. A., & Rubel, D. (2007). Diversity competent group work supervision: An application of the supervision group work model (SGW). *Journal for Specialists in Group Work, 32,* 245–266. doi: 10.1080/01933920701431651

Page, B. (2004). Online group counseling. In J. Delucia-Waack, D. Gerrity, C. Kalodner, & M. Riva (Eds.), *Handbook of group counseling and psychotherapy* (pp. 609–620). Thousand Oaks, CA: Sage.

Page, B. (2011). Online groups. In R. Conyne (Ed.), *The Oxford handbook of group counseling* (pp. 520–533). New York, NY: Oxford University Press.

Pedersen, P. (Ed.). (1991). Multiculturalism as a fourth force in counseling [Special issue]. *Journal of Counseling and Development, 70,* 1.

Peterson, C., & Seligman, M. (2004). *Character strengths and virtues: A handbook and classification.* New York, NY: Oxford University Press.

Pfeiffer, J., & Jones, J. (1983). *The annual handbook for group facilitators.* La Jolla, CA: University Associates.

Pillemer, K. (2012). *30 lessons for living: Tried and true advice from the wisest Americans.* New York, NY: Plume.

Polcin, D. (1991). Prescriptive group leadership. *Journal for Specialists in Group Work, 16,* 8-15.

Polster, M., & Polster, E. (1990). Gestalt therapy. In J. Zeig & W. Munion (Eds.), *What is psychotherapy? Contemporary perspectives* (pp. 103-107). San Francisco, CA: Jossey-Bass.

Population Reference Group. (2012). In the news: U.S. population is now one-third minority. Retrieved from http://www.prb.org/Articles/2006/IntheNewsUSPopulationIsNowOneThirdMinority.aspx?p=1U.S.

Portman, J., & Barnett, J. (1976). *The architect as developer.* New York, NY: McGraw-Hill. Retrieved from http://www.portmanusa.com/_uploads/f28386ed90319842ccc9b2074faf2b73.pdf

Posthuma, B. (2002). *Small groups in counseling and therapy* (4th ed.). Needham Heights, MA: Allyn and Bacon.

Prilleltensky, I. (1997). Values, assumptions, and practices: Assessing the moral implications of psychological discourse and action. *American Psychologist, 52,* 517-535.

Prilleltensky, I. (1999). Critical psychology foundations for the promotion of mental health. *Annual Review of Critical Psychology, 1,* 100-118.

Prilleltensky, I., Dokecki, P., Frieden, G., & Wang, V. (2007). Counseling for wellness and social justice. In E. Aldarondo (Ed.), *Advancing social justice through clinical practice* (pp. 19-42). Mahway, NJ: Lawrence Erlbaum.

Prochaska, J., & DiClemente, C. (2005). The transtheoretical approach. In J. Norcross & M. Goldfried (Eds.), *Handbook of psychotherapy integration* (2nd ed., pp. 147-171). New York, NY: Oxford University Press.

Prochaska, J. O., Johnson, S., & Lee, P. (2009). The transtheoretical model of behavior change. In S. A. Shumaker, J. K. Ockene, & K. A. Riekert (Eds.). *The handbook of behavior change* (3rd ed., pp. 59-83). New York, NY: Springer.

Ramey, L., & Leibert, T. (2011). *How well are students of wellness?* Retrieved from http://counselingoutfitters.com/ vistas/vistas11/Article_42.pdf

Rapin, L. (2004). Guidelines for ethical and legal practice in counseling and psychotherapy groups. In J. DeLucia-Waack, D. Gerrity, C. Kalodner, & M. Riva (Eds.), *Handbook of group counseling and psychotherapy* (pp. 151-165). Thousand Oaks, CA: Sage.

Rapin, L. (2011). Ethics, best practices, and law in group counseling. In R. Conyne (Ed.), *The Oxford handbook of group counseling* (pp. 61-82). New York, NY: Oxford University Press.

Rapin, L., & Conyne, R. (2006). Best practices in group work. In J. Trotzer, The counselor and the group: Integrating theory, training, and practice (4th ed., pp. 291-318). New York, NY: Routledge.

Ratey, J., & Hagerman, E. (2008). *Spark: The revolutionary new science of exercise and the brain.* Boston, MA: Little, Brown & Company.

Ratts, M., Anthony, L., & Santos, K. N. (2010). The Dimensions of Social Justice Model: Transforming traditional group work into a socially just framework. *Journal for Specialists in Group Work, 35,* 160-168. doi: 10.1080/01933921003705974

Rawls, J. (1971). *A theory of justice.* Cambridge, MA: Harvard University Press.

Reddy, W. B. (1994). *Intervention skills: Process consultation for small groups and teams.* San Diego, CA: Pfeiffer & Associates.

Riva, M. (2011). Supervision of group counseling. In R. Conyne (Ed.), *The Oxford handbook of group counseling* (pp. 370–382). New York, NY: Oxford University Press.

Riva, M., Wachtel, M., & Butcher, G. (2000, March). *Understanding group co-therapy relationships: A developmental approach.* Paper presented at the American Counseling Association Annual Convention, Washington, DC.

Riva, M., Wachtel, M., & Lasky, G. (2004). Effective leadership in group counseling and psychotherapy. In J. Delucia-Waack, D. Gerrity, C. Kalodner, & M. Riva (Eds.), *Group counseling and psychotherapy* (pp. 637–640). Thousand Oaks, CA: Sage.

Rivera, E. T., Wilbur, M., Wilbur, J., Phan, L., Garrett, M., & Betz, R. (2004). Supervising and training psychoeducational group leaders. *Journal for Specialists in Group Work, 29,* 377–394. doi: 10.1080/01933920490516134

Rogers, C. (1967). The process of the basic encounter group. In J. F. T. Bugenthal (Ed.), *Challenges of humanistic psychology.* New York, NY: McGraw-Hill.

Roysircar, G. (2008). A response to "Social privilege, social justice, and group counseling: An inquiry": Social privilege: Counselors' competency with systemically determined inequalities. *Journal for Specialists in Group Work, 33,* 377–384.

Rubel, D., & Okech, J. (2011). Qualitative research approaches and group counseling. In R. Conyne (Ed.), *The Oxford handbook of group counseling* (pp. 260–286). New York, NY: Oxford University Press.

Rudes, J., & Guterman, J. (2007). The value of social constructionism for the counseling profession: A reply to Hansen. *Journal of Counseling & Development, 85,* 387–392.

Rutan, S., Stone, W., & Shay, J. (2007). *Psychodynamic group psychotherapy* (4th ed.). New York, NY: Guilford Press.

Saakvitne, K. W., Pearlman, L. A., & Staff of TSI/CAAP. (1996). *Transforming the pain: A workbook on vicarious traumatization.* New York, NY: W. W. Norton.

Sage, A., Zaidman, N., Amichaie-Hamburger, Y., Te'eni, D., & Schwartz, D. (2002). An empirical assessment of the loose–tight leadership model: Quantitative and qualitative analyses. *Journal of Organizational Behavior, 23,* 303–320.

Salazar, C. (Ed.). (2009). *Group work experts share their favorite multicultural activities: A guide to diversity-competent choosing, planning, conducting and processing.* Alexandria, VA: Association for Specialists in Group Work.

Schein, E. (1969). *Process consultation: Its role in organization development.* Reading, MA: Addison-Wesley.

Schein, E. (1998). *Process consultation revisited: Building the helping relationship.* Boston, MA: Addison-Wesley Longman.

Schermer, V. (2010). Mirror neurons: Their implications for group psychotherapy. *International Journal of Group Psychotherapy, 60,* 486–513.

Scholl, R. (2003). Leadership overview. Kingston: University of Rhode Island. Retrieved from http://www.uri.edu/research/lrc/scholl/webnotes/Leadership.htm

Schutz, W. (1958). *FIRO: A three-dimensional theory of interpersonal behavior*. New York, NY: Rinehart.

Schutz, W. (1966). *The interpersonal underworld.* Palo Alto, CA: Science and Behavior Books.

Schmuck, R., & Schmuck, P. (2001). (8th ed.). *Group process in the classroom.* Boston, MA: McGraw-Hill.

Schwarz, R. (2002). *The skilled facilitator: A comprehensive resource for consultants, facilitators, manager, trainers, and coaches.* San Francisco, CA: Jossey-Bass.

Seligman, M., Steen, T., Park, N., & Peterson, C. (2005). Positive psychology progress: Empirical validation of interventions. *American Psychologist, 60,* 410–421.

Seung, S. (2013). *Connectome: How the brain's wiring makes us who we are.* Boston, MA: Mariner Books.

Shallcross, L. (2012). What the future holds for the counseling profession. *Counseling Today, 54,* 32–44.

Shechtman, Z., & Toren, Z. (2009). The effect of leader behavior on processes and outcomes in group counseling. *Group Dynamics: Theory, Research, and Practice, 13,* 218–233. doi: 10.1037/a0015718

Siegel, D. (1999). *The developing mind.* New York, NY: Guilford.

Siegel, D. (2010). Reflections on mind, brain, and relationships in group psychotherapy. Inter*national Journal of Group Psychotherapy, 60,* 483–485.

Singh, A., & Salazar, C. (Eds.). (2011). *Social justice in group work: Practical interventions.* New York, NY: Routledge.

Skinner, B. F. (1974). *About behaviorism.* New York, NY: Knopf.

Sliding Doors. (1998). London, UK: Intermedia Films.

Smith, L., & Shin, R. (2008). Social privilege, social justice, and group counseling. *Journal for Specialists in Group Work, 33,* 351–366.

Solomon, L. (1977). Team development: A training approach. In J. Jones & J. Pfeiffer (Eds.), *The 1977 annual handbook for group facilitators* (pp. 181–193). San Diego, CA: University Associates.

Spitz, H. (1996). *Group psychotherapy and managed mental health care: A clinical guide for providers.* New York, NY: Brunner/Mazel.

Stern, G. (1970). *People in context: Measuring person-environment congruence in education and industry.* New York, NY: Wiley.

Stern, M. (2012, June 18). Maggie Gyllenhaal: On flubbing the lines of perfection (p. 56). *My Favorite Mistake* column. Palm Coast, FL: Newsweek.

Stockton, R., & Morran, D. K. (2011). General research models. In R. Conyne (Ed.), *The Oxford handbook of group counseling* (pp. 231–244). New York, NY: Oxford University Press.

Stockton, R., Morran, D. K., & Nitza, A. (2000). Processing group events: A conceptual map for leaders. *Journal for Specialists in Group Work, 25,* 343–355.

Stockton, R., Morran, D. K., & Krieger, K. (2004). An overview of current research and best practices for training beginning group leaders. In In J. Delucia-Waack, D. Gerrity, C. Kalodner, & M. Riva (Eds.), *Group counseling and psychotherapy* (pp. 65–75). Thousand Oaks, CA: Sage.

Stockton, R., Rohde, R., & Haughey, J. (1992). The effect of structured group exercises on cohesion, engagement, avoidance, and conflict. *Small Group Research, 23,* 155-168. doi: 10.1177/1046496492232001

Sue, D. W., & Sue, D. (2008). *Counseling the culturally diverse: Theory and practice* (5th ed.). New York, NY: Wiley.

Sullivan, H. S. (1953). *The interpersonal theory of psychiatry.* New York, NY: Norton.

Sundstrom, E., DeMeuse, K., & Futrell, D. (1990). Work teams: Applications and effectiveness. *American Psychologist, 45,* 120-133.

Thelen, H. (1954). *Dynamics of groups at work.* Chicago, IL: The University of Chicago Press.

Tinsley, H., Roth, J., & Lease, S. (1989). *Journal of Counseling Psychology, 36,* 48-53.

Toporek, R., Lewis, J., & Crethar, H. (2009). Promoting system change through the *ACA Advocacy Competencies. Journal of Counseling & Development, 87,* 260-268.

Trotzer, J. (2006). *The counselor and the group: Integrating theory, training, and practice* (4th ed.). New York, NY: Routledge.

Trotzer, J. (2011). Personhood of the leader. In R. Conyne (Ed.), *The Oxford handbook of group counseling* (pp. 287-306). New York, NY: Oxford University Press.

Tuckman, B. (1965). Developmental sequence in small groups. *Psychological Bulletin, 63,* 384-399.

Tuckman, B., & Jensen, M. (1977). Stages of small group development revisited. *Group and Organizational Studies, 2,* 419-427.

Tyson, L., Perusse, R., & Whitledge, J. (Eds.). (2004). *Critical incidents in group counseling.* Alexandria, VA: American Counseling Association.

Vera, E. (Ed.). (2012). *The Oxford handbook of prevention.* New York, NY: Oxford University Press.

Vera, E., & Kenny, M. (in press). Social justice and culturally-relevant prevention. In R. Conyne & A. Horne (Eds.), *Prevention practice kit: Action guides for mental health professionals.* Thousand Oaks, CA: Sage.

Vera, E., & Speight, S. (2003). Multicultural competence, social justice, and counseling psychology: Expanding our roles. *The Counseling Psychologist, 31,* 253-272.

Villemaire, D. (2002). *E. A. Burtt, historian and philosopher: A study of the author of the metaphysical foundations of modern physical science.* Dordrecht, The Netherlands: Kluwer Academic.

von Bertalanffy, L. (1956). General systems theory. *General Systems* (Yearbook of the Society for the Advancement of General Systems Theory), *1,* 1-10.

von Bertalanffy, L. (1968). *General systems theory: Foundations, development, application.* New York, NY: Braziller.

Waldo, M. (1985). A curative factor framework for conceptualizing group counseling. *Journal of Counseling and Development, 64,* 52-58.

Waldo, M., Kerne, P., & Van Horn, V. (2007). Therapeutic factors in guidance versus counseling sessions of domestic violence groups. *Journal for Specialists in Group Work, 32,* 346-361. doi: 10.1080/01933920701476672

Waldo, M., Schwartz, J., Horne, A., & Cote, L. (2011). Prevention groups. In R. Conyne (Ed.), *The Oxford handbook of group counseling* (pp. 452–468). New York, NY: Oxford University Press.

Walsh, R. (2011). Lifestyle and mental health. *American Psychologist, 66,* 579–592.

Wampold, B. (2001). *The great psychotherapy debate: Models, methods, and findings.* New York, NY: Routledge.

Wampold, B. (2010). *The basics of psychotherapy: An introduction to theory and practice.* Washington, DC: American Psychological Association.

Ward, D. (2004). The evidence mounts: Group work is effective. *Journal for Specialists in Group Work, 29,* 155–157. doi: 10.1080/01933920490437925

Ward, D. (2006). Classification of groups. *Journal for Specialists in Group Work, 31,* 93–98. doi: 10.1080/01933920500493571

Ward, D. (2009). Group work, developmental stages of. In American Counseling Association (Ed.), The ACA encyclopedia of counseling (pp. 227–229). Alexandria, VA: American Counseling Association.

Ward, D., & Lichy, M. (2004). The effective use of processing in groups. In J. DeLucia-Waack, D. Gerrity, C. Kalodner, & M. Riva (Eds.), *Handbook of group counseling and psychotherapy* (pp. 104–119). Thousand Oaks, CA: Sage.

Ward, D., & Ward, C. (2013). *How to help leaders and members learn from groups.* In R. Conyne (Ed.), *Group work practice kit: Improving the everyday practice of group work.* Thousand Oaks, CA: Sage.

Weinberg, H. (2012). *Group psychotherapy resource guide.* Retrieved February 24, 2012, from http://www.group-psychotherapy.com/index.htm

Weisbord, M. (1978). *Organizational diagnosis.* Reading, MA: Addison-Wesley.

Wheelan, S. (1994). *Group processes: A developmental perspective.* Boston, MA: Allyn & Bacon.

Wheelan, S. (2004). Groups in the workplace. In J. DeLucia-Waack, D. Gerrity, C. Kalodner, & M. Riva (Eds.), *Group handbook of group counseling and psychotherapy* (pp. 401–413). Thousand Oaks, CA: Sage.

Wheelan, S. (Ed.). (2005). *The handbook of group research and practice.* Thousand Oaks, CA: Sage.

Wheelan, S., & Lisk, A. (2000). Cohort effectiveness and the educational achievement of adult undergraduate students. *Small Group Research, 31,* 724–738.

Will, G. (2012). Waiting for the college bubble to pop. Retrieved from www.journalstar.com/news/opinion/editorial/columnists/george-will-waiting-for-the-college-bubble-to-pop/article_5018a202-f014-5455-ac4f-b86b84ca5a2a.html

Wilson, F. R., & Newmeyer, M. (2008). A standards-based inventory for assessing perceived importance of and confidence in using ASGW's core group work skills. *Journal for Specialists in Group Work, 33,* 270–289. doi: 10.1080/01933920802196146

Wilson, F. R., Newmeyer, M., Rapin, L., & Conyne, R. (2007). *Core Group Work Skills Inventory—Importance and Confidence (CGWSI-IC).* Retrieved from http://www.asgw.org/PDF/CGWSI-IC%20Inventory.pdf

Wilson, F. R., Rapin, L., & Haley-Banez, L. (2004). How teaching group work can be guided by foundational documents: Best practice guidelines, diversity principles, training standards. *Journal for Specialists in Group Work, 29,* 19-29. doi: 10:1080/01933920490275321

Wolf, A. (1963). The psychoanalysis of groups. In M. Rosenbaum & M. Berger (Eds.), *Group psychotherapy and group function* (pp. 273-327). New York, NY: Basic Books.

Yalom, I. (1975). *The theory and practice of group psychotherapy* (1st ed.). New York, NY: Basic Books.

Yalom, I. (1985). *The theory and practice of group psychotherapy* (3rd ed.). New York, NY: Basic Books.

Yalom, I. (1995). *The theory and practice of group psychotherapy* (4th ed.). New York, NY: Basic Books.

Yalom, I., & Leszcz, M. (2005). *The theory and practice of group psychotherapy* (5th ed.). New York, NY: Basic Books.

Zaccaro, S., Foti, R., & Kenny, D. (1991). Self-monitoring and trait-based variance in leadership: An investigation of leader flexibility across multiple group situations. *Journal of Applied Psychology, 76,* 308-315.

TRAINING DVDS ●

Group Work

See a number of group work videos from Microtraining Associates/Alexander Street Press (available at www.emicrotraining.com/index.php?cPath=22_82_35):

Afrocentric Approaches to Group Work: I Am Because We Are (S. Pack-Brown, L. Whittington-Clark, & M. Parker, 2002)
Ethnic Sharing: Valuing Diversity (J. Giordano, 1992)
Group Microskills: Encountering Diversity (L. Banez, A. Ivey, & M. Ivey, 2002)

Psychotherapy Group Leadership

Group Therapy: A Live Demonstration with Yalom and Leszcz. (n.d.). American Group Psychotherapy Association. Retrieved from http://member.agpa.org/staticcontent/staticpages/product_info.cfm?SKU=YALOMDVD11_IND&PRODUCT_
For a number of group videos, go to www.psychotherapy.net/learning-centers/approach/group-therapy.

Counseling Group Leadership

The following are available at asgw.org/asgw_training_dvds.htm:

Group Counseling for Children: A Multicultural Approach
(S. Bauman & S. Steen, 2009)

Group Counseling with *Adolescents* (S. Bauman & S. Steen, 2012)

Group Counseling in the Here and Now (P. Carroll, 1985)

Developmental Aspects of Group Counseling (R. Stockton, 1995)

The Bauman and Steen video focused on adolescents also can be found online at www.youtube.com/watch?v=JOpdhvCBZ28.

Group counseling: Strategies and Skills (E. E. Jacobs, R. L. L. Masson, R. L. Harvill, & C. J. Schimmel).

Evolution of a Group: Student Video and Workbook (G. Corey, M. Corey, & R. Haynes, 2000)

Group Counseling: Process and Technique. Fall, K. (n.d.). Microtraining.

Gazda on Groups: Group Counseling. Gazda, G. M. (1992). Microtraining.

Psychoeducation Group Leadership

Leading Groups with Adolescents. DeLucia-Waack, J., & Segrist, A. (2006). Retrieved from http://asgw.org/asgw_training_dvds.htm

Talking Troubles: A Teen Problem Solving Program. Tellerman, J. S. (1998). Verona, Wisconsin: Attainment Co., Inc.

Psychoeducation Group Demonstration: A Career Development Group for International Students. Conyne, R., & Wilson, R. (1999). North Amherst, MA: Microtraining Associates, Inc.

Task Group Leadership

Task Group Demonstration: Learning through Discussion. Conyne, R., & Wilson, R. (1999). North Amherst, MA: Microtraining Associates, Inc.

INDEX

A-B-C-D-E model of human interaction, 150–151
A-B-C model of human interaction, 150
ACA Code of Ethics, 34, 39–40
Academic learning strategy, 22–23
Access, 51
Accountability, 258
Accreditation standards, 56–60, 58 (figure), 263–264
ACES. *See* Association for Counselor Education and Supervision
Action, pausing, 246–247
Adams, J. Q., 177, 201–202
Adjourning stage of group development, 99, 99 (figure), 100
Affective domain, 146–147, 148
Agendas, hidden, 189
Aggressive members, 189
Aggressor role, 88 (figure)
AGPA. *See* American Group Psychotherapy Association
Altruism, 124 (figure)
American Counseling Association (ACA), 34, 39–40
   See also Association for Specialists in Group Work
American Group Psychotherapy Association (AGPA), 10, 99–100
Anthony, L., 169
Apply (Deep Processing Model step), 252 (figure), 253
ASGW. *See* Association for Specialists in Group Work; Group work, ASGW definition of

ASGW Training Standards for Group Counseling, 35–37, 36 (figure), 58–59, 60
Assertive level of process, 75–76, 81
Assessment, 47 (figure), 255–257
Association for Counselor Education and Supervision (ACES), 64–65
Association for Specialists in Group Work (ASGW):
   about, 17
   ASGW Training Standards for Group Counseling, 35–37, 36 (figure), 58–59, 60
   group work, conceptualization of, 10, 11–16
   group work, core competencies in, 11–13
   group work, types of, 14–16
   Multicultural and Social Justice Competence Principles for Group Workers, 49–54, 222–223
   training recommendations, clock hour, 60, 61 (figure)
   See also Group work, ASGW definition of
Association for Specialists in Group Work Best Practice Guidelines:
   domains, 40–46, 41 (figure), 47 (figure)
   group, creating, 121–122
   performing, 43–46, 47 (figure)
   planning, 42–43, 47 (figure)
   Preamble, 40
   processing, 46, 47 (figure), 248

purpose, 40
reflective practice, 244
Associations, professional, 32 (figure), 302
    See also specific associations
Atmosphere, group, 74
Attribution, meaningful, 183, 184,
    185 (figure), 186–188
Autocratic influence style, 73
Autocratic leaders, 117, 191
Avoider role, 86, 88 (figure)
Awareness of self and group members,
    50–51, 52

BASIC I.D., 152–153
Basic skills for group leaders, 200–201
Beck, A., 93
Behaving domain, 152–153
Behavior, imitative, 124 (figure)
Bemak, F., 64–65
Benne, K., 244–245
Bennis, W., 94
Benshoff, J., 245
Best fit, 267
Best practice, 118–121
    See also *Association for Specialists
        in Group Work Best Practice
        Guidelines*
Between-session processing,
    247–249, 250
Blake, R., 192
Blanchard, K., 192
Blocker role, 88 (figure)
Brabender, V., 83, 84, 92
    See also Brabender and Fallon's
        model of group development
Brabender and Fallon's model of group
    development, 103–110
    conflict and rebellion stage, 105–106
    formation and engagement stage, 105
    integration and work stage, 107–108
    intimacy and unity stage, 106–107
    termination stage, 108–110
Brooks, S., 240–241
Brown, N., 70–71, 157

Building blocks of group leadership.
    See Group leader competencies;
    Group leader functions; Group
    leader styles; Group leader types
Burlingame, G., 123, 220

CACREP. *See* Council for the
    Accreditation of Counseling and
    Related Educational Programs
Callanan, P., 226
Caring, 183, 184, 185 (figure), 186–188
Catharsis, 124 (figure)
CGWSI-IC. See *Core Group Work Skills
    Inventory-Importance and
    Confidence*
Change, lasting, 129–130
Choice points, 267–269
Clarifier role, 87 (figure)
Client protection, 39
Climate, group, 122–123, 166
Clock hour training recommendations,
    60, 61 (figure)
Cohen, B., 182
Cohesion, 123, 124 (figure), 219–220,
    220 (figure)
Coleadership, group work, 132–134,
    133 (figure)
Collaboration, 122, 160
Collusion, tacit, 133 (figure)
Communication styles, 51
Competencies, group leader. *See* Group
    leader competencies
Competition, 133 (figure)
Compromiser role, 88 (figure)
Confidentiality, 39
Conflict and rebellion stage of group
    development, 105–106
Confrontive level of process, 76, 81
Consultation, process, 154
Contemporary group development
    models, 93–94
Content, group, 76–79, 80 (figure), 81
    See also Group process
Context, 156, 160, 208, 209 (figure)

Context category of group dynamics, 68, 69
Contextual orientation, 159-161
Contextual perspective, 8, 9
Control, 189
Control and direction category of group dynamics, 68
Conventional level of process, 75, 81
Conyne, R.:
   communication styles, 51
   ecological counseling, 160-161
   Failures in Group Work, 265-266, 269-270
   group counseling leadership definition, 118
   How Personal Growth and Task Groups Work, 269-270
   Journeys to Professional Excellence, 64-65
   performance model, 155-156
   processing, within-session, 245-246
Coordinator role, 87 (figure)
Core Group Work Skills Inventory-Importance and Confidence (CGWSI-IC), 197-200
Corey, G., 226
Corey, M., 226
Council for the Accreditation of Counseling and Related Educational Programs (CACREP), 56, 57-60, 58 (figure), 263-264
Counseling, group. *See* Group counseling
Covering, in group work coleadership, 133 (figure)
Craig, D., 203
Creativity, 211-214
Critical incidents, 266-269
Crowell, J., 160-161
Cutting off strategy, 228, 229-230
Cyclical models of group development, 93

Decision-making procedures, 73
Deep Processing Model, 249, 251-253, 252 (figure)

Democratic influence style, 73
Democratic leaders, 97-98, 117, 191
Development, group. *See* Group development
Developmental perspective, 84
Development and organization category of group dynamics, 68
Diedrich, L., 51
Dimensions of Social Justice Model, 169
Discover (Deep Processing Model step), 252-253, 252 (figure)
Diversity, 143, 222-224
Division of responsibilities, in group work coleadership, 133 (figure)
Doctoral degree standards, 60
Domains:
   affective, 146-147, 148
   behaving, 152-153
   thinking, 147-150
   thinking-acting-doing, 150-152
Dominator role, 88 (figure)
Donigian, J., 79, 142
Drawing out strategy, 228, 229
Dynamics, group. *See* Group dynamics
Dysfunctional roles, 85, 86, 88 (figure)

Ecological assessment, 47 (figure)
Ecological orientation, 160-161
Effectiveness of group work, 10-11
Ellerbee, L., 3
Ellis, A., 150-151
Emotional stimulation, 183, 184, 185 (figure), 186-188
Empowerment, 117, 166-169
Encounter groups study:
   about, 180-182
   group leader functions, 182-183, 184, 185 (figure)
   group leader types, 192-193, 194-195
Encounter tapes, 182
Encourager role, 85, 87 (figure)
Energizer role, 87 (figure)
Energizers (group leader type), 192, 193
Enhancing, 166

Equity, 51

Esalen electric, 182

Ettin, M., 182

Evaluator role, 87 (figure)

Evolve (Deep Processing Model step), 252 (figure), 253

Executive function, 183, 184, 185 (figure), 186-188

Exercises, pre-planned/structured, 230-232, 231 (figure)

Existential factors, 124 (figure)

Existential theory, 147-150

Experiential learning, 22, 156-158, 158 (figure)

Experiments, intuitive, 232-233

Facilitating interaction, 190, 216, 217 (figure), 218-219

Faherty, J., 123

Failures, 264-266

Failures in Group Work (Conyne), 265-266, 269-270

Fallon, A. *See* Brabender and Fallon's model of group development

Families, 40, 124 (figure)

Feedback, 77-79, 106-107, 133 (figure)

Feelings, observing, 74

Fidler, J., 182

Final stage of group development, 99, 99 (figure), 100

First experiences with group leadership, 178-179, 180

Flexibility, 116, 207

Focusing, 227-228

Follower role, 88 (figure)

Formation and engagement stage of group development, 105

Forming stage of group development, 99, 99 (figure), 100

Forsyth, D., 66, 91, 117

Frost, R., 267-268

Fuhriman, G., 220

Functions:
    executive, 183, 184, 185 (figure), 186-188

maintenance, 26, 73-74

task, 26, 73

See also Group leader functions

Gatekeeper role, 86, 87 (figure)

Gestalt theory, 147, 148

Gestalt therapy, 182

Gladding, S., 70

Gladwell, M., 263, 264

Glass, J., 245

Goals, 25-27

Goethe, J. W. von, 203

Golant, M., 184, 190

Goodman, M., 3

Gorky, A., 211, 212

Group atmosphere, 74

Group climate, 122-123, 166

Group content, 76-79, 80 (figure), 81
    See also Group process

Group counseling:
    about, 14-15, 16
    intervention case illustration, 281-287
    training recommendations, clock hour, 61 (figure)
    videos, training, 119
    See also Group counseling and group psychotherapy theories; Group counseling leadership definition

Group counseling and group psychotherapy theories, 145-153
    affective domain, 146-147, 148
    BASIC I.D., 152-153
    behaving domain, 152-153
    existential theory, 147-150
    gestalt theory, 147, 148
    person-centered theory, 146-147
    psychoanalytic theory, 146
    Rational-Emotive Behavior Therapy, 150-152
    thinking-acting-doing domain, 150-152
    thinking domain, 147-150

Group counseling leadership definition, 118-130
   best practice and good professional judgment, 118-121
   cohesion, 123
   collaboration with members, 122
   definition, 118
   group, creating, 121-122
   group climate, building and maintaining positive, 122-123
   growth and change, lasting, 129-130
   here-and-now interaction, nurturing, 125-127
   processing, 128-129
   therapeutic factors, 123-125, 124 (figure)
Group development, 91-111
   about, 83-84, 91-92
   American Group Psychotherapy Association model, 99-100
   Brabender and Fallon's model, 103-110
   contemporary models, 93-94
   cyclical models, 93
   framework, guidance by, 215
   importance, 92
   Jones' model, 101-103
   process orientation, 165
   progressive stage models, 94-98
   Tuckman's model, 99, 99 (figure)
Group dynamics, 64-70
   context category, 68, 69
   control and direction category, 68
   defined, 66
   development and organization category, 68
   maintenance and conflict category, 68, 69
   process orientation, 165-166
   strengths and limitations, 66-67, 69-70
   working in groups category, 68-69
Group leader competencies, 193, 195-201
   about, 193, 195-197, 195 (figure)
   basic skills for group leaders, 200-201
   Core Group Work Skills Inventory-Importance and Confidence, 197-200
Group leader functions, 182-191
   caring, 183, 184, 185 (figure), 186-188
   emotional stimulation, 183, 184, 185 (figure), 186-188
   empirically derived functions, 182-184, 185-188, 185 (figure)
   executive function, 183, 184, 185 (figure), 186-188
   facilitating interaction, 190
   guiding interaction, 191
   initiating interaction, 190-191
   meaningful attribution, 183, 184, 185 (figure), 186-188
   meaningful group processes, 184, 190
   problem situations in groups, 189
   promoting interaction, 190
   questionnaire, 186-188
Group leader methods, 204-225
   about, 204-205, 205 (figure)
   cohesion, building, 219-220, 220 (figure)
   connection and interaction, facilitating, 216, 217 (figure), 218-219
   context, rounding group leadership in, 208, 209 (figure)
   creativity and spontaneity, 211-214
   diversity, multiculturalism, and social justice, endorsing, 222-224
   group development framework, guidance by, 215
   group work advantages, adapting, 225
   intentionality, 209-211
   online and social media groups, 218-219
   personhood, drawing from, 205-208
   therapeutic factors, 221-222
Group leadership, first experiences with, 178-179, 180

Group leader strategies and techniques,
226-234
about, 226-227
exercises, pre-planned/structured,
230-232, 231 (figure)
experiments, intuitive, 232-233
focusing, 227-228
interaction, shifting, 228-230
lecturettes, psychoeducation,
233-234
*Multicultural and Social Justice
Competence Principles for
Group Workers,* 52
Group leader styles, 191-193, 194-195
Group leader types, 192-193, 194-195
Group member roles, 84-86, 87-88
(figure), 89
Group perspective, 7, 8
Group process, 70-83
assertive level, 75-76, 81
balancing with content, 76-79,
80 (figure)
confrontive level, 76, 81
conventional level, 75, 81
defined, 70-71
feedback, giving, 77-79
Hill Interaction Matrix, 75-76
meaningful, 184, 190
*Modified Grid for Processing
Experiences and Events in
Group Work,* 80-83, 82 (figure),
245-246
observing, 71-75
processing events and experiences
in group work, 79-83, 82
(figure), 245-246
speculative level, 76, 81
Group psychotherapy:
about, 15, 16
group work leadership, 134-135
intervention case illustration,
287-294
training recommendations, clock
hour, 61 (figure)

See also Group counseling and
group psychotherapy theories
Groups:
ACA Code of Ethics, 40
creating, 121-122
importance, 302
qualities, 144-145, 144 (figure)
as "safe place," 49-50
ubiquity of, 5-7
Group work:
advantages, 225
components, 35-36, 36 (figure)
conceptualization, 10, 11-16
core competencies, 11-13
core curricular experiences, 58-59,
58 (figure)
effectiveness, 10-11
importance, xxiv, 298
nature, xxv-xxvi
perspectives underlying, 7-9
purposes, xxvi
types, xxvi, 14-16
as umbrella term, 10
See also Group work, ASGW
definition of; *specific topics*
Group work, ASGW definition of, 17-27
about, 17
as broad professional practice, 17-18
as giving help or accomplishing tasks
in group setting, 18
goals, 25-27
group theory and process, application
of, 18-21
interdependent collection of
people, 24
practitioner, capable professional, 21-24
See also Association for Specialists in
Group Work
Group work coleadership, 132-134,
133 (figure)
Group work leadership:
coleadership, 132-134, 133 (figure)
defined, 130-132
general statements about, 134-135

group development stages and,
96-98
leadership, generally, 116-117
See also specific topics
Group work theories, 139-176
group counseling and group
psychotherapy theories, 145-153
importance, 139-141
limitations, 142
need for, 142-145, 144 (figure)
overarching, 145, 170, 171-172
personal theory, 140, 170, 172-174
psychoeducational group theory,
156-158, 158 (figure)
task group theory, 154-156
transtheoretical orientations, 158-170
Growth, lasting, 129-130
Guiding interaction, 191
Gyllenhaal, M., 264-265

Hackman, R., 155
Haley-Banez, L., 30, 34
Hanson, P., 71-75
Harmonizer role, 87 (figure)
Harvill, R., 70, 200-201, 227
Healing, 166
Help-seeker role, 88 (figure)
Herlihy, B., 143
Hersey, P., 192
Hidden agendas, 189
High context communication, 51
Hill, W. F., 75-76, 84
Hill Interaction Matrix (HIM), 75-76
Hoffman, H., 211-212
Hope, 124 (figure)
*How Personal Growth and Task
Groups Work* (Conyne), 269-270
Hulse-Killacky, D., 79, 142

Identity, professional, 298-299, 301-303
"I" level of content, 81
Imitative behavior, 124 (figure)
Impersonals (group leader type), 193
Incidents, critical, 266-269

Individual person perspective, 7, 8
Individual roles, 85, 86, 88 (figure)
Influence, 72-73
Information, imparting, 124 (figure),
233-234
Information giver role, 87 (figure)
Information seeker role, 85, 87 (figure)
Initiating interaction, 190-191
Initiator role, 87 (figure)
Integration and work stage of group
development, 107-108
Intentionality, 209-211
Interaction:
A-B-C-D-E model, 150-151
A-B-C model, 150
facilitating, 190, 216, 217 (figure),
218-219
guiding, 191
here-and-now, 125-127
initiating, 190-191
promoting, 190
shifting by loosening and tightening,
228-230
Interactive orientation, 163
Interconnection, 9, 160, 216,
217 (figure), 218
*International Journal of Group
Psychotherapy,* 164, 300
Internships, 59-60, 263-264
Interpersonal factors, in multicultural
competency and social justice, 51
Interpersonal goals, 26
Interpersonal learning, 124 (figure)
Interpersonal neurobiology (IPNB),
163-164, 300-301
Interpersonal orientation, 161-163
Interpersonal perspective, 7, 8-9
Interpersonal process, leadership
as, 117
Interventions, 261-295
about, 261-262
counseling group illustration,
281-287
leader choices in group, 269-270

practice, 263–266
processing, 266–269, 267 (figure)
psychoeducation group illustration,
275–281
psychotherapy group illustration,
287–294
task group illustration, 270–275
Intimacy and unity stage of group
development, 106–107
Intrapersonal awareness, 50–51, 52
Intuitive experiments, 232–233
IPNB. *See* Interpersonal neurobiology
"It" level of content, 81
Ivey, A., 164

Jacobs, E., 70, 200–201, 227
Jencius, M., 218
Jensen, M., 99, 99 (figure)
Johnson, D., 192
Johnson, J., 220
Joker role, 88 (figure)
Jones, J., 101–103, 101 (figure)
*Journal for Specialists in Group
Work,* 36
Journals, 32 (figure), 258
See also specific journals
Journeys to Professional Excellence
(Conyne & Bemak, editors),
64–65

Keys, A., 240
Killacky, J., 79
Kivlighan, D. M., Jr., 125
Kolb, D., 157
Kubler-Ross, E., 261

Laissez-faire influence style, 73
Laissez-faire leaders, 117, 191, 193
Lao Tse, 115, 135
Leader incompatibility, in group work
coleadership, 133 (figure)
Leaders:
autocratic, 117, 191
democratic, 97–98, 117, 191

laissez-faire, 117, 191, 193
maintenance, 88 (figure)
self-focused, 88 (figure)
task, 88 (figure)
Leadership, generally, 116–117
See also Group work leadership
Leadership Grid, 192
Leader-type roles, 88 (figure)
Learning, 22–24, 124 (figure), 156–158,
158 (figure)
Learning strategies, 22–24
Lease, S., 183
Lecturettes, psychoeducation,
233–234
Lessons learned, 240–244
Leszcz, M., 221, 230–231, 233
Lewin, K., 66, 117, 139, 160, 245
Liberatory Critical Consciousness, 169
Lichy, M., 245
Lieberman, M., 184, 190
See also Encounter groups study
Life line exercise, 232
Lippitt, R., 117
Looping back, 128–129, 239
Low context communication, 51

Mackenzie, K., 93
Maintenance and conflict category of
group dynamics, 68, 69
Maintenance functions, 26, 73–74
Maintenance leaders, 88 (figure)
Maintenance roles, 85–86, 87–88
(figure)
Managers (group leader type), 193
Marathon, 182
Masson, R., 70, 200–201, 227
MBSR. *See* Mindfulness-Based Stress
Reduction
McClendon, D. T., 123
MCT. *See* Multicultural counseling and
therapy
Meaning, 47 (figure), 161
Meaningful attribution, 183, 184,
185 (figure), 186–188

Meaningful group processes, 184, 190
Meditation, 257–258
Members:
    aggressive, 189
    awareness of, 50–51, 52
    goals, outcome-oriented, 25
    goals, process-oriented, 25
    roles, 84–86, 87–88 (figure), 89
    screening of prospective, 39
    silent, 189
Membership, observing, 74
Methods, group leader. *See* Group
    leader methods
Miles, M. *See* Encounter groups study
Mindfulness-Based Stress Reduction
    (MBSR), 152–153
Mistakes, 264–266
Modeling, 133 (figure)
Model-setting participant (group leader
    type), 231
*Modified Grid for Processing
    Experiences and Events in Group
    Work*, 80–83, 82 (figure), 245–246
Monopolizer case study, 281–287
Monopolizer role, 86, 88 (figure)
Morran, D. K., 245
Mouton, J., 192
*Multicultural and Social Justice
    Competence Principles for Group
    Workers* (Association for
    Specialists in Group Work), 49–54
    awareness of self and group
        members, 52
    competency principle, 222–223
    groups as "safe place," 49–50
    interpersonal factors, 51
    intrapersonal awareness, 50–51
    social justice advocacy, 52
    social justice factors, 51
    strategies and skills, 52
Multicultural counseling and therapy
    (MCT), 161
Multicultural-diversity
    perspective, 8, 9

Multiculturalism, 49–51, 169,
    222–224
Multicultural orientation, 161

Naiveté, 169
National Training Laboratories (NTL),
    244–245
Network model of group leadership,
    24, 216, 217 (figure)
Neurobiology, 163–164, 300–301
Newmeyer, M., 160–161
Nitza, A., 245
Norming stage of group development,
    99, 99 (figure), 100
Norms, 74–75
NTL. *See* National Training
    Laboratories

Observation guidelines, 71–75
Observation learning strategy, 22
Oklahoma City Thunder professional
    hockey team, 240–241
Online and social media, 162–163,
    218–219
Openness, 208
Opinion giver role, 87 (figure)
Opinion seeker role, 87 (figure)
Orientations, transtheoretical.
    See Transtheoretical orientations
Orient role, 87 (figure)
Outcome-oriented group goals, 25
Outcome-oriented individual member
    goals, 25

Page, B., 218–219
Parks, R., 50
PARS model. *See* Process, Activity,
    Relationship, and Self model
Participation, 51, 72
Pausing the action, 246–247
Peacemaker influence style, 73
Peer relationships, 40
Performance models, 155–156
Performing, 43–46, 47 (figure)

Performing stage of group development, 99, 99 (figure), 100
Personal goals, 26
Personal growth groups, 182
Personal theory, 140, 170, 172–174
Person-centered theory, 146–147
Personhood of group leaders, 205–208, 223
Perspectives underlying group work, 7–9, 84, 154
PGTM. *See* Purposeful Group Techniques Model
Planning, 42–43, 47 (figure)
Playfulness, 213
Polcin, D., 143
Portman, J., 63, 89
Positive Psychology, 168, 264
Power and control, 189
Practice:
    best, 118–121
    interventions, 263–266
    professional, 17–18, 258
    reflective, 47 (figure), 244–250
    See also *Association for Specialists in Group Work Best Practice Guidelines* ; Processing
Practicum, 59–60, 263–264
Pratt, J., 233
Preparation, 220, 220 (figure), 263–264
Presence, 207
Prevention, 167–169
Prilleltensky, I., 223
Problem situations in groups, 189
Process. *See* Group process
Process, Activity, Relationship, and Self (PARS) model, 245
Process consultation, 154
Processing:
    Association for Specialists in Group Work Best Practice Guidelines, 46, 47 (figure)
    between-session, 247–249, 250
    end of session, 247, 248

events and experiences in group work, 79–83, 82 (figure), 245–246
group counseling leadership definition, 128–129
interventions, 266–269, 267 (figure)
Modified Grid for Processing Experiences and Events in Group Work, 80–83, 82 (figure), 245–246
within-session, 244–247, 248, 249
Process observer role, 86, 88 (figure)
Process orientation, 25, 165–166
Process-oriented group goals, 25
Process-oriented individual member goals, 25
Producing, 170
Professional associations, 32 (figure), 302
    See also specific associations
Professional identity, 298–299, 301–303
Professional practice, 17–18, 258
Program development and evaluation, 47 (figure)
Progressive stage models of group development, 94–98
Promoting interaction, 190
Providers (group leader type), 192, 193, 194–195
Psychoanalytically oriented groups, 182
Psychoanalytic theory, 146
Psychodrama, 182
Psychoeducation groups:
    about, 14, 15–16
    group work leadership definition, 130
    intervention case illustration, 275–281
    theory, 156–158, 158 (figure)
    training recommendations, clock hour, 61 (figure)
    videos, training, 130
Psychoeducation lecturettes, 233–234
Psychological issues, linking group development with, 95–96

Psychotherapy, group. *See* Group psychotherapy
Punctuated Equilibrium Model, 93–94
Purposeful Group Techniques Model (PGTM), 266, 267 (figure)
Purposive orientation, 166–170

Questionnaire, group leader functions, 186–188

Rand, J., 155–156
Rapin, L., 30, 34, 39–40, 155–156
Rational-Emotive Behavior Therapy, 150–152
Ratts, M., 143, 169
Reflecting, 239–260
  about, 239
  between-session processing, 247–249, 250
  Deep Processing Model, 249, 251–253, 252 (figure)
  in group work practice, 240–250
  on group work practice, 251–258
  importance, 300
  lessons learned, 240–244
  professional practice and accountability, 258
  self-care, 254–258
  within-session processing, 244–247, 248, 249
Reflective practice, 47 (figure), 244–250
  See also Processing
Relationships leadership style, 191–192
Rescuer role, 86, 88 (figure)
Responsibilities, division of, in group work coleadership, 133 (figure)
"Road Not Taken, The" (Frost), 267–268
Roles:
  dysfunctional, 85, 86, 88 (figure)
  group member, 84–86, 87–88 (figure), 89
  individual, 85, 86, 88 (figure)
  leader-type, 88 (figure)
  maintenance, 85–86, 87–88 (figure)
  task, 85, 87 (figure)
  See also specific roles
Roth, J., 183
Ruby and Oren Principle, 302
Russell, J. M., 226

Salazar, C., 53
Santos, K. N., 169
SCAMPER model, 212–213
Schedule, processing, 47 (figure)
Schimmel, C., 70, 200–201, 227
Schwarz, R., 135, 155
Screening of prospective group members, 39
Self-awareness, 50–51, 52
Self-care, 254–258
Self-confessor role, 88 (figure)
Self-focused leaders, 88 (figure)
Self-reflective loop, 128–129, 239
Seneca, 239
Shallcross, L., 143
Shepard, H., 94
Silent members, 189
Situational Leadership model, 192
Skills, basic, for group leaders, 200–201
Sliding Doors (movie), 268
Social Engineers (group leader type), 192–193
Socializing techniques development, 124 (figure)
Social justice, 49–51, 52, 168–169, 222–224
Social media, 162–163, 218–219
Social psychology perspective, 154
Social system maintenance, 161
Special interest pleader role, 88 (figure)
Speculative level of process, 76, 81
Spontaneity, 211–214
Standard setter role, 88 (figure)
Stockton, R., 245
Storming stage of group development, 99, 99 (figure), 100

Strategies and techniques, group leader. *See* Group leader strategies and techniques
Styles:
    communication, 51
    group leader, 191-193, 194-195
Summarizer role, 85, 87 (figure)
Supervision learning strategy, 23
Sustainability, 161
Synanon, 182
Systemic orientation, 159-160

Task coordination, lack of, 133 (figure)
Task functions, 26, 73
Task groups:
    about, 14, 15
    goals, 26-27
    group work leadership, 135
    group work leadership definition, 131-132
    intervention case illustration, 270-275
    theory, 154-156
    training recommendations, clock hour, 61 (figure)
    videos, training, 131
Task leaders, 88 (figure)
Task leadership style, 191-192
Task roles, 85, 87 (figure)
Team-based learning, 156-157, 157-158, 158 (figure)
Teams, 135, 154-155
    See also Task groups
Technical expert role, 231
Technician role, 85, 87 (figure)
Techniques, group leader. *See* Group leader strategies and techniques
"Telephone switchboard" model of group leadership, 24, 216, 217 (figure)
Termination, 99, 99 (figure), 100, 108-110, 189
T-groups, 182, 244-245
Theory, defined, 140

See also Group work theories; *specific theories*
Theory of Reasoned Action and Planned Behavior (TRA/PB), 167-168
Therapeutic conditions and dynamics, 47 (figure)
Therapeutic factors, 123-125, 124 (figure), 221-222
Therapeutic Life Changes (TLC), 164, 276
Thinking-acting-doing domain, 150-152
Thinking domain, 147-150
Thompson, E., 265
Tinsley, H., 183
TLC. *See* Therapeutic Life Changes
Training recommendations, clock hour, 60, 61 (figure)
Training videos, 119, 130, 131
Transactional analysis, 182
Transpose/Record (Deep Processing Model step), 252, 252 (figure)
Transtheoretical Model of Behavior Change (TTM), 167
Transtheoretical orientations, 158-170
    about, 158-159, 159 (figure)
    contextual orientation, 159-161
    ecological orientation, 160-161
    interactive orientation, 163
    interpersonal neurobiology orientation, 163-164, 300-301
    interpersonal orientation, 161-163
    multicultural orientation, 161
    process orientation, 165-166
    purposive orientation, 166-170
    systemic orientation, 159-160
TRA/PB. *See* Theory of Reasoned Action and Planned Behavior
Trotzer, J., 190-191, 201, 205
TTM. *See* Transtheoretical Model of Behavior Change
Tuckman, B., 99, 99 (figure)
Types, group leader, 192-193, 194-195

Universality, 124 (figure), 298
"Us" level of content, 81

Videos, training, 119, 130, 131
von Bertalanffy, L., 159-160

Wallace, M., 243
Ward, C., 98
Ward, D., 98, 245
Washington, G., 297, 299
"Web of life," 9, 216, 217 (figure), 218
Weisbord, M., 155
"We" level of content, 81
Wellness, 51
What to Look for in Groups
       (Hanson), 71-75
White, R. K., 117
Will, G., 223-224

Wilson, F. R., 30, 34
Within-session processing, 244-247,
       248, 249
Work groups. *See* Task groups
Working in groups category of group
       dynamics, 68-69
Worksheet, self-care assessment, 255-257

Yalom, I.:
    exercises, structured, 230-231
    interactive orientation, 163
    processing, 128
    therapeutic factors, 123, 124 (figure),
       221, 233
    See also Encounter groups study
"Yes, but" *versus* "Yes, and", 214
"You" level of content, 81
Youngman, H., 261

ABOUT THE AUTHOR

Robert K. Conyne is professor emeritus from the University of Cincinnati and a licensed psychologist, clinical counselor, and fellow of the Association for Specialists in Group Work (ASGW) and the American Psychological Association (APA). He has 40 years of professional experience as a university professor and department head, psychologist, counselor, administrator, researcher, consultant, and trainer. Currently, he volunteers as an American Red Cross disaster mental health specialist and works as a military family life consultant. He has received many awards, including Eminent Career Award from AGSW and Lifetime Achievement Award in Prevention from APA. He served as president of the Association for Specialists in Group Work (1996) and the Society of Group Psychology and Group Psychotherapy (2009). With over 200 scholarly publications and presentations, including 13 books in his areas of expertise (group work, prevention, and ecological counseling), Bob is recognized as a major contributor in both counseling and counseling psychology.

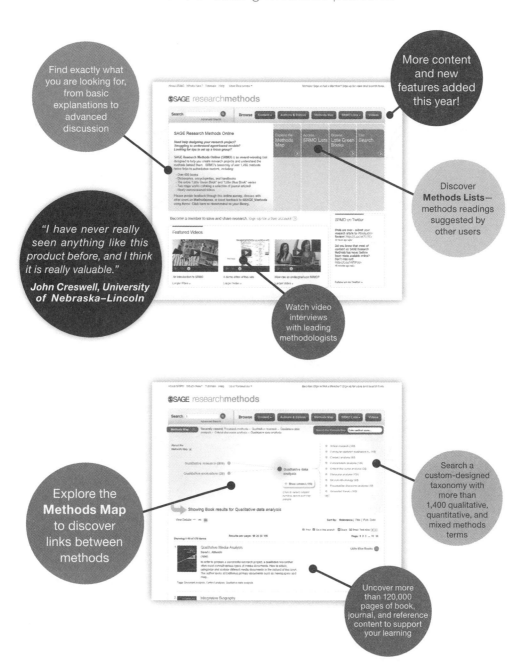

⑤SAGE research**methods**

The essential online tool for researchers from the world's leading methods publisher

Find exactly what you are looking for, from basic explanations to advanced discussion

More content and new features added this year!

"*I have never really seen anything like this product before, and I think it is really valuable.*"
John Creswell, University of Nebraska–Lincoln

Discover **Methods Lists**—methods readings suggested by other users

Watch video interviews with leading methodologists

Explore the **Methods Map** to discover links between methods

Search a custom-designed taxonomy with more than 1,400 qualitative, quantitative, and mixed methods terms

Uncover more than 120,000 pages of book, journal, and reference content to support your learning

Find out more at
www.sageresearchmethods.com